MARVEL STUDIOS

# CAPTAIN MARVEL

## PRELUDE

## MS. MARVEL (1977) #1
WRITER/EDITOR: **GENE COLAN**
PENCILER: **JOHN BUSCEMA**
INKER: **JOE SINNOTT**
COLORIST: **MARIE SEVERIN**
LETTERER: **JOHN COSTANZA**

## MS. MARVEL (2006) #1
WRITER: **BRIAN REED**
PENCILER: **ROBERTO DE LA TORRE**
INKER: **JIMMY PALMIOTTI**
COLORIST: **CHRIS SOTOMAYOR**
LETTERER: **DAVE SHARPE**
COVER ART: **FRANK CHO**
ASSISTANT EDITORS: **MOLLY LAZER & AUBREY SITTERSON**
EDITOR: **ANDY SCHMIDT**

## CAPTAIN MARVEL (2012) #1
WRITER: **KELLY SUE DeCONNICK**
ARTIST: **DEXTER SOY**
LETTERER: **VC'S JOE CARAMAGNA**
COVER ART: **ED McGUINNESS, DEXTER VINES & JAVIER RODRÍGUEZ**
ASSISTANT EDITOR: **ELLIE PYLE**
ASSOCIATE EDITOR: **SANA AMANAT**
SENIOR EDITOR: **STEPHEN WACKER**

## GENERATIONS: CAPTAIN MARVEL & CAPTAIN MAR-VELL #1
WRITER: **MARGARET STOHL**
ARTIST: **BRENT SCHOONOVER**
COLOR ARTIST: **JORDAN BOYD**
LETTERER: **VC'S JOE CARAMAGNA**
COVER ART: **DAVID NAKAYAMA**
EDITOR: **CHARLES BEACHAM**
SUPERVISING EDITOR: **SANA AMANAT**

## THE LIFE OF CAPTAIN MARVEL #1
WRITER: **MARGARET STOHL**
PENCILER, PRESENT DAY: **CARLOS PACHECO**
INKER, PRESENT DAY: **RAFAEL FONTERIZ**
COLORIST, PRESENT DAY: **MARCIO MENYZ**
ARTIST, FLASHBACKS: **MARGUERITE SAUVAGE**
LETTERER: **VC'S CLAYTON COWLES**
COVER ART: **JULIAN TOTINO TEDESCO**
EDITOR: **SARAH BRUNSTAD**
CONSULTING EDITOR: **SANA AMANAT**
EXECUTIVE EDITOR: **TOM BREVOORT**

**MARVEL'S CAPTAIN MARVEL PRELUDE.** Contains material originally published in magazine form as MARVEL'S CAPTAIN MARVEL PRELUDE #1, MS. MARVEL (1977) #1, MS. MARVEL (2006) #1, CAPTAIN MARVEL (2012) #1, GENERATIONS: CAPTAIN MARVEL & CAPTAIN MAR-VELL #1 and THE LIFE OF CAPTAIN MARVEL #1. First printing 2019. ISBN 978-1-302-91494-3. Published by MARVEL WORLDWIDE, INC., a subsidiary of MARVEL ENTERTAINMENT, LLC. OFFICE OF PUBLICATION: 135 West 50th Street, New York, NY 10020. Copyright © 2019 MARVEL No similarity between any of the names, characters, persons, and/or institutions in this magazine with those of any living or dead person or institution is intended, and any such similarity which may exist is purely coincidental. **Printed in the U.S.A.** DAN BUCKLEY, President, Marvel Entertainment; JOHN NEE, Publisher; JOE QUESADA, Chief Creative Officer; TOM BREVOORT, SVP of Publishing; DAVID BOGART, SVP of Business Affairs & Operations, Publishing & Partnership; DAVID GABRIEL, SVP of Sales & Marketing, Publishing; JEFF YOUNGQUIST, VP of Production & Special Projects; DAN CARR, Executive Director of Publishing Technology; ALEX MORALES, Director of Publishing Operations; DAN EDINGTON, Managing Editor; SUSAN CRESPI, Production Manager; STAN LEE, Chairman Emeritus. For information regarding advertising in Marvel Comics or on Marvel.com, please contact Vit DeBellis, Custom Solutions & Integrated Advertising Manager, at vdebellis@marvel.com. For Marvel subscription inquiries, please call 888-511-5480. Manufactured between 12/14/2018 and 1/15/2019 by LSC COMMUNICATIONS INC., KENDALLVILLE, IN, USA.

# MARVEL STUDIOS

# CAPTAIN MARVEL

## PRELUDE

WRITER: **WILL CORONA PILGRIM**

ARTIST: **ANDREA DI VITO**

COLOR ARTIST: **LAURA VILLARI**

LETTERER: **VC'S TRAVIS LANHAM**

ASSISTANT EDITOR: **LAUREN AMARO**

EDITOR: **MARK BASSO**


**FOR MARVEL STUDIOS**
MANAGER, PRODUCTION & DEVELOPMENT: **MICHELLE MOMPLAISIR**
MANAGER, PRODUCTION & DEVELOPMENT: **BOJAN VUČIĆEVIĆ**
EXECUTIVE, PRODUCTION & DEVELOPMENT: **JONATHAN SCHWARTZ**
EXECUTIVE, PRODUCTION & DEVELOPMENT: **TRINH TRAN**
PRESIDENT: **KEVIN FEIGE**


COLLECTION EDITOR: JENNIFER GRÜNWALD
ASSISTANT EDITOR: CAITLIN O'CONNELL
ASSOCIATE MANAGING EDITOR: KATERI WOODY
EDITOR, SPECIAL PROJECTS: MARK D. BEAZLEY
VP PRODUCTION & SPECIAL PROJECTS: JEFF YOUNGQUIST
SVP PRINT, SALES & MARKETING: DAVID GABRIEL

EDITOR IN CHIEF: C.B. CEBULSKI
CHIEF CREATIVE OFFICER: JOE QUESADA
PRESIDENT: DAN BUCKLEY

**MARVEL'S
CAPTAIN MARVEL**

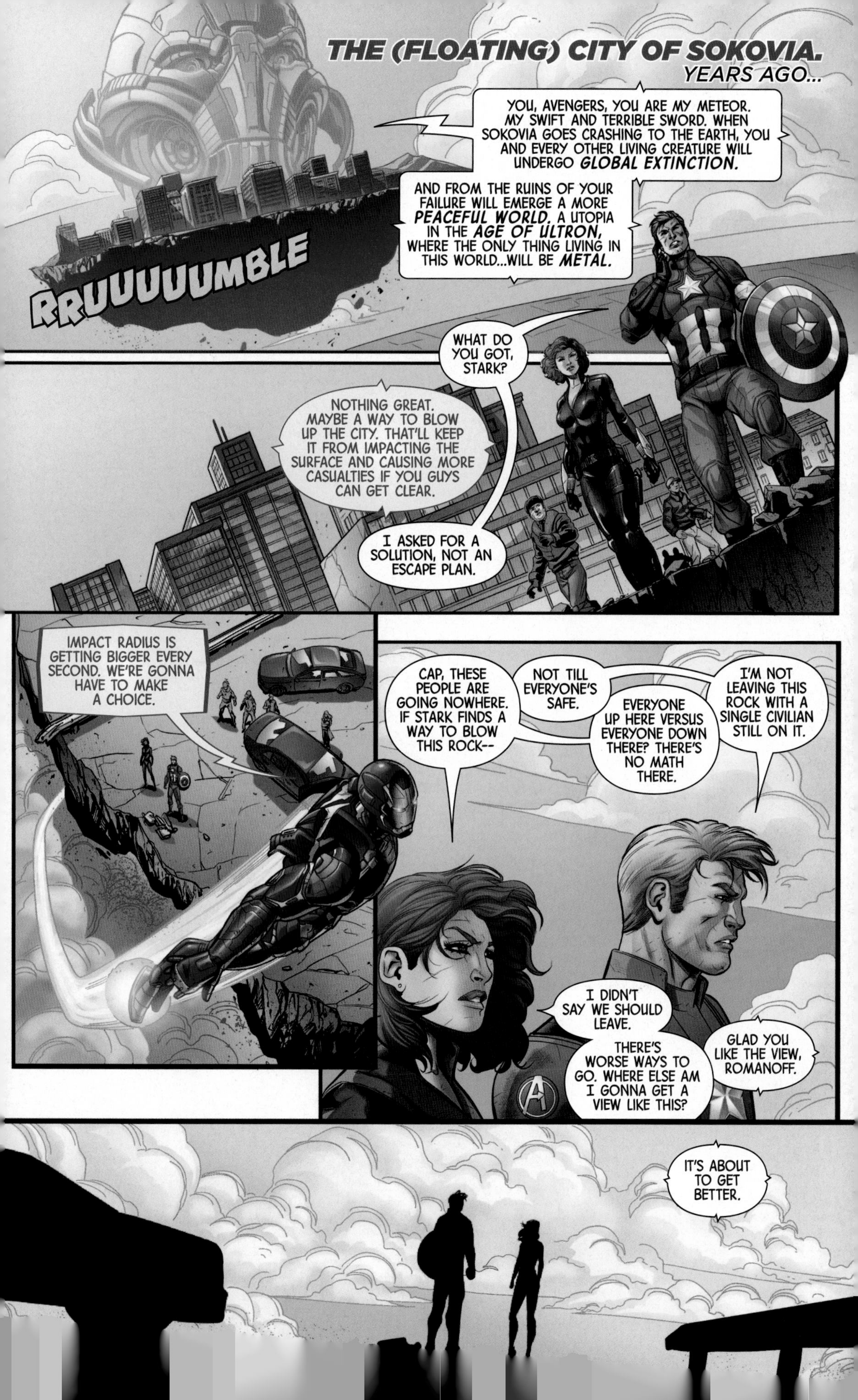
THE (FLOATING) CITY OF SOKOVIA.
YEARS AGO...
YOU, AVENGERS, YOU ARE MY METEOR. MY SWIFT AND TERRIBLE SWORD. WHEN SOKOVIA GOES CRASHING TO THE EARTH, YOU AND EVERY OTHER LIVING CREATURE WILL UNDERGO GLOBAL EXTINCTION.
AND FROM THE RUINS OF YOUR FAILURE WILL EMERGE A MORE PEACEFUL WORLD. A UTOPIA IN THE AGE OF ULTRON, WHERE THE ONLY THING LIVING IN THIS WORLD...WILL BE METAL.
RRUUUUUMBLE
WHAT DO YOU GOT, STARK?
NOTHING GREAT. MAYBE A WAY TO BLOW UP THE CITY. THAT'LL KEEP IT FROM IMPACTING THE SURFACE AND CAUSING MORE CASUALTIES IF YOU GUYS CAN GET CLEAR.
I ASKED FOR A SOLUTION, NOT AN ESCAPE PLAN.
IMPACT RADIUS IS GETTING BIGGER EVERY SECOND. WE'RE GONNA HAVE TO MAKE A CHOICE.
CAP, THESE PEOPLE ARE GOING NOWHERE. IF STARK FINDS A WAY TO BLOW THIS ROCK--
NOT TILL EVERYONE'S SAFE.
EVERYONE UP HERE VERSUS EVERYONE DOWN THERE? THERE'S NO MATH THERE.
I'M NOT LEAVING THIS ROCK WITH A SINGLE CIVILIAN STILL ON IT.
I DIDN'T SAY WE SHOULD LEAVE.
THERE'S WORSE WAYS TO GO. WHERE ELSE AM I GONNA GET A VIEW LIKE THIS?
GLAD YOU LIKE THE VIEW, ROMANOFF.
IT'S ABOUT TO GET BETTER.

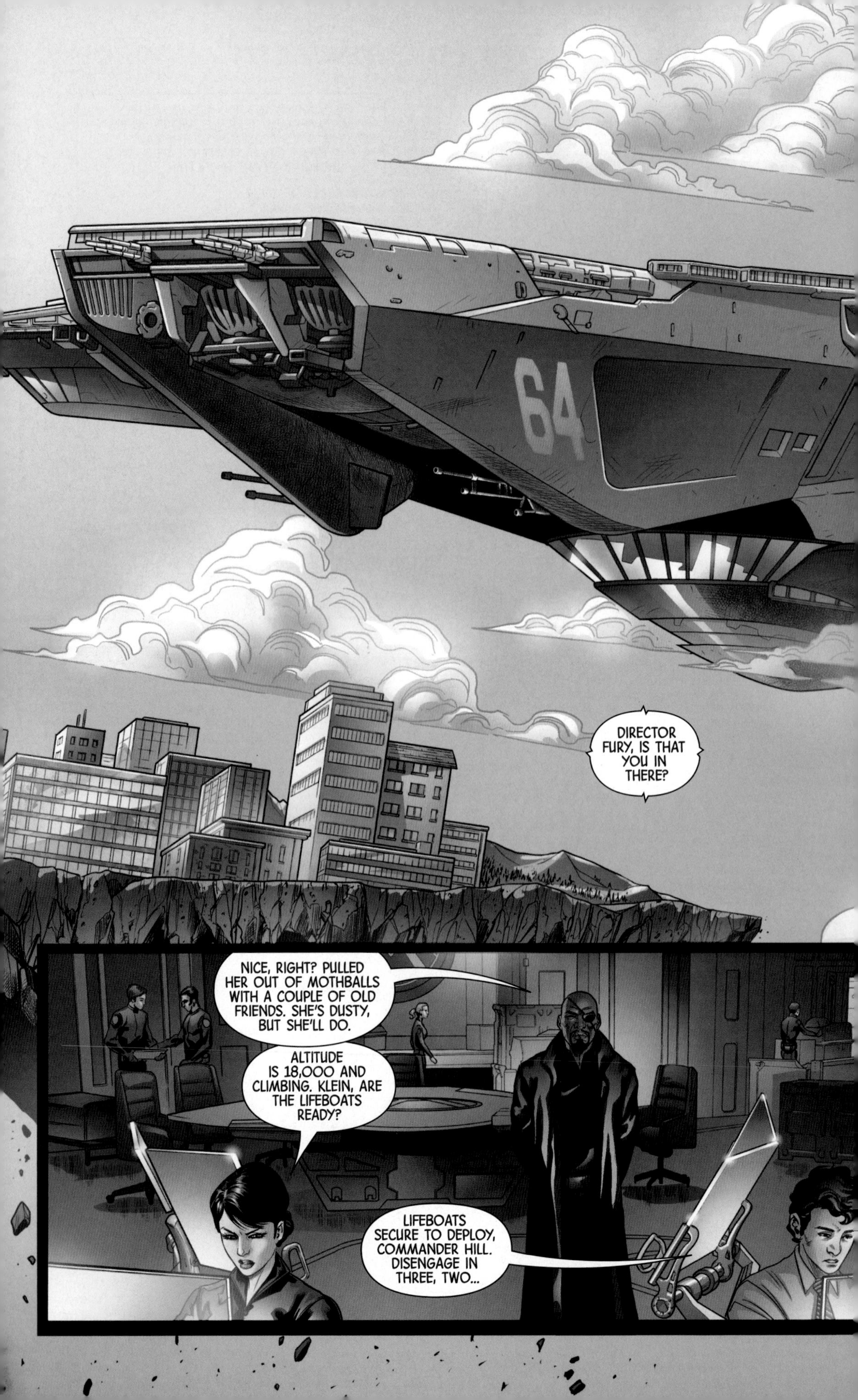
DIRECTOR FURY, IS THAT YOU IN THERE?
NICE, RIGHT? PULLED HER OUT OF MOTHBALLS WITH A COUPLE OF OLD FRIENDS. SHE'S DUSTY, BUT SHE'LL DO.
ALTITUDE IS 18,000 AND CLIMBING. KLEIN, ARE THE LIFEBOATS READY?
LIFEBOATS SECURE TO DEPLOY, COMMANDER HILL. DISENGAGE IN THREE, TWO...

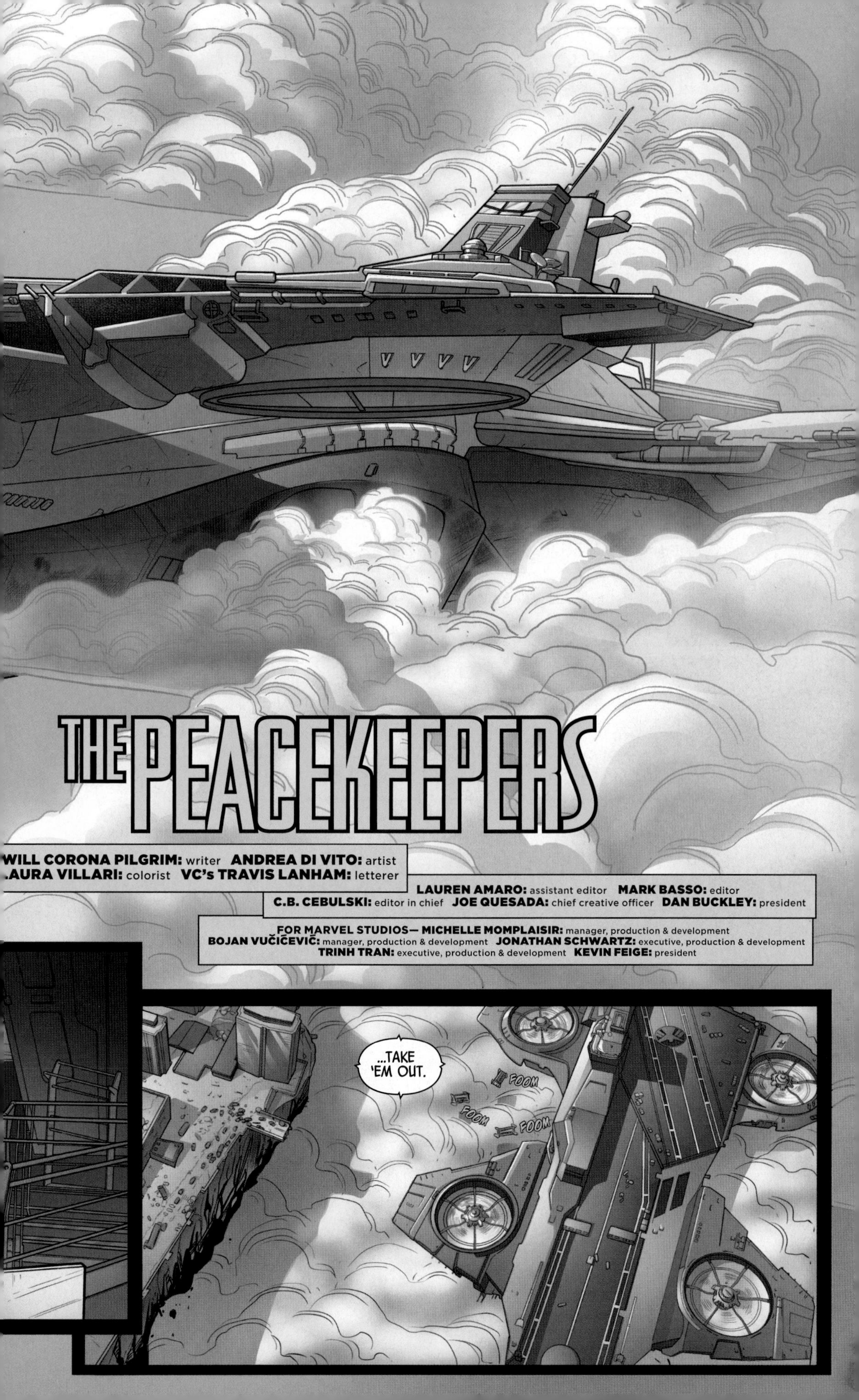
THE PEACEKEEPERS
WILL CORONA PILGRIM: writer ANDREA DI VITO: artist
AURA VILLARI: colorist VC's TRAVIS LANHAM: letterer
LAUREN AMARO: assistant editor MARK BASSO: editor
C.B. CEBULSKI: editor in chief JOE QUESADA: chief creative officer DAN BUCKLEY: president
FOR MARVEL STUDIOS— MICHELLE MOMPLAISIR: manager, production & development
BOJAN VUČIČEVIČ: manager, production & development JONATHAN SCHWARTZ: executive, production & development
TRINH TRAN: executive, production & development KEVIN FEIGE: president
...TAKE 'EM OUT.
FOOM
FOOM
FOOM

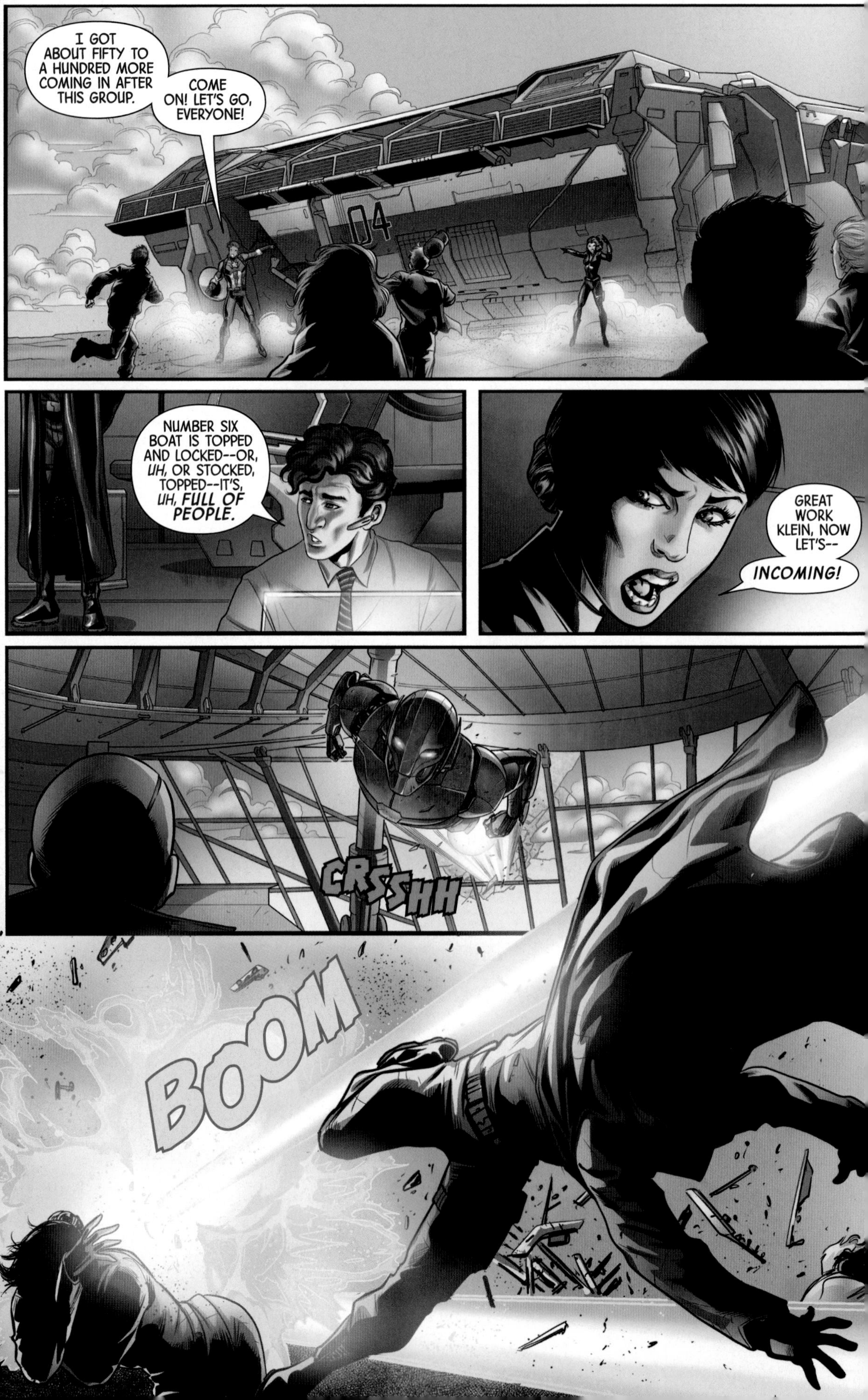
I GOT ABOUT FIFTY TO A HUNDRED MORE COMING IN AFTER THIS GROUP.
COME ON! LET'S GO, EVERYONE!
NUMBER SIX BOAT IS TOPPED AND LOCKED--OR, *UH*, OR STOCKED, TOPPED--IT'S, *UH*, ***FULL OF PEOPLE.***
GREAT WORK KLEIN, NOW LET'S--
***INCOMING!***
CRSSHH
BOOM

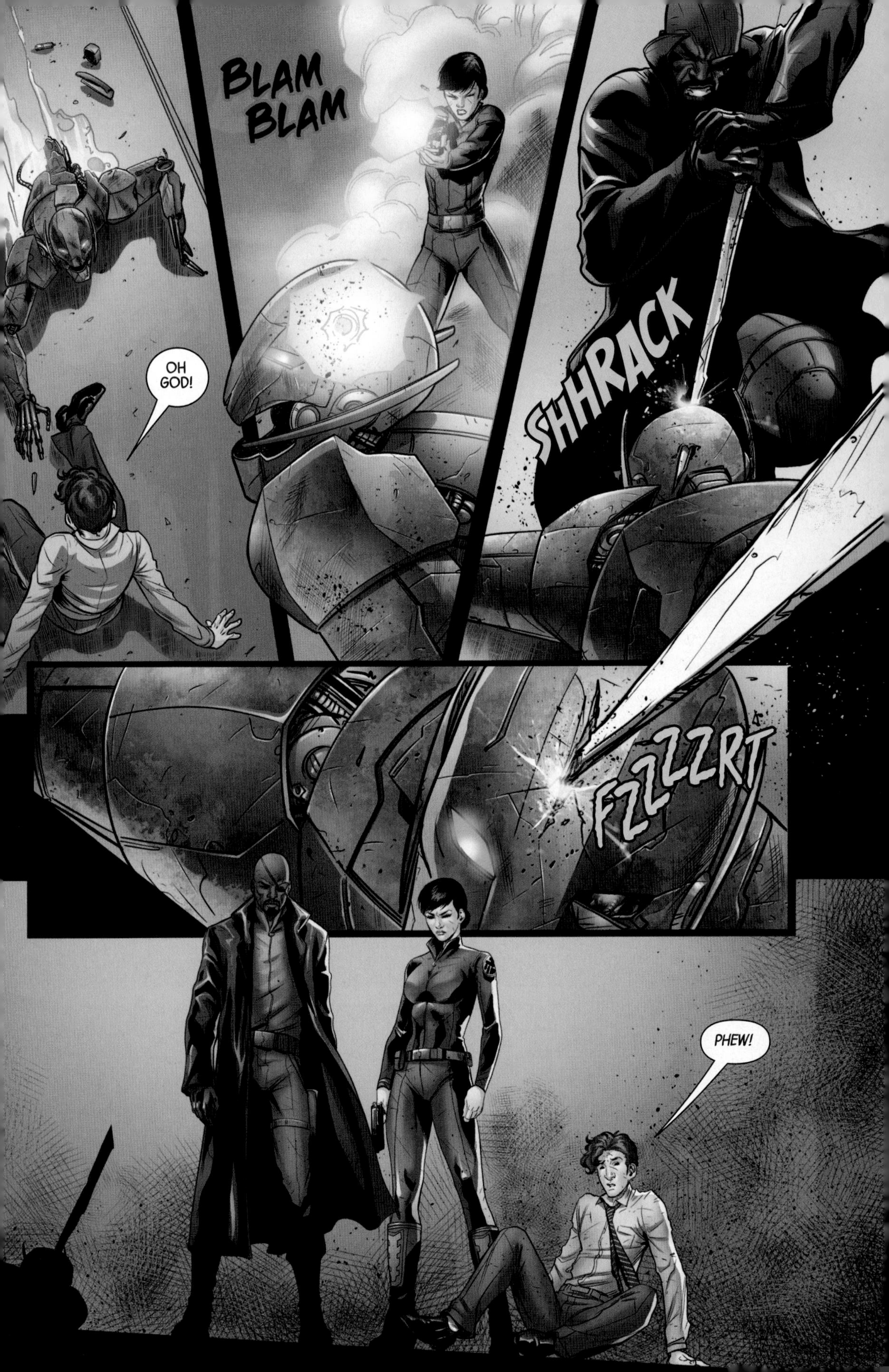
OH GOD!
BLAM BLAM
SHHRACK
FZZZZRT
PHEW!

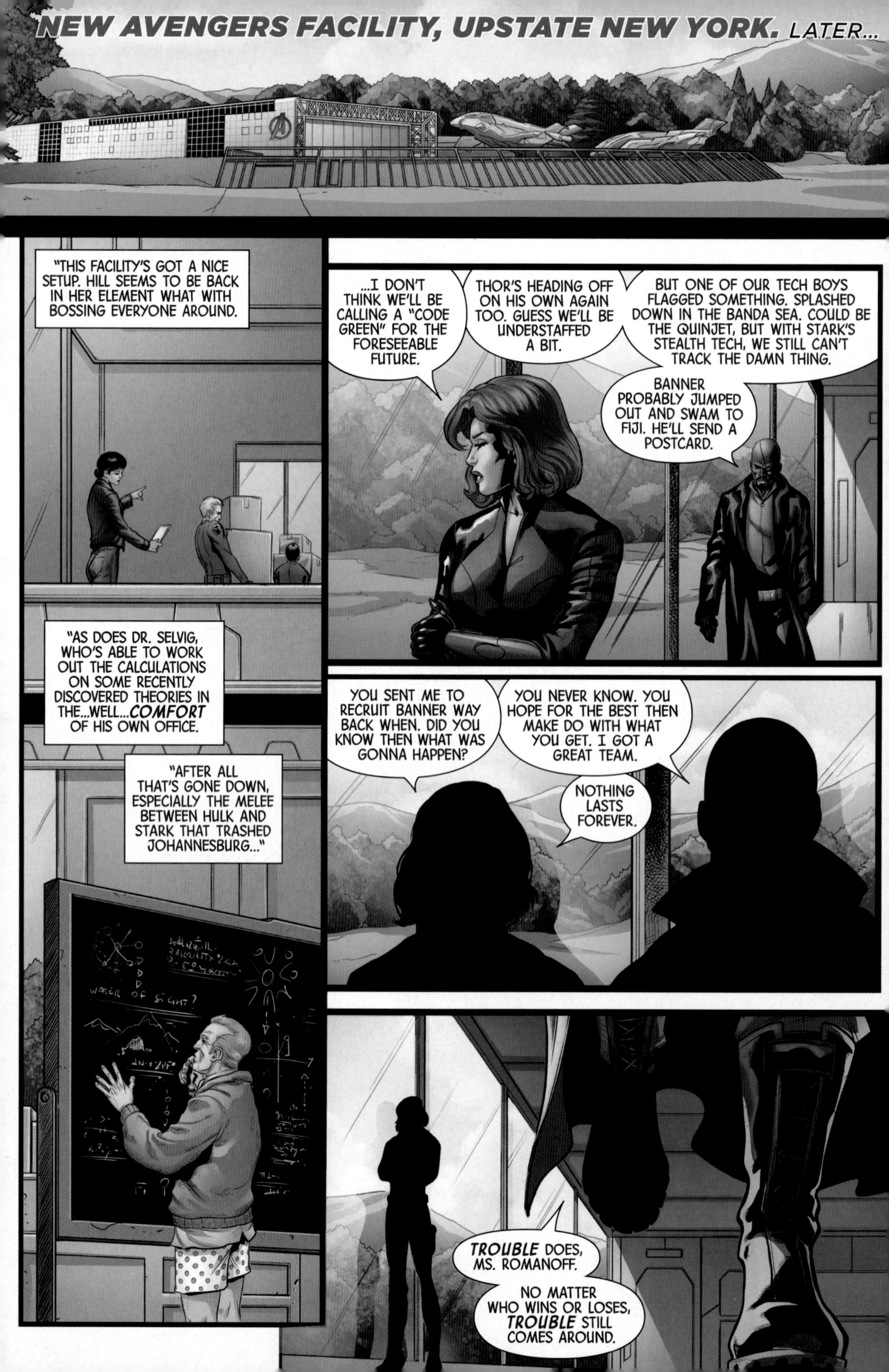
NEW AVENGERS FACILITY, UPSTATE NEW YORK. LATER...
"THIS FACILITY'S GOT A NICE SETUP. HILL SEEMS TO BE BACK IN HER ELEMENT WHAT WITH BOSSING EVERYONE AROUND.
...I DON'T THINK WE'LL BE CALLING A "CODE GREEN" FOR THE FORESEEABLE FUTURE.
THOR'S HEADING OFF ON HIS OWN AGAIN TOO. GUESS WE'LL BE UNDERSTAFFED A BIT.
BUT ONE OF OUR TECH BOYS FLAGGED SOMETHING. SPLASHED DOWN IN THE BANDA SEA. COULD BE THE QUINJET, BUT WITH STARK'S STEALTH TECH, WE STILL CAN'T TRACK THE DAMN THING.
BANNER PROBABLY JUMPED OUT AND SWAM TO FIJI. HE'LL SEND A POSTCARD.
"AS DOES DR. SELVIG, WHO'S ABLE TO WORK OUT THE CALCULATIONS ON SOME RECENTLY DISCOVERED THEORIES IN THE...WELL...COMFORT OF HIS OWN OFFICE.
YOU SENT ME TO RECRUIT BANNER WAY BACK WHEN. DID YOU KNOW THEN WHAT WAS GONNA HAPPEN?
YOU NEVER KNOW. YOU HOPE FOR THE BEST THEN MAKE DO WITH WHAT YOU GET. I GOT A GREAT TEAM.
NOTHING LASTS FOREVER.
"AFTER ALL THAT'S GONE DOWN, ESPECIALLY THE MELEE BETWEEN HULK AND STARK THAT TRASHED JOHANNESBURG..."
WATER OF SIGHT?
TROUBLE DOES, MS. ROMANOFF.
NO MATTER WHO WINS OR LOSES, TROUBLE STILL COMES AROUND.

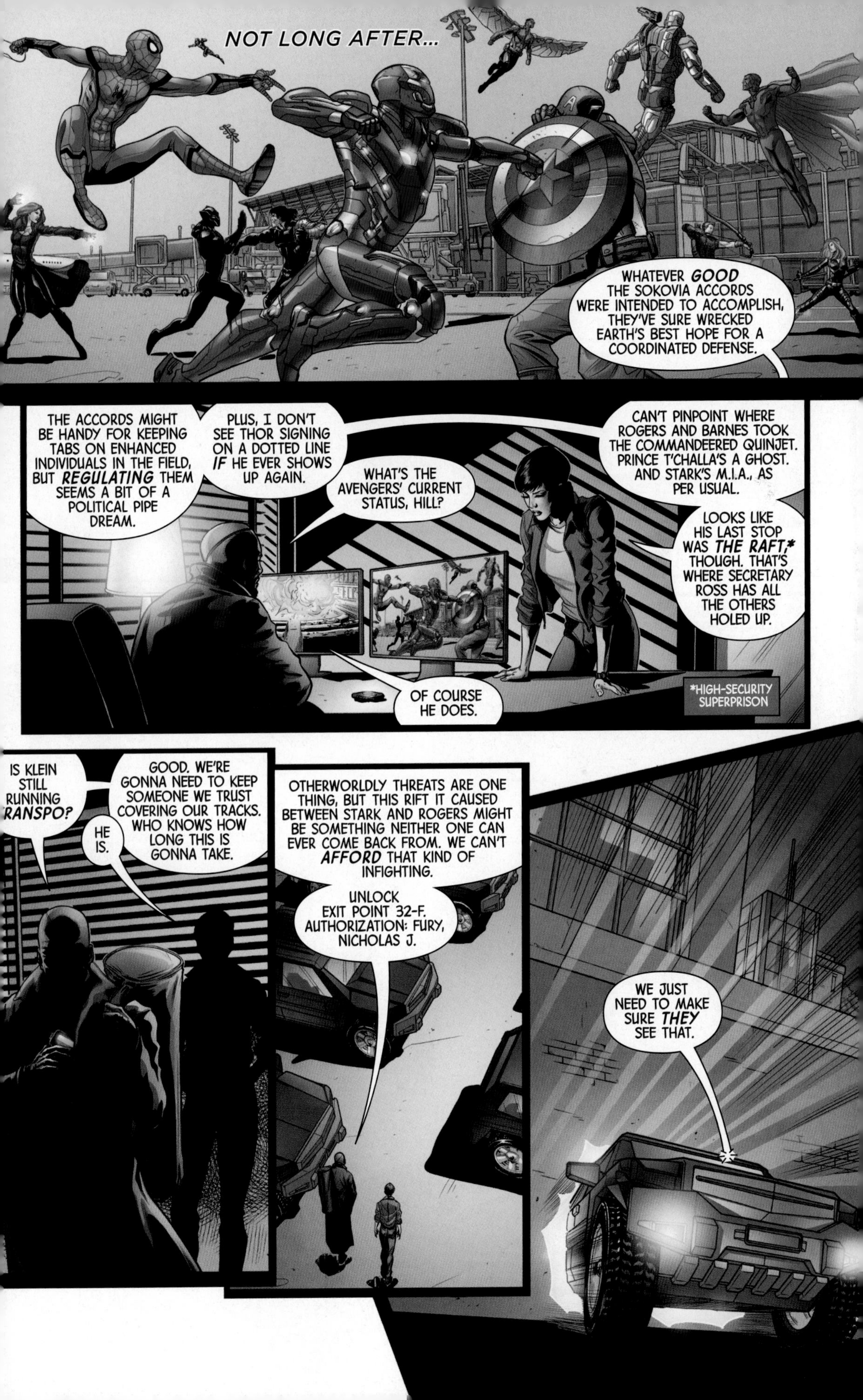
NOT LONG AFTER...
WHATEVER GOOD THE SOKOVIA ACCORDS WERE INTENDED TO ACCOMPLISH, THEY'VE SURE WRECKED EARTH'S BEST HOPE FOR A COORDINATED DEFENSE.
THE ACCORDS MIGHT BE HANDY FOR KEEPING TABS ON ENHANCED INDIVIDUALS IN THE FIELD, BUT REGULATING THEM SEEMS A BIT OF A POLITICAL PIPE DREAM.
PLUS, I DON'T SEE THOR SIGNING ON A DOTTED LINE IF HE EVER SHOWS UP AGAIN.
WHAT'S THE AVENGERS' CURRENT STATUS, HILL?
CAN'T PINPOINT WHERE ROGERS AND BARNES TOOK THE COMMANDEERED QUINJET. PRINCE T'CHALLA'S A GHOST. AND STARK'S M.I.A., AS PER USUAL.
LOOKS LIKE HIS LAST STOP WAS THE RAFT,* THOUGH. THAT'S WHERE SECRETARY ROSS HAS ALL THE OTHERS HOLED UP.
OF COURSE HE DOES.
*HIGH-SECURITY SUPERPRISON
IS KLEIN STILL RUNNING RANSPO?
HE IS.
GOOD. WE'RE GONNA NEED TO KEEP SOMEONE WE TRUST COVERING OUR TRACKS. WHO KNOWS HOW LONG THIS IS GONNA TAKE.
OTHERWORLDLY THREATS ARE ONE THING, BUT THIS RIFT IT CAUSED BETWEEN STARK AND ROGERS MIGHT BE SOMETHING NEITHER ONE CAN EVER COME BACK FROM. WE CAN'T AFFORD THAT KIND OF INFIGHTING.
UNLOCK EXIT POINT 32-F. AUTHORIZATION: FURY, NICHOLAS J.
WE JUST NEED TO MAKE SURE THEY SEE THAT.

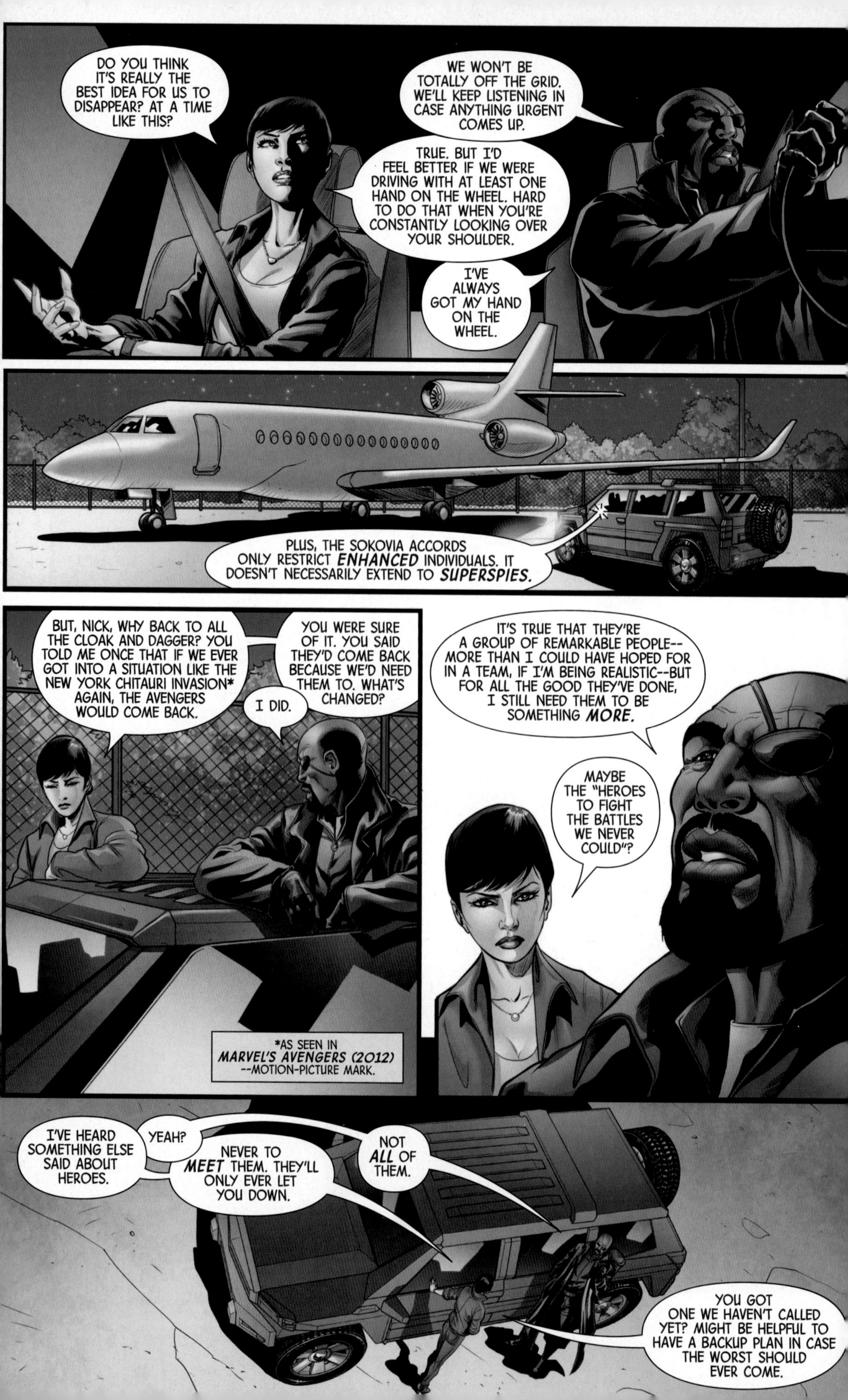
DO YOU THINK IT'S REALLY THE BEST IDEA FOR US TO DISAPPEAR? AT A TIME LIKE THIS?
WE WON'T BE TOTALLY OFF THE GRID. WE'LL KEEP LISTENING IN CASE ANYTHING URGENT COMES UP.
TRUE. BUT I'D FEEL BETTER IF WE WERE DRIVING WITH AT LEAST ONE HAND ON THE WHEEL. HARD TO DO THAT WHEN YOU'RE CONSTANTLY LOOKING OVER YOUR SHOULDER.
I'VE ALWAYS GOT MY HAND ON THE WHEEL.
PLUS, THE SOKOVIA ACCORDS ONLY RESTRICT ENHANCED INDIVIDUALS. IT DOESN'T NECESSARILY EXTEND TO SUPERSPIES.
BUT, NICK, WHY BACK TO ALL THE CLOAK AND DAGGER? YOU TOLD ME ONCE THAT IF WE EVER GOT INTO A SITUATION LIKE THE NEW YORK CHITAURI INVASION* AGAIN, THE AVENGERS WOULD COME BACK.
I DID.
YOU WERE SURE OF IT. YOU SAID THEY'D COME BACK BECAUSE WE'D NEED THEM TO. WHAT'S CHANGED?
*AS SEEN IN MARVEL'S AVENGERS (2012) --MOTION-PICTURE MARK.
IT'S TRUE THAT THEY'RE A GROUP OF REMARKABLE PEOPLE-- MORE THAN I COULD HAVE HOPED FOR IN A TEAM, IF I'M BEING REALISTIC--BUT FOR ALL THE GOOD THEY'VE DONE, I STILL NEED THEM TO BE SOMETHING MORE.
MAYBE THE "HEROES TO FIGHT THE BATTLES WE NEVER COULD"?
I'VE HEARD SOMETHING ELSE SAID ABOUT HEROES.
YEAH?
NEVER TO MEET THEM. THEY'LL ONLY EVER LET YOU DOWN.
NOT ALL OF THEM.
YOU GOT ONE WE HAVEN'T CALLED YET? MIGHT BE HELPFUL TO HAVE A BACKUP PLAN IN CASE THE WORST SHOULD EVER COME.

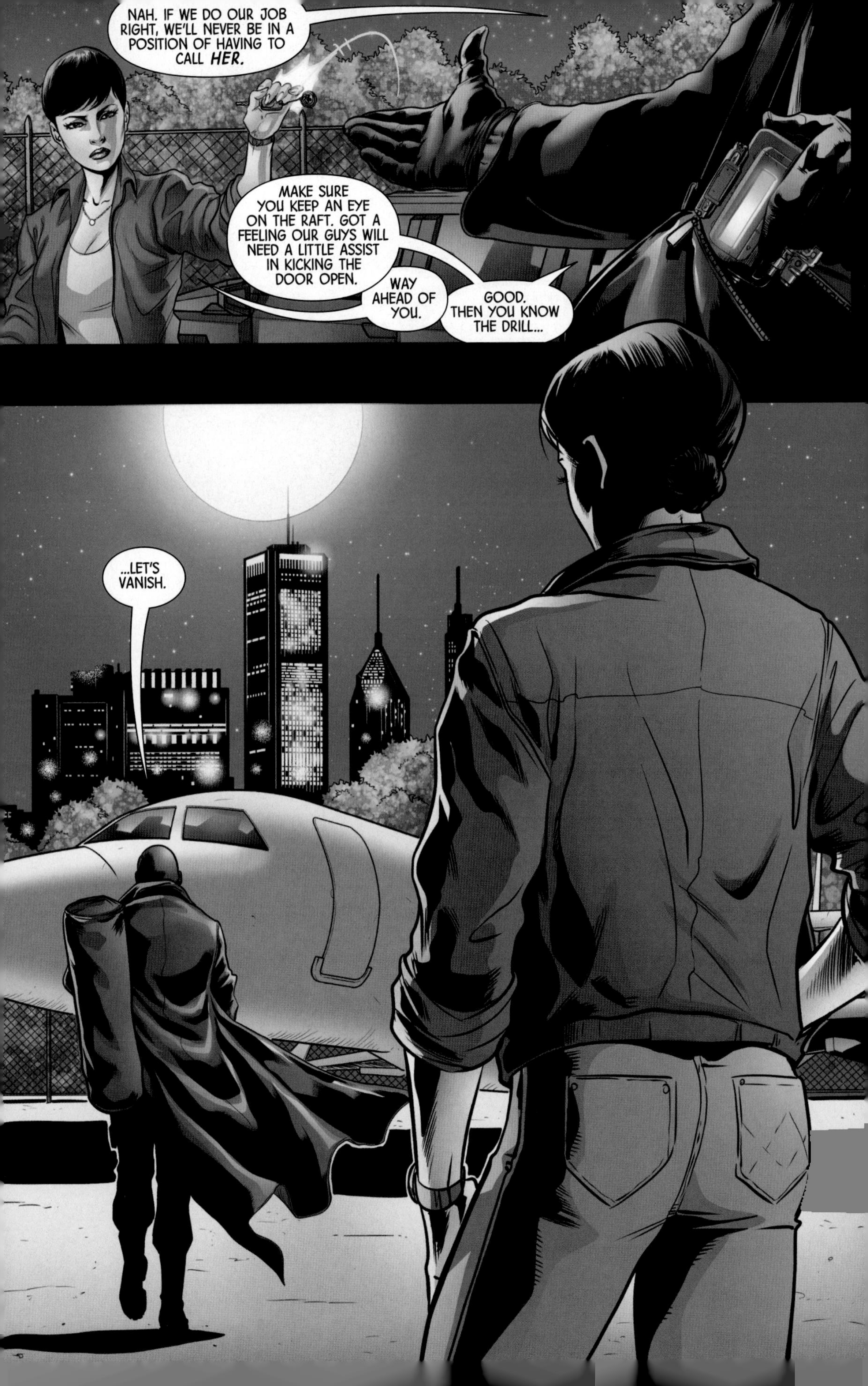
NAH. IF WE DO OUR JOB RIGHT, WE'LL NEVER BE IN A POSITION OF HAVING TO CALL HER.
MAKE SURE YOU KEEP AN EYE ON THE RAFT. GOT A FEELING OUR GUYS WILL NEED A LITTLE ASSIST IN KICKING THE DOOR OPEN.
WAY AHEAD OF YOU.
GOOD. THEN YOU KNOW THE DRILL...
...LET'S VANISH.

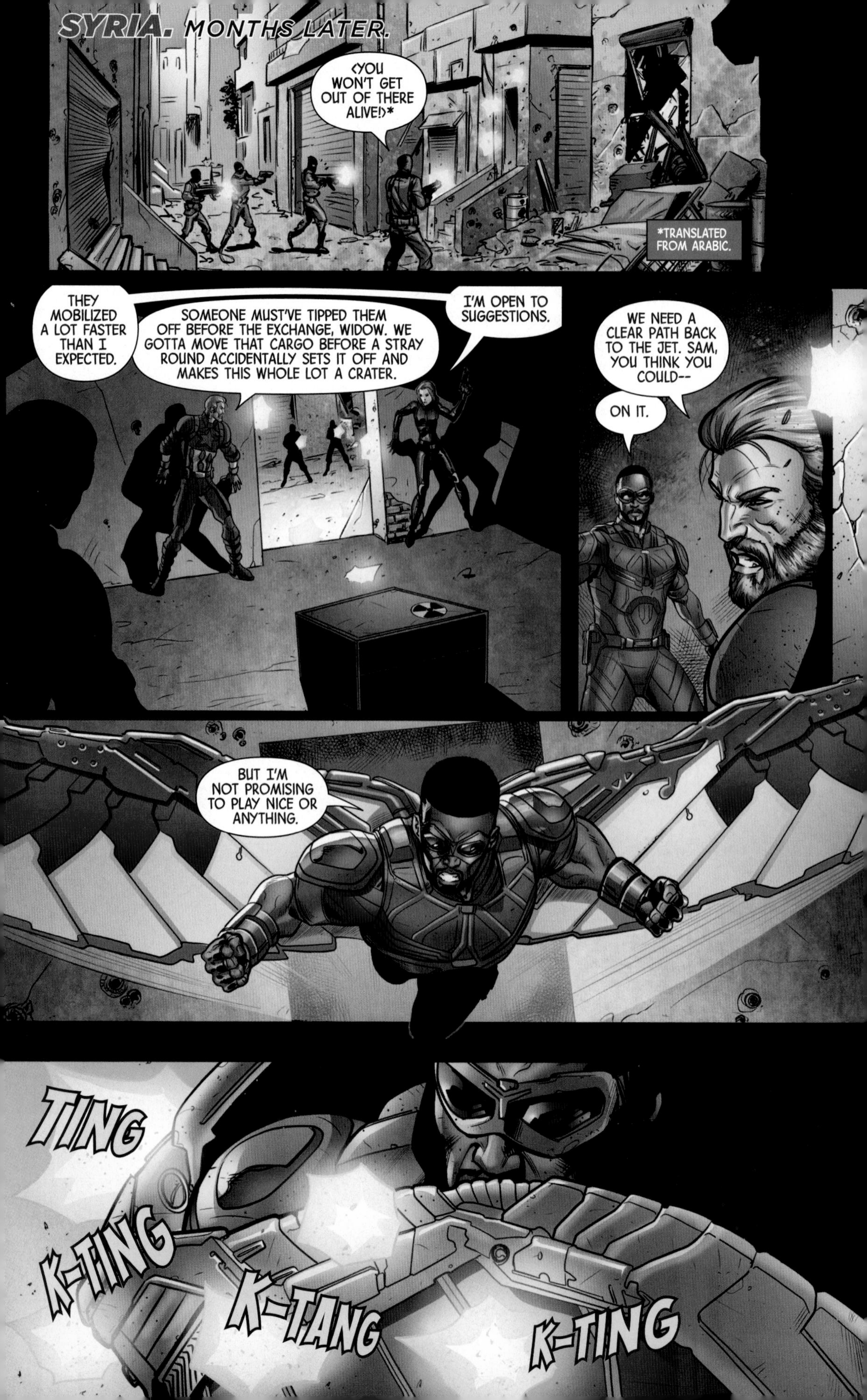
SYRIA. MONTHS LATER.
‹YOU WON'T GET OUT OF THERE ALIVE!›*
*TRANSLATED FROM ARABIC.
THEY MOBILIZED A LOT FASTER THAN I EXPECTED.
SOMEONE MUST'VE TIPPED THEM OFF BEFORE THE EXCHANGE, WIDOW. WE GOTTA MOVE THAT CARGO BEFORE A STRAY ROUND ACCIDENTALLY SETS IT OFF AND MAKES THIS WHOLE LOT A CRATER.
I'M OPEN TO SUGGESTIONS.
WE NEED A CLEAR PATH BACK TO THE JET. SAM, YOU THINK YOU COULD--
ON IT.
BUT I'M NOT PROMISING TO PLAY NICE OR ANYTHING.
TING
K-TING
K-TANG
K-TING

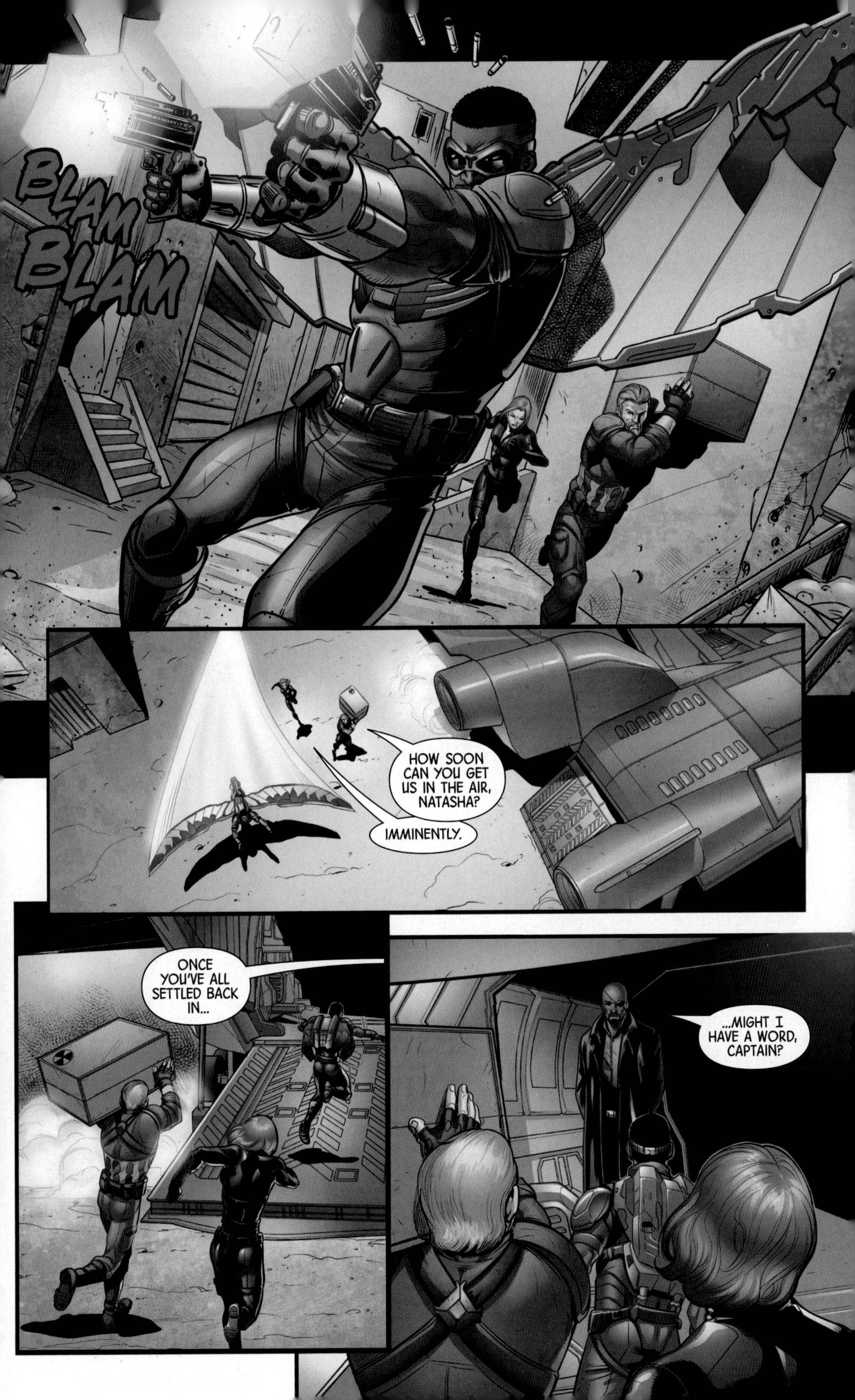
BLAM
BLAM
HOW SOON CAN YOU GET US IN THE AIR, NATASHA?
IMMINENTLY.
ONCE YOU'VE ALL SETTLED BACK IN...
...MIGHT I HAVE A WORD, CAPTAIN?

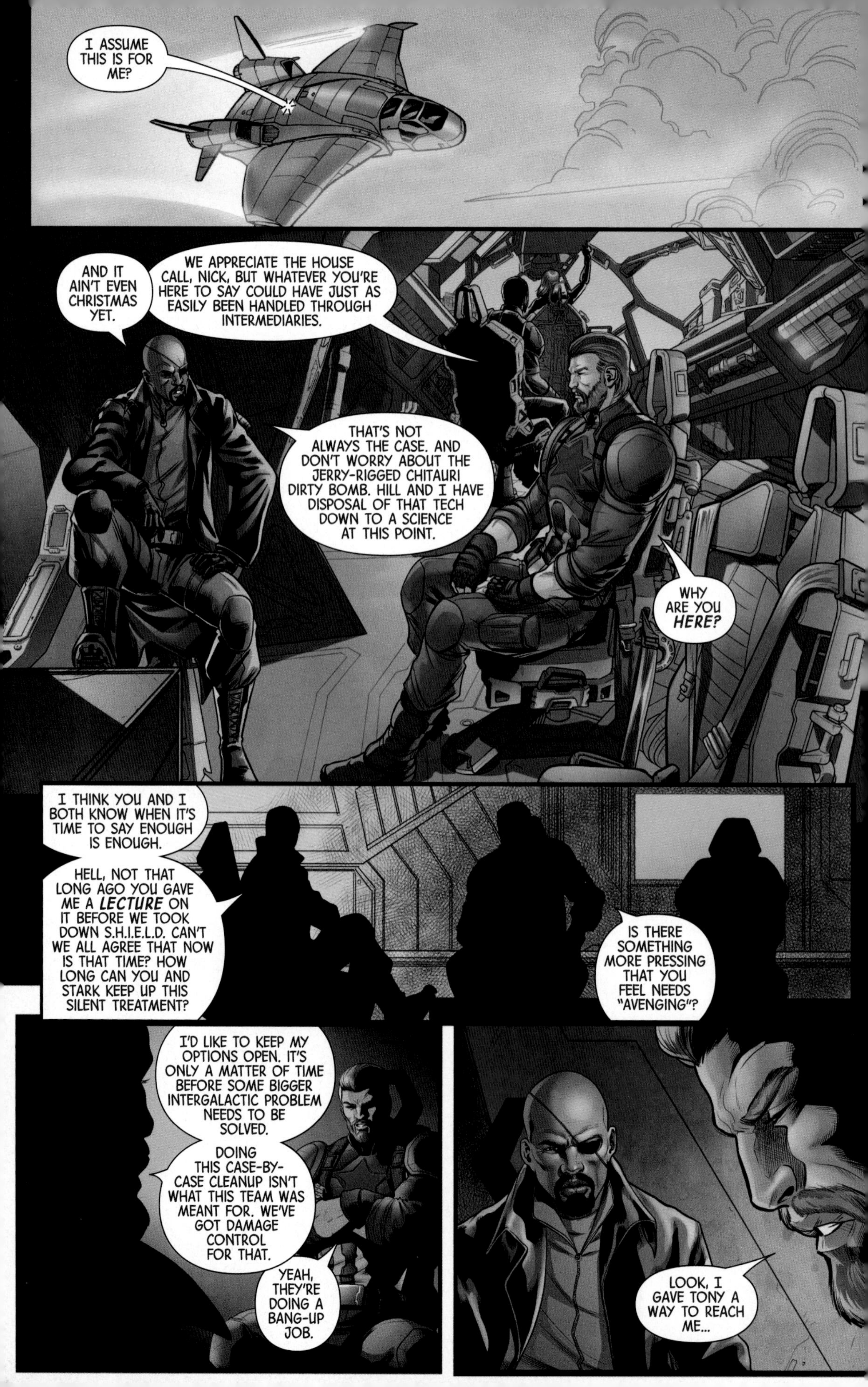
I ASSUME THIS IS FOR ME?
AND IT AIN'T EVEN CHRISTMAS YET.
WE APPRECIATE THE HOUSE CALL, NICK, BUT WHATEVER YOU'RE HERE TO SAY COULD HAVE JUST AS EASILY BEEN HANDLED THROUGH INTERMEDIARIES.
THAT'S NOT ALWAYS THE CASE. AND DON'T WORRY ABOUT THE JERRY-RIGGED CHITAURI DIRTY BOMB. HILL AND I HAVE DISPOSAL OF THAT TECH DOWN TO A SCIENCE AT THIS POINT.
WHY ARE YOU *HERE?*
I THINK YOU AND I BOTH KNOW WHEN IT'S TIME TO SAY ENOUGH IS ENOUGH.
HELL, NOT THAT LONG AGO YOU GAVE ME A *LECTURE* ON IT BEFORE WE TOOK DOWN S.H.I.E.L.D. CAN'T WE ALL AGREE THAT NOW IS THAT TIME? HOW LONG CAN YOU AND STARK KEEP UP THIS SILENT TREATMENT?
IS THERE SOMETHING MORE PRESSING THAT YOU FEEL NEEDS "AVENGING"?
I'D LIKE TO KEEP MY OPTIONS OPEN. IT'S ONLY A MATTER OF TIME BEFORE SOME BIGGER INTERGALACTIC PROBLEM NEEDS TO BE SOLVED.
DOING THIS CASE-BY-CASE CLEANUP ISN'T WHAT THIS TEAM WAS MEANT FOR. WE'VE GOT DAMAGE CONTROL FOR THAT.
YEAH, THEY'RE DOING A BANG-UP JOB.
LOOK, I GAVE TONY A WAY TO REACH ME...

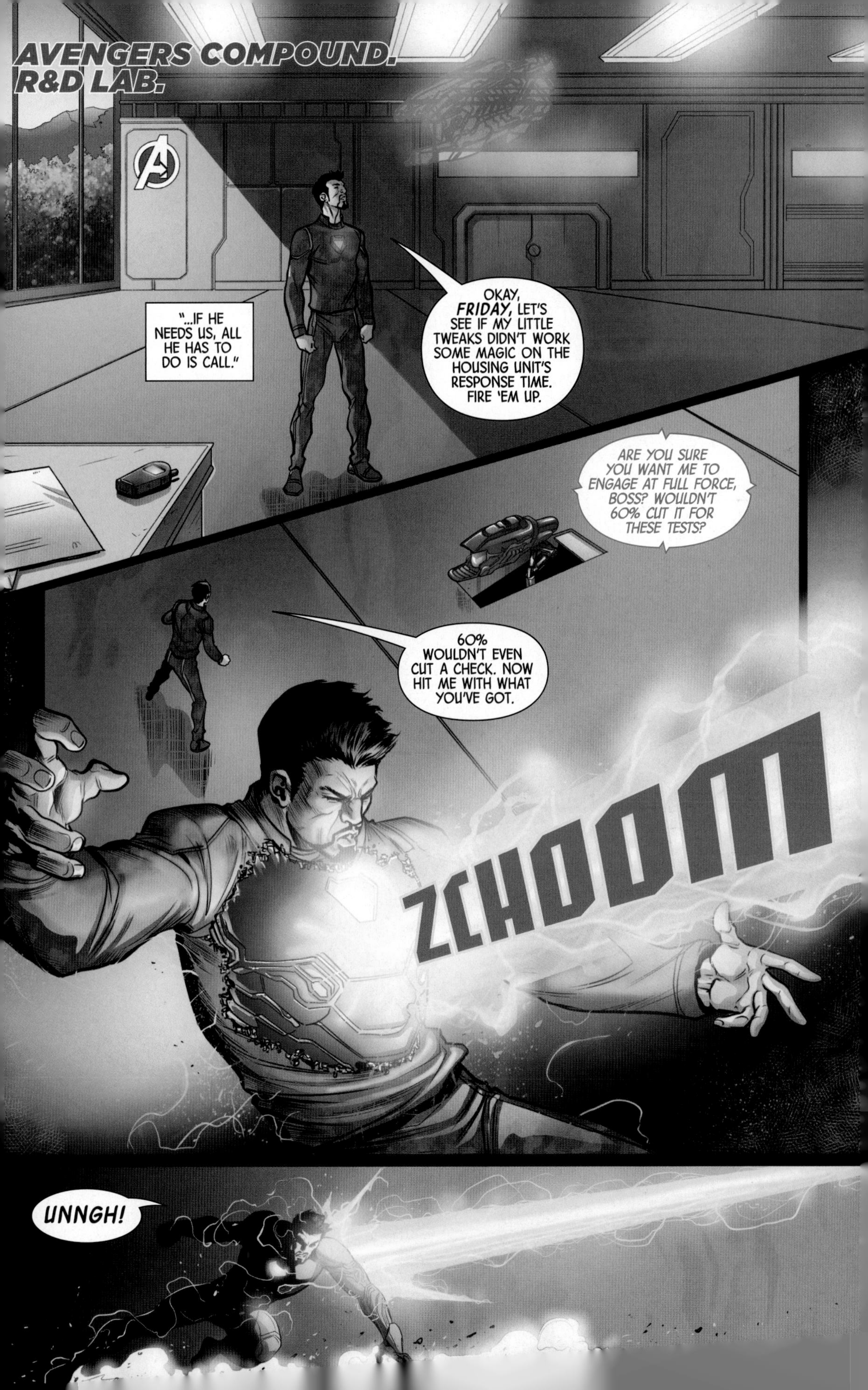
AVENGERS COMPOUND. R&D LAB.
"...IF HE NEEDS US, ALL HE HAS TO DO IS CALL."
OKAY, FRIDAY, LET'S SEE IF MY LITTLE TWEAKS DIDN'T WORK SOME MAGIC ON THE HOUSING UNIT'S RESPONSE TIME. FIRE 'EM UP.
ARE YOU SURE YOU WANT ME TO ENGAGE AT FULL FORCE, BOSS? WOULDN'T 60% CUT IT FOR THESE TESTS?
60% WOULDN'T EVEN CUT A CHECK. NOW HIT ME WITH WHAT YOU'VE GOT.
ZCHOOM
UNNGH!

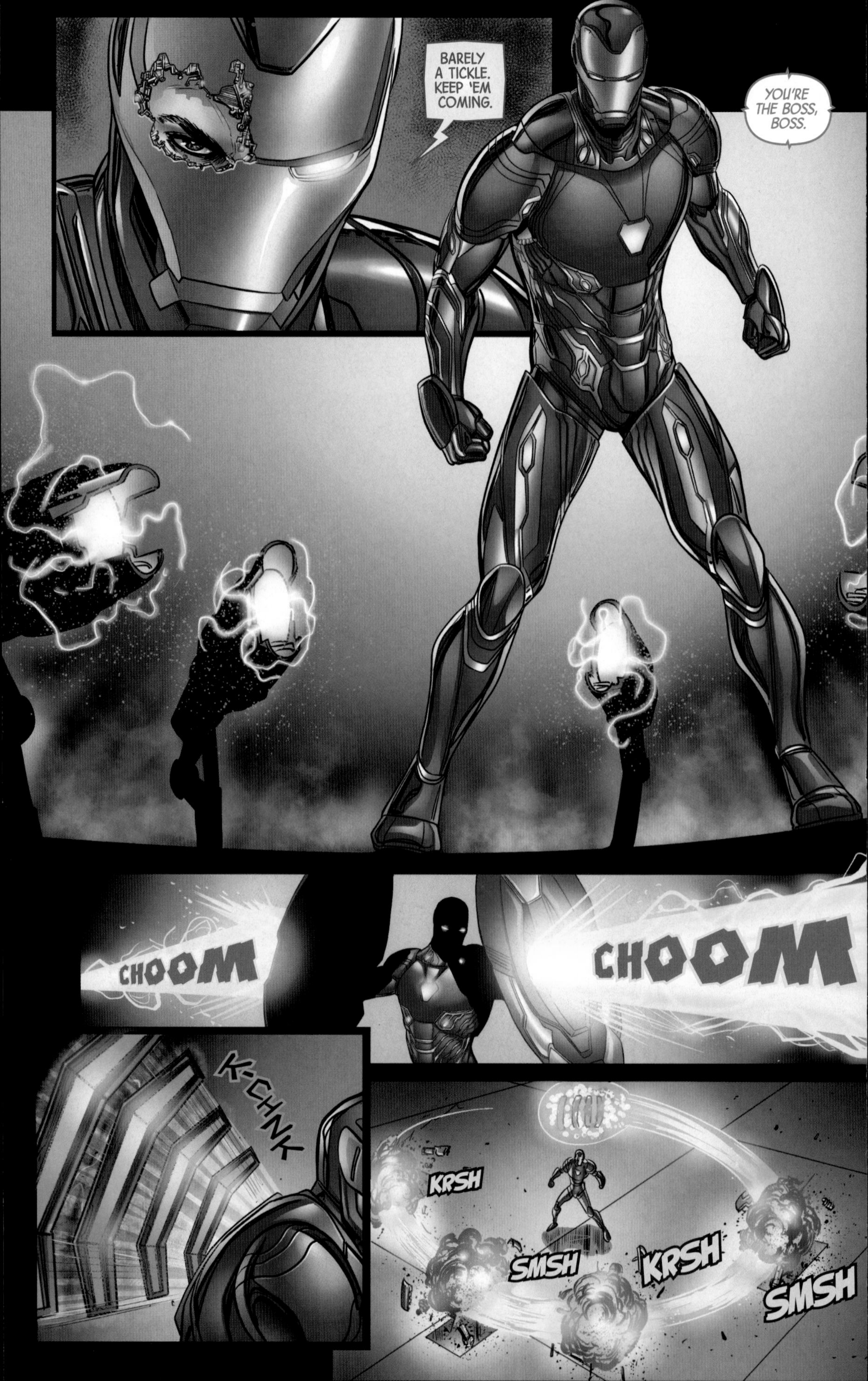
BARELY A TICKLE. KEEP 'EM COMING.
YOU'RE THE BOSS, BOSS.
CHOOM
CHOOM
K-CHNK
KRSH
SMSH
KRSH
SMSH

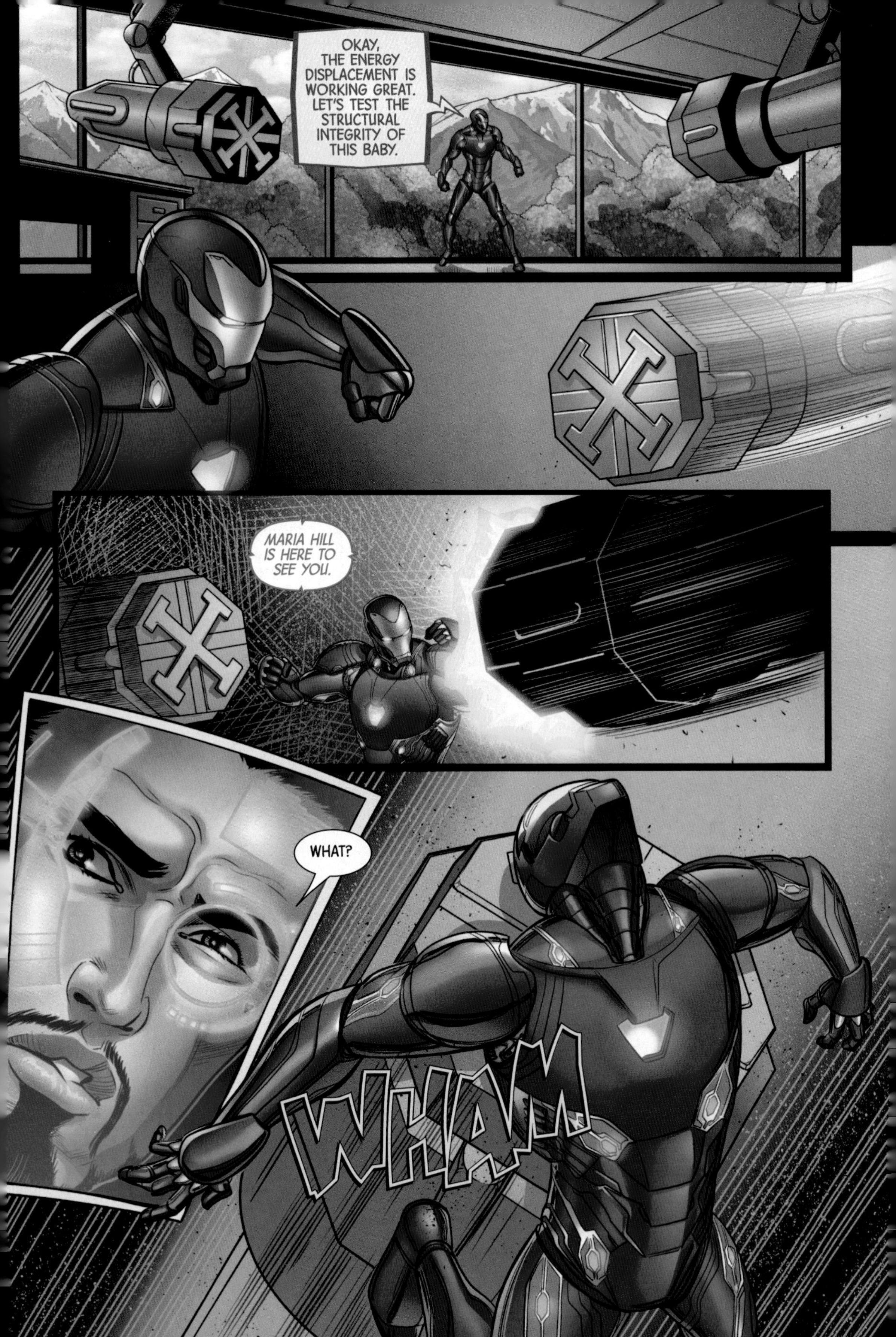
OKAY, THE ENERGY DISPLACEMENT IS WORKING GREAT. LET'S TEST THE STRUCTURAL INTEGRITY OF THIS BABY.
MARIA HILL IS HERE TO SEE YOU.
WHAT?
WHAM

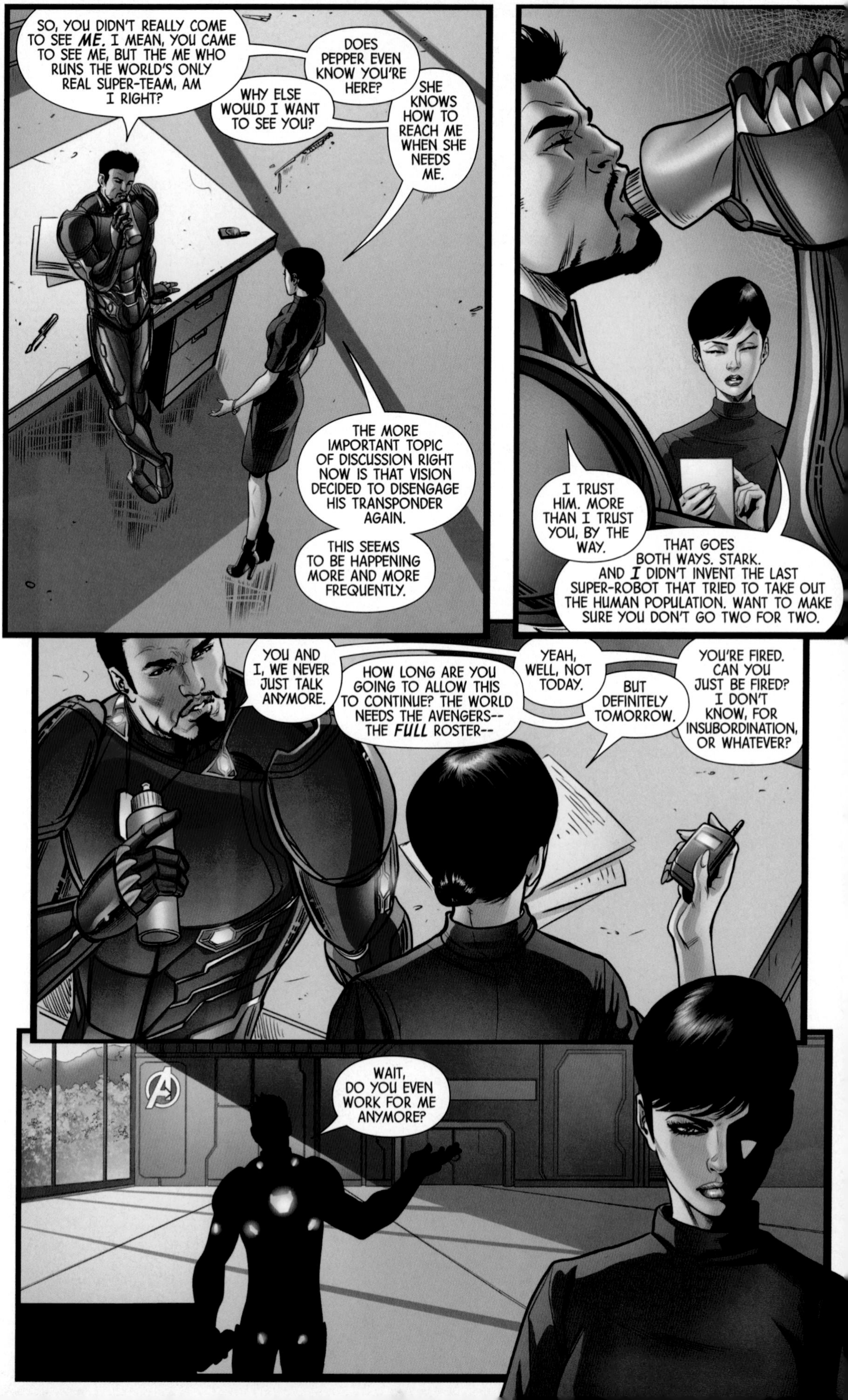

SO, YOU DIDN'T REALLY COME TO SEE *ME*. I MEAN, YOU CAME TO SEE ME, BUT THE ME WHO RUNS THE WORLD'S ONLY REAL SUPER-TEAM, AM I RIGHT?
DOES PEPPER EVEN KNOW YOU'RE HERE?
WHY ELSE WOULD I WANT TO SEE YOU?
SHE KNOWS HOW TO REACH ME WHEN SHE NEEDS ME.
THE MORE IMPORTANT TOPIC OF DISCUSSION RIGHT NOW IS THAT VISION DECIDED TO DISENGAGE HIS TRANSPONDER AGAIN.
THIS SEEMS TO BE HAPPENING MORE AND MORE FREQUENTLY.
I TRUST HIM. MORE THAN I TRUST YOU, BY THE WAY.
THAT GOES BOTH WAYS. STARK. AND *I* DIDN'T INVENT THE LAST SUPER-ROBOT THAT TRIED TO TAKE OUT THE HUMAN POPULATION. WANT TO MAKE SURE YOU DON'T GO TWO FOR TWO.
YOU AND I, WE NEVER JUST TALK ANYMORE.
HOW LONG ARE YOU GOING TO ALLOW THIS TO CONTINUE? THE WORLD NEEDS THE AVENGERS-- THE *FULL* ROSTER--
YEAH, WELL, NOT TODAY.
BUT DEFINITELY TOMORROW.
YOU'RE FIRED. CAN YOU JUST BE FIRED? I DON'T KNOW, FOR INSUBORDINATION, OR WHATEVER?
WAIT, DO YOU EVEN WORK FOR ME ANYMORE?

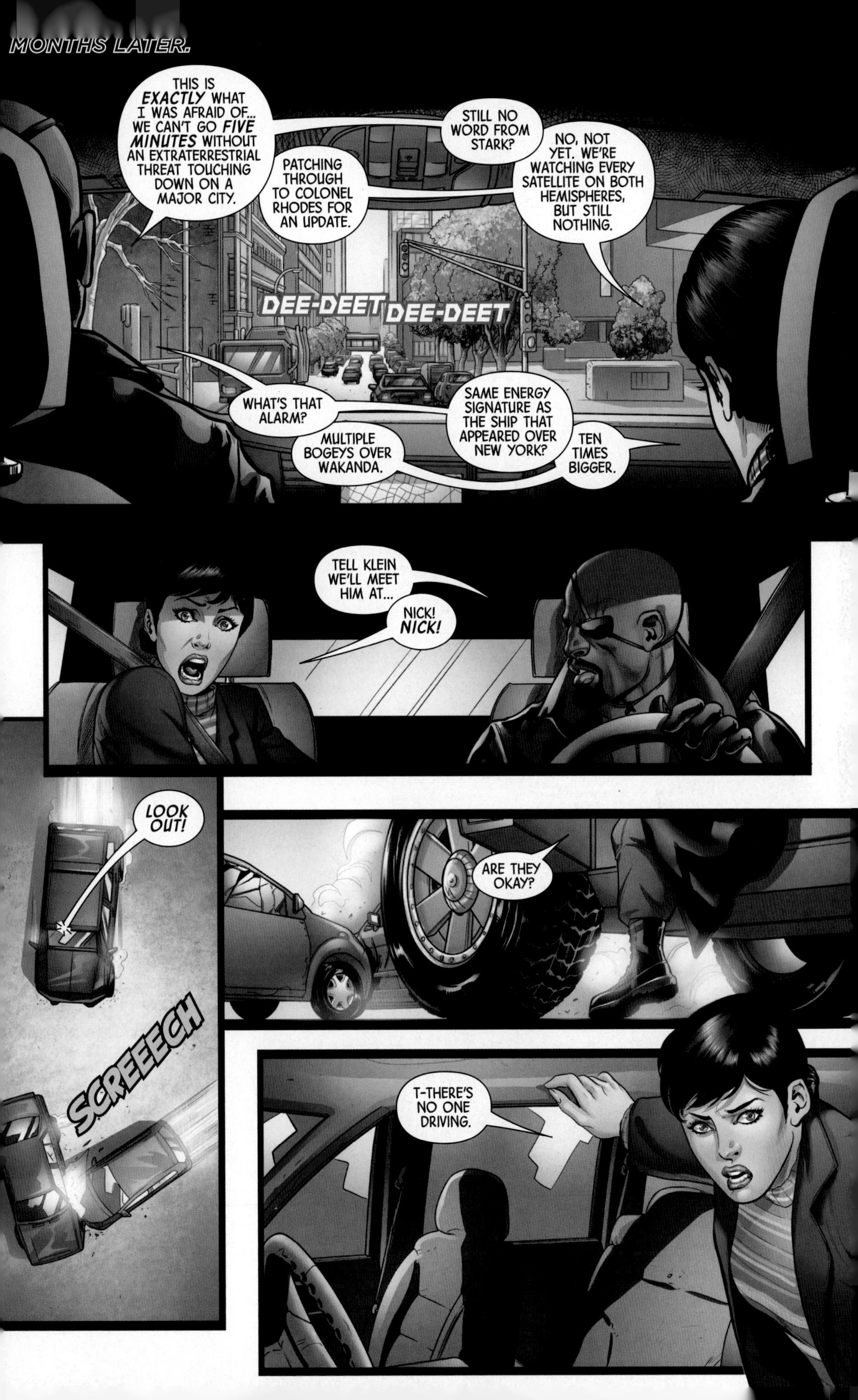
MONTHS LATER.
THIS IS EXACTLY WHAT I WAS AFRAID OF... WE CAN'T GO FIVE MINUTES WITHOUT AN EXTRATERRESTRIAL THREAT TOUCHING DOWN ON A MAJOR CITY.
STILL NO WORD FROM STARK?
PATCHING THROUGH TO COLONEL RHODES FOR AN UPDATE.
NO, NOT YET. WE'RE WATCHING EVERY SATELLITE ON BOTH HEMISPHERES, BUT STILL NOTHING.
DEE-DEET DEE-DEET
WHAT'S THAT ALARM?
MULTIPLE BOGEYS OVER WAKANDA.
SAME ENERGY SIGNATURE AS THE SHIP THAT APPEARED OVER NEW YORK?
TEN TIMES BIGGER.
TELL KLEIN WE'LL MEET HIM AT...
NICK! NICK!
LOOK OUT!
SCREEECH
ARE THEY OKAY?
T-THERE'S NO ONE DRIVING.

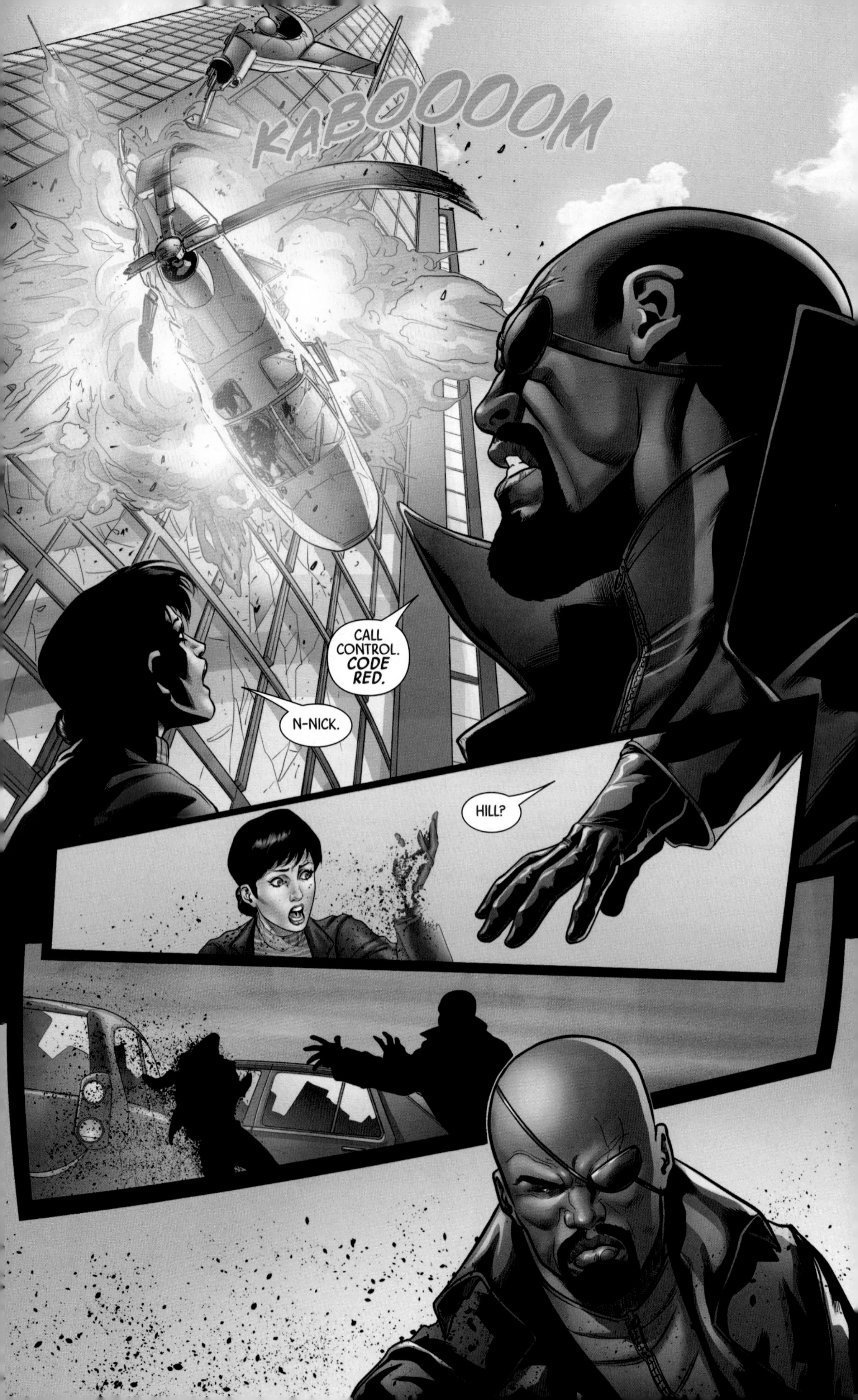
KABOOOOM
CALL CONTROL. CODE RED.
N-NICK.
HILL?

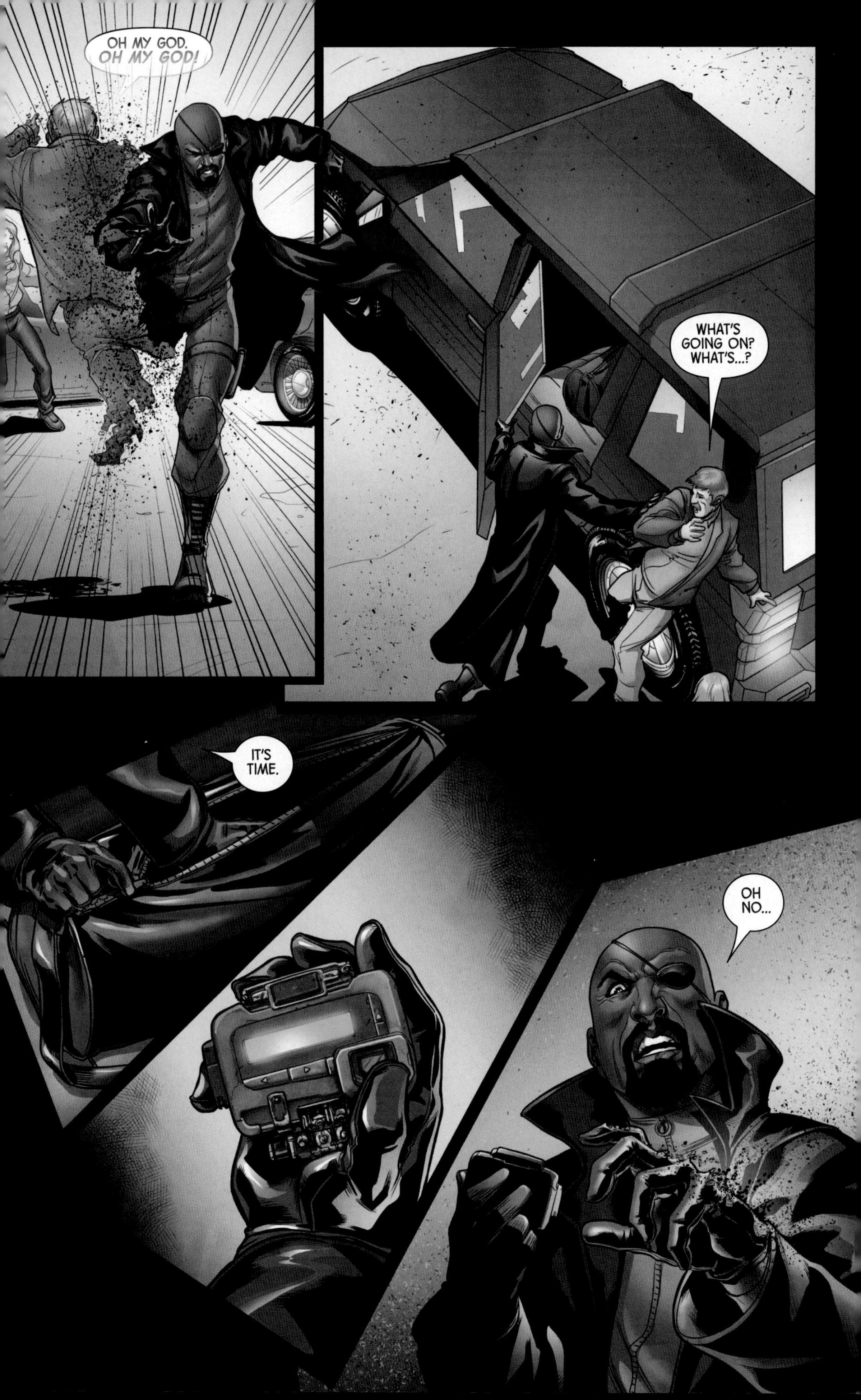
OH MY GOD. OH MY GOD!
WHAT'S GOING ON? WHAT'S...?
IT'S TIME.
OH NO...

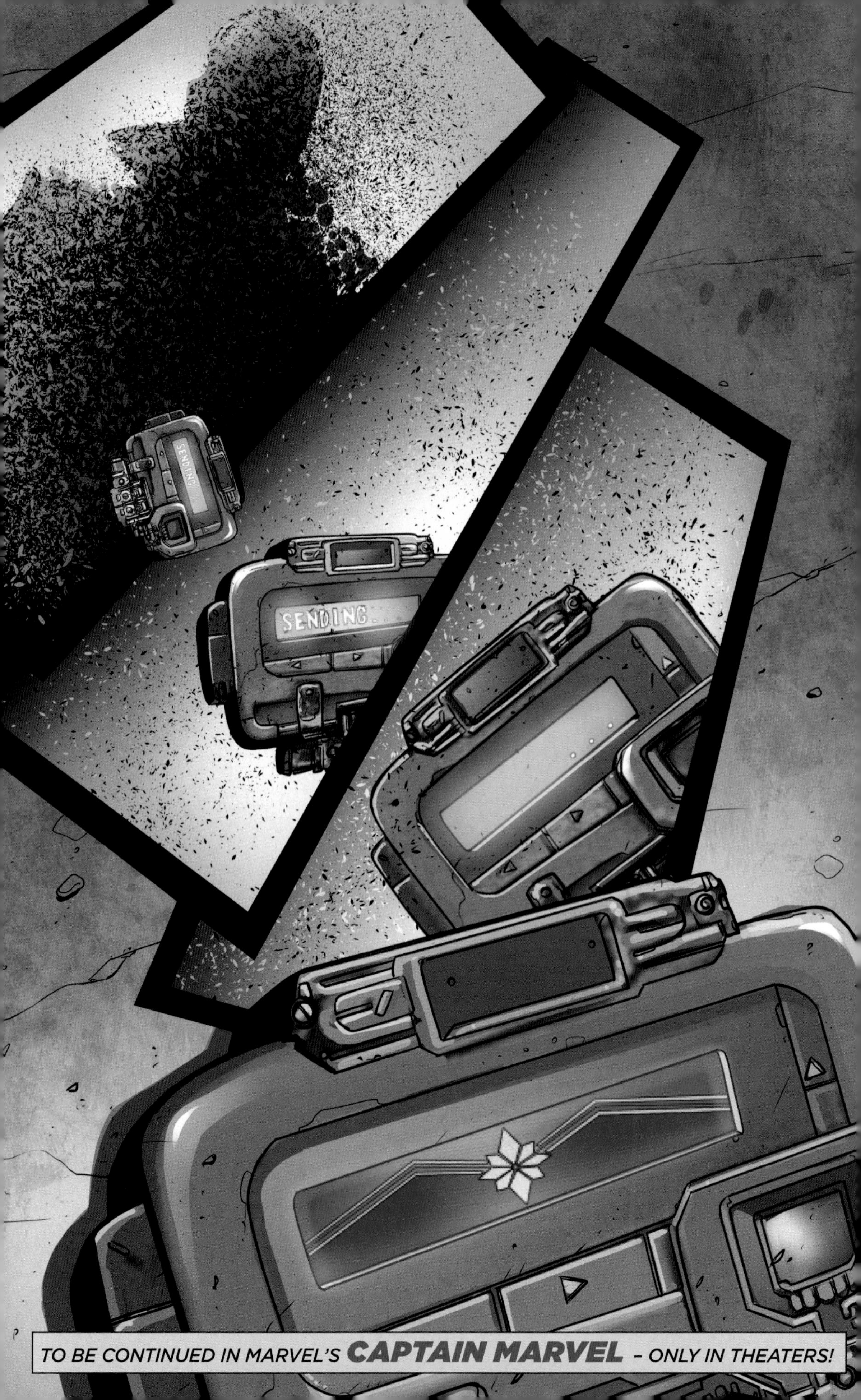
SENDING
SENDING...
TO BE CONTINUED IN MARVEL'S CAPTAIN MARVEL - ONLY IN THEATERS!

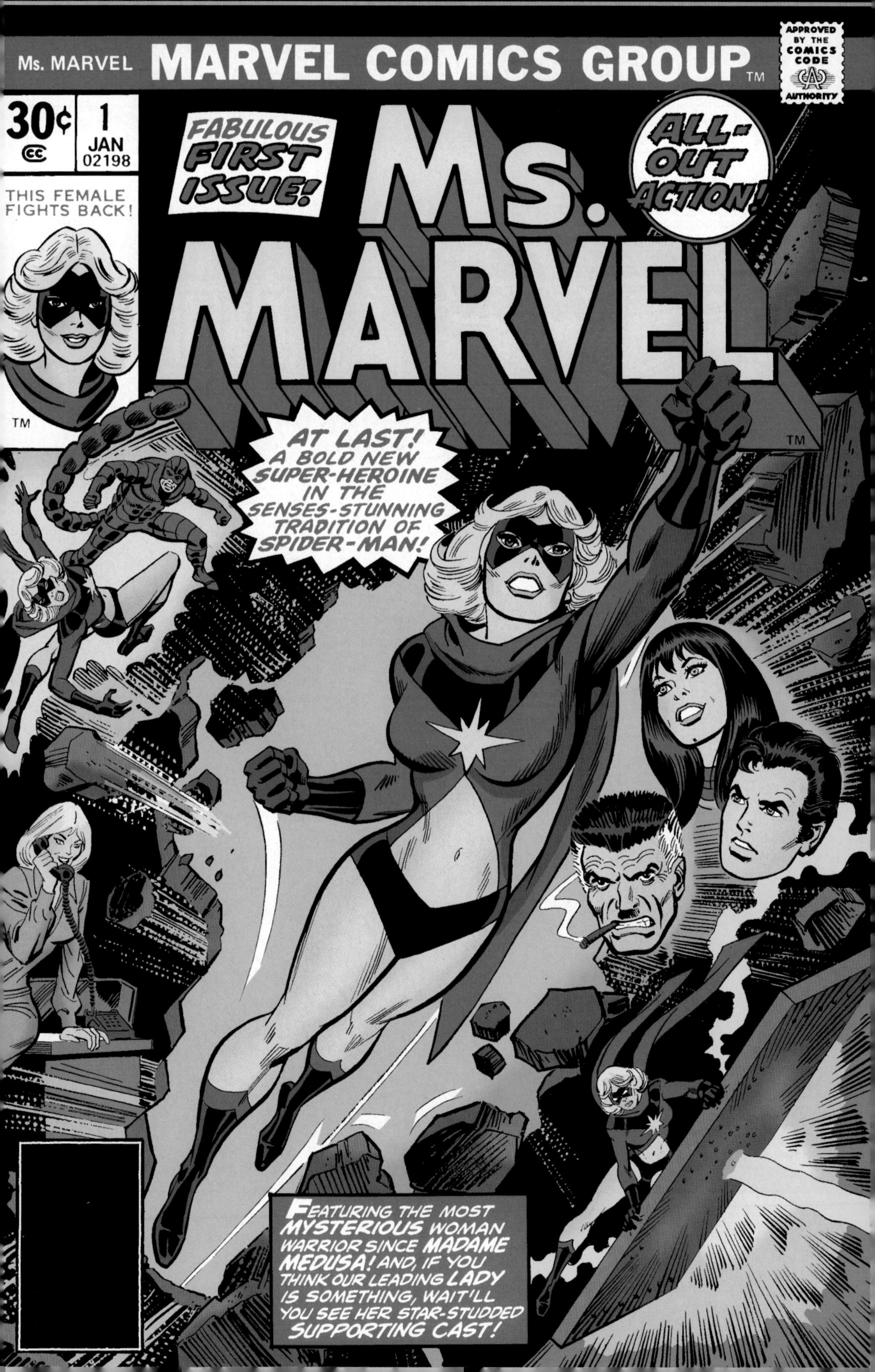

Ms. MARVEL
MARVEL COMICS GROUP TM
APPROVED BY THE COMICS CODE AUTHORITY
30¢ 1 JAN 02198
THIS FEMALE FIGHTS BACK!
TM
FABULOUS FIRST ISSUE!
Ms. MARVEL
ALL-OUT ACTION!
TM
AT LAST! A BOLD NEW SUPER-HEROINE IN THE SENSES-STUNNING TRADITION OF SPIDER-MAN!
FEATURING THE MOST MYSTERIOUS WOMAN WARRIOR SINCE MADAME MEDUSA! AND, IF YOU THINK OUR LEADING LADY IS SOMETHING, WAIT'LL YOU SEE HER STAR-STUDDED SUPPORTING CAST!


IN HER FIRST SOLO SERIES, CAROL DANVERS MUST CONTEND WITH THE SCIENTISTS OF A.I.M. AND THE SCORPION.

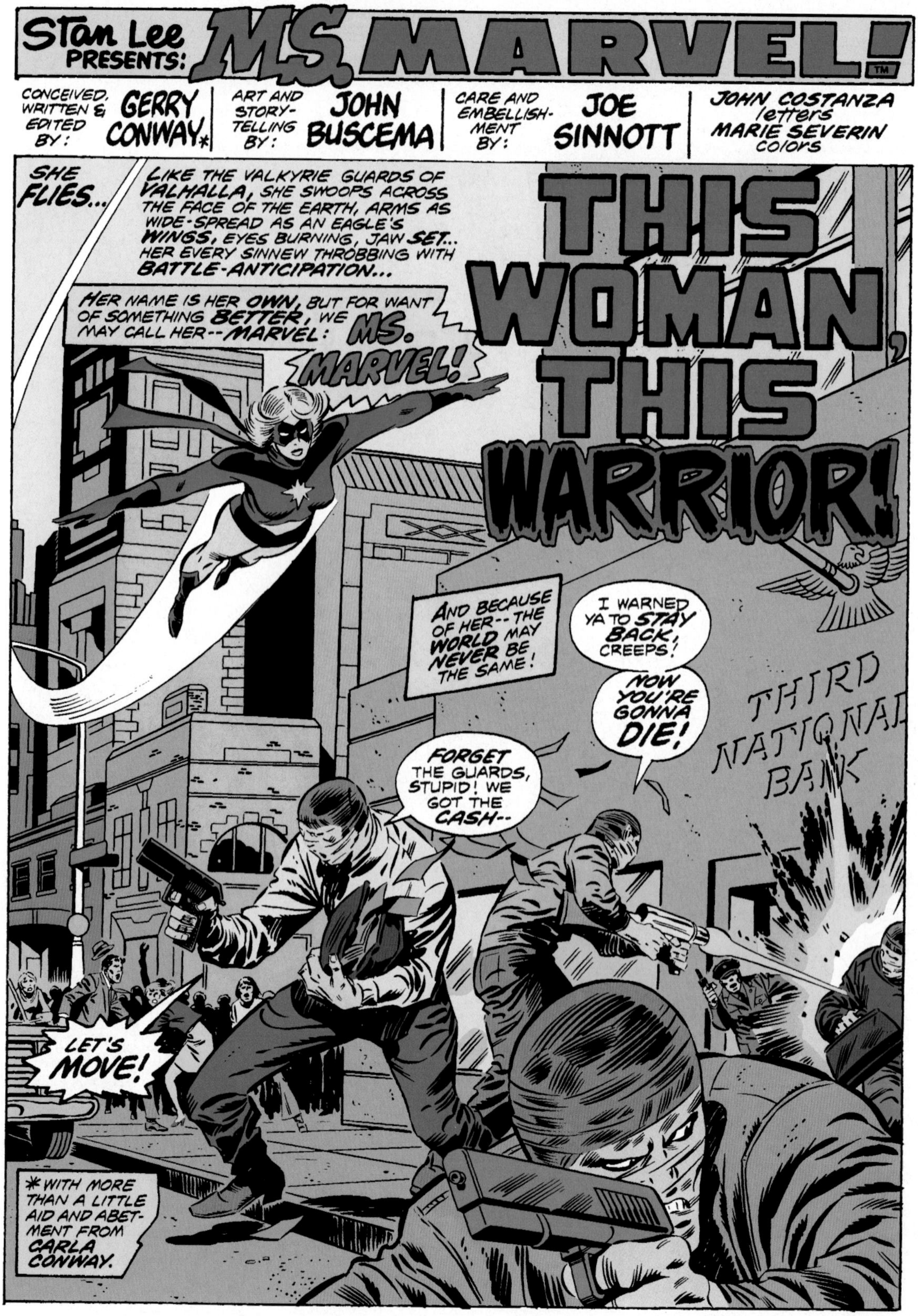
Stan Lee PRESENTS: MS. MARVEL!™
CONCEIVED, WRITTEN & EDITED BY: GERRY CONWAY*
ART AND STORY-TELLING BY: JOHN BUSCEMA
CARE AND EMBELLISH-MENT BY: JOE SINNOTT
JOHN COSTANZA letters
MARIE SEVERIN colors
SHE FLIES...
LIKE THE VALKYRIE GUARDS OF VALHALLA, SHE SWOOPS ACROSS THE FACE OF THE EARTH, ARMS AS WIDE-SPREAD AS AN EAGLE'S WINGS, EYES BURNING, JAW SET... HER EVERY SINNEW THROBBING WITH BATTLE-ANTICIPATION...
THIS WOMAN, THIS WARRIOR!
HER NAME IS HER OWN, BUT FOR WANT OF SOMETHING BETTER, WE MAY CALL HER--MARVEL: MS. MARVEL!
AND BECAUSE OF HER--THE WORLD MAY NEVER BE THE SAME!
I WARNED YA TO STAY BACK, CREEPS!
NOW YOU'RE GONNA DIE!
THIRD NATIONAL BANK
FORGET THE GUARDS, STUPID! WE GOT THE CASH--
LET'S MOVE!
*WITH MORE THAN A LITTLE AID AND ABETMENT FROM CARLA CONWAY.

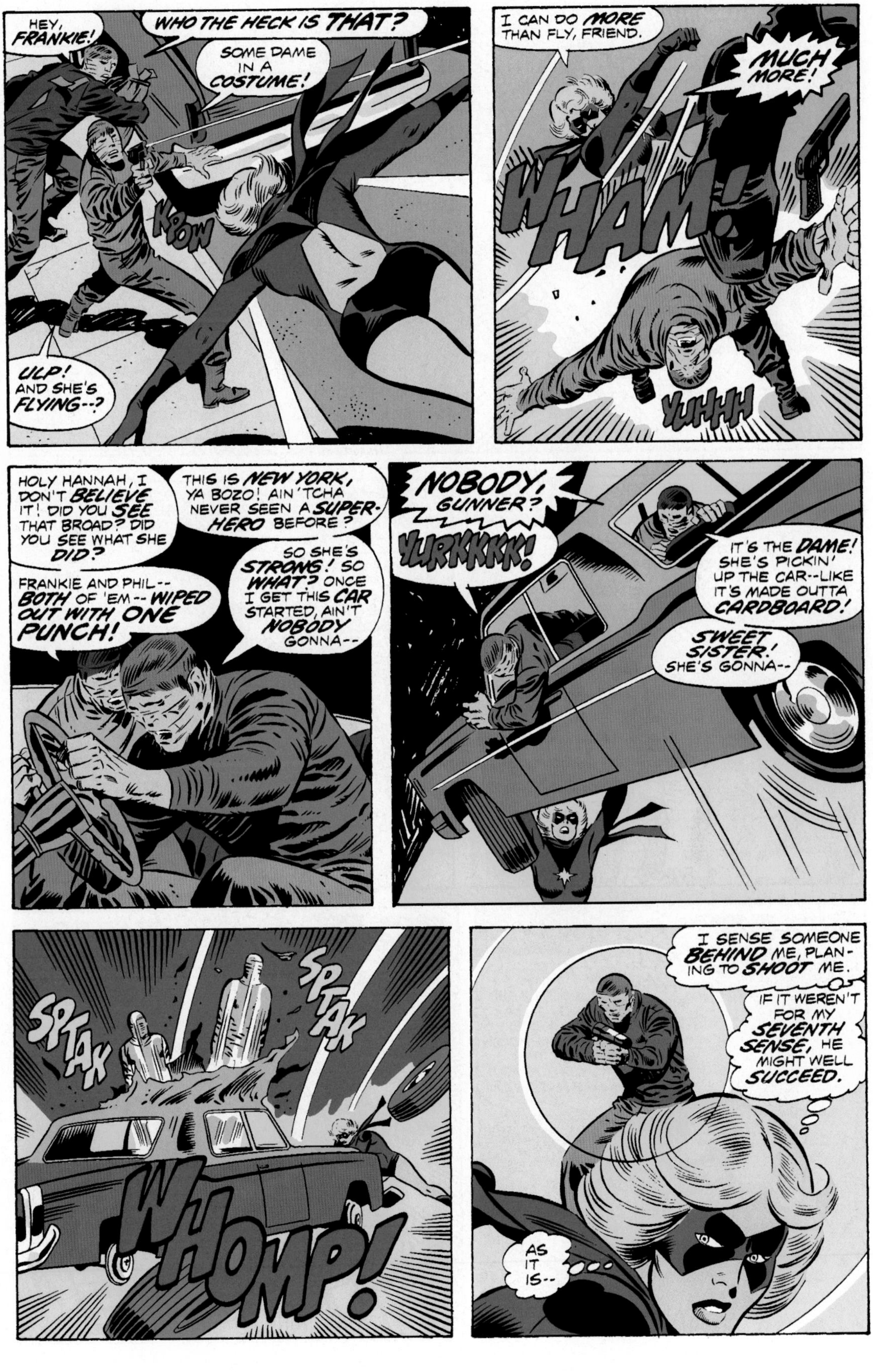

HEY, FRANKIE!
WHO THE HECK IS THAT?
SOME DAME IN A COSTUME!
KBOOM
ULP! AND SHE'S FLYING--?
I CAN DO MORE THAN FLY, FRIEND.
MUCH MORE!
WHAM!
YUHHH
HOLY HANNAH, I DON'T BELIEVE IT! DID YOU SEE THAT BROAD? DID YOU SEE WHAT SHE DID?
THIS IS NEW YORK, YA BOZO! AIN'TCHA NEVER SEEN A SUPER-HERO BEFORE?
FRANKIE AND PHIL-- BOTH OF 'EM -- WIPED OUT WITH ONE PUNCH!
SO SHE'S STRONG! SO WHAT? ONCE I GET THIS CAR STARTED, AIN'T NOBODY GONNA--
NOBODY, GUNNER?
YURKKKK!
IT'S THE DAME! SHE'S PICKIN' UP THE CAR--LIKE IT'S MADE OUTTA CARDBOARD!
SWEET SISTER! SHE'S GONNA--
SPTAK
SPTAK
WHOMP!
I SENSE SOMEONE BEHIND ME, PLAN-ING TO SHOOT ME.
IF IT WEREN'T FOR MY SEVENTH SENSE, HE MIGHT WELL SUCCEED.
AS IT IS--

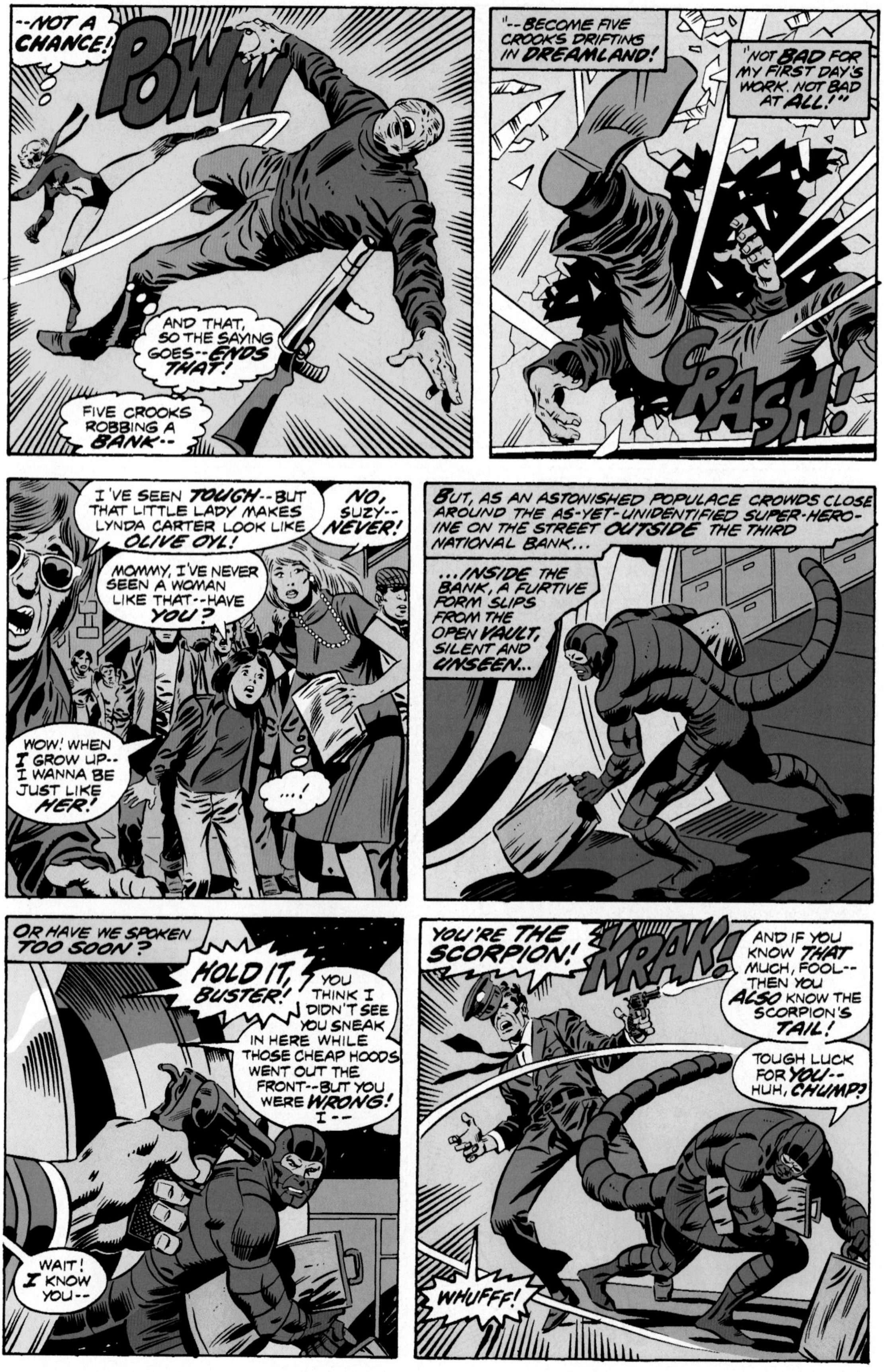
--NOT A CHANCE!
POWW
AND THAT, SO THE SAYING GOES--ENDS THAT!
FIVE CROOKS ROBBING A BANK--
"--BECOME FIVE CROOKS DRIFTING IN DREAMLAND!
"NOT BAD FOR MY FIRST DAY'S WORK. NOT BAD AT ALL!"
CRASH!
I'VE SEEN TOUGH--BUT THAT LITTLE LADY MAKES LYNDA CARTER LOOK LIKE OLIVE OYL!
NO, SUZY--NEVER!
MOMMY, I'VE NEVER SEEN A WOMAN LIKE THAT--HAVE YOU?
WOW! WHEN I GROW UP--I WANNA BE JUST LIKE HER!
...!
BUT, AS AN ASTONISHED POPULACE CROWDS CLOSE AROUND THE AS-YET-UNIDENTIFIED SUPER-HEROINE ON THE STREET OUTSIDE THE THIRD NATIONAL BANK...
...INSIDE THE BANK, A FURTIVE FORM SLIPS FROM THE OPEN VAULT, SILENT AND UNSEEN...
OR HAVE WE SPOKEN TOO SOON?
HOLD IT, BUSTER!
YOU THINK I DIDN'T SEE YOU SNEAK IN HERE WHILE THOSE CHEAP HOODS WENT OUT THE FRONT--BUT YOU WERE WRONG! I--
WAIT! I KNOW YOU--
YOU'RE THE SCORPION!
KRAK!
AND IF YOU KNOW THAT MUCH, FOOL--THEN YOU ALSO KNOW THE SCORPION'S TAIL!
TOUGH LUCK FOR YOU--HUH, CHUMP?
WHUFFF!

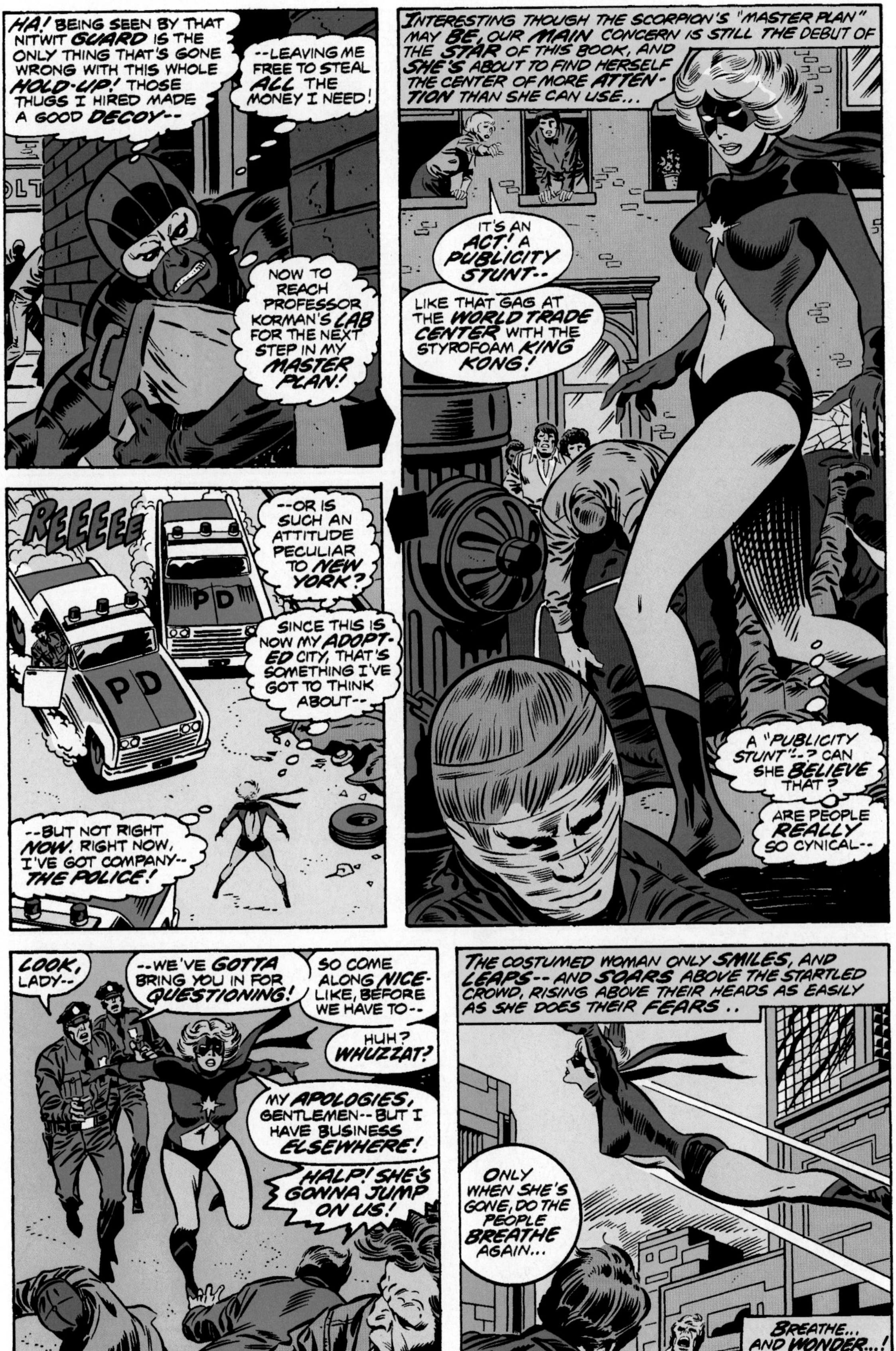
HA! BEING SEEN BY THAT NITWIT GUARD IS THE ONLY THING THAT'S GONE WRONG WITH THIS WHOLE HOLD-UP! THOSE THUGS I HIRED MADE A GOOD DECOY--
--LEAVING ME FREE TO STEAL ALL THE MONEY I NEED!
NOW TO REACH PROFESSOR KORMAN'S LAB FOR THE NEXT STEP IN MY MASTER PLAN!
INTERESTING THOUGH THE SCORPION'S "MASTER PLAN" MAY BE, OUR MAIN CONCERN IS STILL THE DEBUT OF THE STAR OF THIS BOOK, AND SHE'S ABOUT TO FIND HERSELF THE CENTER OF MORE ATTENTION THAN SHE CAN USE...
IT'S AN ACT! A PUBLICITY STUNT--
LIKE THAT GAG AT THE WORLD TRADE CENTER WITH THE STYROFOAM KING KONG!
A "PUBLICITY STUNT"--? CAN SHE BELIEVE THAT?
ARE PEOPLE REALLY SO CYNICAL--
--OR IS SUCH AN ATTITUDE PECULIAR TO NEW YORK?
SINCE THIS IS NOW MY ADOPTED CITY, THAT'S SOMETHING I'VE GOT TO THINK ABOUT--
REEEEEE
PD
PD
--BUT NOT RIGHT NOW. RIGHT NOW, I'VE GOT COMPANY-- THE POLICE!
LOOK, LADY--
--WE'VE GOTTA BRING YOU IN FOR QUESTIONING!
SO COME ALONG NICE-LIKE, BEFORE WE HAVE TO--
HUH? WHUZZAT?
MY APOLOGIES, GENTLEMEN-- BUT I HAVE BUSINESS ELSEWHERE!
HALP! SHE'S GONNA JUMP ON US!
THE COSTUMED WOMAN ONLY SMILES, AND LEAPS-- AND SOARS ABOVE THE STARTLED CROWD, RISING ABOVE THEIR HEADS AS EASILY AS SHE DOES THEIR FEARS..
ONLY WHEN SHE'S GONE, DO THE PEOPLE BREATHE AGAIN...
BREATHE... AND WONDER...!

ONE HOUR LATER, IN A *PROJECTION ROOM* LOCATED WITHIN THE OFFICES OF THE *DAILY BUGLE* BUILDING...

LET ME GET THIS *STRAIGHT,* MR. JAMESON: YOU WANT TO HIRE ME AS AN *EDITOR* FOR A NEW MAGAZINE CALLED "WOMAN"--

--AND YOU WANT MY FIRST ISSUE TO BE AN *EXPOSE* OF-- *HER?*

*RIGHT.*

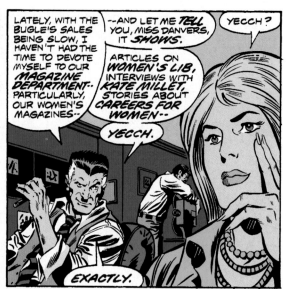

LATELY, WITH THE BUGLE'S SALES BEING SLOW, I HAVEN'T HAD THE TIME TO DEVOTE MYSELF TO OUR *MAGAZINE DEPARTMENT--* PARTICULARLY, OUR WOMEN'S MAGAZINES--

--AND LET ME *TELL* YOU, MISS DANVERS, IT *SHOWS.*

ARTICLES ON *WOMEN'S LIB,* INTERVIEWS WITH *KATE MILLET,* STORIES ABOUT *CAREERS FOR WOMEN--*

YECCH?

*YECCH.*

*EXACTLY.*

THE WAY *I* SEE IT, A WOMAN'S MAGAZINE SHOULD HAVE ARTICLES THAT ARE *USEFUL--*

--LIKE *NEW DIETS,* AND *FASHIONS,* AND *RECIPES.* THINGS LIKE THAT.

SO HOW DOES THIS NEW *SUPER-HEROINE* FIT IN?

UNDER *FASHION?*

NAW, THIS IS SOME-THING *ELSE.* SOMETHING *MORE IMPORTANT.*

I *HATE* SUPER-HEROES, MISS DANVERS. *HATE* THEM!

SO YOU WANT TO HIRE ME. AND YOU WANT ME TO EDIT A WOMAN'S MAGAZINE *YOUR* WAY-- INCLUDING A FEATURE ON THIS *SUPER-WOMAN.*

OKAY, MR. JAMESON-- WHAT ABOUT MY *SALARY?*

*SALARY?*

SURE--AS IN *WEEKLY PAYCHECK?*

*HMMMM...*

I REALIZE I'M NOT WHAT YOU CALL *PRIME* MATERIAL--

--SINCE I'VE ONLY BEEN *WRITING* FOR A YEAR, AFTER LEAVING THE *SECURITY FIELD.* *

BUT I *DO* HAVE SOME-THING OF A *REPUTA-TION* NOW--

AND REPS COST *MONEY.*

*MONEY?* EH...?

* EVERYONE REMEMBER *CAROL DANVERS,* CAPE KENNEDY SECURITY CHIEF FROM *CAPTAIN MARVEL* #1-18? --GER.

TWENTY THOUSAND?

TWENTY-TWO?

TWENTY-FIVE?

*BLAST IT!* HOW CAN I *ARGUE* MONEY WITH A *WOMAN?*

*THIRTY.*

*THIRTY!*

*THIRTY!*

ALL RIGHT, ALL RIGHT-- *THIRTY!*

AND ONE THING *MORE,* JONAH... MY NAME IS *MS.* CAROL DANVERS.

AND AS FAR AS *DIETS* AND *RECIPES* GO--

*FORGET* IT.

*HURRUMPH!*

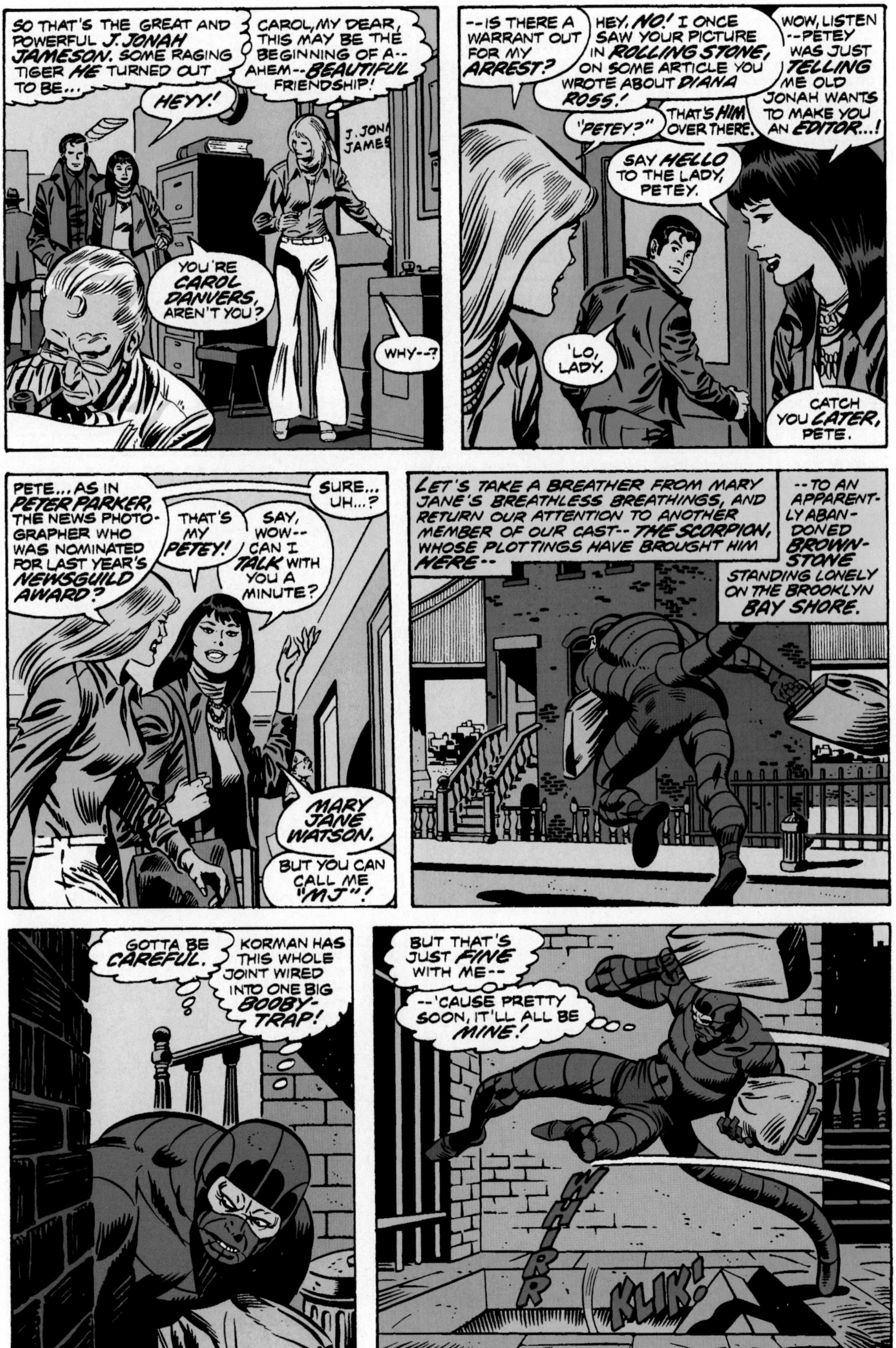
SO THAT'S THE GREAT AND POWERFUL J. JONAH JAMESON. SOME RAGING TIGER HE TURNED OUT TO BE...
CAROL, MY DEAR, THIS MAY BE THE BEGINNING OF A-- AHEM--BEAUTIFUL FRIENDSHIP!
HEYY!
YOU'RE CAROL DANVERS, AREN'T YOU?
WHY--?
--IS THERE A WARRANT OUT FOR MY ARREST?
HEY, NO! I ONCE SAW YOUR PICTURE IN ROLLING STONE, ON SOME ARTICLE YOU WROTE ABOUT DIANA ROSS!
WOW, LISTEN --PETEY WAS JUST TELLING ME OLD JONAH WANTS TO MAKE YOU AN EDITOR...!
"PETEY?"
THAT'S HIM OVER THERE.
SAY HELLO TO THE LADY, PETEY.
'LO, LADY.
CATCH YOU LATER, PETE.
PETE... AS IN PETER PARKER, THE NEWS PHOTOGRAPHER WHO WAS NOMINATED FOR LAST YEAR'S NEWSGUILD AWARD?
SURE... UH...?
THAT'S MY PETEY!
SAY, WOW--CAN I TALK WITH YOU A MINUTE?
MARY JANE WATSON.
BUT YOU CAN CALL ME "MJ"!
LET'S TAKE A BREATHER FROM MARY JANE'S BREATHLESS BREATHINGS, AND RETURN OUR ATTENTION TO ANOTHER MEMBER OF OUR CAST--THE SCORPION, WHOSE PLOTTINGS HAVE BROUGHT HIM HERE--
--TO AN APPARENTLY ABANDONED BROWNSTONE STANDING LONELY ON THE BROOKLYN BAY SHORE.
GOTTA BE CAREFUL.
KORMAN HAS THIS WHOLE JOINT WIRED INTO ONE BIG BOOBY-TRAP!
BUT THAT'S JUST FINE WITH ME--
--'CAUSE PRETTY SOON, IT'LL ALL BE MINE!
WHIRR
KLIK!

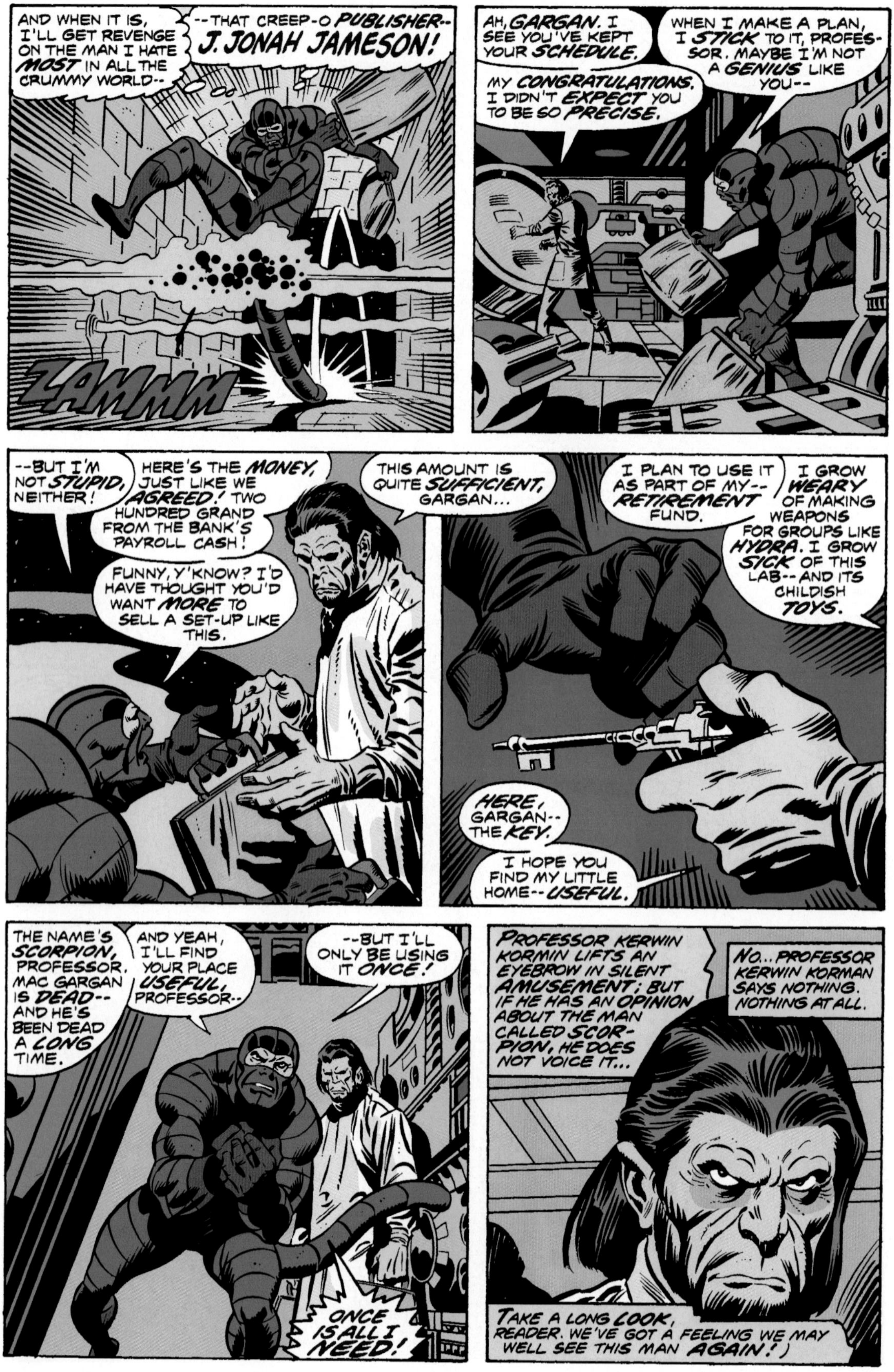
AND WHEN IT IS, I'LL GET REVENGE ON THE MAN I HATE MOST IN ALL THE CRUMMY WORLD--
--THAT CREEP-O PUBLISHER-- J. JONAH JAMESON!
ZAMMM
AH, GARGAN. I SEE YOU'VE KEPT YOUR SCHEDULE.
MY CONGRATULATIONS. I DIDN'T EXPECT YOU TO BE SO PRECISE.
WHEN I MAKE A PLAN, I STICK TO IT, PROFESSOR. MAYBE I'M NOT A GENIUS LIKE YOU--
--BUT I'M NOT STUPID, NEITHER!
HERE'S THE MONEY, JUST LIKE WE AGREED! TWO HUNDRED GRAND FROM THE BANK'S PAYROLL CASH!
FUNNY, Y'KNOW? I'D HAVE THOUGHT YOU'D WANT MORE TO SELL A SET-UP LIKE THIS.
THIS AMOUNT IS QUITE SUFFICIENT, GARGAN...
I PLAN TO USE IT AS PART OF MY-- RETIREMENT FUND.
I GROW WEARY OF MAKING WEAPONS FOR GROUPS LIKE HYDRA. I GROW SICK OF THIS LAB--AND ITS CHILDISH TOYS.
HERE, GARGAN-- THE KEY.
I HOPE YOU FIND MY LITTLE HOME--USEFUL.
THE NAME'S SCORPION, PROFESSOR. MAC GARGAN IS DEAD-- AND HE'S BEEN DEAD A LONG TIME.
AND YEAH, I'LL FIND YOUR PLACE USEFUL, PROFESSOR--
--BUT I'LL ONLY BE USING IT ONCE!
ONCE IS ALL I NEED!
PROFESSOR KERWIN KORMIN LIFTS AN EYEBROW IN SILENT AMUSEMENT; BUT IF HE HAS AN OPINION ABOUT THE MAN CALLED SCORPION, HE DOES NOT VOICE IT...
NO...PROFESSOR KERWIN KORMAN SAYS NOTHING. NOTHING AT ALL.
TAKE A LONG LOOK, READER. WE'VE GOT A FEELING WE MAY WELL SEE THIS MAN AGAIN!)

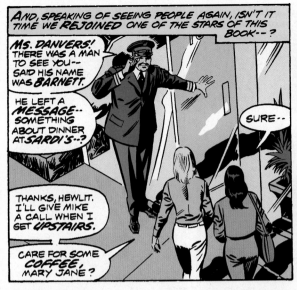

AND, SPEAKING OF SEEING PEOPLE AGAIN, ISN'T IT TIME WE REJOINED ONE OF THE STARS OF THIS BOOK--?

MS. DANVERS! THERE WAS A MAN TO SEE YOU-- SAID HIS NAME WAS BARNETT.

HE LEFT A MESSAGE-- SOMETHING ABOUT DINNER AT SARDI'S--?

SURE--

THANKS, HEWLIT. I'LL GIVE MIKE A CALL WHEN I GET UPSTAIRS.

CARE FOR SOME COFFEE, MARY JANE?

--I'VE NEVER HAD COFFEE IN A CENTRAL PARK PENTHOUSE BEFORE!

THEY DON'T, MJ-- BUT SOME LUCKY WRITERS DO.

SAY, HOW DO YOU AFFORD A FAN-TASSTIC LAYOUT LIKE THIS? DO EDITORS MAKE THAT MUCH MONEY..?

ROYALTIES FROM MY FIRST BOOK-- ABOUT THE SPACE INDUSTRY.

WOW...

...THAT'S RIGHT. YOU WERE A SECURITY CONSULTANT AT CAPE KENNEDY, WEREN'T YOU?

I REMEMBER READING ABOUT YOU IN THE PAPERS, WHEN THAT WEIRD CAPTAIN MARVEL GUY FIRST SHOWED UP ON EARTH. *

WHY'D YOU LEAVE ALL THAT, CAROL-- AND HOWCUM YOU BECAME A WRITER?

NOT BECAUSE I WANTED TO, MJ--

* AGAIN, CM #1. --GER.

--BUT BECAUSE I HAD TO.

CAPTAIN MARVEL'S APPEARANCE AT THE CAPE-- AND MY INABILITY TO CAPTURE HIM-- JUST ABOUT DESTROYED MY SECURITY FIELD CAREER.

I KEPT TRYING TO HOLD IT TOGETHER, UNTIL I FINALLY WENT BACK TO MY FIRST LOVE--

WRITING.

TURNS OUT I HAVE MORE TALENT FOR THE PEN THEN THE SWORD-- AND I'LL TELL YOU, I'M A LOT HAPPIER THAN--

OHHHH

CAROL!

KRASH

I-I'M ALL RIGHT, MARY JANE. J-JUST A MIGRANE HEADACHE...

I'VE BEEN GETTING A LOT OF THEM... SINCE COMING TO NEW YORK...

YOU WANT ME TO CALL A DOCTOR?

NO!

NO... I'M SORRY ... BUT YOU BETTER JUST GO...

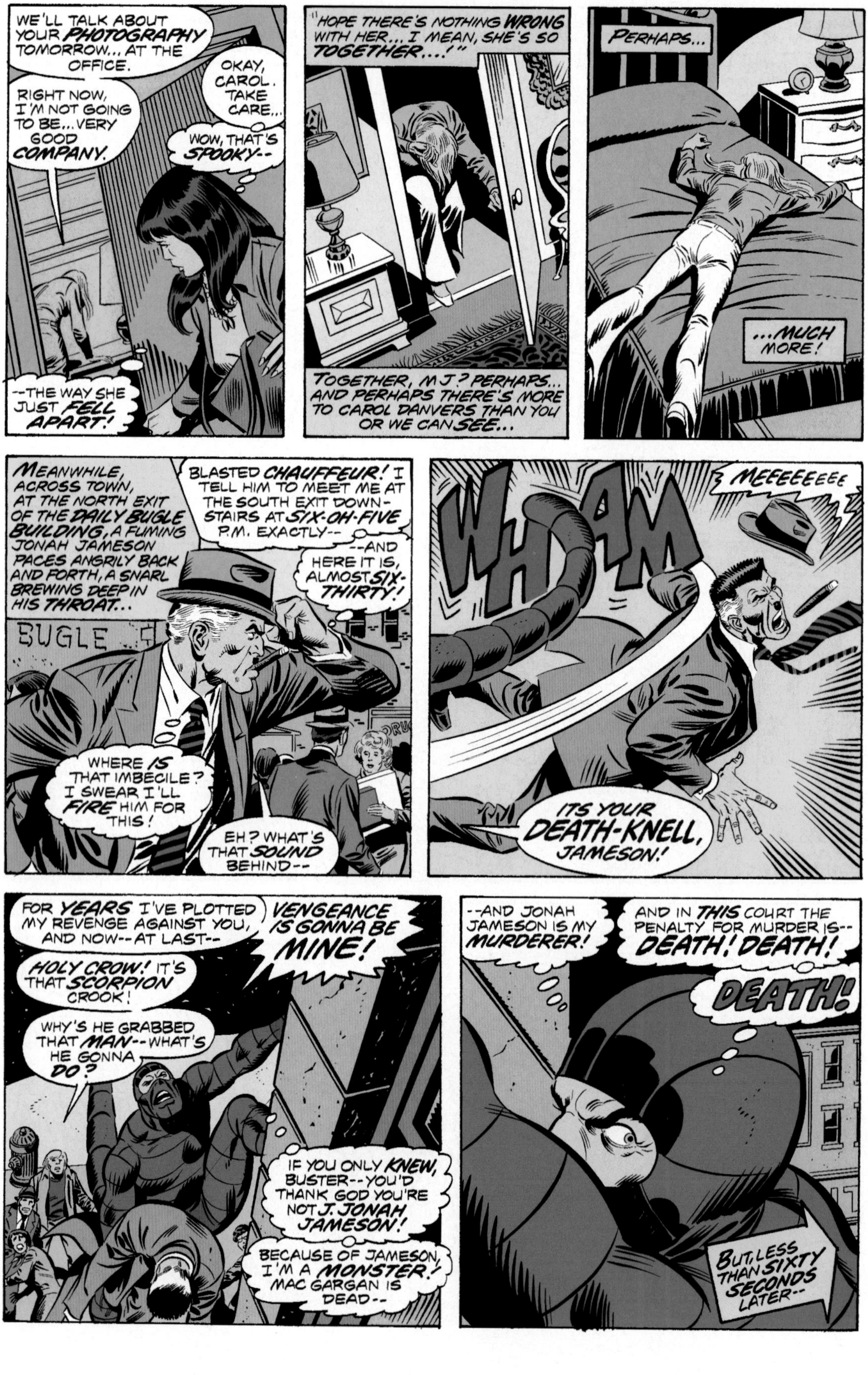
WE'LL TALK ABOUT YOUR PHOTOGRAPHY TOMORROW... AT THE OFFICE.
RIGHT NOW, I'M NOT GOING TO BE... VERY GOOD COMPANY.
OKAY, CAROL. TAKE CARE...
WOW, THAT'S SPOOKY--
--THE WAY SHE JUST FELL APART!
"HOPE THERE'S NOTHING WRONG WITH HER... I MEAN, SHE'S SO TOGETHER...!"
TOGETHER, M J.? PERHAPS... AND PERHAPS THERE'S MORE TO CAROL DANVERS THAN YOU OR WE CAN SEE...
PERHAPS...
...MUCH MORE!
MEANWHILE, ACROSS TOWN, AT THE NORTH EXIT OF THE DAILY BUGLE BUILDING, A FUMING JONAH JAMESON PACES ANGRILY BACK AND FORTH, A SNARL BREWING DEEP IN HIS THROAT...
BLASTED CHAUFFEUR! I TELL HIM TO MEET ME AT THE SOUTH EXIT DOWN-STAIRS AT SIX-OH-FIVE P.M. EXACTLY--
--AND HERE IT IS, ALMOST SIX-THIRTY!
BUGLE
WHERE IS THAT IMBECILE? I SWEAR I'LL FIRE HIM FOR THIS!
EH? WHAT'S THAT SOUND BEHIND--
WHAM
MEEEEEEEEE
ITS YOUR DEATH-KNELL, JAMESON!
FOR YEARS I'VE PLOTTED MY REVENGE AGAINST YOU, AND NOW--AT LAST--
VENGEANCE IS GONNA BE MINE!
HOLY CROW! IT'S THAT SCORPION CROOK!
WHY'S HE GRABBED THAT MAN--WHAT'S HE GONNA DO?
IF YOU ONLY KNEW, BUSTER--YOU'D THANK GOD YOU'RE NOT J. JONAH JAMESON!
BECAUSE OF JAMESON, I'M A MONSTER! MAC GARGAN IS DEAD--
--AND JONAH JAMESON IS MY MURDERER!
AND IN THIS COURT THE PENALTY FOR MURDER IS-- DEATH! DEATH!
DEATH!
BUT, LESS THAN SIXTY SECONDS LATER--

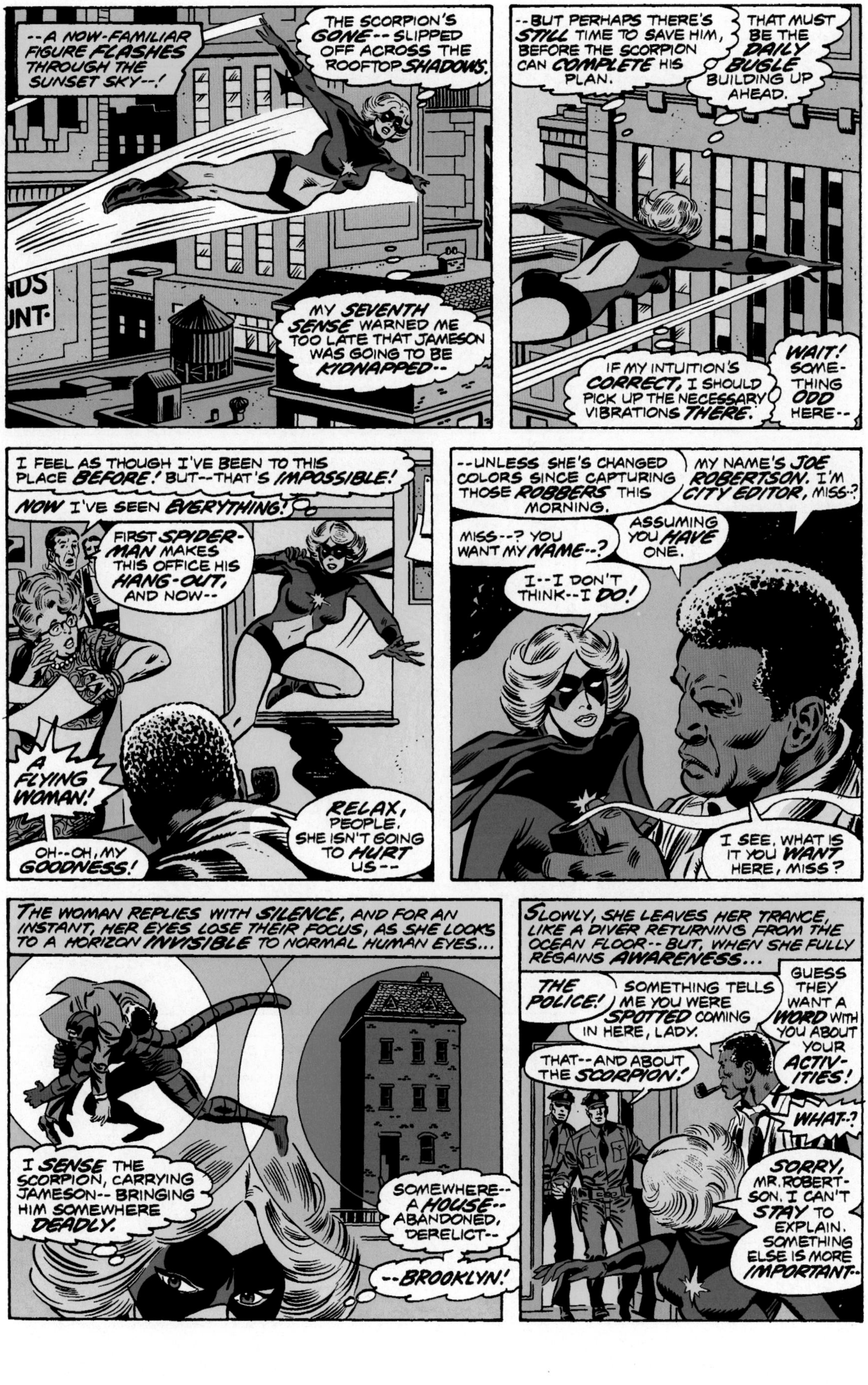
--A NOW-FAMILIAR FIGURE FLASHES THROUGH THE SUNSET SKY--!
THE SCORPION'S GONE--SLIPPED OFF ACROSS THE ROOFTOP SHADOWS.
MY SEVENTH SENSE WARNED ME TOO LATE THAT JAMESON WAS GOING TO BE KIDNAPPED--
--BUT PERHAPS THERE'S STILL TIME TO SAVE HIM, BEFORE THE SCORPION CAN COMPLETE HIS PLAN.
THAT MUST BE THE DAILY BUGLE BUILDING UP AHEAD.
IF MY INTUITION'S CORRECT, I SHOULD PICK UP THE NECESSARY VIBRATIONS THERE.
WAIT! SOMETHING ODD HERE--
I FEEL AS THOUGH I'VE BEEN TO THIS PLACE BEFORE! BUT--THAT'S IMPOSSIBLE!
NOW I'VE SEEN EVERYTHING!
FIRST SPIDER-MAN MAKES THIS OFFICE HIS HANG-OUT, AND NOW--
A FLYING WOMAN!
OH--OH, MY GOODNESS!
RELAX, PEOPLE. SHE ISN'T GOING TO HURT US--
--UNLESS SHE'S CHANGED COLORS SINCE CAPTURING THOSE ROBBERS THIS MORNING.
MY NAME'S JOE ROBERTSON. I'M CITY EDITOR, MISS-?
MISS--? YOU WANT MY NAME--?
ASSUMING YOU HAVE ONE.
I--I DON'T THINK--I DO!
I SEE. WHAT IS IT YOU WANT HERE, MISS?
THE WOMAN REPLIES WITH SILENCE, AND FOR AN INSTANT, HER EYES LOSE THEIR FOCUS, AS SHE LOOKS TO A HORIZON INVISIBLE TO NORMAL HUMAN EYES...
I SENSE THE SCORPION, CARRYING JAMESON--BRINGING HIM SOMEWHERE DEADLY.
SOMEWHERE--A HOUSE--ABANDONED, DERELICT--
--BROOKLYN!
SLOWLY, SHE LEAVES HER TRANCE, LIKE A DIVER RETURNING FROM THE OCEAN FLOOR--BUT, WHEN SHE FULLY REGAINS AWARENESS...
THE POLICE!
SOMETHING TELLS ME YOU WERE SPOTTED COMING IN HERE, LADY.
GUESS THEY WANT A WORD WITH YOU ABOUT YOUR ACTIVITIES!
THAT--AND ABOUT THE SCORPION!
WHAT-?
SORRY, MR. ROBERTSON. I CAN'T STAY TO EXPLAIN. SOMETHING ELSE IS MORE IMPORTANT--

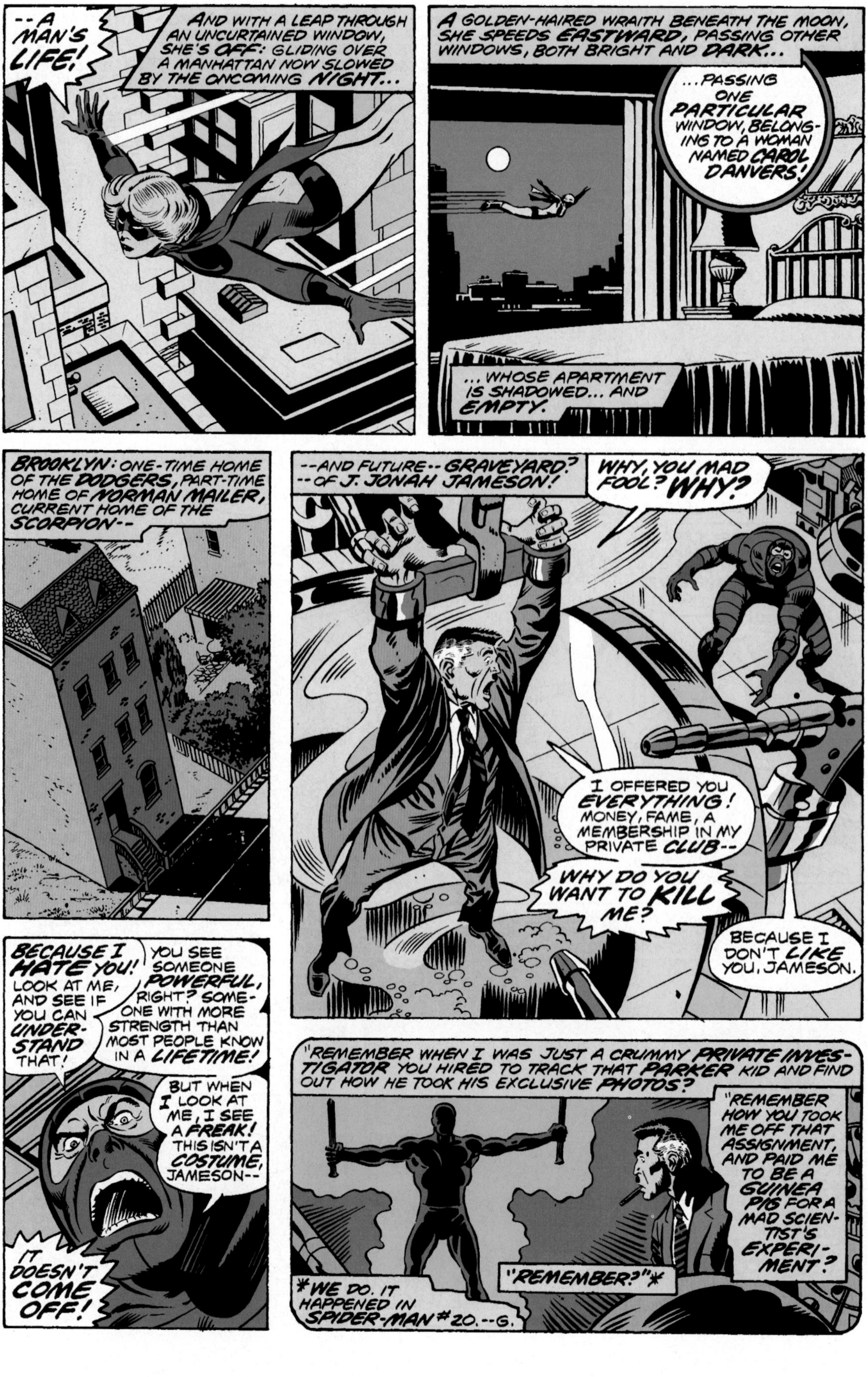
--A MAN'S LIFE!
AND WITH A LEAP THROUGH AN UNCURTAINED WINDOW, SHE'S OFF: GLIDING OVER A MANHATTAN NOW SLOWED BY THE ONCOMING NIGHT...
A GOLDEN-HAIRED WRAITH BENEATH THE MOON, SHE SPEEDS EASTWARD, PASSING OTHER WINDOWS, BOTH BRIGHT AND DARK...
...PASSING ONE PARTICULAR WINDOW, BELONGING TO A WOMAN NAMED CAROL DANVERS!
...WHOSE APARTMENT IS SHADOWED... AND EMPTY.
BROOKLYN: ONE-TIME HOME OF THE DODGERS, PART-TIME HOME OF NORMAN MAILER, CURRENT HOME OF THE SCORPION--
--AND FUTURE--GRAVEYARD? --OF J. JONAH JAMESON!
WHY, YOU MAD FOOL? WHY?
I OFFERED YOU EVERYTHING! MONEY, FAME, A MEMBERSHIP IN MY PRIVATE CLUB--
WHY DO YOU WANT TO KILL ME?
BECAUSE I DON'T LIKE YOU, JAMESON.
BECAUSE I HATE YOU! LOOK AT ME, AND SEE IF YOU CAN UNDERSTAND THAT!
YOU SEE SOMEONE POWERFUL, RIGHT? SOMEONE WITH MORE STRENGTH THAN MOST PEOPLE KNOW IN A LIFETIME!
BUT WHEN I LOOK AT ME, I SEE A FREAK! THIS ISN'T A COSTUME, JAMESON--
IT DOESN'T COME OFF!
"REMEMBER WHEN I WAS JUST A CRUMMY PRIVATE INVESTIGATOR YOU HIRED TO TRACK THAT PARKER KID AND FIND OUT HOW HE TOOK HIS EXCLUSIVE PHOTOS?
"REMEMBER HOW YOU TOOK ME OFF THAT ASSIGNMENT, AND PAID ME TO BE A GUINEA PIG FOR A MAD SCIENTIST'S EXPERIMENT?
"REMEMBER?"*
*WE DO. IT HAPPENED IN SPIDER-MAN #20.--G.

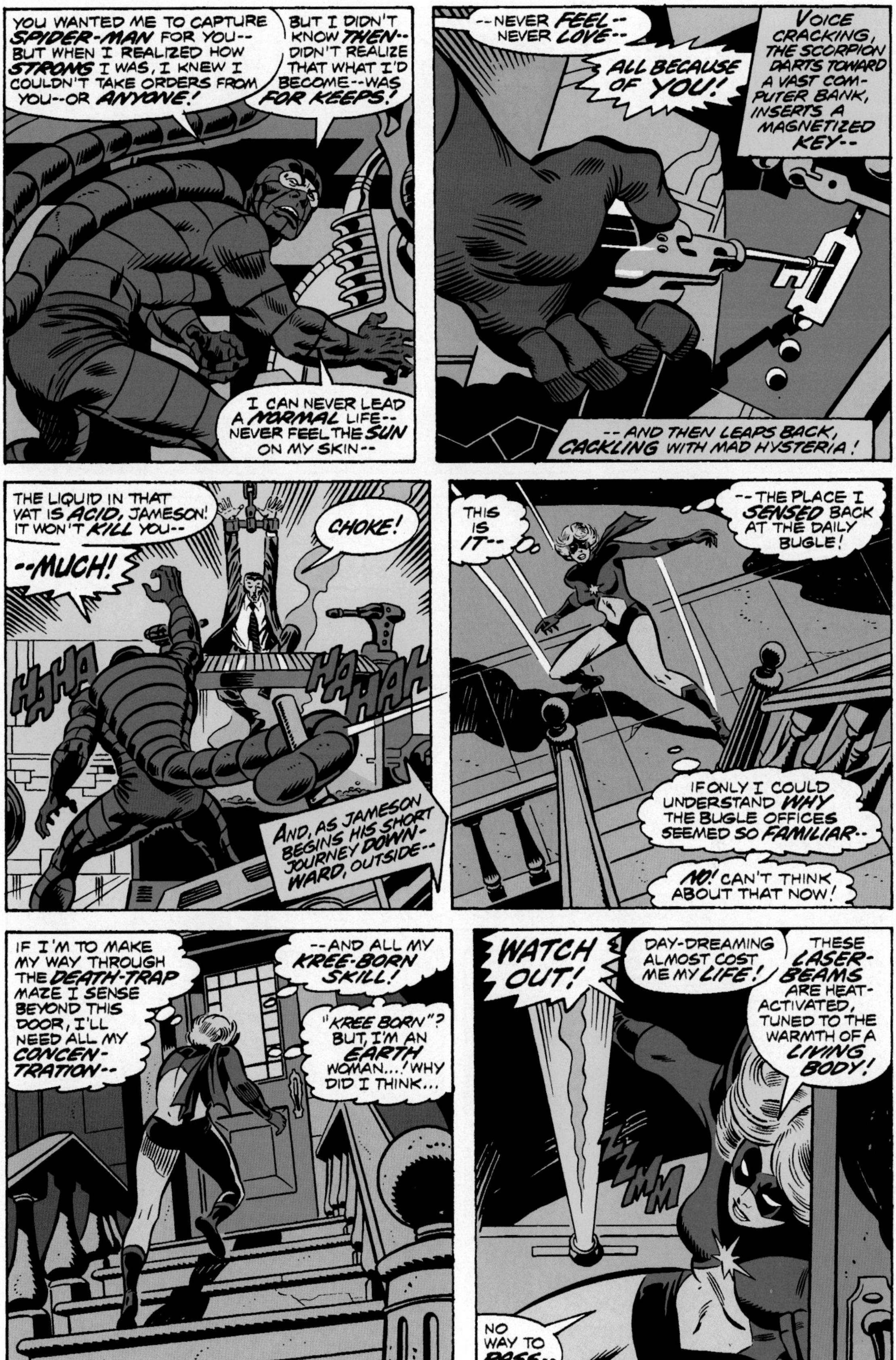
YOU WANTED ME TO CAPTURE SPIDER-MAN FOR YOU-- BUT WHEN I REALIZED HOW STRONG I WAS, I KNEW I COULDN'T TAKE ORDERS FROM YOU--OR ANYONE!
BUT I DIDN'T KNOW THEN-- DIDN'T REALIZE THAT WHAT I'D BECOME--WAS FOR KEEPS!
I CAN NEVER LEAD A NORMAL LIFE-- NEVER FEEL THE SUN ON MY SKIN--
--NEVER FEEL-- NEVER LOVE--
ALL BECAUSE OF YOU!
VOICE CRACKING, THE SCORPION DARTS TOWARD A VAST COMPUTER BANK, INSERTS A MAGNETIZED KEY--
--AND THEN LEAPS BACK, CACKLING WITH MAD HYSTERIA!
THE LIQUID IN THAT VAT IS ACID, JAMESON! IT WON'T KILL YOU--
--MUCH!
CHOKE!
HAHA
HAHAHAH
AND, AS JAMESON BEGINS HIS SHORT JOURNEY DOWNWARD, OUTSIDE--
THIS IS IT--
--THE PLACE I SENSED BACK AT THE DAILY BUGLE!
IF ONLY I COULD UNDERSTAND WHY THE BUGLE OFFICES SEEMED SO FAMILIAR--
NO! CAN'T THINK ABOUT THAT NOW!
IF I'M TO MAKE MY WAY THROUGH THE DEATH-TRAP MAZE I SENSE BEYOND THIS DOOR, I'LL NEED ALL MY CONCENTRATION--
--AND ALL MY KREE-BORN SKILL!
"KREE BORN"? BUT, I'M AN EARTH WOMAN...! WHY DID I THINK...
WATCH OUT!
DAY-DREAMING ALMOST COST ME MY LIFE!
THESE LASER-BEAMS ARE HEAT-ACTIVATED, TUNED TO THE WARMTH OF A LIVING BODY!
ZZMM
NO WAY TO PASS--

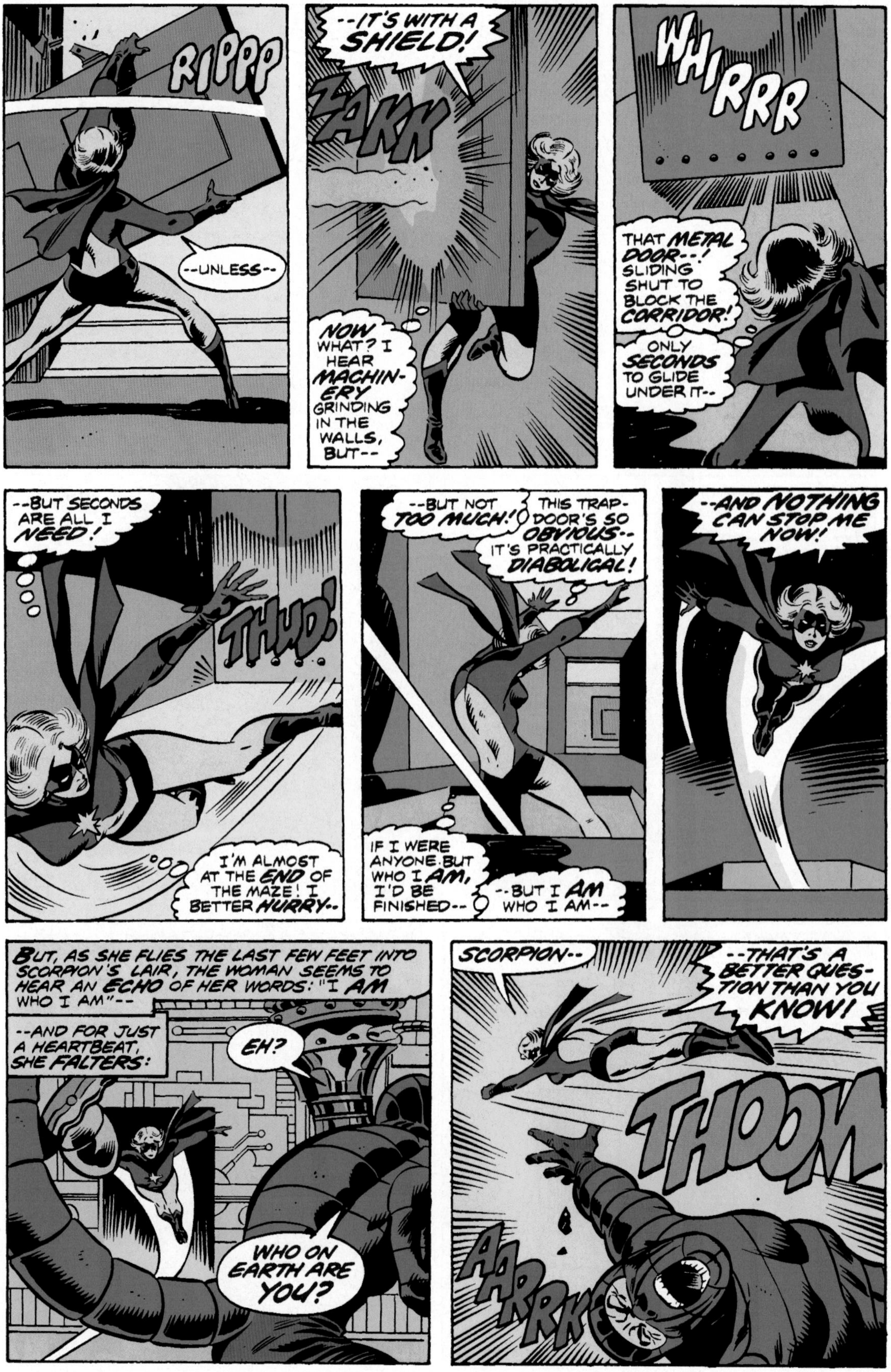
RIPPP
--UNLESS--
--IT'S WITH A SHIELD!
ZAKK
NOW, WHAT? I HEAR MACHIN-ERY GRINDING IN THE WALLS, BUT--
WHIRRR
THAT METAL DOOR--! SLIDING SHUT TO BLOCK THE CORRIDOR!
ONLY SECONDS TO GLIDE UNDER IT--
--BUT SECONDS ARE ALL I NEED!
THUD!
I'M ALMOST AT THE END OF THE MAZE! I BETTER HURRY--
--BUT NOT TOO MUCH!
THIS TRAP-DOOR'S SO OBVIOUS-- IT'S PRACTICALLY DIABOLICAL!
IF I WERE ANYONE BUT WHO I AM, I'D BE FINISHED--
--BUT I AM WHO I AM--
--AND NOTHING CAN STOP ME NOW!
BUT, AS SHE FLIES THE LAST FEW FEET INTO SCORPION'S LAIR, THE WOMAN SEEMS TO HEAR AN ECHO OF HER WORDS: "I AM WHO I AM"--
--AND FOR JUST A HEARTBEAT, SHE FALTERS:
EH?
WHO ON EARTH ARE YOU?
SCORPION--
--THAT'S A BETTER QUES-TION THAN YOU KNOW!
THOOM
AARRKK

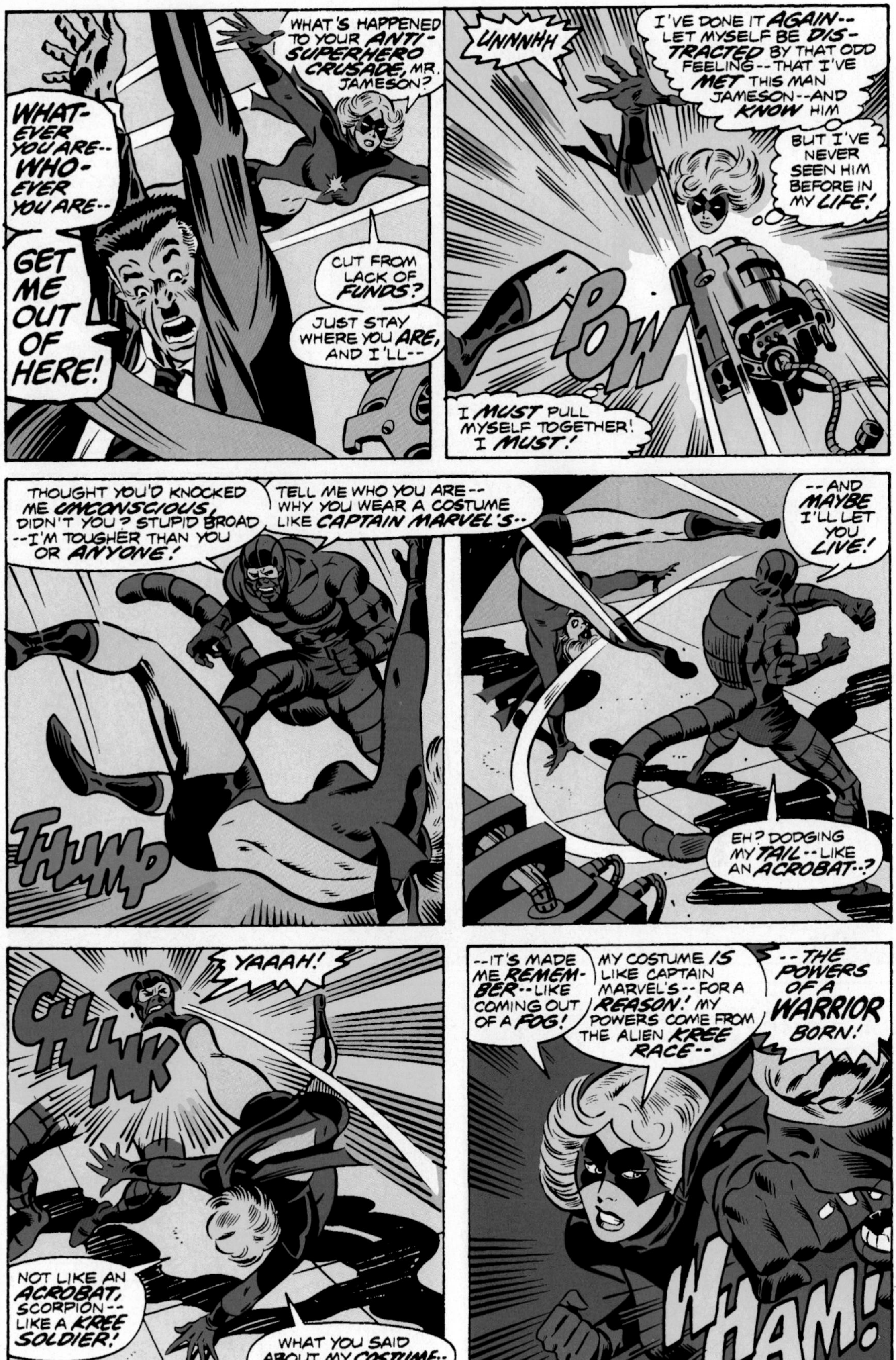
WHAT'S HAPPENED TO YOUR ANTI-SUPERHERO CRUSADE, MR. JAMESON?
WHAT-EVER YOU ARE-- WHO-EVER YOU ARE--
GET ME OUT OF HERE!
CUT FROM LACK OF FUNDS?
JUST STAY WHERE YOU ARE, AND I'LL--
UNNNHH
I'VE DONE IT AGAIN-- LET MYSELF BE DIS-TRACTED BY THAT ODD FEELING--THAT I'VE MET THIS MAN JAMESON--AND KNOW HIM
BUT I'VE NEVER SEEN HIM BEFORE IN MY LIFE!
POW
I MUST PULL MYSELF TOGETHER! I MUST!
THOUGHT YOU'D KNOCKED ME UNCONSCIOUS, DIDN'T YOU? STUPID BROAD --I'M TOUGHER THAN YOU OR ANYONE!
TELL ME WHO YOU ARE-- WHY YOU WEAR A COSTUME LIKE CAPTAIN MARVEL'S--
THUMP
--AND MAYBE I'LL LET YOU LIVE!
EH? DODGING MY TAIL--LIKE AN ACROBAT--?
YAAAH!
CHUNK
NOT LIKE AN ACROBAT, SCORPION-- LIKE A KREE SOLDIER!
WHAT YOU SAID ABOUT MY COSTUME--
--IT'S MADE ME REMEM-BER--LIKE COMING OUT OF A FOG!
MY COSTUME IS LIKE CAPTAIN MARVEL'S--FOR A REASON! MY POWERS COME FROM THE ALIEN KREE RACE--
--THE POWERS OF A WARRIOR BORN!
WHAM!

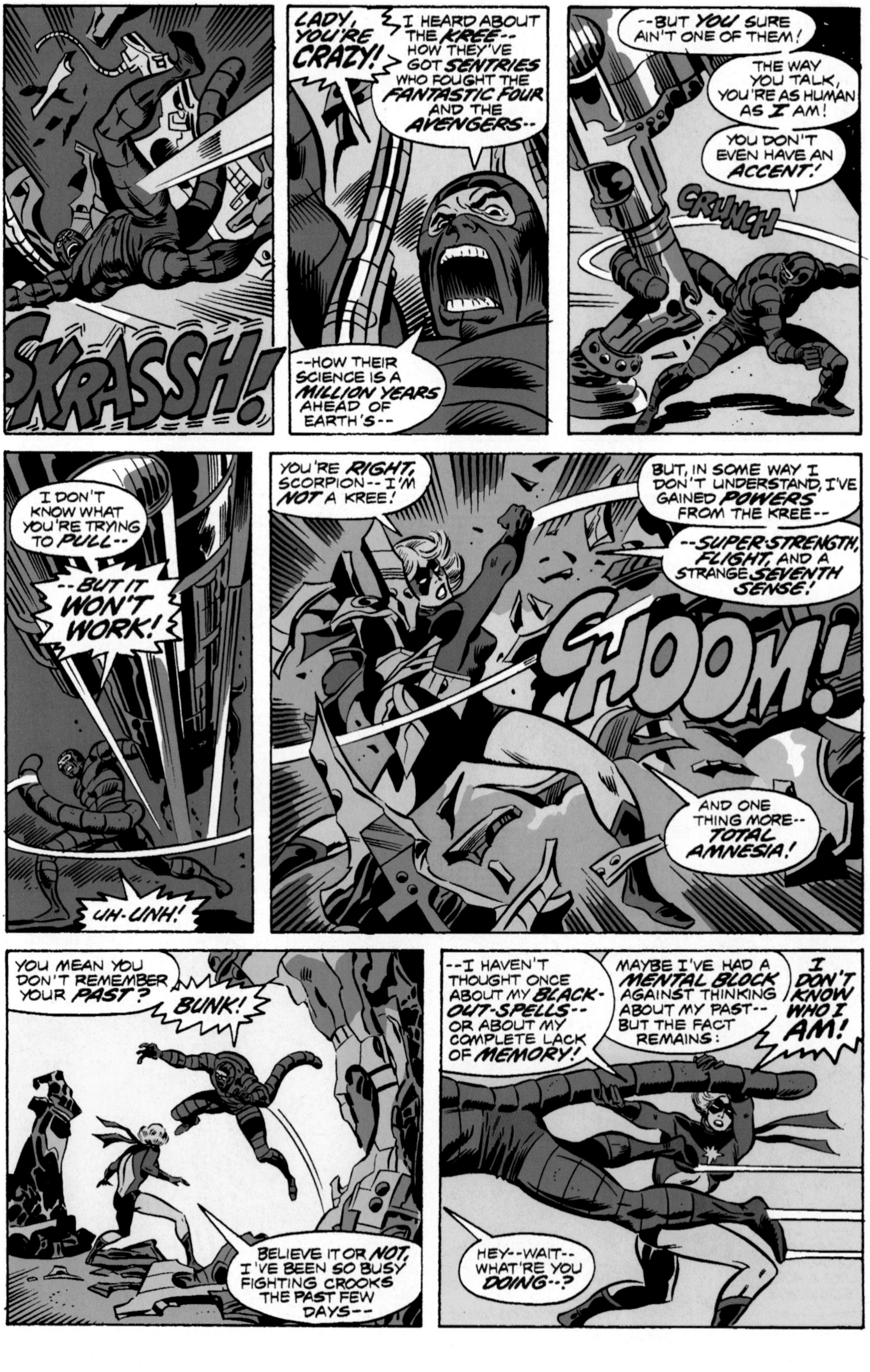
SKRASSH!
LADY, YOU'RE CRAZY!
I HEARD ABOUT THE KREE-- HOW THEY'VE GOT SENTRIES WHO FOUGHT THE FANTASTIC FOUR AND THE AVENGERS--
--HOW THEIR SCIENCE IS A MILLION YEARS AHEAD OF EARTH'S--
--BUT YOU SURE AIN'T ONE OF THEM!
THE WAY YOU TALK, YOU'RE AS HUMAN AS I AM!
YOU DON'T EVEN HAVE AN ACCENT!
CRUNCH
I DON'T KNOW WHAT YOU'RE TRYING TO PULL--
--BUT IT WON'T WORK!
UH-UNH!
YOU'RE RIGHT, SCORPION--I'M NOT A KREE!
BUT, IN SOME WAY I DON'T UNDERSTAND, I'VE GAINED POWERS FROM THE KREE--
--SUPER-STRENGTH, FLIGHT, AND A STRANGE SEVENTH SENSE!
CHOOM!
AND ONE THING MORE-- TOTAL AMNESIA!
YOU MEAN YOU DON'T REMEMBER YOUR PAST?
BUNK!
BELIEVE IT OR NOT, I'VE BEEN SO BUSY FIGHTING CROOKS THE PAST FEW DAYS--
--I HAVEN'T THOUGHT ONCE ABOUT MY BLACK-OUT-SPELLS-- OR ABOUT MY COMPLETE LACK OF MEMORY!
MAYBE I'VE HAD A MENTAL BLOCK AGAINST THINKING ABOUT MY PAST-- BUT THE FACT REMAINS:
I DON'T KNOW WHO I AM!
HEY--WAIT-- WHAT'RE YOU DOING--?

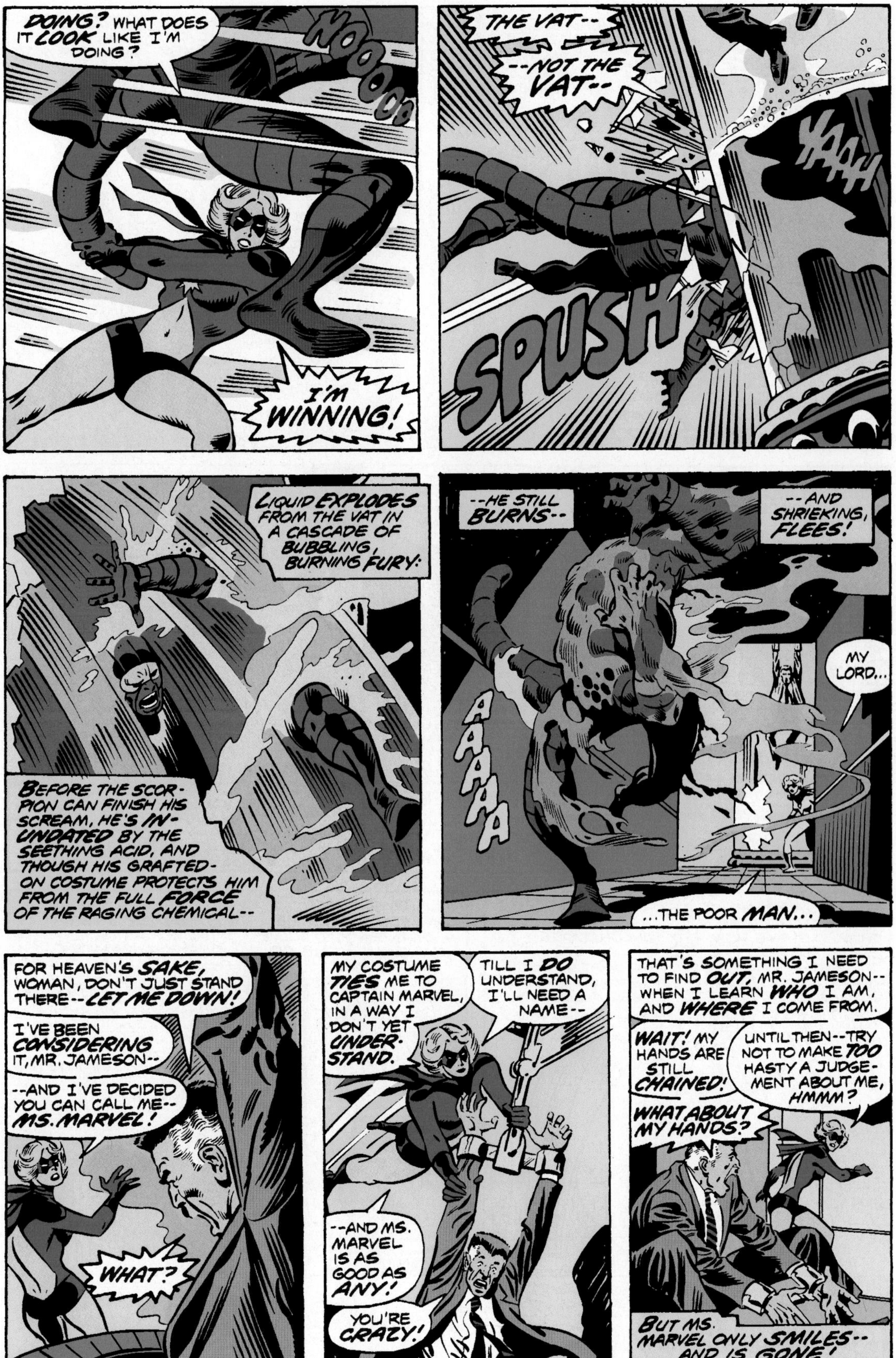

DOING? WHAT DOES IT LOOK LIKE I'M DOING?
NOOOOO
I'M WINNING!
THE VAT--
--NOT THE VAT--
YAAH
SPUSH
LIQUID EXPLODES FROM THE VAT IN A CASCADE OF BUBBLING, BURNING FURY:
BEFORE THE SCORPION CAN FINISH HIS SCREAM, HE'S INUNDATED BY THE SEETHING ACID, AND THOUGH HIS GRAFTED-ON COSTUME PROTECTS HIM FROM THE FULL FORCE OF THE RAGING CHEMICAL--
--HE STILL BURNS--
--AND SHRIEKING, FLEES!
AAAAA
MY LORD...
...THE POOR MAN...
FOR HEAVEN'S SAKE, WOMAN, DON'T JUST STAND THERE--LET ME DOWN!
I'VE BEEN CONSIDERING IT, MR. JAMESON--
--AND I'VE DECIDED YOU CAN CALL ME--MS. MARVEL!
WHAT?
MY COSTUME TIES ME TO CAPTAIN MARVEL, IN A WAY I DON'T YET UNDERSTAND.
TILL I DO UNDERSTAND, I'LL NEED A NAME--
--AND MS. MARVEL IS AS GOOD AS ANY!
YOU'RE CRAZY!
THAT'S SOMETHING I NEED TO FIND OUT, MR. JAMESON--WHEN I LEARN WHO I AM, AND WHERE I COME FROM.
WAIT! MY HANDS ARE STILL CHAINED!
UNTIL THEN--TRY NOT TO MAKE TOO HASTY A JUDGEMENT ABOUT ME, HMMM?
WHAT ABOUT MY HANDS?
BUT MS. MARVEL ONLY SMILES--AND IS GONE!

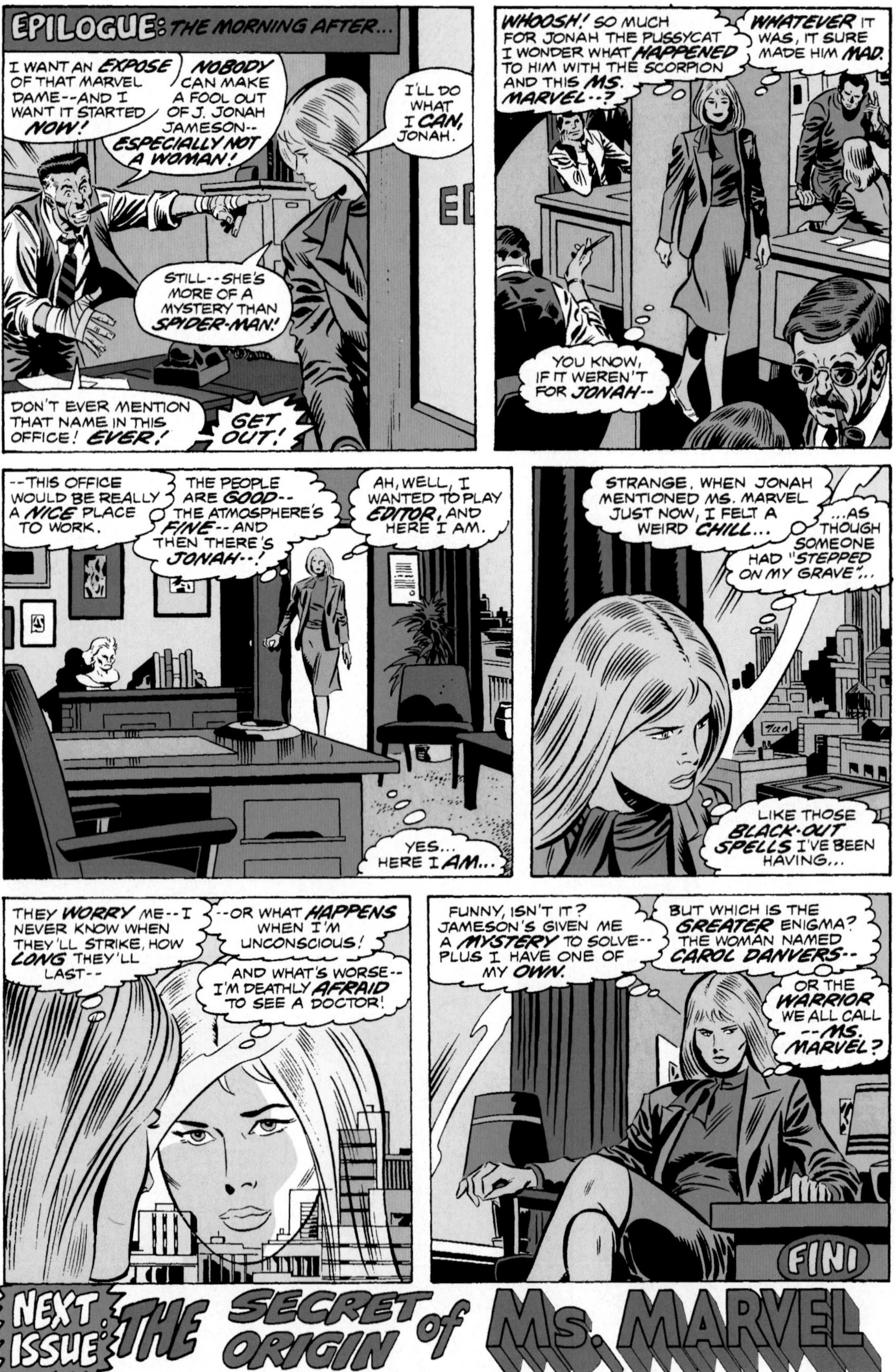
EPILOGUE: THE MORNING AFTER...
I WANT AN EXPOSE OF THAT MARVEL DAME--AND I WANT IT STARTED NOW!
NOBODY CAN MAKE A FOOL OUT OF J. JONAH JAMESON--ESPECIALLY NOT A WOMAN!
I'LL DO WHAT I CAN, JONAH.
STILL--SHE'S MORE OF A MYSTERY THAN SPIDER-MAN!
DON'T EVER MENTION THAT NAME IN THIS OFFICE! EVER!
GET OUT!
WHOOSH! SO MUCH FOR JONAH THE PUSSYCAT I WONDER WHAT HAPPENED TO HIM WITH THE SCORPION AND THIS MS. MARVEL--?
WHATEVER IT WAS, IT SURE MADE HIM MAD.
YOU KNOW, IF IT WEREN'T FOR JONAH--
--THIS OFFICE WOULD BE REALLY A NICE PLACE TO WORK.
THE PEOPLE ARE GOOD--THE ATMOSPHERE'S FINE--AND THEN THERE'S JONAH--!
AH, WELL, I WANTED TO PLAY EDITOR, AND HERE I AM.
YES... HERE I AM...
STRANGE. WHEN JONAH MENTIONED MS. MARVEL JUST NOW, I FELT A WEIRD CHILL...
...AS THOUGH SOMEONE HAD "STEPPED ON MY GRAVE"...
LIKE THOSE BLACK-OUT SPELLS I'VE BEEN HAVING...
THEY WORRY ME--I NEVER KNOW WHEN THEY'LL STRIKE, HOW LONG THEY'LL LAST--
--OR WHAT HAPPENS WHEN I'M UNCONSCIOUS!
AND WHAT'S WORSE--I'M DEATHLY AFRAID TO SEE A DOCTOR!
FUNNY, ISN'T IT? JAMESON'S GIVEN ME A MYSTERY TO SOLVE--PLUS I HAVE ONE OF MY OWN.
BUT WHICH IS THE GREATER ENIGMA? THE WOMAN NAMED CAROL DANVERS--
--OR THE WARRIOR WE ALL CALL--MS. MARVEL?
FINI
NEXT ISSUE: THE SECRET ORIGIN of MS. MARVEL

**CONTINUED IN *MS. MARVEL EPIC COLLECTION: THIS WOMAN ,THIS WARRIOR* TPB.**

CAROL DANVERS IS EXPERIENCING AN IDENTITY CRISIS AS SHE STRIVES TO ESTABLISH HER OWN IDENTITY. COMPLICATING MATTERS IS AN ALIEN INVASION!

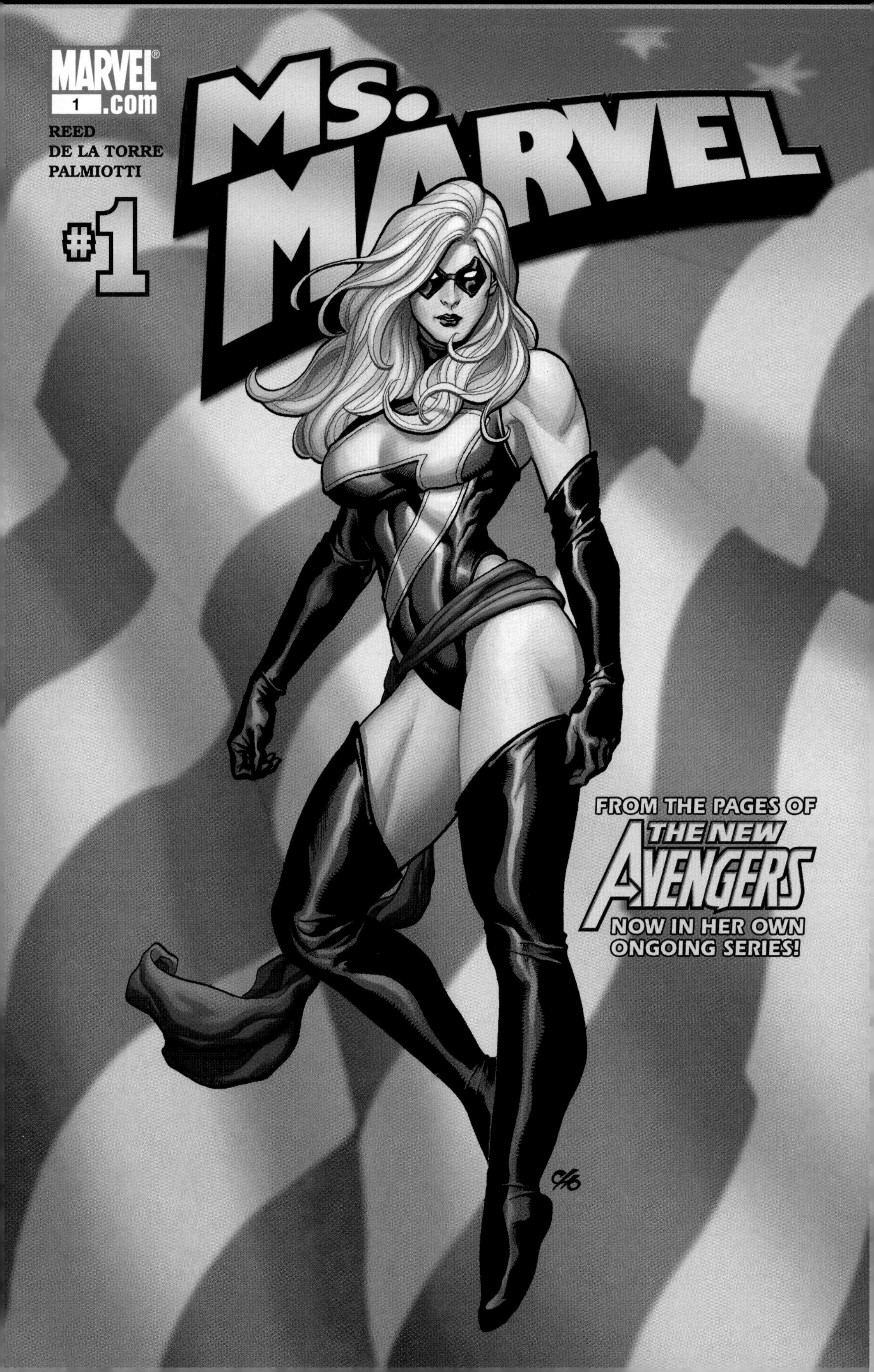

MARVEL
1 .com
REED
DE LA TORRE
PALMIOTTI
MS. MARVEL
#1
FROM THE PAGES OF
THE NEW AVENGERS
NOW IN HER OWN ONGOING SERIES!

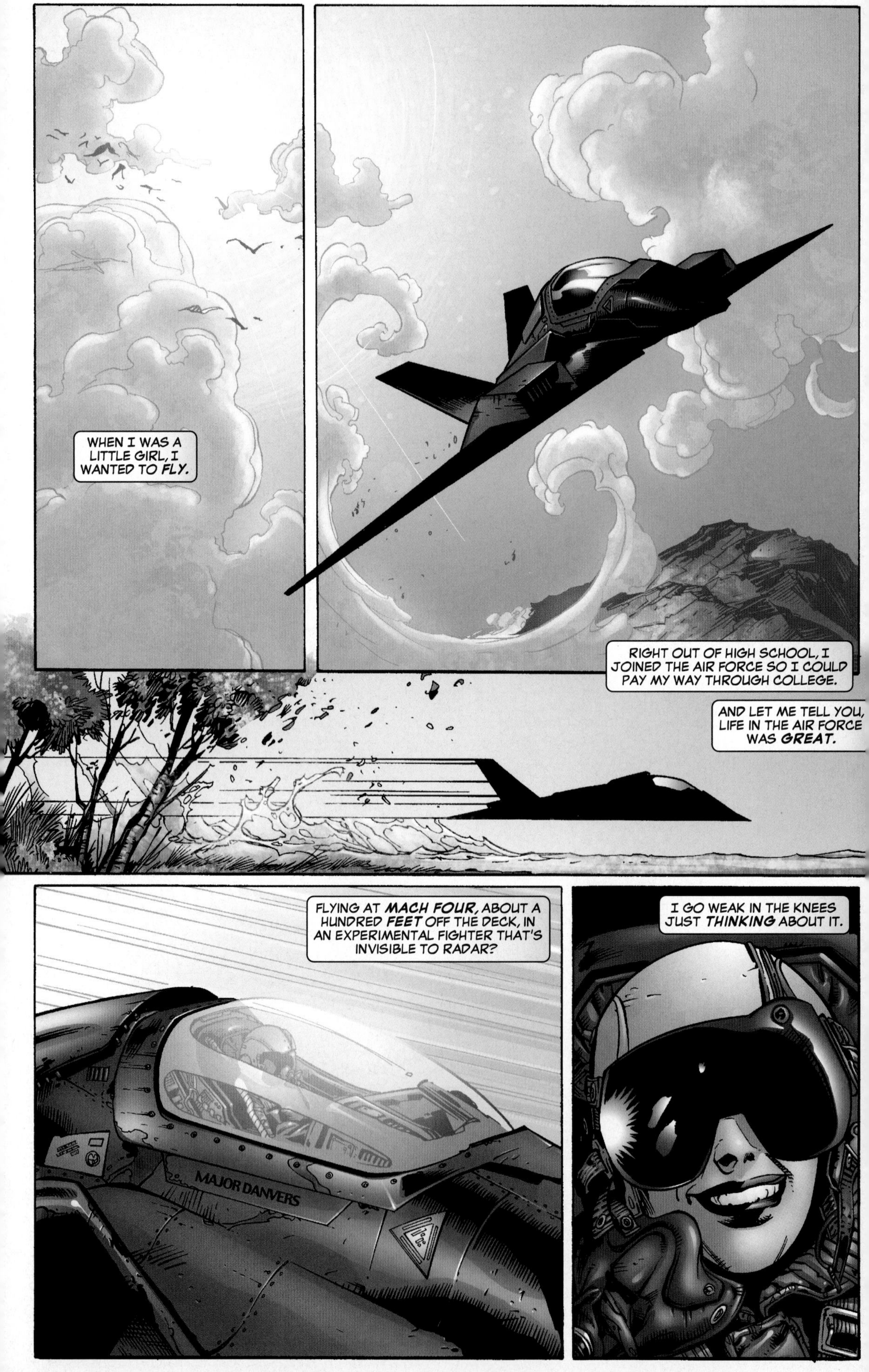
WHEN I WAS A LITTLE GIRL, I WANTED TO FLY.
RIGHT OUT OF HIGH SCHOOL, I JOINED THE AIR FORCE SO I COULD PAY MY WAY THROUGH COLLEGE.
AND LET ME TELL YOU, LIFE IN THE AIR FORCE WAS GREAT.
FLYING AT MACH FOUR, ABOUT A HUNDRED FEET OFF THE DECK, IN AN EXPERIMENTAL FIGHTER THAT'S INVISIBLE TO RADAR?
MAJOR DANVERS
I GO WEAK IN THE KNEES JUST THINKING ABOUT IT.

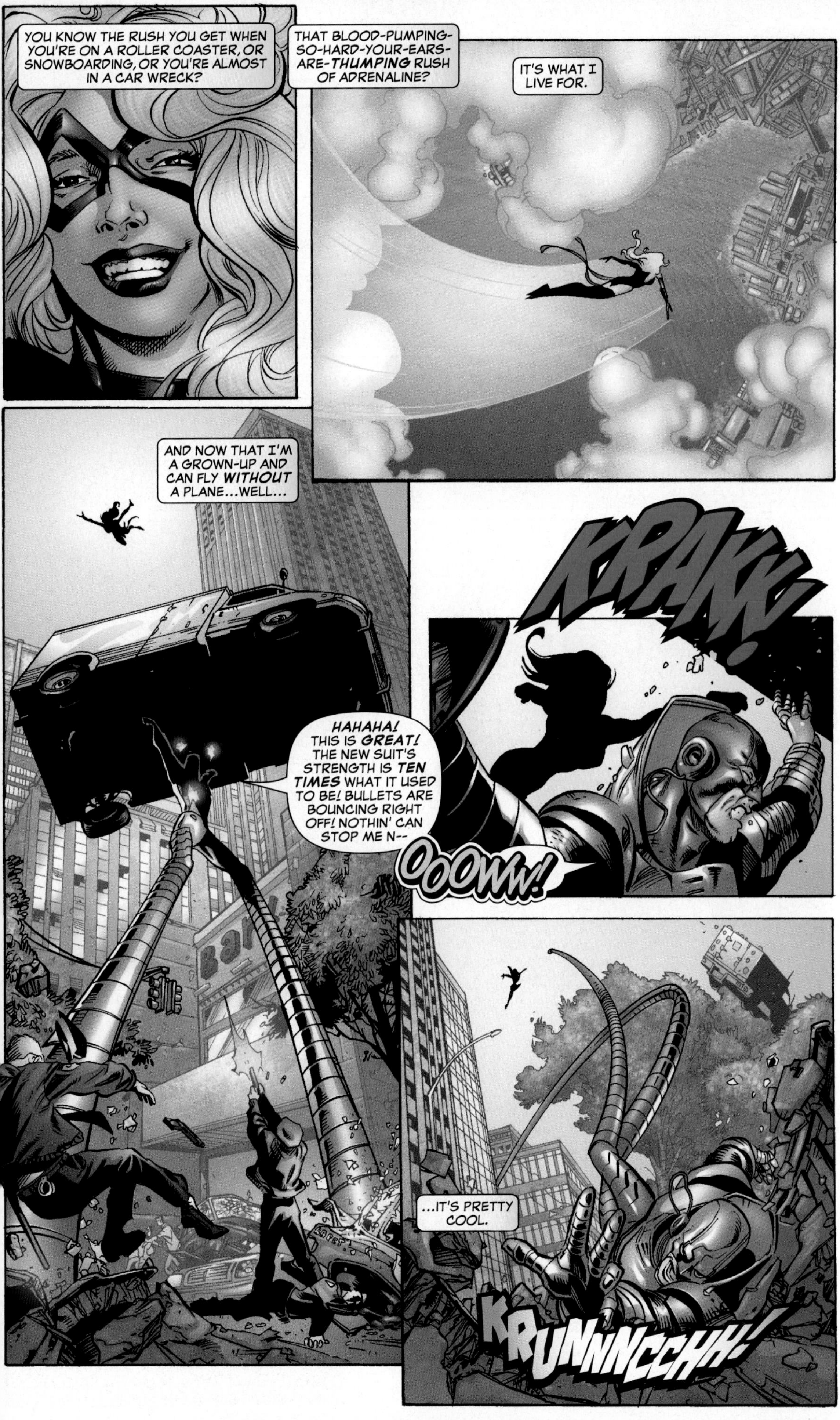
YOU KNOW THE RUSH YOU GET WHEN YOU'RE ON A ROLLER COASTER, OR SNOWBOARDING, OR YOU'RE ALMOST IN A CAR WRECK?
THAT BLOOD-PUMPING-SO-HARD-YOUR-EARS-ARE-*THUMPING* RUSH OF ADRENALINE?
IT'S WHAT I LIVE FOR.
AND NOW THAT I'M A GROWN-UP AND CAN FLY *WITHOUT* A PLANE...WELL...
*HAHAHA!* THIS IS *GREAT!* THE NEW SUIT'S STRENGTH IS *TEN TIMES* WHAT IT USED TO BE! BULLETS ARE BOUNCING RIGHT OFF! NOTHIN' CAN STOP ME N--
KRAKK!
OOOWW!
...IT'S PRETTY COOL.
KRUNNNCCHH!

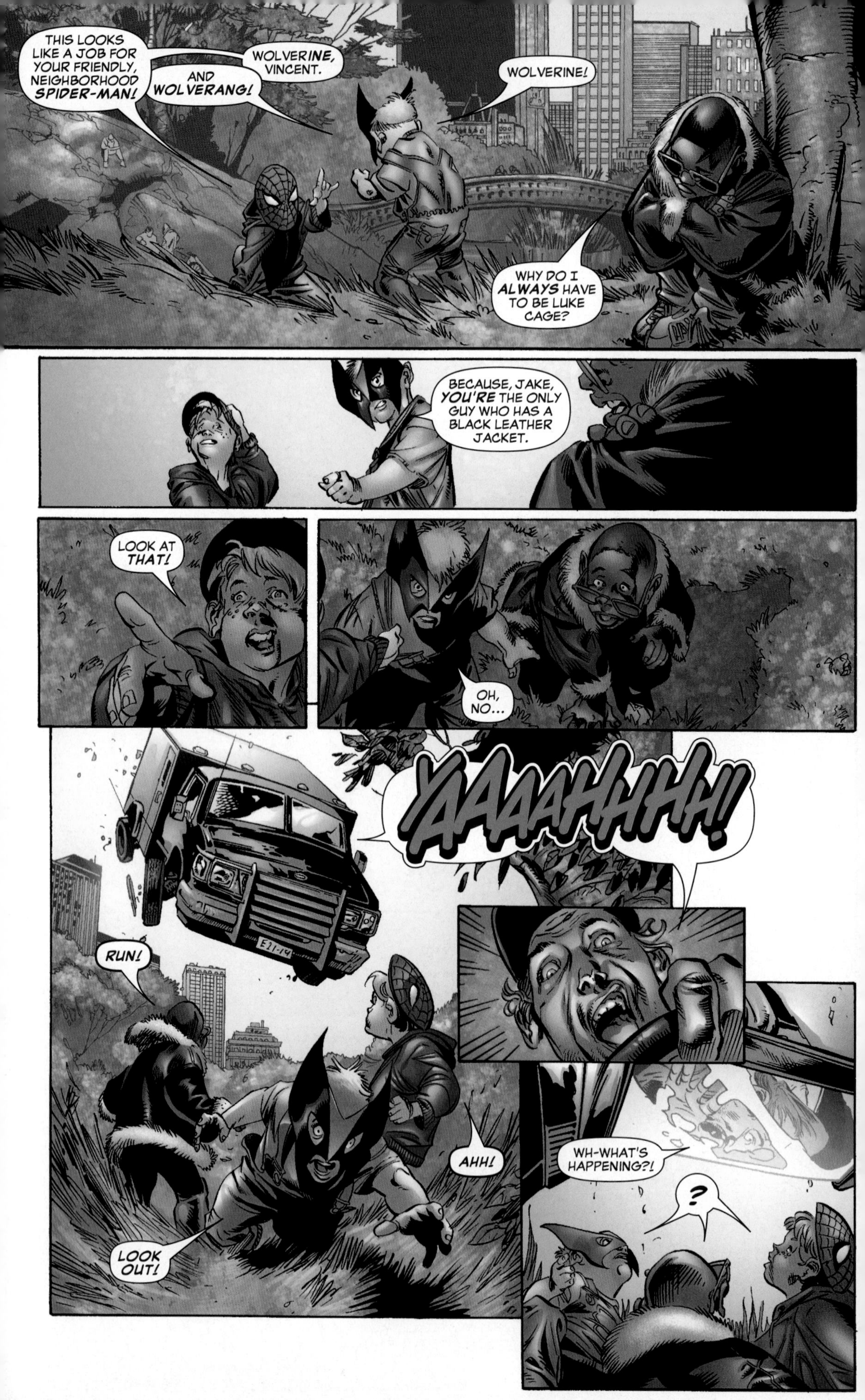
THIS LOOKS LIKE A JOB FOR YOUR FRIENDLY, NEIGHBORHOOD SPIDER-MAN!
WOLVERINE, VINCENT.
AND WOLVERANG!
WOLVERINE!
WHY DO I ALWAYS HAVE TO BE LUKE CAGE?
BECAUSE, JAKE, YOU'RE THE ONLY GUY WHO HAS A BLACK LEATHER JACKET.
LOOK AT THAT!
OH, NO...
YAAAAHHHH!
RUN!
AHH!
LOOK OUT!
WH-WHAT'S HAPPENING?!
?

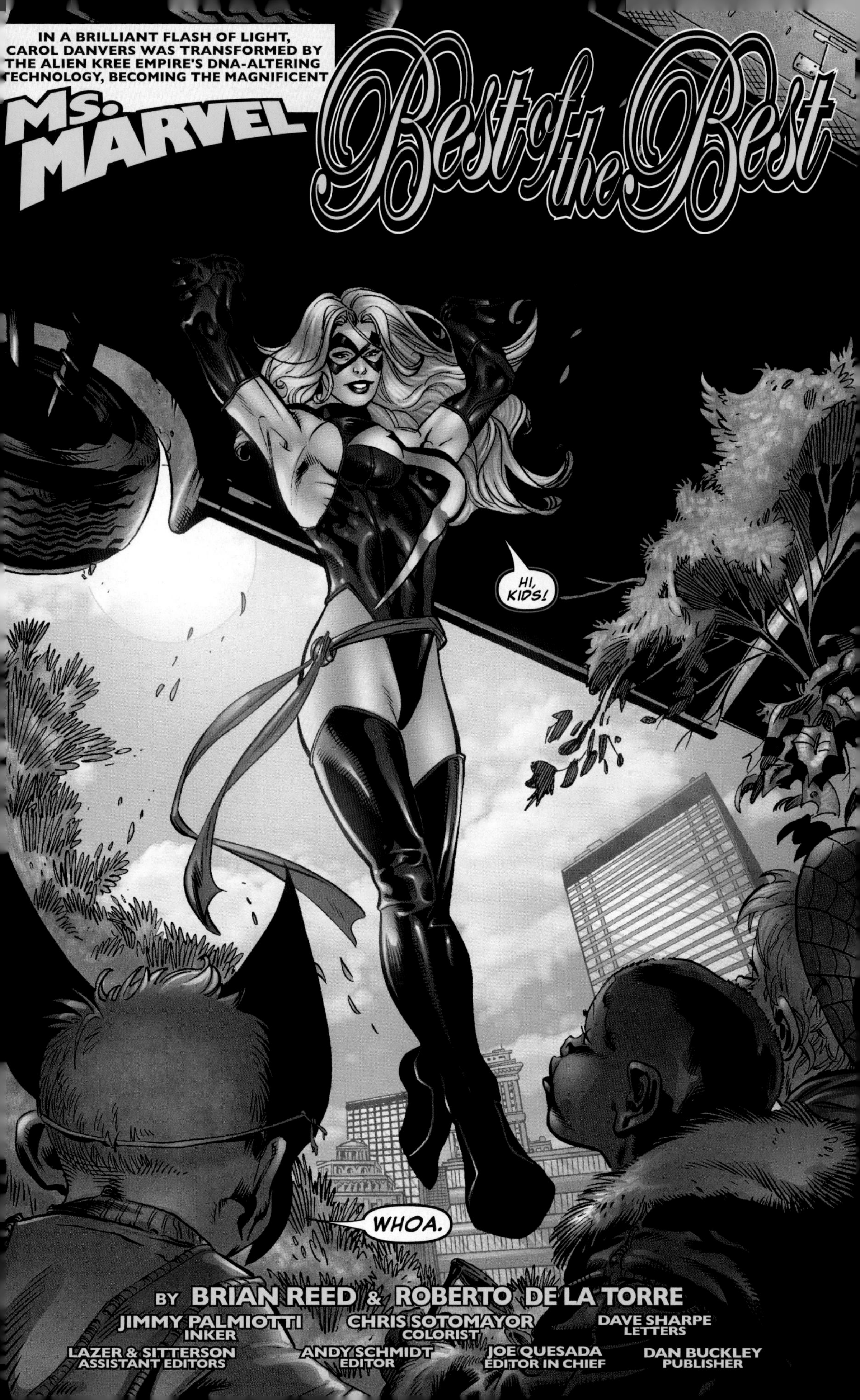
IN A BRILLIANT FLASH OF LIGHT, CAROL DANVERS WAS TRANSFORMED BY THE ALIEN KREE EMPIRE'S DNA-ALTERING TECHNOLOGY, BECOMING THE MAGNIFICENT
MS. MARVEL
Best of the Best
HI, KIDS!
WHOA.
BY BRIAN REED & ROBERTO DE LA TORRE
JIMMY PALMIOTTI INKER
CHRIS SOTOMAYOR COLORIST
DAVE SHARPE LETTERS
LAZER & SITTERSON ASSISTANT EDITORS
ANDY SCHMIDT EDITOR
JOE QUESADA EDITOR IN CHIEF
DAN BUCKLEY PUBLISHER

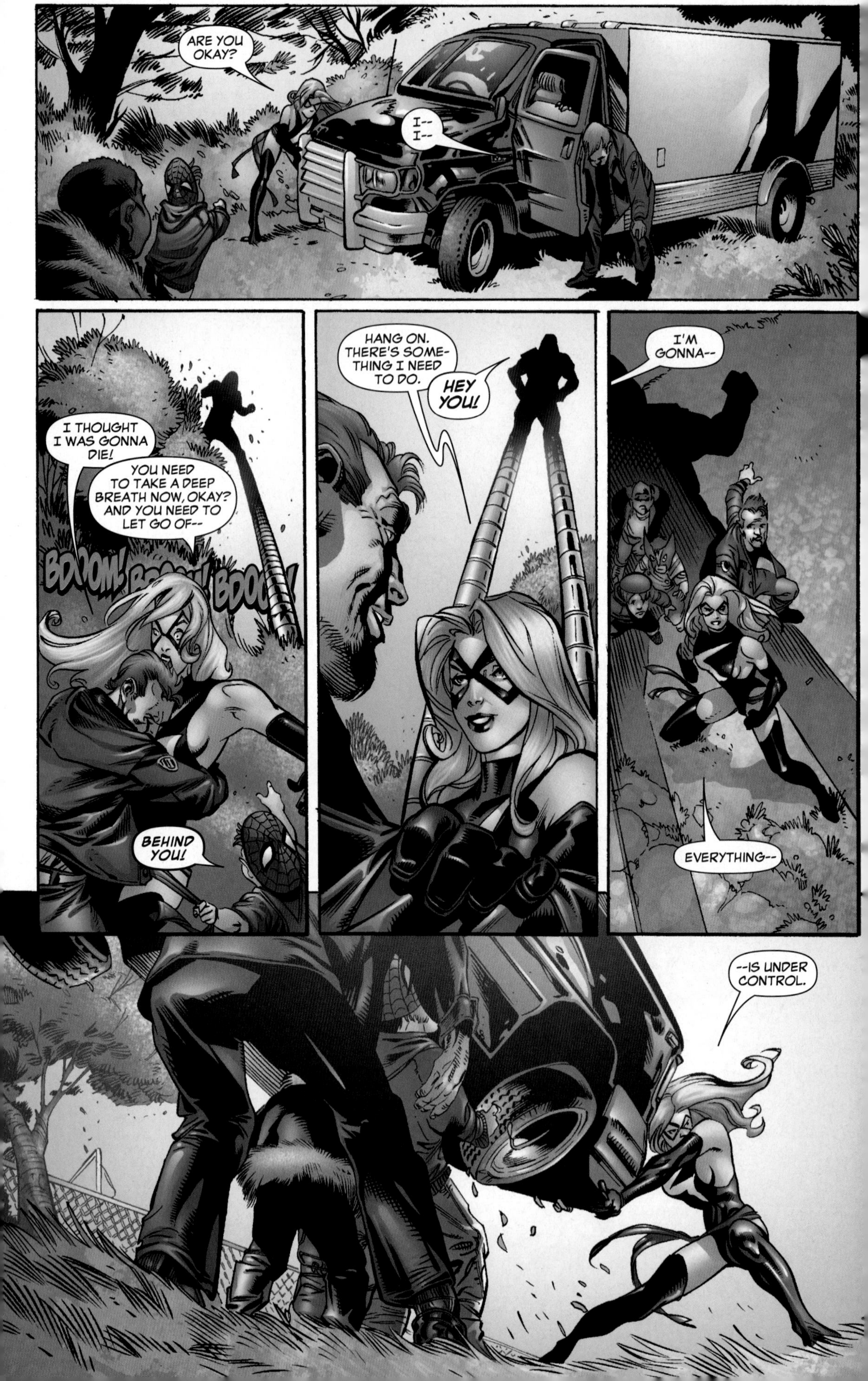
ARE YOU OKAY?
I-- I--
I THOUGHT I WAS GONNA DIE!
YOU NEED TO TAKE A DEEP BREATH NOW, OKAY? AND YOU NEED TO LET GO OF--
BDOOM! BDOOM! BDOOM!
BEHIND YOU!
HANG ON. THERE'S SOMETHING I NEED TO DO.
HEY YOU!
I'M GONNA--
EVERYTHING--
--IS UNDER CONTROL.

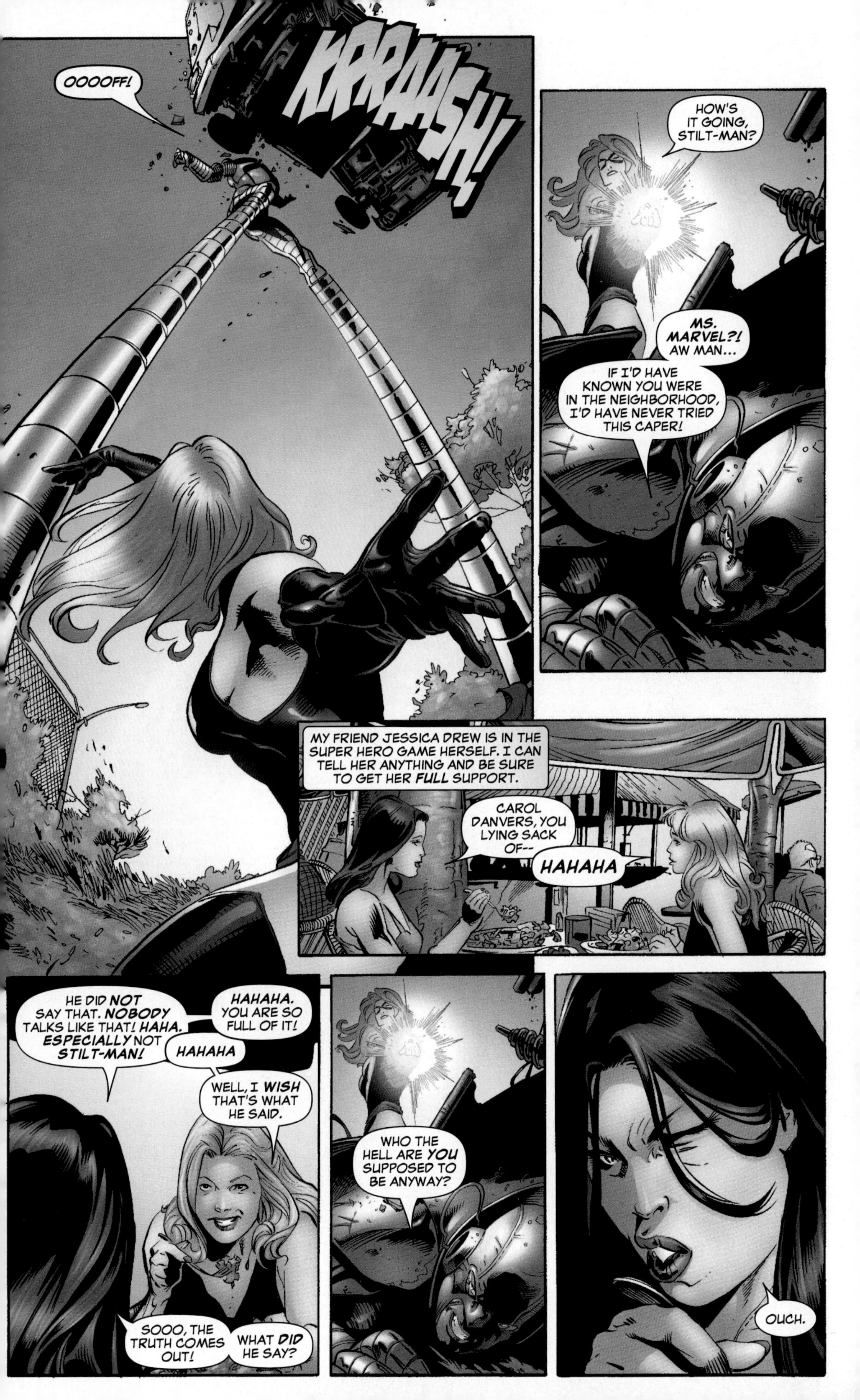
OOOOFF!
KRRAASH!
HOW'S IT GOING, STILT-MAN?
MS. MARVEL?! AW MAN...
IF I'D HAVE KNOWN YOU WERE IN THE NEIGHBORHOOD, I'D HAVE NEVER TRIED THIS CAPER!
MY FRIEND JESSICA DREW IS IN THE SUPER HERO GAME HERSELF. I CAN TELL HER ANYTHING AND BE SURE TO GET HER FULL SUPPORT.
CAROL DANVERS, YOU LYING SACK OF--
HAHAHA
HE DID NOT SAY THAT. NOBODY TALKS LIKE THAT! HAHA. ESPECIALLY NOT STILT-MAN!
HAHAHA. YOU ARE SO FULL OF IT!
HAHAHA
WELL, I WISH THAT'S WHAT HE SAID.
SOOO, THE TRUTH COMES OUT!
WHAT DID HE SAY?
WHO THE HELL ARE YOU SUPPOSED TO BE ANYWAY?
OUCH.

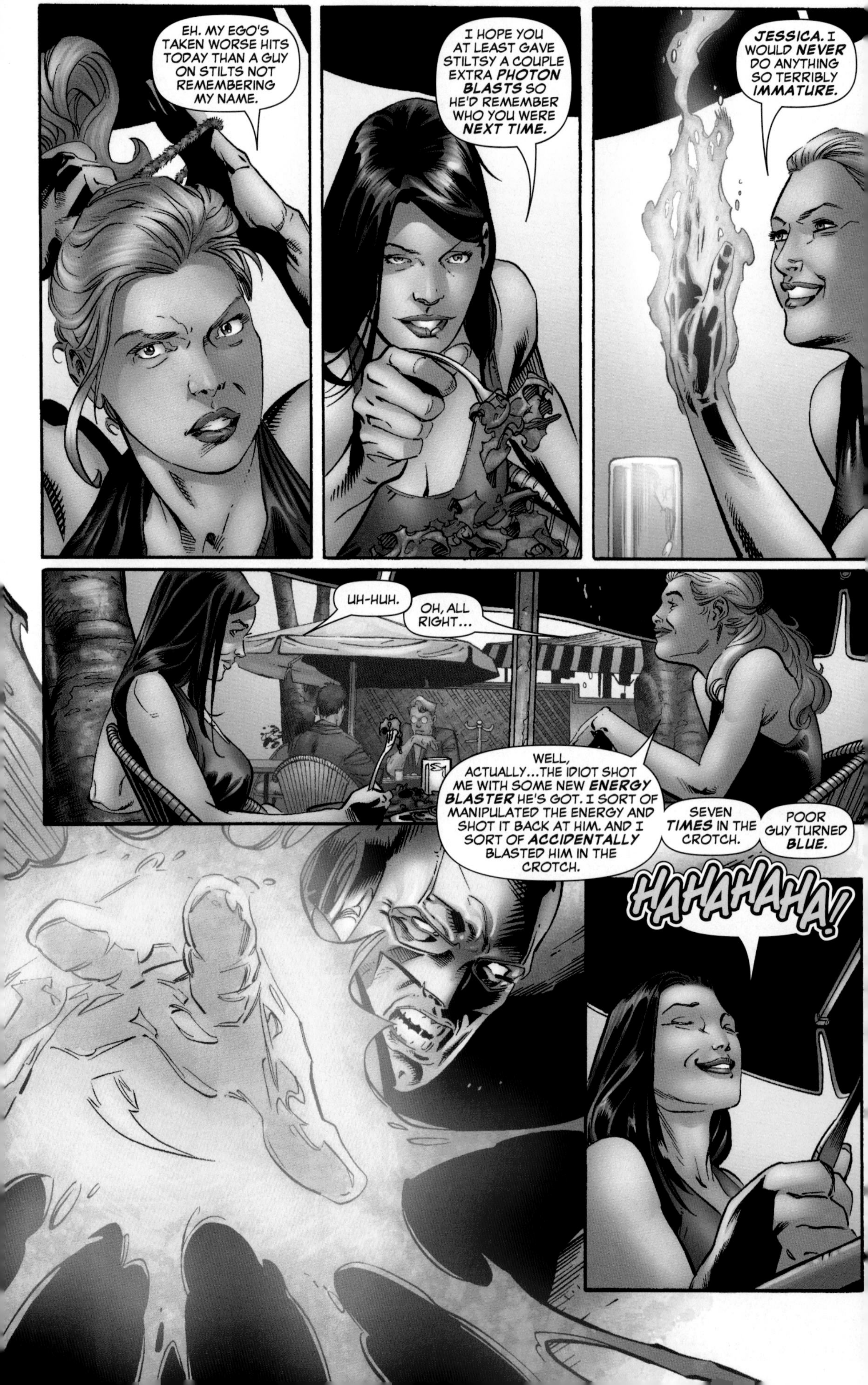
EH. MY EGO'S TAKEN WORSE HITS TODAY THAN A GUY ON STILTS NOT REMEMBERING MY NAME.
I HOPE YOU AT LEAST GAVE STILTSY A COUPLE EXTRA PHOTON BLASTS SO HE'D REMEMBER WHO YOU WERE NEXT TIME.
JESSICA. I WOULD NEVER DO ANYTHING SO TERRIBLY IMMATURE.
UH-HUH.
OH, ALL RIGHT...
WELL, ACTUALLY...THE IDIOT SHOT ME WITH SOME NEW ENERGY BLASTER HE'S GOT. I SORT OF MANIPULATED THE ENERGY AND SHOT IT BACK AT HIM. AND I SORT OF ACCIDENTALLY BLASTED HIM IN THE CROTCH.
SEVEN TIMES IN THE CROTCH.
POOR GUY TURNED BLUE.
HAHAHAHA!

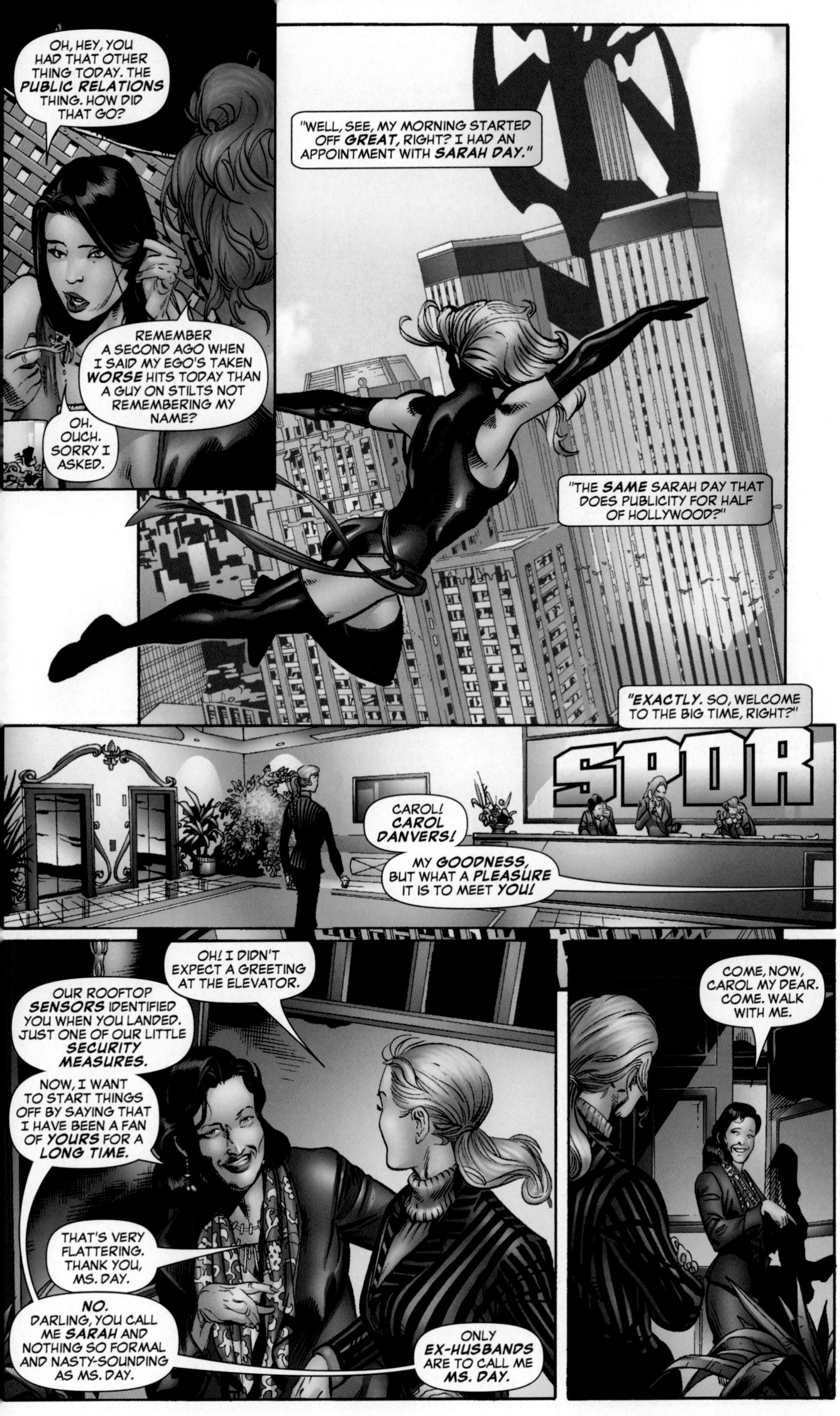
OH, HEY, YOU HAD THAT OTHER THING TODAY. THE PUBLIC RELATIONS THING. HOW DID THAT GO?
REMEMBER A SECOND AGO WHEN I SAID MY EGO'S TAKEN WORSE HITS TODAY THAN A GUY ON STILTS NOT REMEMBERING MY NAME?
OH. OUCH. SORRY I ASKED.
"WELL, SEE, MY MORNING STARTED OFF GREAT, RIGHT? I HAD AN APPOINTMENT WITH SARAH DAY."
"THE SAME SARAH DAY THAT DOES PUBLICITY FOR HALF OF HOLLYWOOD?"
"EXACTLY. SO, WELCOME TO THE BIG TIME, RIGHT?"
SPDR
CAROL! CAROL DANVERS!
MY GOODNESS, BUT WHAT A PLEASURE IT IS TO MEET YOU!
OH! I DIDN'T EXPECT A GREETING AT THE ELEVATOR.
OUR ROOFTOP SENSORS IDENTIFIED YOU WHEN YOU LANDED. JUST ONE OF OUR LITTLE SECURITY MEASURES.
NOW, I WANT TO START THINGS OFF BY SAYING THAT I HAVE BEEN A FAN OF YOURS FOR A LONG TIME.
THAT'S VERY FLATTERING. THANK YOU, MS. DAY.
NO. DARLING, YOU CALL ME SARAH AND NOTHING SO FORMAL AND NASTY-SOUNDING AS MS. DAY.
ONLY EX-HUSBANDS ARE TO CALL ME MS. DAY.
COME, NOW, CAROL MY DEAR. COME. WALK WITH ME.

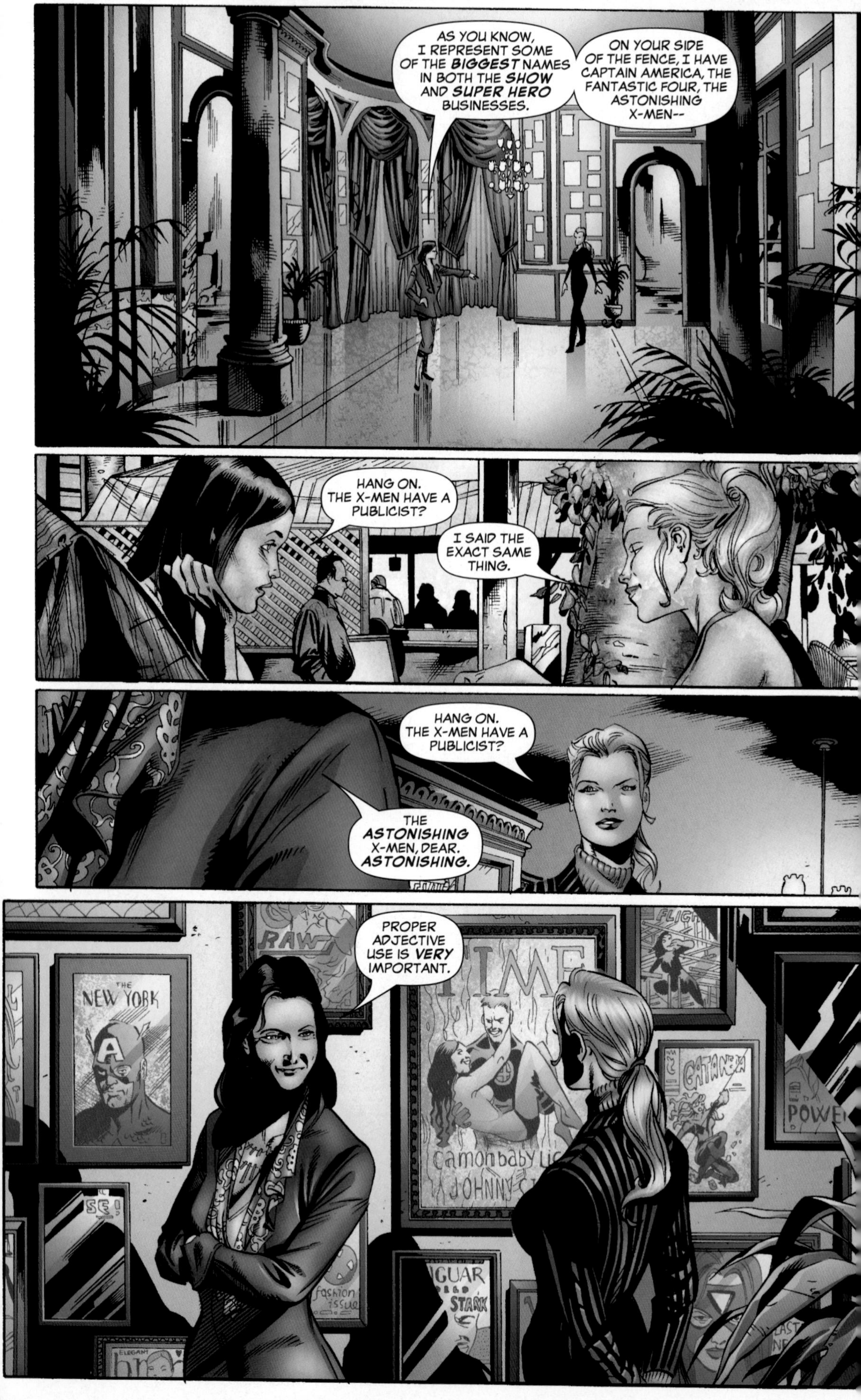
AS YOU KNOW, I REPRESENT SOME OF THE **BIGGEST** NAMES IN BOTH THE **SHOW** AND **SUPER HERO** BUSINESSES.
ON YOUR SIDE OF THE FENCE, I HAVE CAPTAIN AMERICA, THE FANTASTIC FOUR, THE ASTONISHING X-MEN--
HANG ON. THE X-MEN HAVE A PUBLICIST?
I SAID THE EXACT SAME THING.
HANG ON. THE X-MEN HAVE A PUBLICIST?
THE **ASTONISHING** X-MEN, DEAR. **ASTONISHING.**
PROPER ADJECTIVE USE IS **VERY** IMPORTANT.
THE NEW YORK
TIME
RAW
POWE
STARK
fashion issue

SO, HERE'S WHAT I KNOW ABOUT YOU, AND TELL ME IF I'M LEAVING ANYTHING OUT.

EX-AIR FORCE. EX-NASA. EX-AVENGER. AND, AS OF LATE LAST WEEK, EX-HOMELAND SECURITY.

YOU QUIT YOUR HOMELAND SECURITY POST?

I'LL GET TO THAT IN A MINUTE.

YOU BEGAN YOUR SUPER HERO CAREER AS "MS. MARVEL", A NAME I QUITE LIKED, BUT HAVE ALSO GONE BY THE LESS COMPELLING TITLES OF "BINARY" AND, MORE RECENTLY, THE RATHER DREADFUL "WARBIRD".

ALL THE WHILE YOU'VE BEEN WEARING A COSTUME THAT, WELL, COULD BE MORE THAN IT IS, IF I MAY BE FRANK.

ALTHOUGH I DO LIKE THE BOOTS. NOT EVERYONE HAS THE LEGS FOR THEM. YOU DO.

LET'S SEE, WHAT ELSE DO I KNOW? OH, OF COURSE, YOU PUBLISHED A FEW NOVELS THAT GOT SOME ATTENTION.

AND NOW... WHAT?

I, UM--

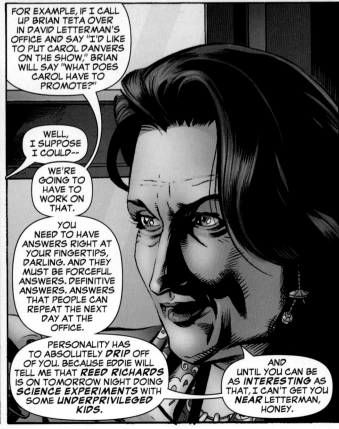

FOR EXAMPLE, IF I CALL UP BRIAN TETA OVER IN DAVID LETTERMAN'S OFFICE AND SAY "I'D LIKE TO PUT CAROL DANVERS ON THE SHOW," BRIAN WILL SAY "WHAT DOES CAROL HAVE TO PROMOTE?"

WELL, I SUPPOSE I COULD--

WE'RE GOING TO HAVE TO WORK ON THAT.

YOU NEED TO HAVE ANSWERS RIGHT AT YOUR FINGERTIPS, DARLING. AND THEY MUST BE FORCEFUL ANSWERS. DEFINITIVE ANSWERS. ANSWERS THAT PEOPLE CAN REPEAT THE NEXT DAY AT THE OFFICE.

PERSONALITY HAS TO ABSOLUTELY DRIP OFF OF YOU. BECAUSE EDDIE WILL TELL ME THAT REED RICHARDS IS ON TOMORROW NIGHT DOING SCIENCE EXPERIMENTS WITH SOME UNDERPRIVILEGED KIDS.

AND UNTIL YOU CAN BE AS INTERESTING AS THAT, I CAN'T GET YOU NEAR LETTERMAN, HONEY.

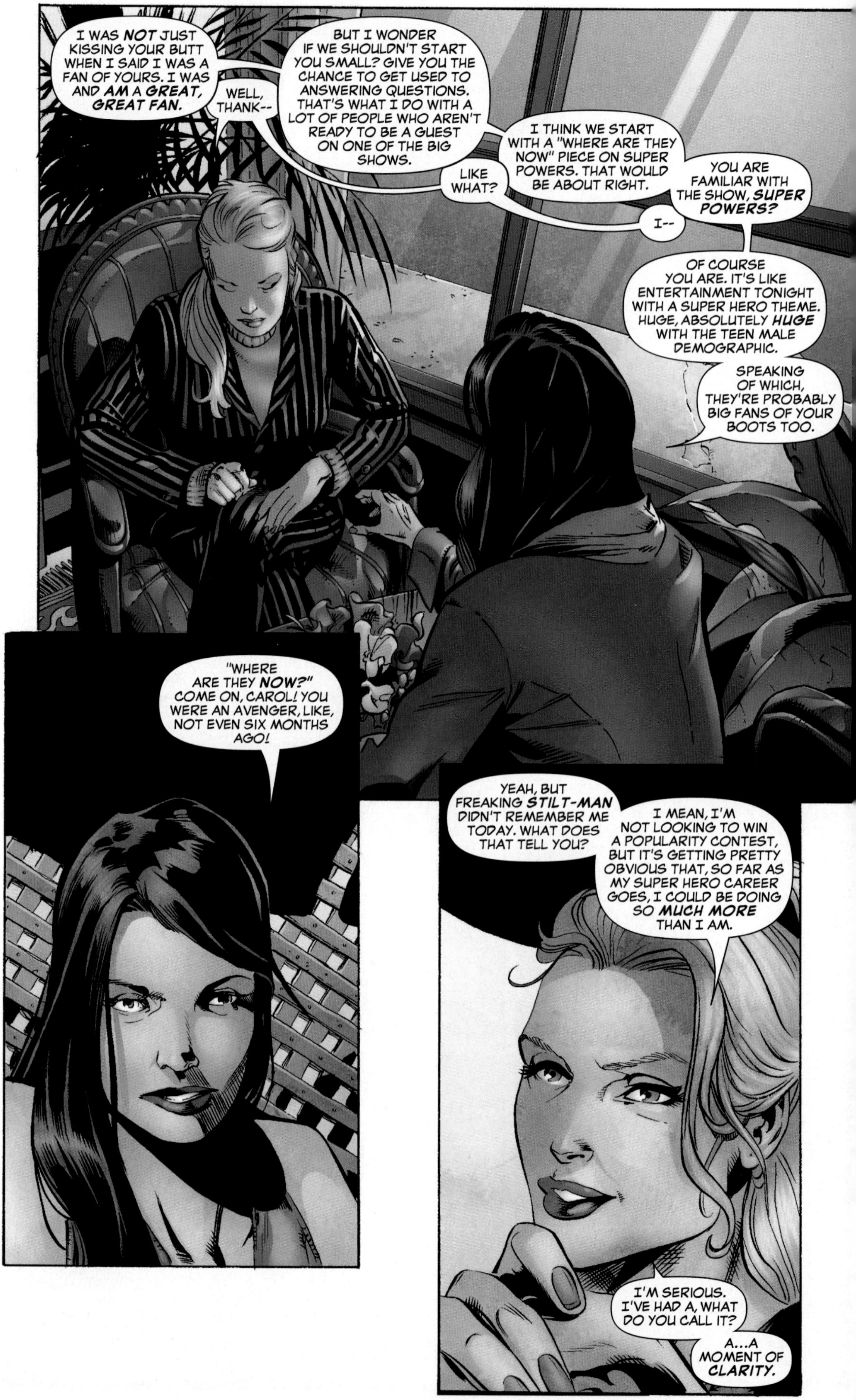
I WAS NOT JUST KISSING YOUR BUTT WHEN I SAID I WAS A FAN OF YOURS. I WAS AND AM A GREAT, GREAT FAN.
WELL, THANK--
BUT I WONDER IF WE SHOULDN'T START YOU SMALL? GIVE YOU THE CHANCE TO GET USED TO ANSWERING QUESTIONS. THAT'S WHAT I DO WITH A LOT OF PEOPLE WHO AREN'T READY TO BE A GUEST ON ONE OF THE BIG SHOWS.
LIKE WHAT?
I THINK WE START WITH A "WHERE ARE THEY NOW" PIECE ON SUPER POWERS. THAT WOULD BE ABOUT RIGHT.
I--
YOU ARE FAMILIAR WITH THE SHOW, SUPER POWERS?
OF COURSE YOU ARE. IT'S LIKE ENTERTAINMENT TONIGHT WITH A SUPER HERO THEME. HUGE, ABSOLUTELY HUGE WITH THE TEEN MALE DEMOGRAPHIC.
SPEAKING OF WHICH, THEY'RE PROBABLY BIG FANS OF YOUR BOOTS TOO.
"WHERE ARE THEY NOW?" COME ON, CAROL! YOU WERE AN AVENGER, LIKE, NOT EVEN SIX MONTHS AGO!
YEAH, BUT FREAKING STILT-MAN DIDN'T REMEMBER ME TODAY. WHAT DOES THAT TELL YOU?
I MEAN, I'M NOT LOOKING TO WIN A POPULARITY CONTEST, BUT IT'S GETTING PRETTY OBVIOUS THAT, SO FAR AS MY SUPER HERO CAREER GOES, I COULD BE DOING SO MUCH MORE THAN I AM.
I'M SERIOUS. I'VE HAD A, WHAT DO YOU CALL IT?
A...A MOMENT OF CLARITY.

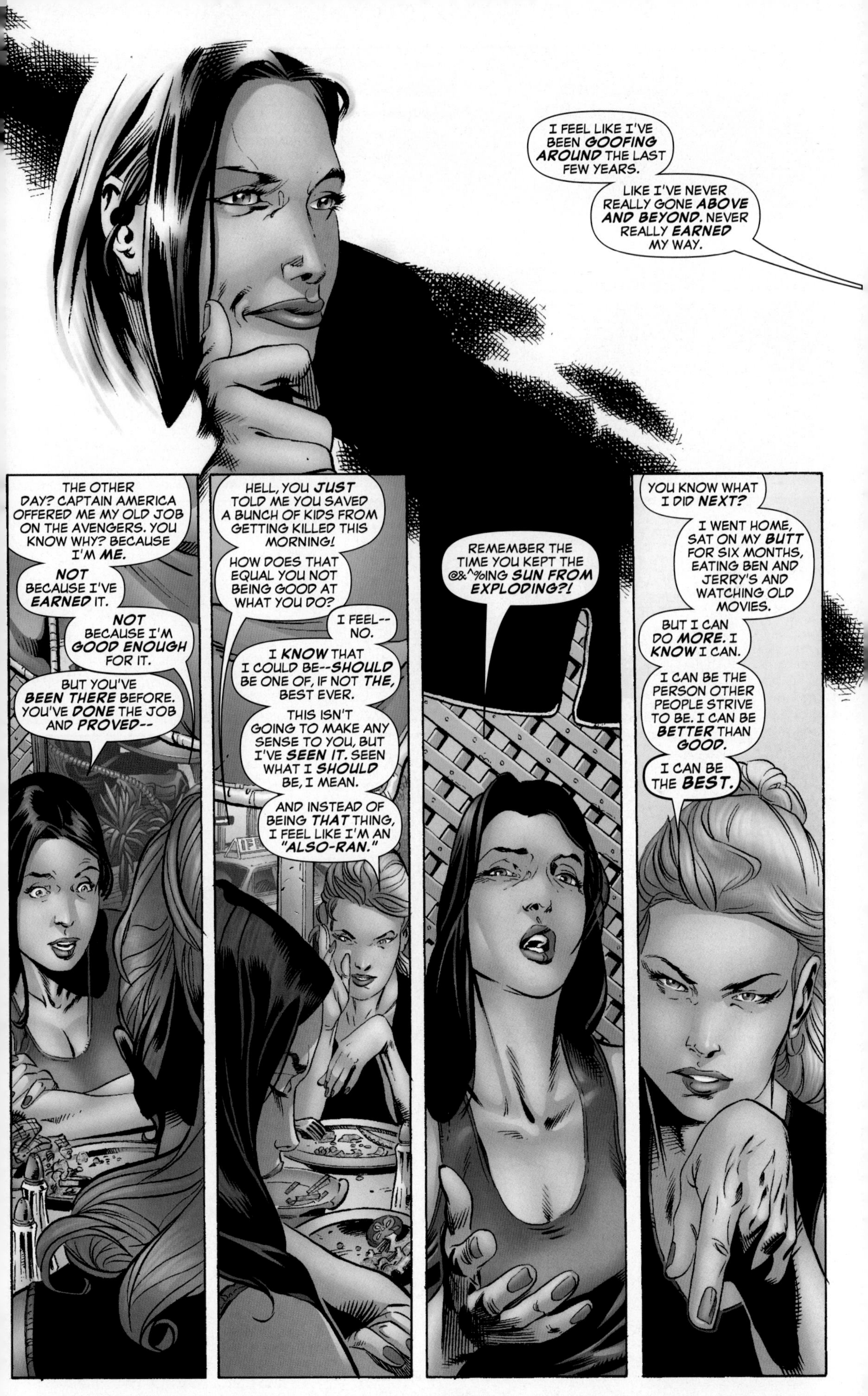
I FEEL LIKE I'VE BEEN GOOFING AROUND THE LAST FEW YEARS.
LIKE I'VE NEVER REALLY GONE ABOVE AND BEYOND. NEVER REALLY EARNED MY WAY.
THE OTHER DAY? CAPTAIN AMERICA OFFERED ME MY OLD JOB ON THE AVENGERS. YOU KNOW WHY? BECAUSE I'M ME.
NOT BECAUSE I'VE EARNED IT.
NOT BECAUSE I'M GOOD ENOUGH FOR IT.
BUT YOU'VE BEEN THERE BEFORE. YOU'VE DONE THE JOB AND PROVED--
HELL, YOU JUST TOLD ME YOU SAVED A BUNCH OF KIDS FROM GETTING KILLED THIS MORNING!
HOW DOES THAT EQUAL YOU NOT BEING GOOD AT WHAT YOU DO?
I FEEL-- NO.
I KNOW THAT I COULD BE--SHOULD BE ONE OF, IF NOT THE, BEST EVER.
THIS ISN'T GOING TO MAKE ANY SENSE TO YOU, BUT I'VE SEEN IT. SEEN WHAT I SHOULD BE, I MEAN.
AND INSTEAD OF BEING THAT THING, I FEEL LIKE I'M AN "ALSO-RAN."
REMEMBER THE TIME YOU KEPT THE @&^%ING SUN FROM EXPLODING?!
YOU KNOW WHAT I DID NEXT?
I WENT HOME, SAT ON MY BUTT FOR SIX MONTHS, EATING BEN AND JERRY'S AND WATCHING OLD MOVIES.
BUT I CAN DO MORE. I KNOW I CAN.
I CAN BE THE PERSON OTHER PEOPLE STRIVE TO BE. I CAN BE BETTER THAN GOOD.
I CAN BE THE BEST.

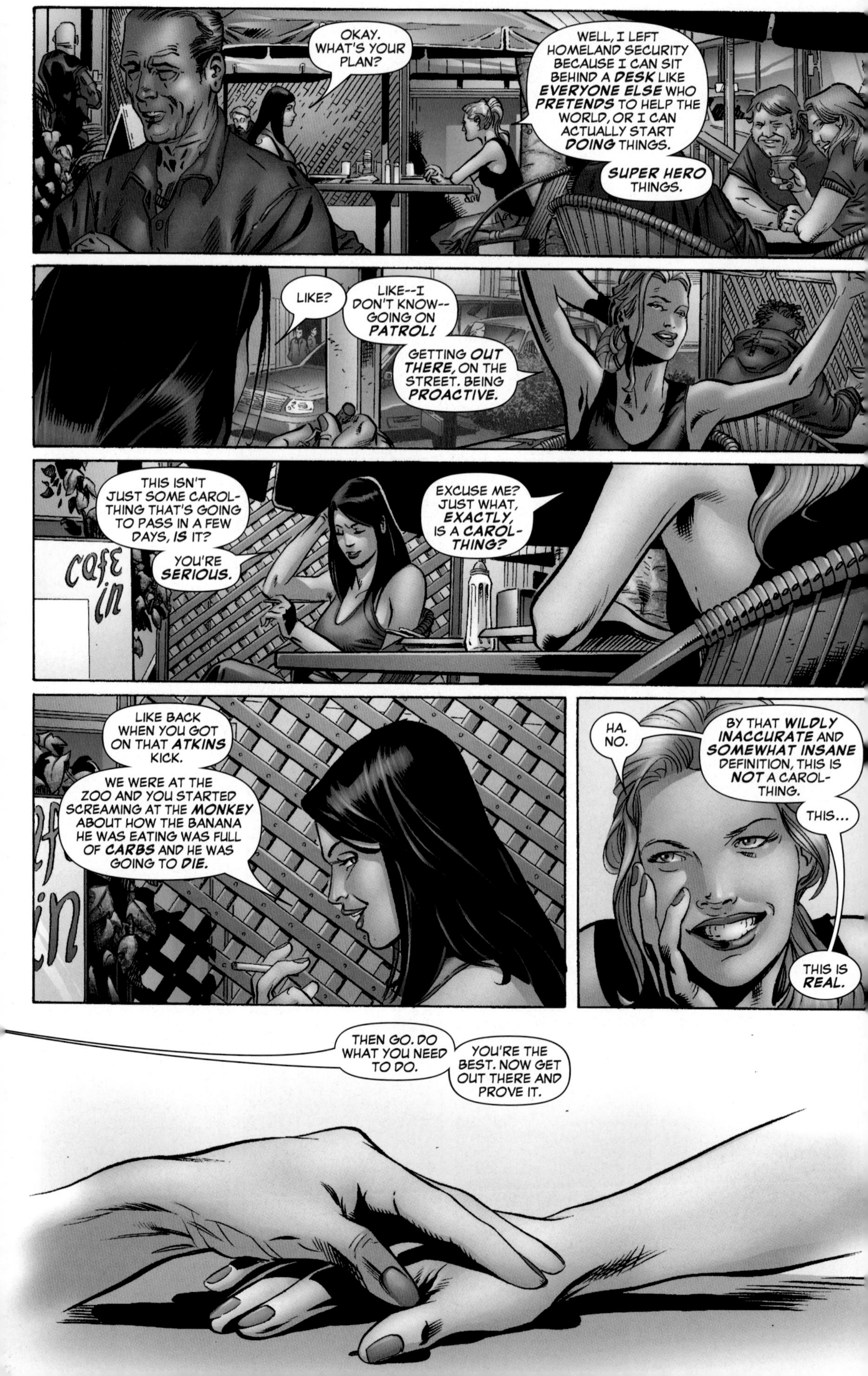
OKAY. WHAT'S YOUR PLAN?
WELL, I LEFT HOMELAND SECURITY BECAUSE I CAN SIT BEHIND A DESK LIKE EVERYONE ELSE WHO PRETENDS TO HELP THE WORLD, OR I CAN ACTUALLY START DOING THINGS.
SUPER HERO THINGS.
LIKE?
LIKE--I DON'T KNOW--GOING ON PATROL!
GETTING OUT THERE, ON THE STREET. BEING PROACTIVE.
THIS ISN'T JUST SOME CAROL-THING THAT'S GOING TO PASS IN A FEW DAYS, IS IT?
YOU'RE SERIOUS.
EXCUSE ME? JUST WHAT, EXACTLY, IS A CAROL-THING?
cafe in
LIKE BACK WHEN YOU GOT ON THAT ATKINS KICK.
WE WERE AT THE ZOO AND YOU STARTED SCREAMING AT THE MONKEY ABOUT HOW THE BANANA HE WAS EATING WAS FULL OF CARBS AND HE WAS GOING TO DIE.
HA. NO.
BY THAT WILDLY INACCURATE AND SOMEWHAT INSANE DEFINITION, THIS IS NOT A CAROL-THING.
THIS...
THIS IS REAL.
THEN GO. DO WHAT YOU NEED TO DO.
YOU'RE THE BEST. NOW GET OUT THERE AND PROVE IT.

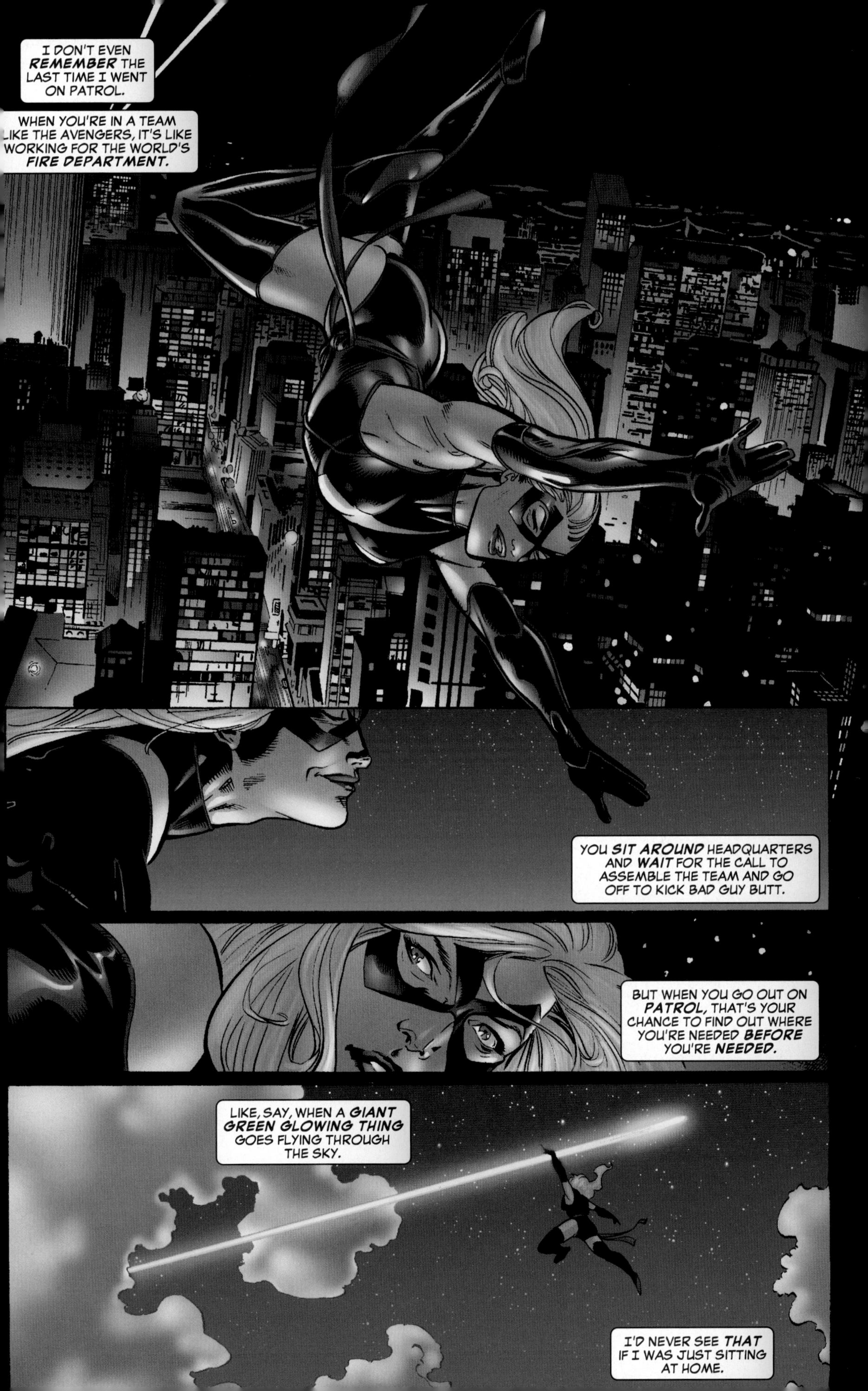
I DON'T EVEN REMEMBER THE LAST TIME I WENT ON PATROL.
WHEN YOU'RE IN A TEAM LIKE THE AVENGERS, IT'S LIKE WORKING FOR THE WORLD'S FIRE DEPARTMENT.
YOU SIT AROUND HEADQUARTERS AND WAIT FOR THE CALL TO ASSEMBLE THE TEAM AND GO OFF TO KICK BAD GUY BUTT.
BUT WHEN YOU GO OUT ON PATROL, THAT'S YOUR CHANCE TO FIND OUT WHERE YOU'RE NEEDED BEFORE YOU'RE NEEDED.
LIKE, SAY, WHEN A GIANT GREEN GLOWING THING GOES FLYING THROUGH THE SKY.
I'D NEVER SEE THAT IF I WAS JUST SITTING AT HOME.

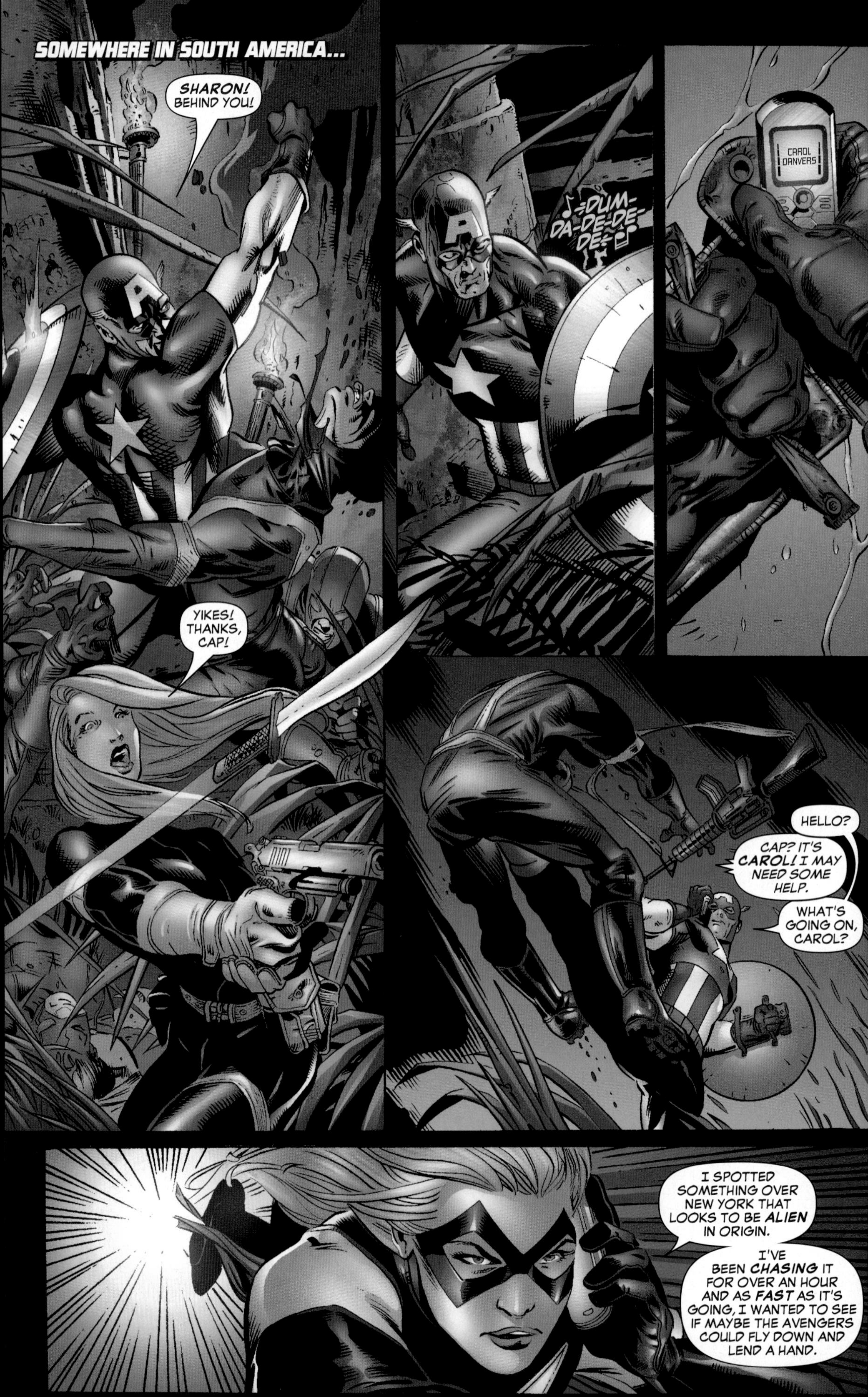
SOMEWHERE IN SOUTH AMERICA...
SHARON! BEHIND YOU!
YIKES! THANKS, CAP!
DUM-DA-DE-DE-DE-
CAROL DANVERS
HELLO?
CAP? IT'S CAROL! I MAY NEED SOME HELP.
WHAT'S GOING ON, CAROL?
I SPOTTED SOMETHING OVER NEW YORK THAT LOOKS TO BE ALIEN IN ORIGIN.
I'VE BEEN CHASING IT FOR OVER AN HOUR AND AS FAST AS IT'S GOING, I WANTED TO SEE IF MAYBE THE AVENGERS COULD FLY DOWN AND LEND A HAND.

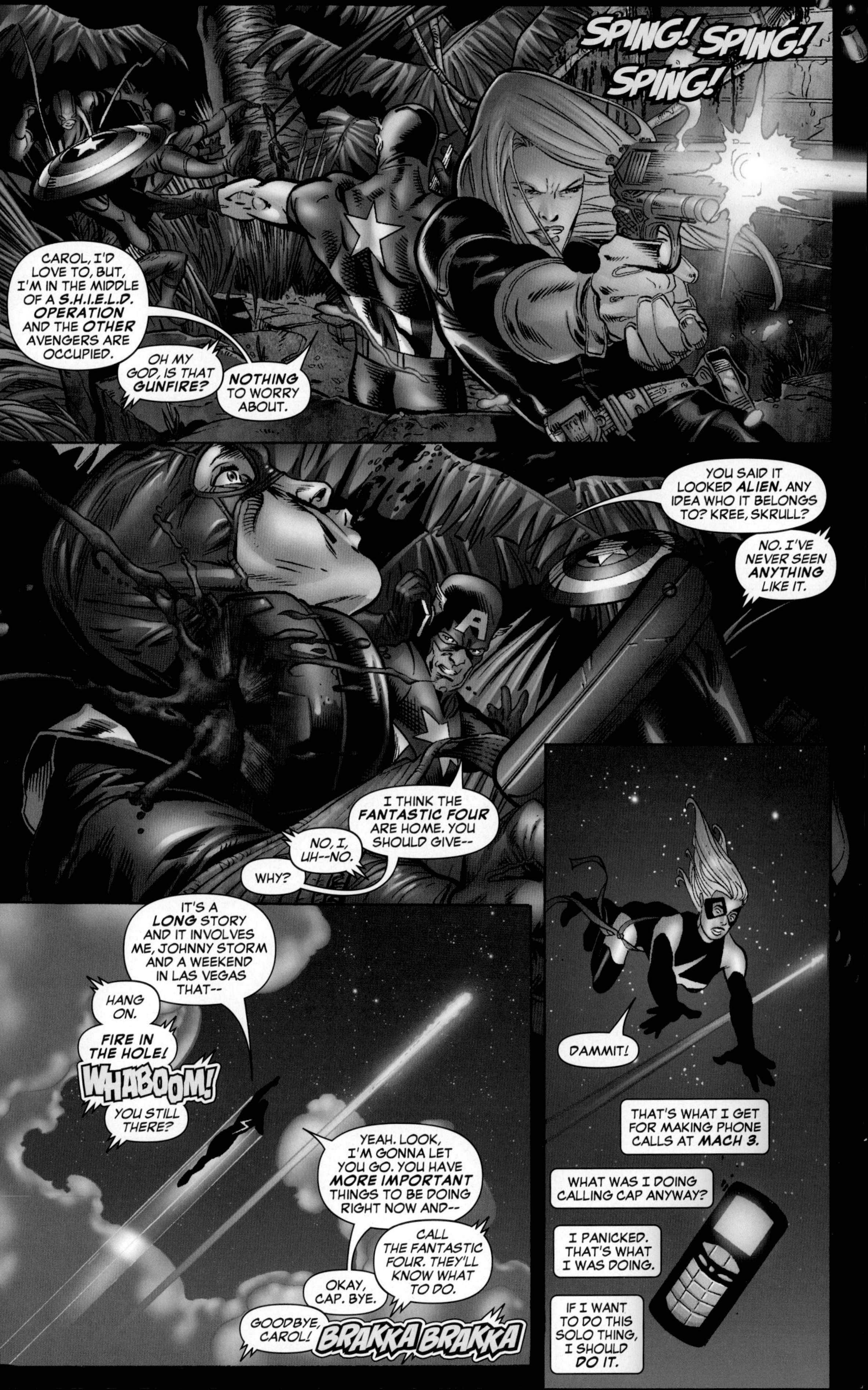
SPING! SPING! SPING!
CAROL, I'D LOVE TO, BUT, I'M IN THE MIDDLE OF A S.H.I.E.L.D. OPERATION AND THE OTHER AVENGERS ARE OCCUPIED.
OH MY GOD, IS THAT GUNFIRE?
NOTHING TO WORRY ABOUT.
YOU SAID IT LOOKED ALIEN. ANY IDEA WHO IT BELONGS TO? KREE, SKRULL?
NO. I'VE NEVER SEEN ANYTHING LIKE IT.
I THINK THE FANTASTIC FOUR ARE HOME. YOU SHOULD GIVE--
NO, I, UH--NO.
WHY?
IT'S A LONG STORY AND IT INVOLVES ME, JOHNNY STORM AND A WEEKEND IN LAS VEGAS THAT--
HANG ON.
FIRE IN THE HOLE!
WHABOOM!
YOU STILL THERE?
YEAH. LOOK, I'M GONNA LET YOU GO. YOU HAVE MORE IMPORTANT THINGS TO BE DOING RIGHT NOW AND--
CALL THE FANTASTIC FOUR. THEY'LL KNOW WHAT TO DO.
OKAY, CAP. BYE.
GOODBYE, CAROL!
BRAKKA BRAKKA
DAMMIT!
THAT'S WHAT I GET FOR MAKING PHONE CALLS AT MACH 3.
WHAT WAS I DOING CALLING CAP ANYWAY?
I PANICKED. THAT'S WHAT I WAS DOING.
IF I WANT TO DO THIS SOLO THING, I SHOULD DO IT.

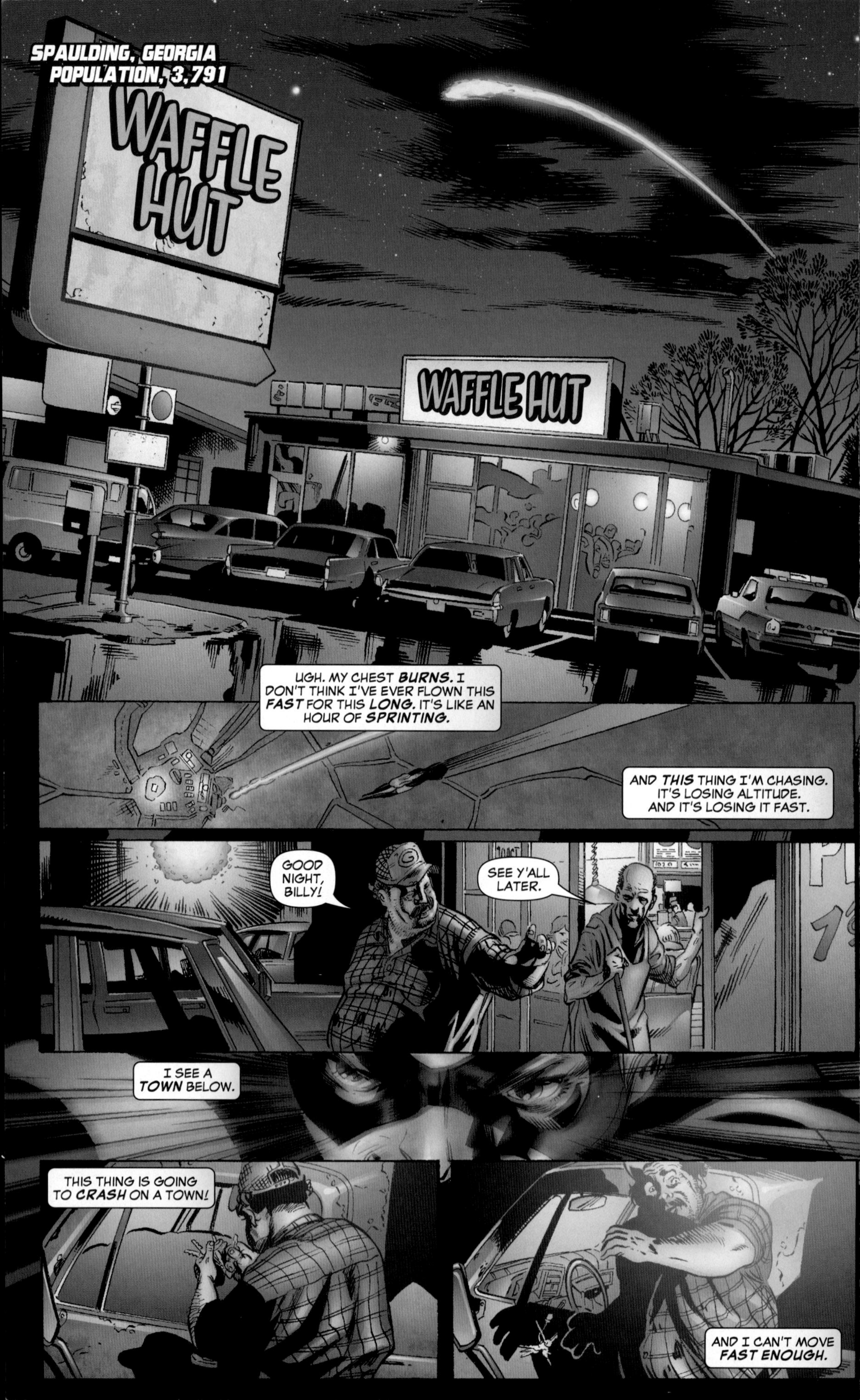
SPAULDING, GEORGIA
POPULATION, 3,791
WAFFLE HUT
WAFFLE HUT
UGH. MY CHEST BURNS. I DON'T THINK I'VE EVER FLOWN THIS FAST FOR THIS LONG. IT'S LIKE AN HOUR OF SPRINTING.
AND THIS THING I'M CHASING. IT'S LOSING ALTITUDE. AND IT'S LOSING IT FAST.
GOOD NIGHT, BILLY!
SEE Y'ALL LATER.
I SEE A TOWN BELOW.
THIS THING IS GOING TO CRASH ON A TOWN!
AND I CAN'T MOVE FAST ENOUGH.

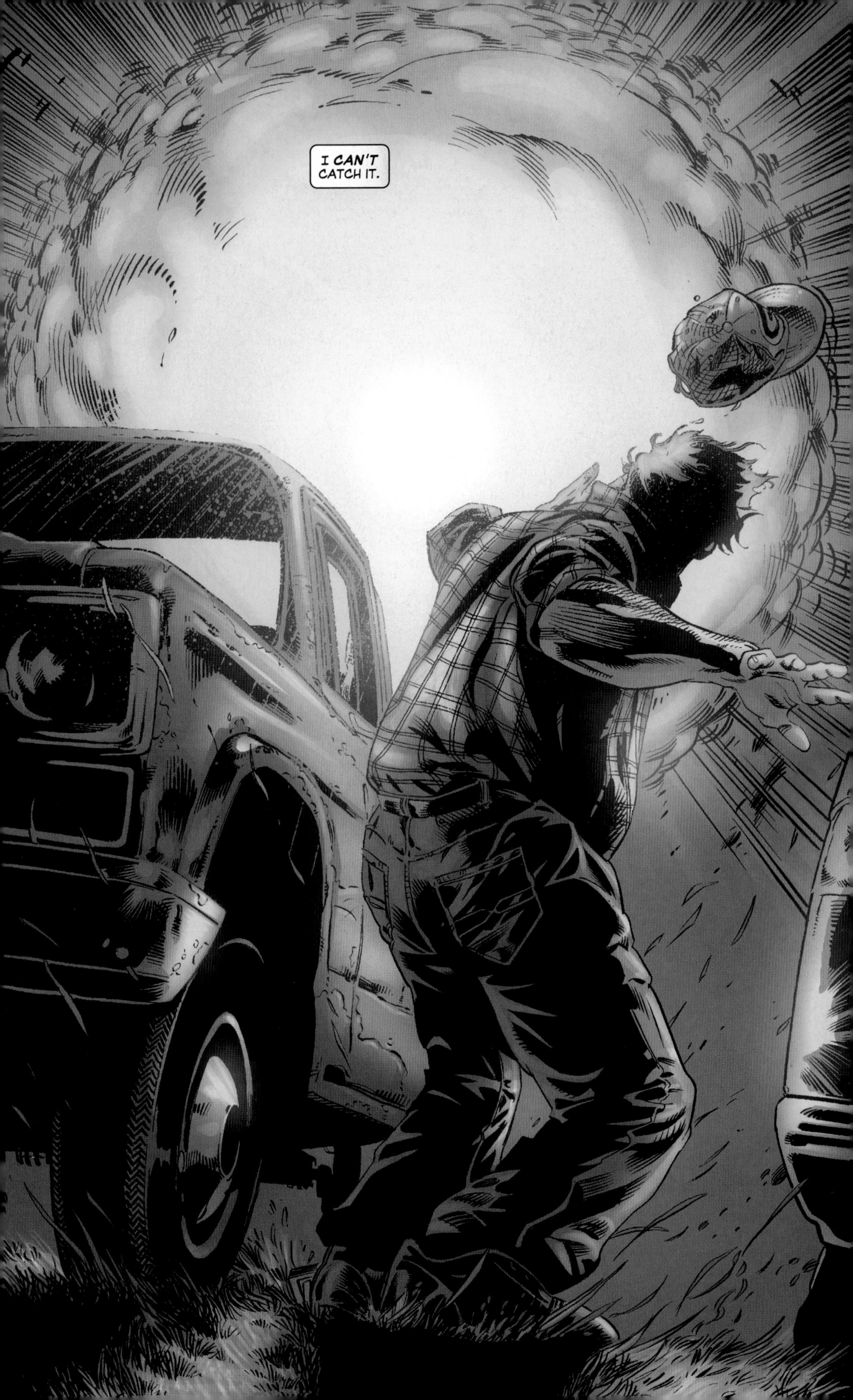
I CAN'T CATCH IT.

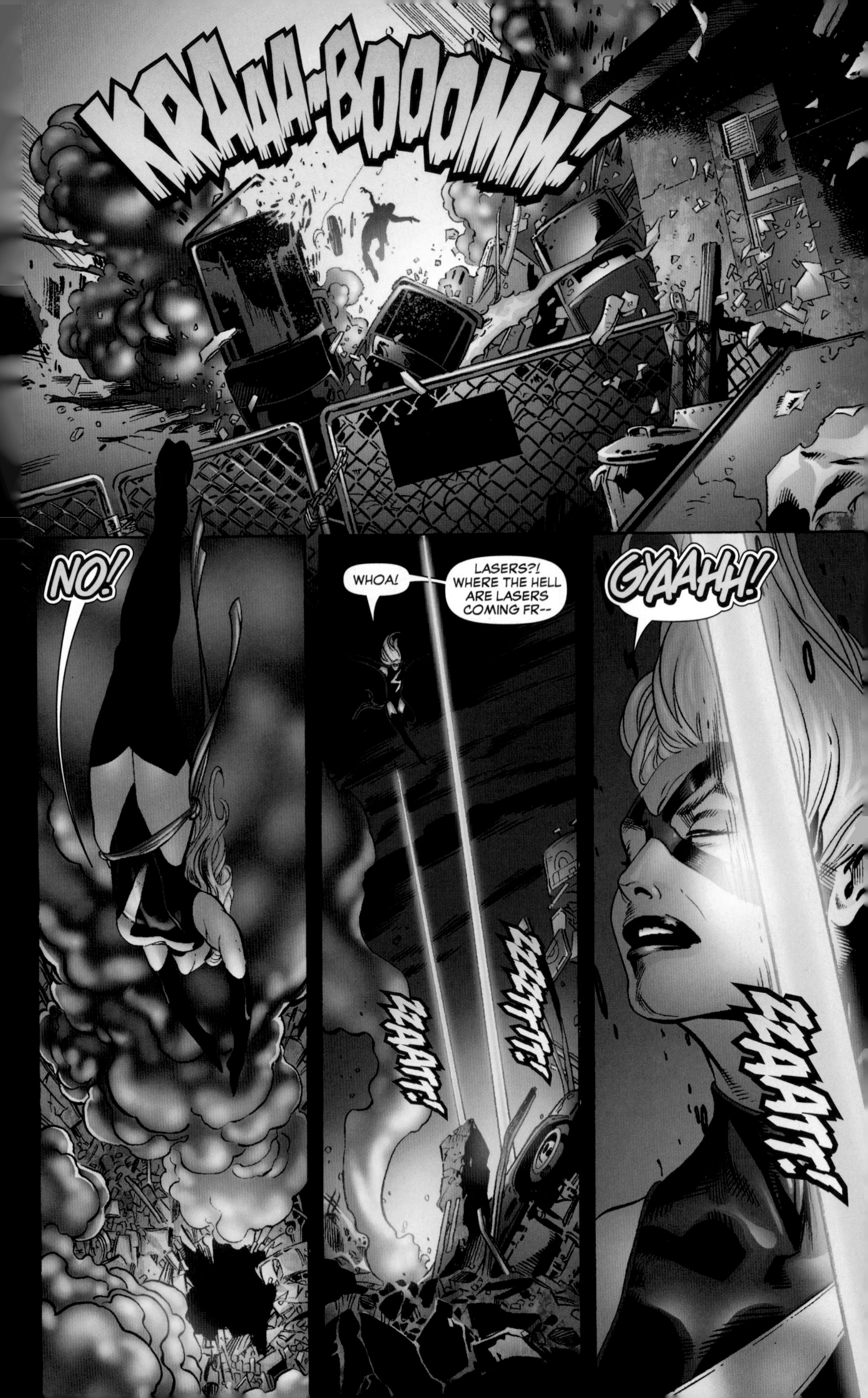
KRAAA-BOOOMM!
NO!
WHOA!
LASERS?! WHERE THE HELL ARE LASERS COMING FR--
ZZAAT!
ZZZZTTT!
GYAAHH!
ZZAAT!

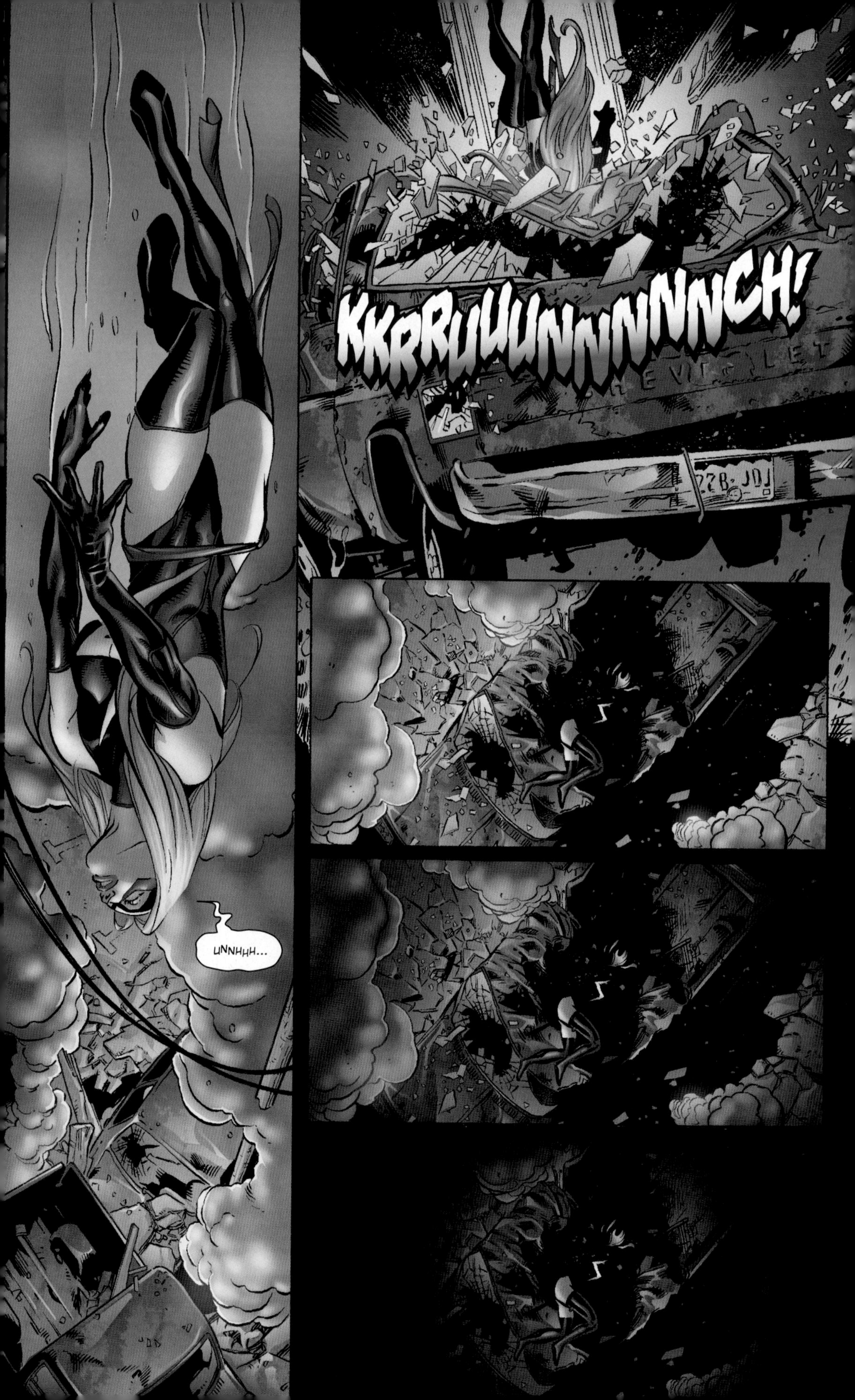

KKRUUUNNNNNCH!
UNNHHH...

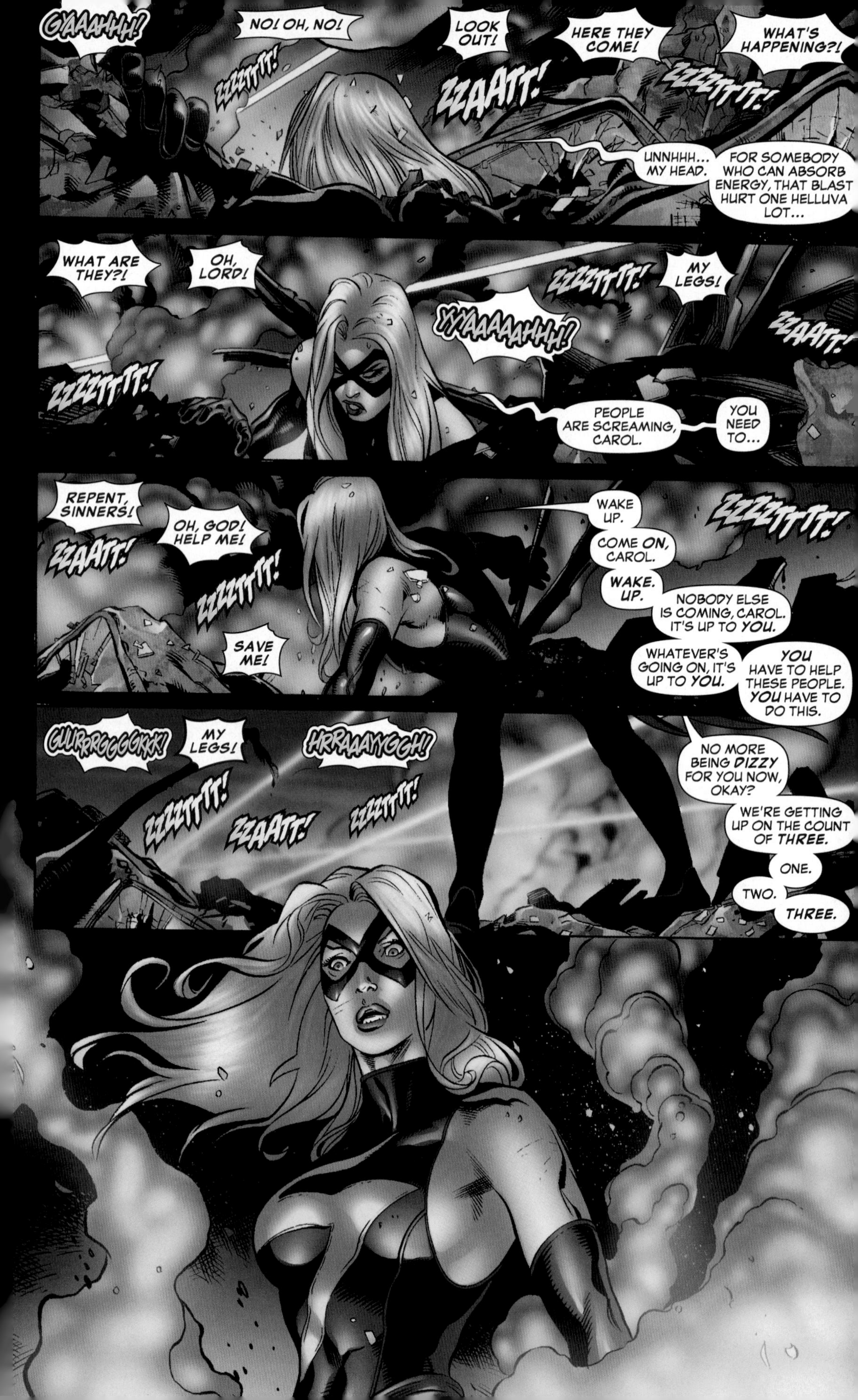
GYAAAHHH!
NO! OH, NO!
LOOK OUT!
HERE THEY COME!
WHAT'S HAPPENING?!
ZZZZTTTT!
ZZAATT!
ZZZZTTTTT!
UNNHHH... MY HEAD.
FOR SOMEBODY WHO CAN ABSORB ENERGY, THAT BLAST HURT ONE HELLUVA LOT...
WHAT ARE THEY?!
OH, LORD!
ZZZZTTTT!
MY LEGS!
YYAAAAAHHH!
ZZAATT!
ZZZZTTTT!
PEOPLE ARE SCREAMING, CAROL.
YOU NEED TO...
REPENT, SINNERS!
ZZAATT!
OH, GOD! HELP ME!
ZZZZTTTT!
SAVE ME!
WAKE UP.
ZZZZTTTT!
COME ON, CAROL.
WAKE. UP.
NOBODY ELSE IS COMING, CAROL. IT'S UP TO YOU.
WHATEVER'S GOING ON, IT'S UP TO YOU.
YOU HAVE TO HELP THESE PEOPLE. YOU HAVE TO DO THIS.
GUURRGGGKK!
MY LEGS!
HRRAAAYYGGH!
ZZZZTTTT!
ZZAATT!
ZZZZTTTT!
NO MORE BEING DIZZY FOR YOU NOW, OKAY?
WE'RE GETTING UP ON THE COUNT OF THREE.
ONE.
TWO.
THREE.

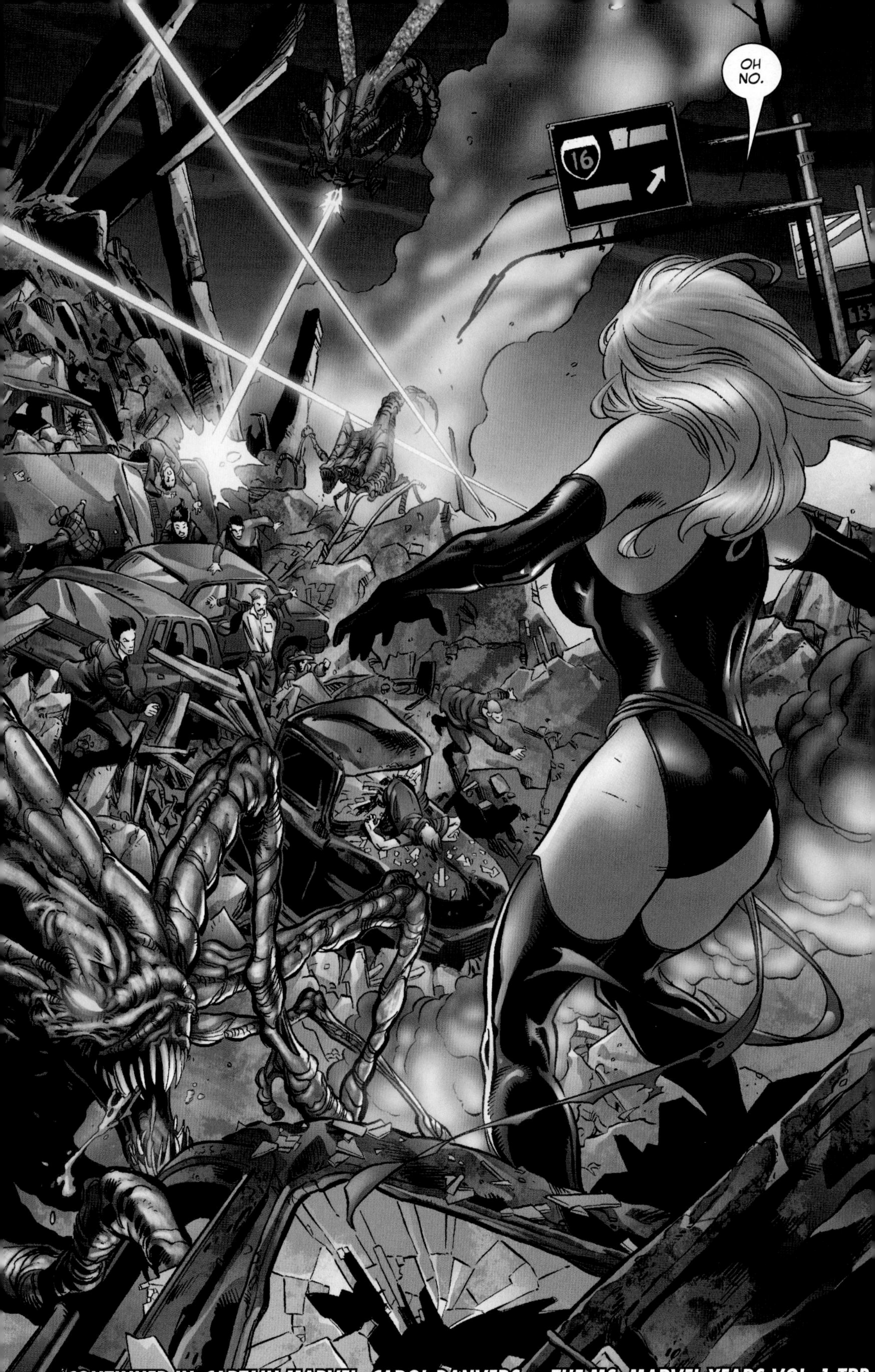
OH NO.
16

CONTINUED IN *CAPTAIN MARVEL: CAROL DANVERS — THE MS. MARVEL YEARS VOL. 1 TPB*

EARTH'S MIGHTIEST HERO
CAPTAIN MARVEL
#1
MARVEL
DECONNICK
SOY

FINAL ☆☆☆☆

# DAILY BUGLE®

SINCE 1897 ☆☆☆☆ $1.00 (in NYC) $1.50 (outside city)

## SPECIAL COMMEMORATIVE ISSUE!

NSIDE: BLONDE BOMBSHELL BRAVES BOSTON! DAREDEVIL SPOTTINGS CONFIRMED IN LATVERIA! LIZARDS LOOSE IN MANHATTAN! MORE...

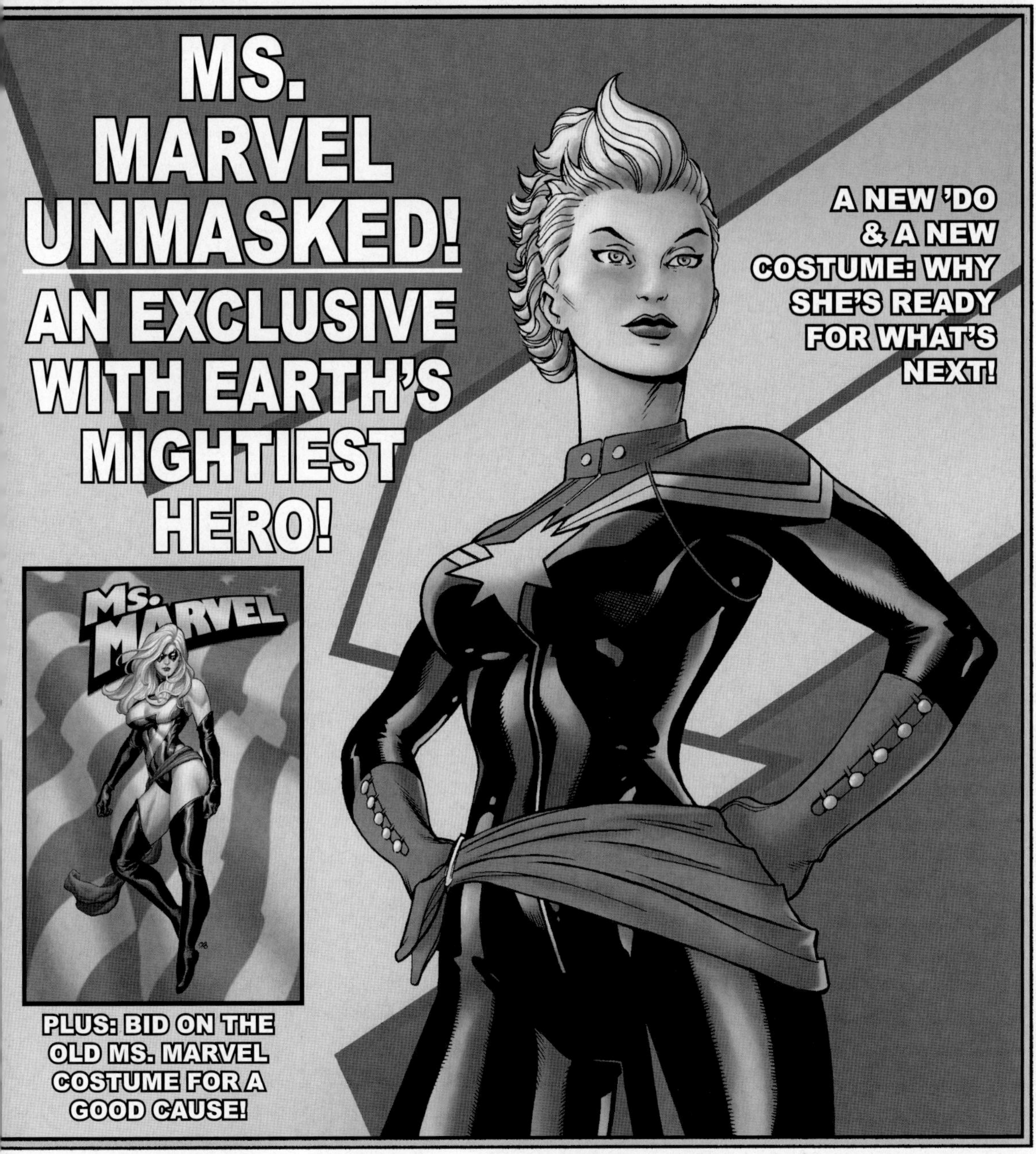
MS. MARVEL UNMASKED!
AN EXCLUSIVE WITH EARTH'S MIGHTIEST HERO!
A NEW 'DO & A NEW COSTUME: WHY SHE'S READY FOR WHAT'S NEXT!
MS. MARVEL
PLUS: BID ON THE OLD MS. MARVEL COSTUME FOR A GOOD CAUSE!

KELLY SUE DeCONNICK
WRITER

DEXTER SOY
ARTIST

ED McGUINNESS, DEXTER VINES & JAVIER RODRIGUEZ
COVER

VC'S JOE CARAMAGNA
LETTERER

ELLIE PYLE
ASSISTANT EDITOR

SANA AMANAT
ASSOCIATE EDITOR

STEPHEN WACKER
EDITOR

AXEL ALONSO
EDITOR IN CHIEF

JOE QUESADA
CHIEF CREATIVE OFFICER

DAN BUCKLEY
PUBLISHER

ALAN FINE
EXEC. PRODUCER

CAPTAIN MARVEL COSTUME DESIGNED BY JAMIE McKELVIE

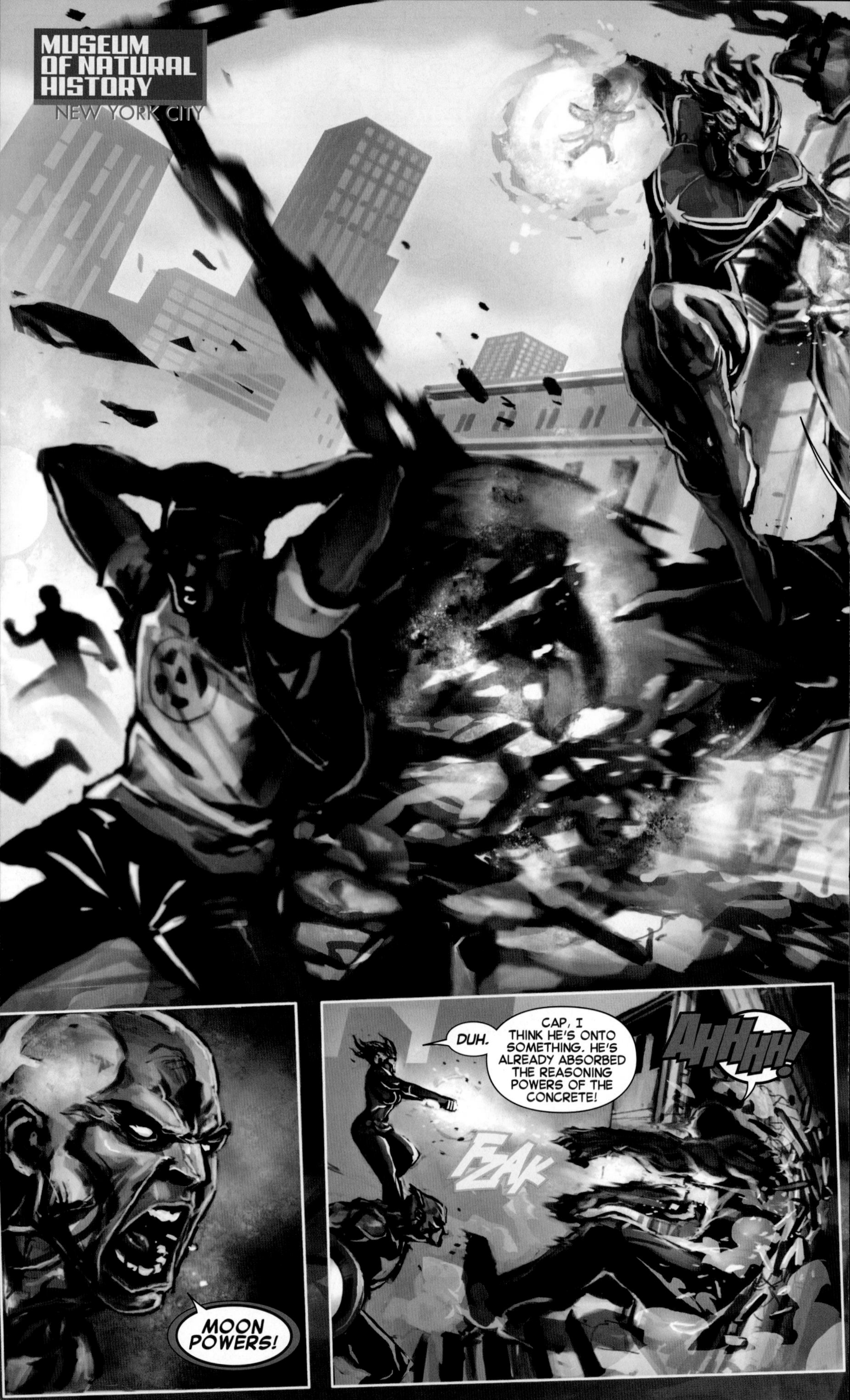
MUSEUM OF NATURAL HISTORY
NEW YORK CITY
MOON POWERS!
DUH.
CAP, I THINK HE'S ONTO SOMETHING. HE'S ALREADY ABSORBED THE REASONING POWERS OF THE CONCRETE!
AHHHH!
FZAK

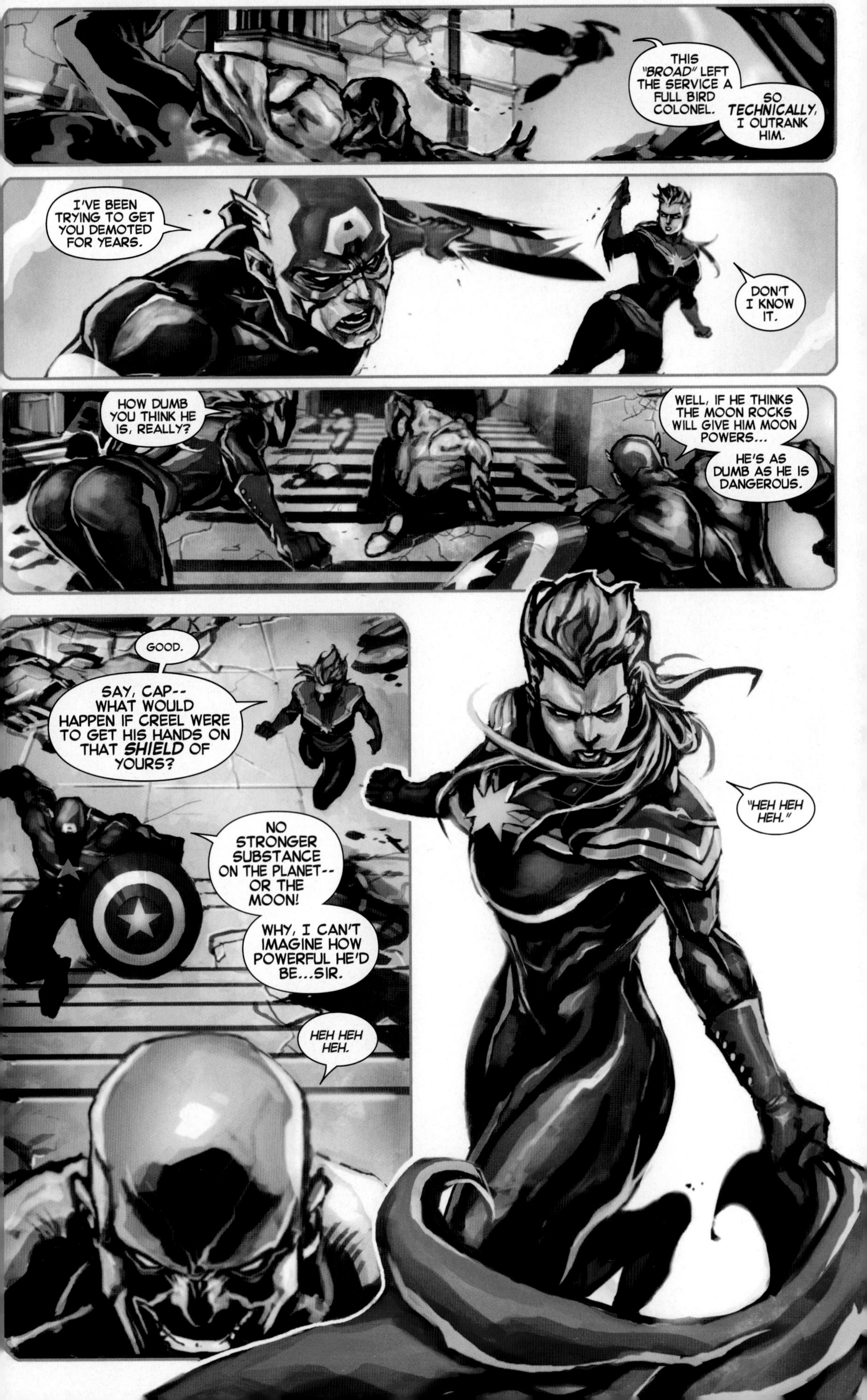
THIS "BROAD" LEFT THE SERVICE A FULL BIRD COLONEL.
SO TECHNICALLY, I OUTRANK HIM.
I'VE BEEN TRYING TO GET YOU DEMOTED FOR YEARS.
DON'T I KNOW IT.
HOW DUMB YOU THINK HE IS, REALLY?
WELL, IF HE THINKS THE MOON ROCKS WILL GIVE HIM MOON POWERS...
HE'S AS DUMB AS HE IS DANGEROUS.
GOOD.
SAY, CAP-- WHAT WOULD HAPPEN IF CREEL WERE TO GET HIS HANDS ON THAT SHIELD OF YOURS?
NO STRONGER SUBSTANCE ON THE PLANET-- OR THE MOON!
WHY, I CAN'T IMAGINE HOW POWERFUL HE'D BE...SIR.
"HEH HEH HEH."
HEH HEH HEH.

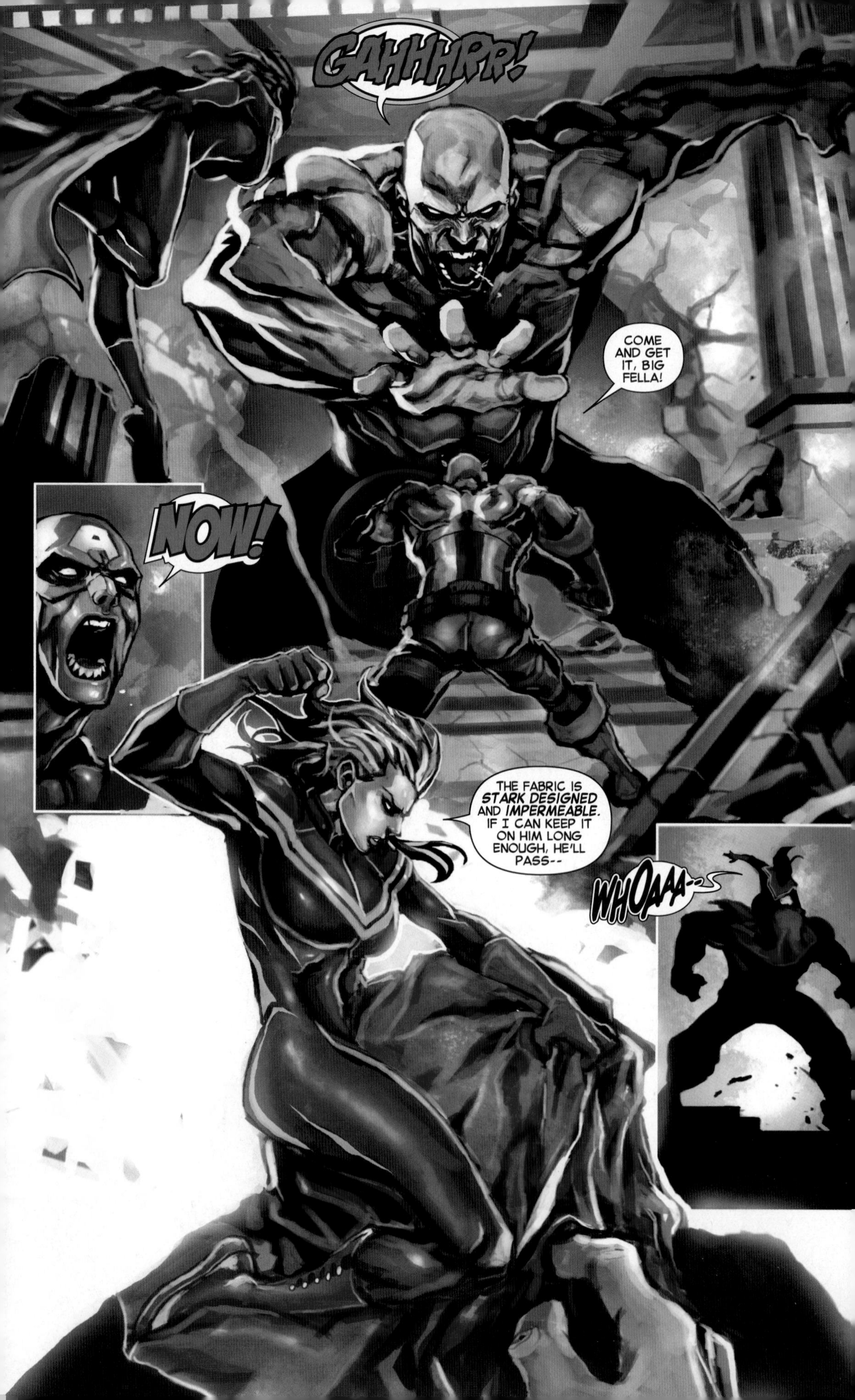
GAHHHRR!
COME AND GET IT, BIG FELLA!
NOW!
THE FABRIC IS STARK DESIGNED AND IMPERMEABLE. IF I CAN KEEP IT ON HIM LONG ENOUGH, HE'LL PASS--
WHOAAA--

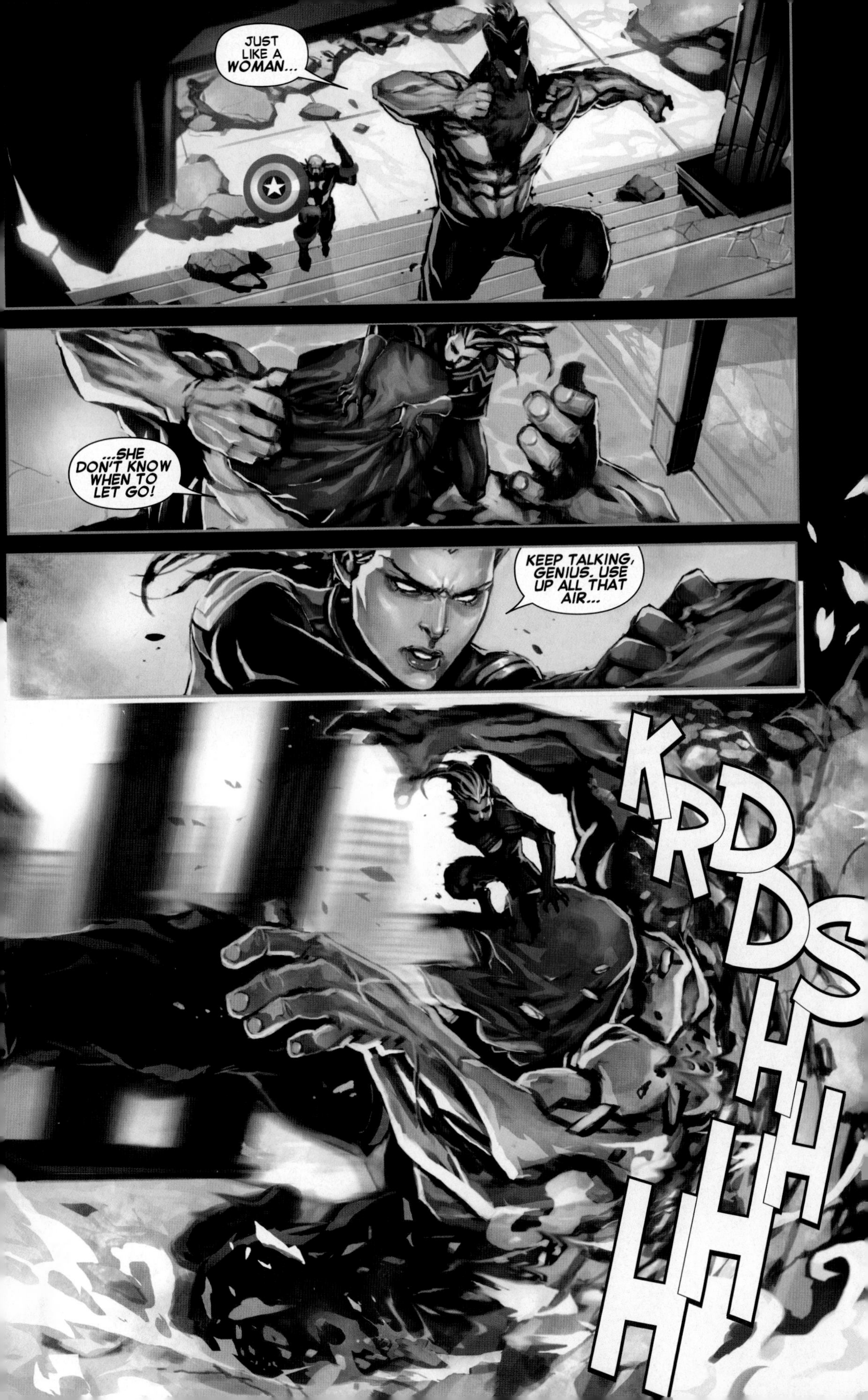
JUST LIKE A WOMAN...
...SHE DON'T KNOW WHEN TO LET GO!
KEEP TALKING, GENIUS. USE UP ALL THAT AIR...
KRDDSHHHHH

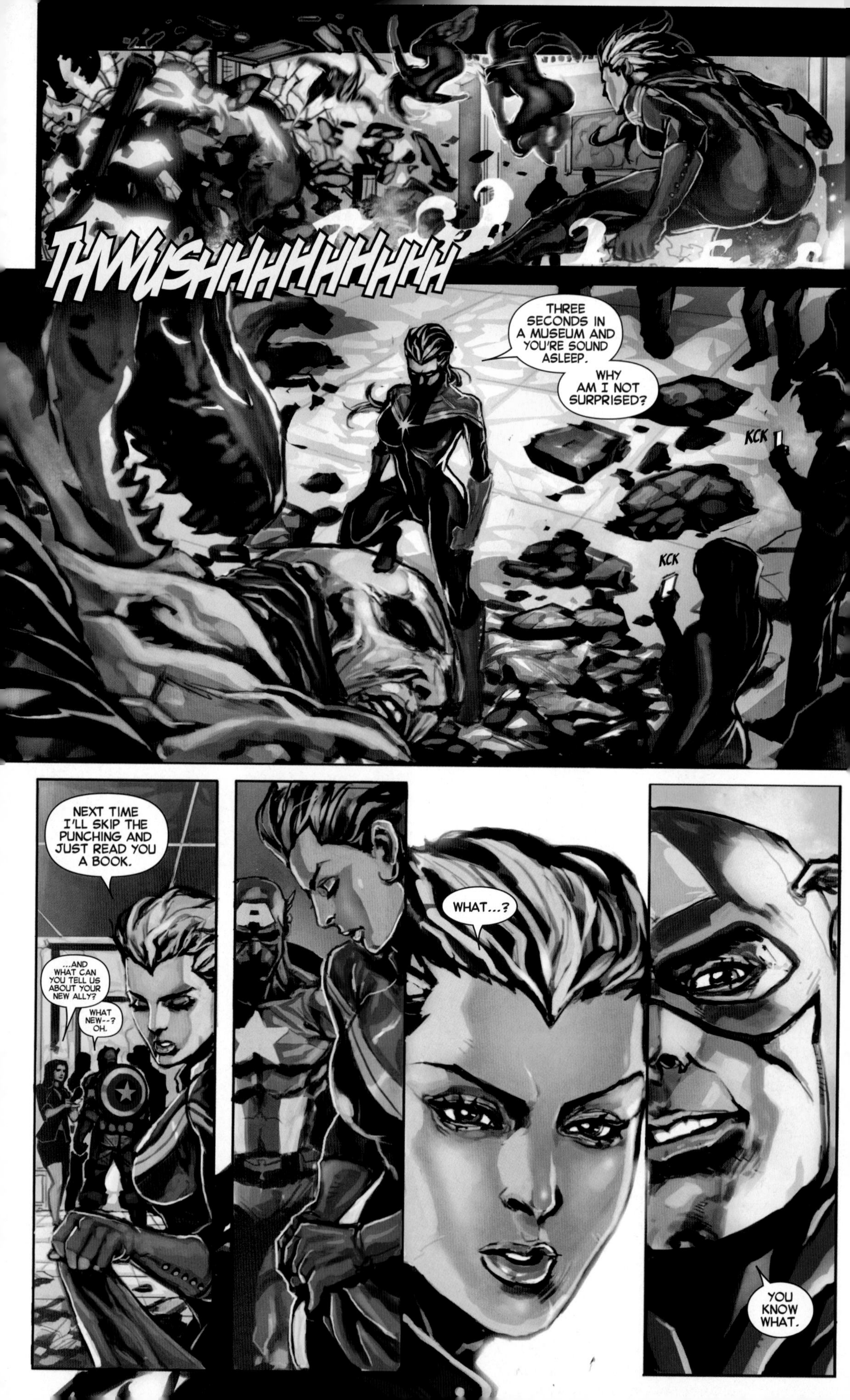
THWUSHHHHHHHH
THREE SECONDS IN A MUSEUM AND YOU'RE SOUND ASLEEP.
WHY AM I NOT SURPRISED?
KCK
KCK
NEXT TIME I'LL SKIP THE PUNCHING AND JUST READ YOU A BOOK.
...AND WHAT CAN YOU TELL US ABOUT YOUR NEW ALLY?
WHAT NEW--? OH.
WHAT...?
YOU KNOW WHAT.

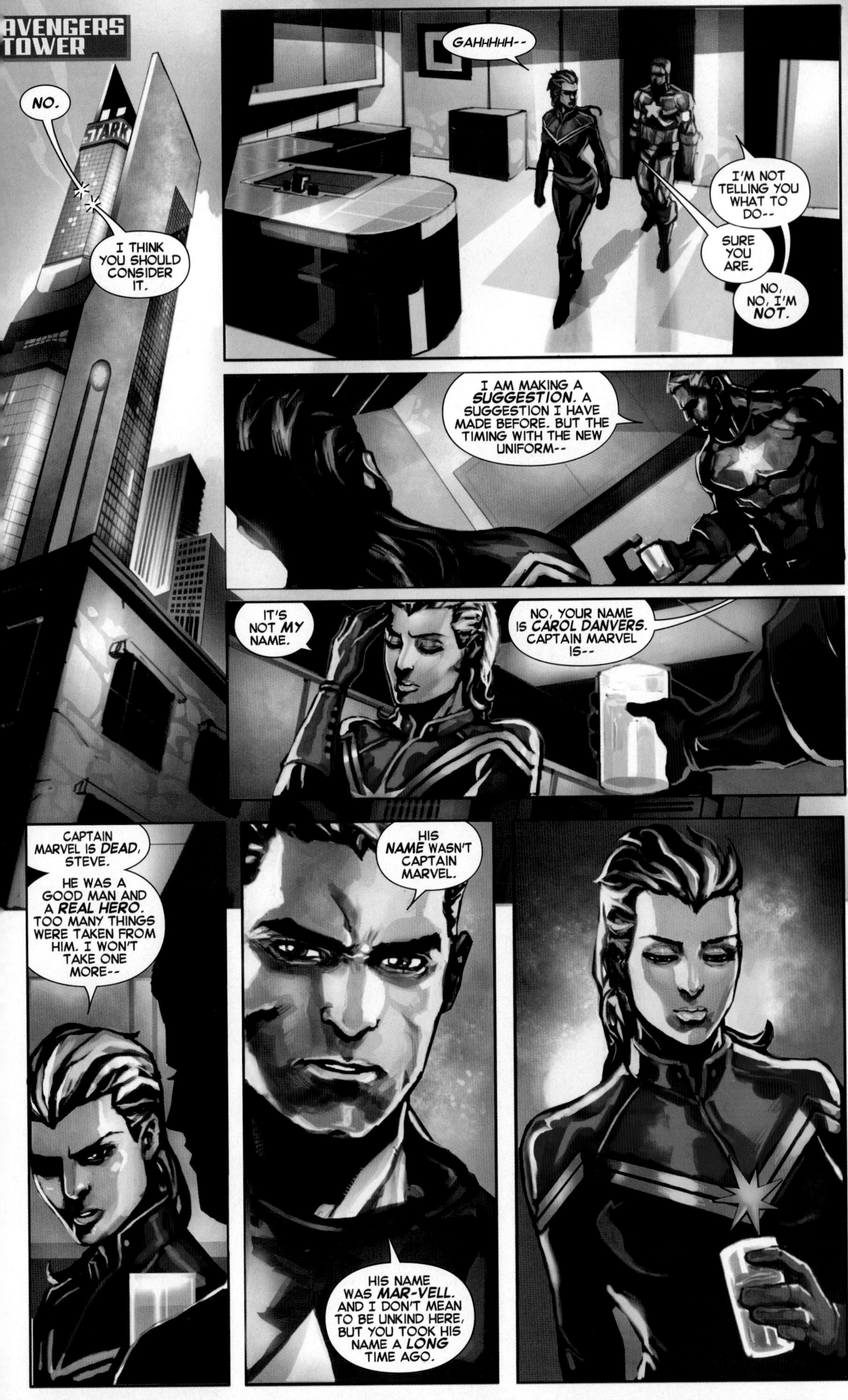
AVENGERS TOWER
STARK
NO.
I THINK YOU SHOULD CONSIDER IT.
GAHHHHH--
I'M NOT TELLING YOU WHAT TO DO--
SURE YOU ARE.
NO, NO, I'M NOT.
I AM MAKING A SUGGESTION. A SUGGESTION I HAVE MADE BEFORE. BUT THE TIMING WITH THE NEW UNIFORM--
IT'S NOT MY NAME.
NO, YOUR NAME IS CAROL DANVERS. CAPTAIN MARVEL IS--
CAPTAIN MARVEL IS DEAD, STEVE.
HE WAS A GOOD MAN AND A REAL HERO. TOO MANY THINGS WERE TAKEN FROM HIM. I WON'T TAKE ONE MORE--
HIS NAME WASN'T CAPTAIN MARVEL.
HIS NAME WAS MAR-VELL. AND I DON'T MEAN TO BE UNKIND HERE, BUT YOU TOOK HIS NAME A LONG TIME AGO.

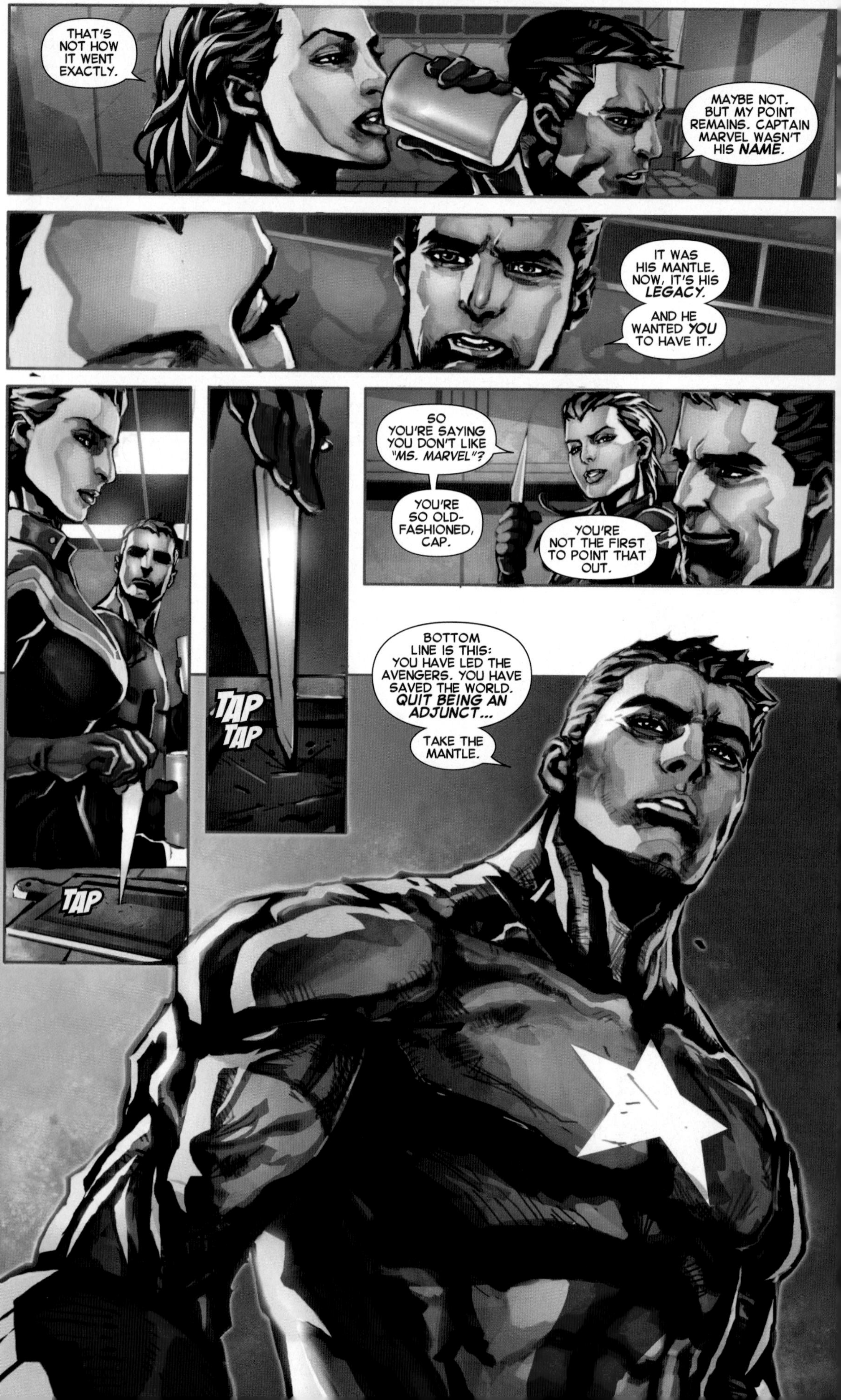
THAT'S NOT HOW IT WENT EXACTLY.
MAYBE NOT. BUT MY POINT REMAINS. CAPTAIN MARVEL WASN'T HIS NAME.
IT WAS HIS MANTLE. NOW, IT'S HIS LEGACY.
AND HE WANTED YOU TO HAVE IT.
TAP
TAP TAP
SO YOU'RE SAYING YOU DON'T LIKE "MS. MARVEL"?
YOU'RE SO OLD-FASHIONED, CAP.
YOU'RE NOT THE FIRST TO POINT THAT OUT.
BOTTOM LINE IS THIS: YOU HAVE LED THE AVENGERS. YOU HAVE SAVED THE WORLD. QUIT BEING AN ADJUNCT...
TAKE THE MANTLE.

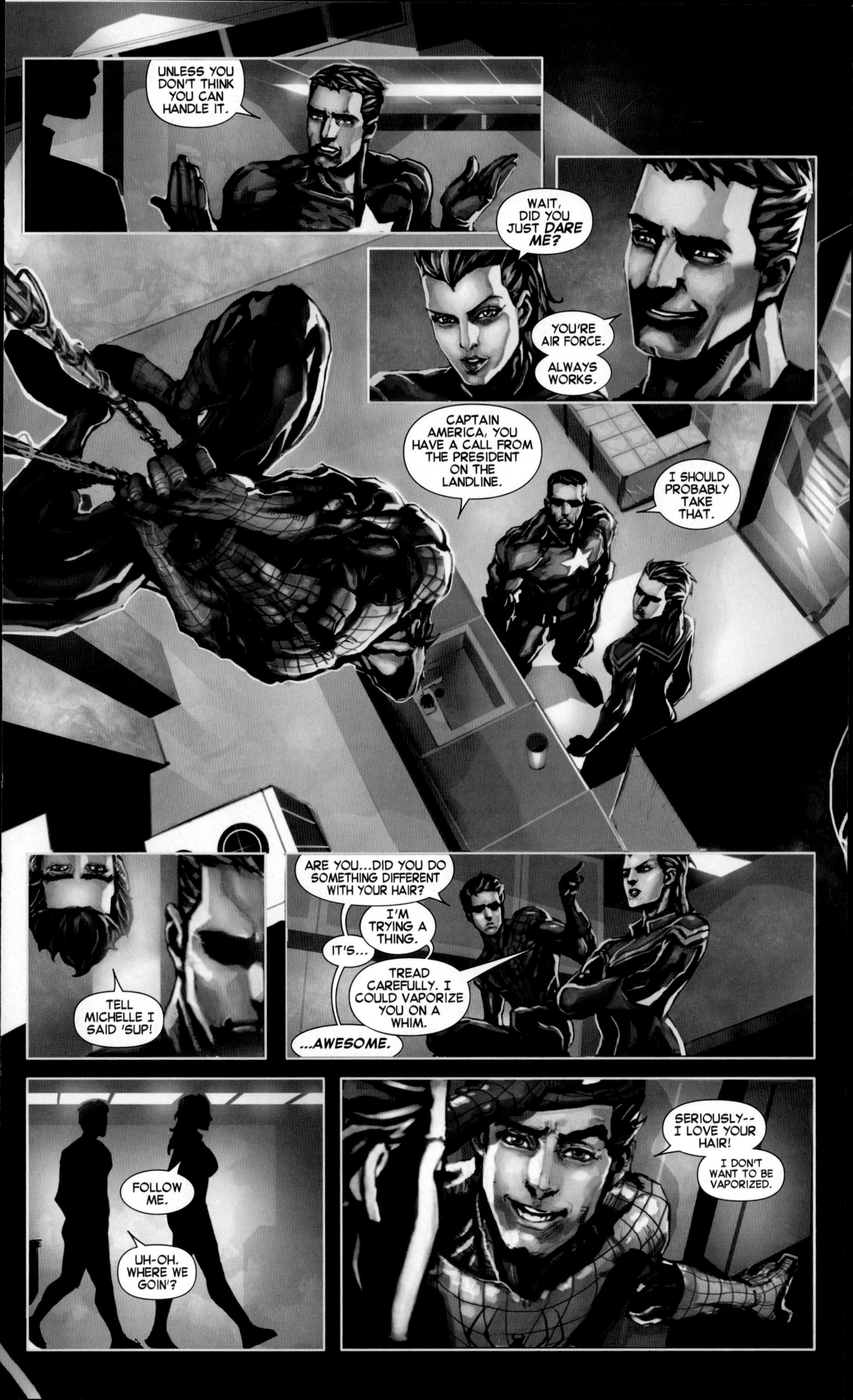
UNLESS YOU DON'T THINK YOU CAN HANDLE IT.
WAIT, DID YOU JUST DARE ME?
YOU'RE AIR FORCE.
ALWAYS WORKS.
CAPTAIN AMERICA, YOU HAVE A CALL FROM THE PRESIDENT ON THE LANDLINE.
I SHOULD PROBABLY TAKE THAT.
TELL MICHELLE I SAID 'SUP!
ARE YOU...DID YOU DO SOMETHING DIFFERENT WITH YOUR HAIR?
I'M TRYING A THING.
IT'S...
TREAD CAREFULLY. I COULD VAPORIZE YOU ON A WHIM.
...AWESOME.
FOLLOW ME.
UH-OH. WHERE WE GOIN'?
SERIOUSLY-- I LOVE YOUR HAIR!
I DON'T WANT TO BE VAPORIZED.

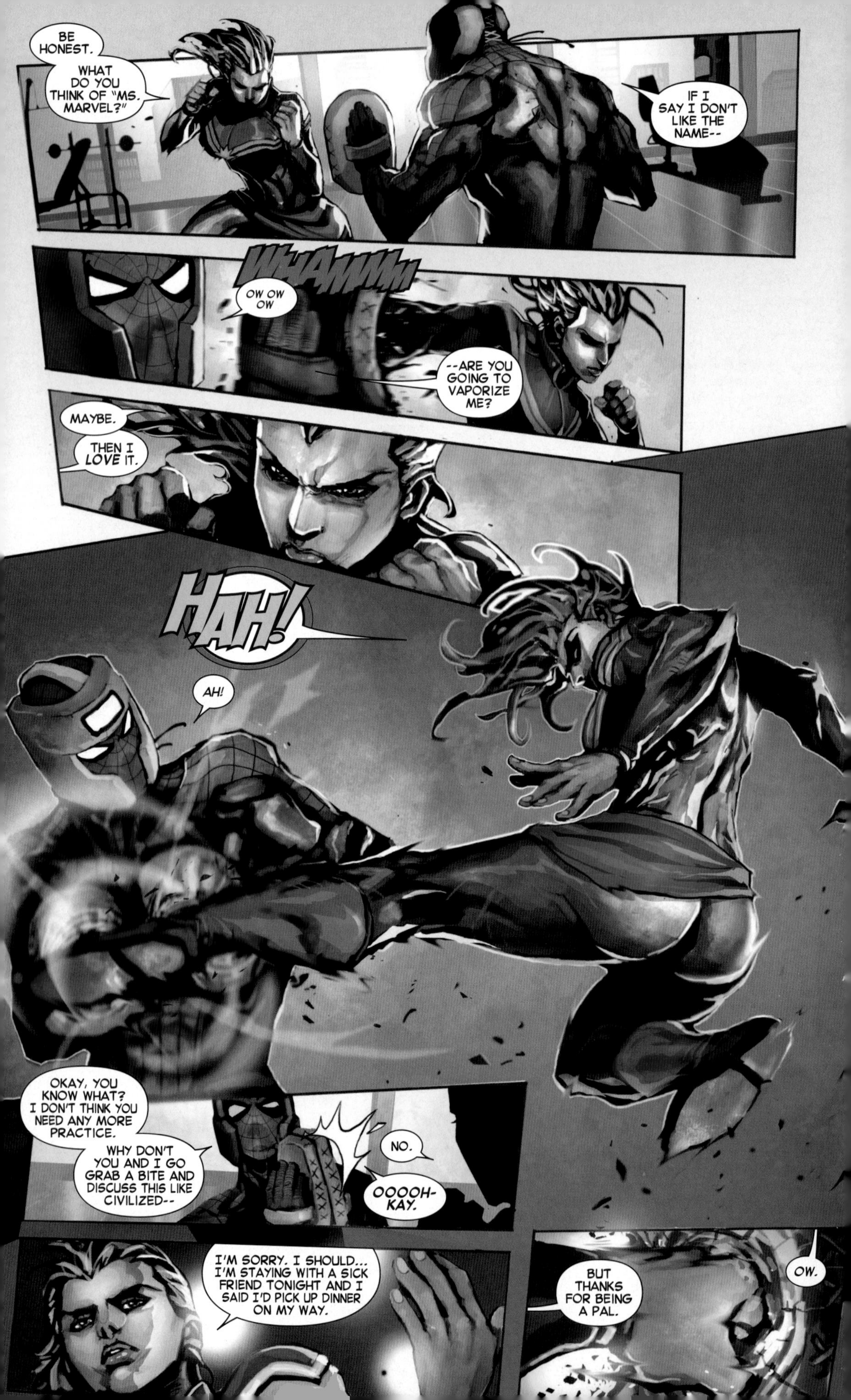
BE HONEST.
WHAT DO YOU THINK OF "MS. MARVEL?"
IF I SAY I DON'T LIKE THE NAME--
WHAMMMM
OW OW OW
--ARE YOU GOING TO VAPORIZE ME?
MAYBE.
THEN I LOVE IT.
HAH!
AH!
OKAY, YOU KNOW WHAT? I DON'T THINK YOU NEED ANY MORE PRACTICE.
WHY DON'T YOU AND I GO GRAB A BITE AND DISCUSS THIS LIKE CIVILIZED--
NO.
OOOOH-KAY.
I'M SORRY. I SHOULD... I'M STAYING WITH A SICK FRIEND TONIGHT AND I SAID I'D PICK UP DINNER ON MY WAY.
BUT THANKS FOR BEING A PAL.
OW.

I WAS A LUCKY KID BECAUSE I HAD TWO HEROES--MY DAD AND A PILOT NAMED HELEN COBB.

HELEN HELD FIFTEEN SPEED RECORDS WHEN SHE RETIRED.

FIFTEEN.

I'M NOT PRONE TO ENVY. BUT THOSE RECORDS...

I ENVY THOSE RECORDS.

I CAN FLY. FAST.

REAL FAST.

BUT THESE "ABILITIES" COME AT A COST. FOR ONE THING, I'LL NEVER BE ALLOWED TO HOLD A RECORD LIKE HELEN'S.

I CAN'T EVEN COMPETE. WOULDN'T BE A FAIR FIGHT.

I LOST MY SHOT WHEN I WAS CAUGHT IN THE BLAST OF THAT ALIEN PSYCHE-MAGNETRON DEVICE.

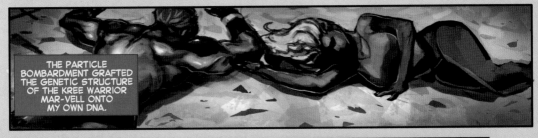

THE PARTICLE BOMBARDMENT GRAFTED THE GENETIC STRUCTURE OF THE KREE WARRIOR MAR-VELL ONTO MY OWN DNA.

IT'S A HELL OF A REWARD...BUT IT ERASED WHAT I LOVED MOST...

...THE RISK.

ONE MINUTE, FIFTY-EIGHT SECONDS FROM BROADWAY TO THE END OF OUR ATMOSPHERE, A NEW PERSONAL BEST.

LUCKY ME.

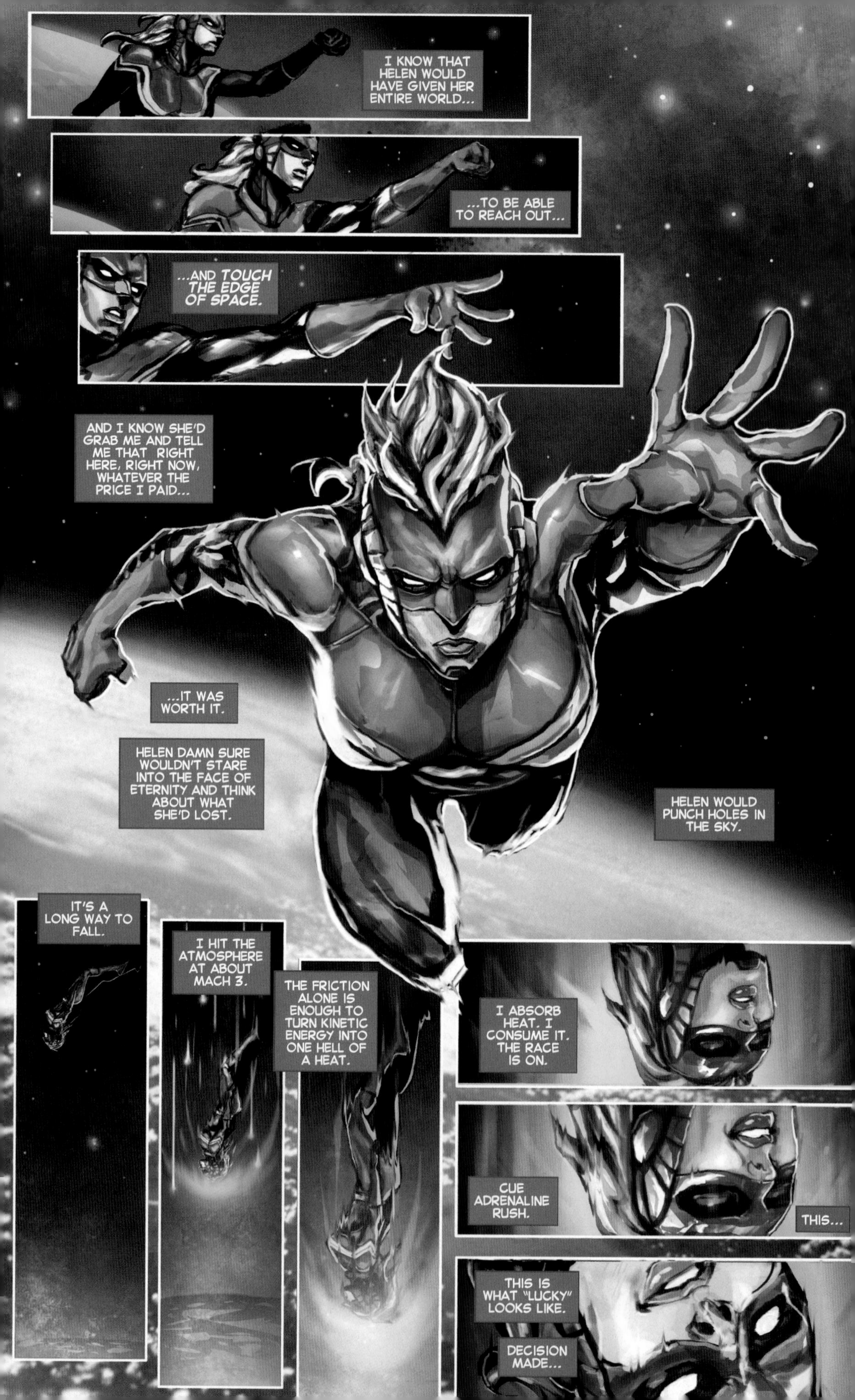
I KNOW THAT HELEN WOULD HAVE GIVEN HER ENTIRE WORLD...
...TO BE ABLE TO REACH OUT...
...AND TOUCH THE EDGE OF SPACE.
AND I KNOW SHE'D GRAB ME AND TELL ME THAT RIGHT HERE, RIGHT NOW, WHATEVER THE PRICE I PAID...
...IT WAS WORTH IT.
HELEN DAMN SURE WOULDN'T STARE INTO THE FACE OF ETERNITY AND THINK ABOUT WHAT SHE'D LOST.
HELEN WOULD PUNCH HOLES IN THE SKY.
IT'S A LONG WAY TO FALL.
I HIT THE ATMOSPHERE AT ABOUT MACH 3.
THE FRICTION ALONE IS ENOUGH TO TURN KINETIC ENERGY INTO ONE HELL OF A HEAT.
I ABSORB HEAT. I CONSUME IT. THE RACE IS ON.
CUE ADRENALINE RUSH.
THIS...
THIS IS WHAT "LUCKY" LOOKS LIKE.
DECISION MADE...

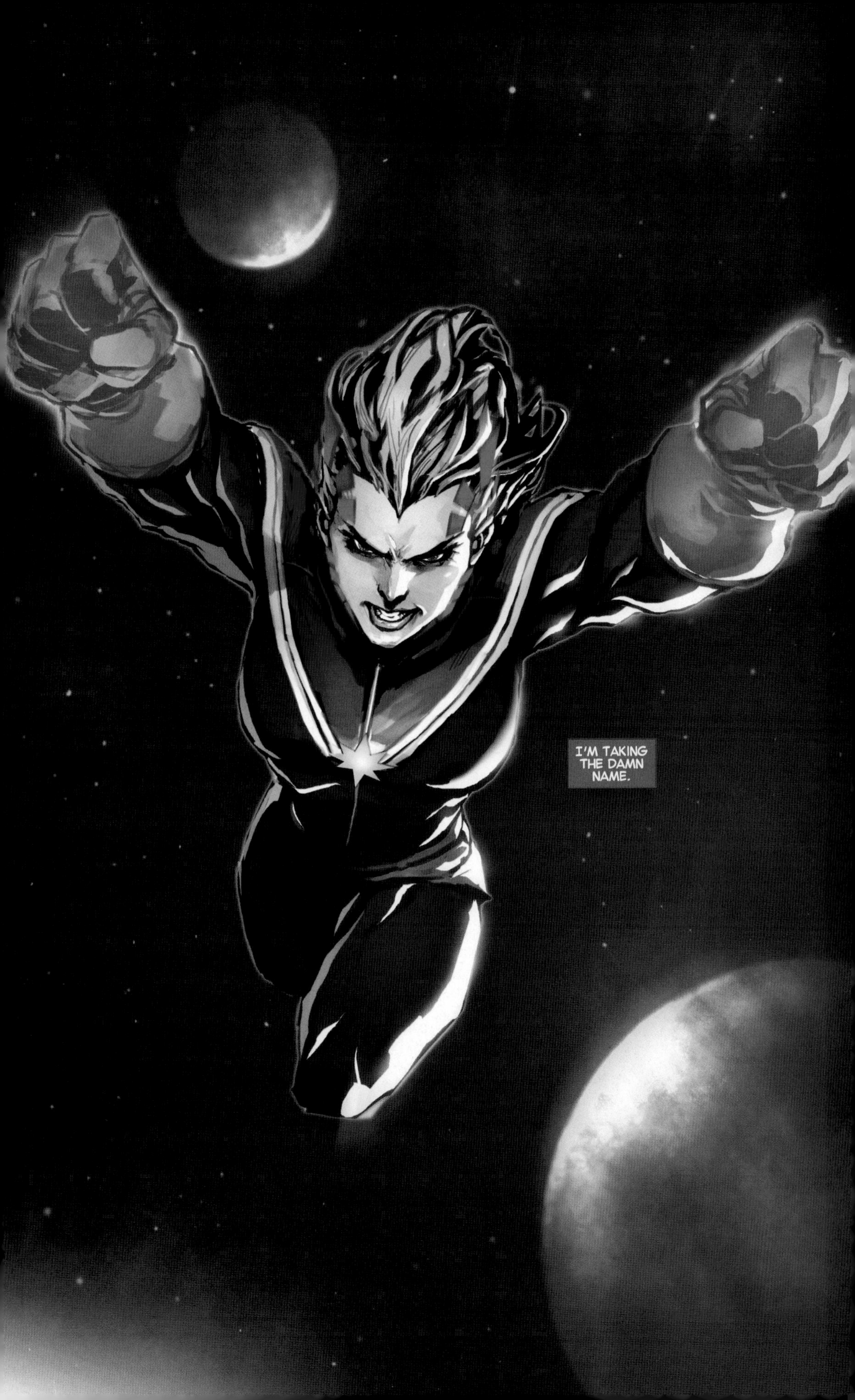
I'M TAKING THE DAMN NAME.

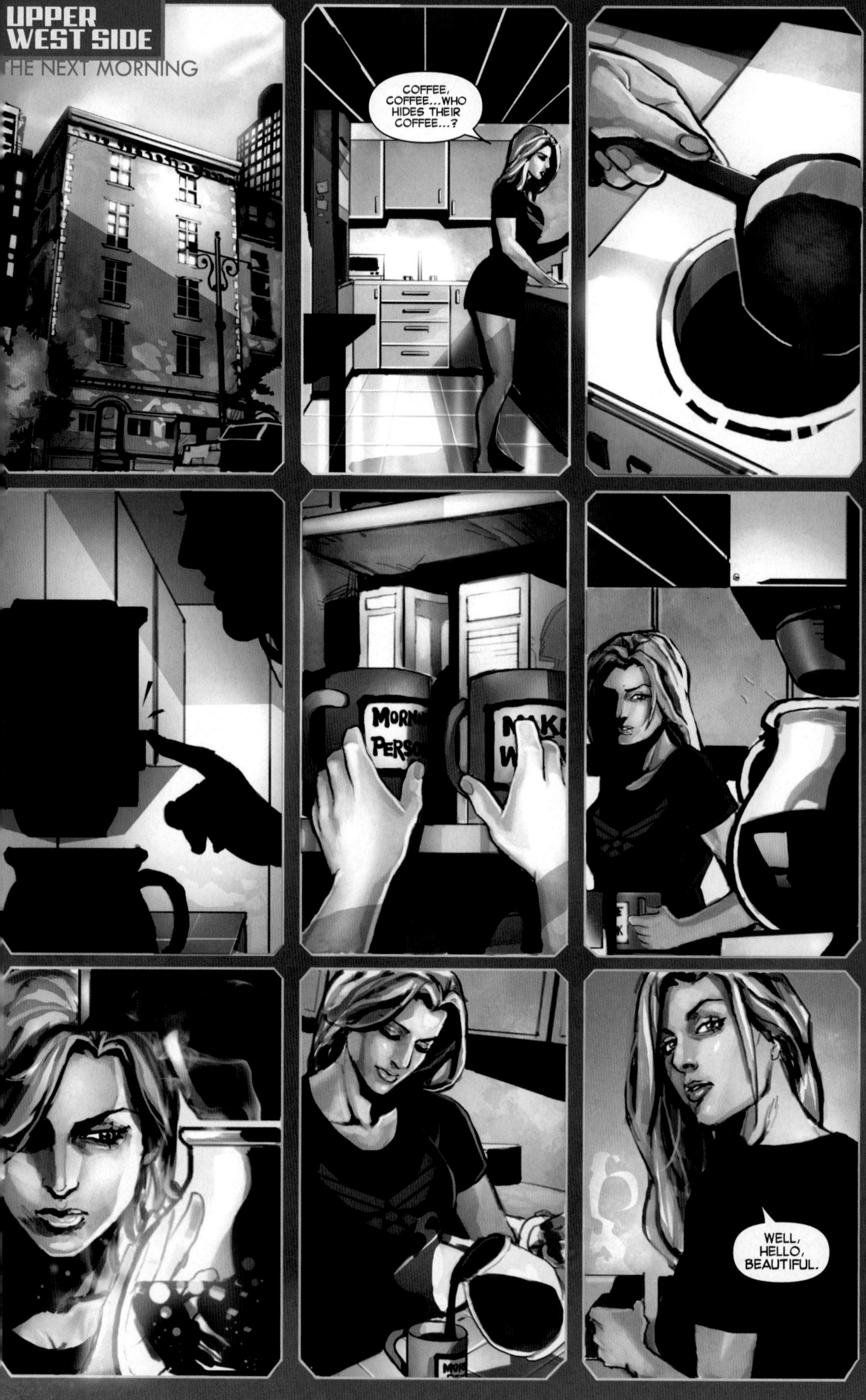
UPPER WEST SIDE
THE NEXT MORNING
COFFEE, COFFEE...WHO HIDES THEIR COFFEE...?
WELL, HELLO, BEAUTIFUL.

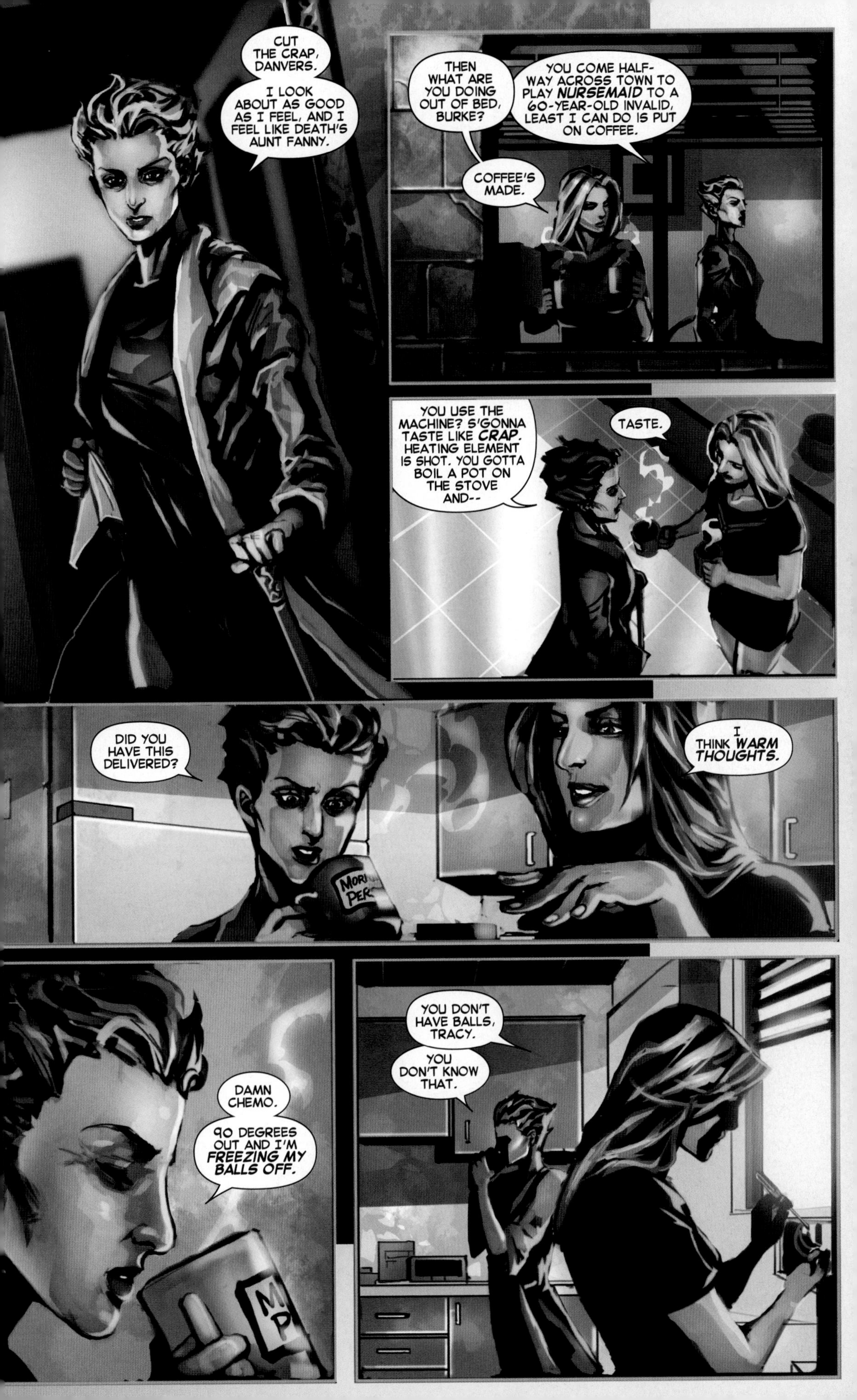
CUT THE CRAP, DANVERS.
I LOOK ABOUT AS GOOD AS I FEEL, AND I FEEL LIKE DEATH'S AUNT FANNY.
THEN WHAT ARE YOU DOING OUT OF BED, BURKE?
COFFEE'S MADE.
YOU COME HALF-WAY ACROSS TOWN TO PLAY NURSEMAID TO A 60-YEAR-OLD INVALID, LEAST I CAN DO IS PUT ON COFFEE.
YOU USE THE MACHINE? S'GONNA TASTE LIKE CRAP. HEATING ELEMENT IS SHOT. YOU GOTTA BOIL A POT ON THE STOVE AND--
TASTE.
DID YOU HAVE THIS DELIVERED?
I THINK WARM THOUGHTS.
DAMN CHEMO.
90 DEGREES OUT AND I'M FREEZING MY BALLS OFF.
YOU DON'T HAVE BALLS, TRACY.
YOU DON'T KNOW THAT.

MY PRESENCE IN THE APARTMENT SHOULD RAISE THE TEMPERATURE 2-3 DEGREES, FOR WHATEVER THAT'S WORTH.

AND I THINK I'VE GOT THE COFFEE MAKER PROBLEM FIXED. SZZT

REALLY? I DON'T REMEMBER FEELING A DIFFERENCE AT THE MAGAZINE WHEN YOU WORKED FOR ME.

YOU WORKED FOR *ME*.

KEEP TELLING YOURSELF THAT.

I MADE SOME CALLS AFTER YOU WENT TO BED. THE LANDLORD'S SENDING A GUY OVER TO LOOK AT THE THERMOSTAT LATER TODAY.

I HAVEN'T EVEN BEEN ABLE TO GET THAT TIGHT BASTARD TO ANSWER THE PHONE!

I RESORTED TO THREATS.

I *STARTED* WITH THREATS.

I MUST BE MORE INTIMIDATING THAN YOU.

LIKE HELL.

DO YOU NOT EAT? THERE'S NOTHING IN HERE. MAKE ME A LIST AND I'LL RUN OUT--

CAROL... HAVE YOU SEEN THE PAPER?

OH. YEAH. THAT--

NO, NOT *THAT*--

**DAILY BUGLE**
SINCE 1897
NEW YORK'S FINEST DAILY NEWSPAPER
FINAL $1.00 (in NYC) $1.50 (outside city)

New Captain Marvel! And he's a She!

Iconic Pilot Dies in Fire at Historic Aviation Club

at Historic Aviation Club

*HELEN COBB, PILOT*
POWDER PUFF DERBY WINNER, 1958.
FROM BUGLE FILE PHOTO.

*THAT.*

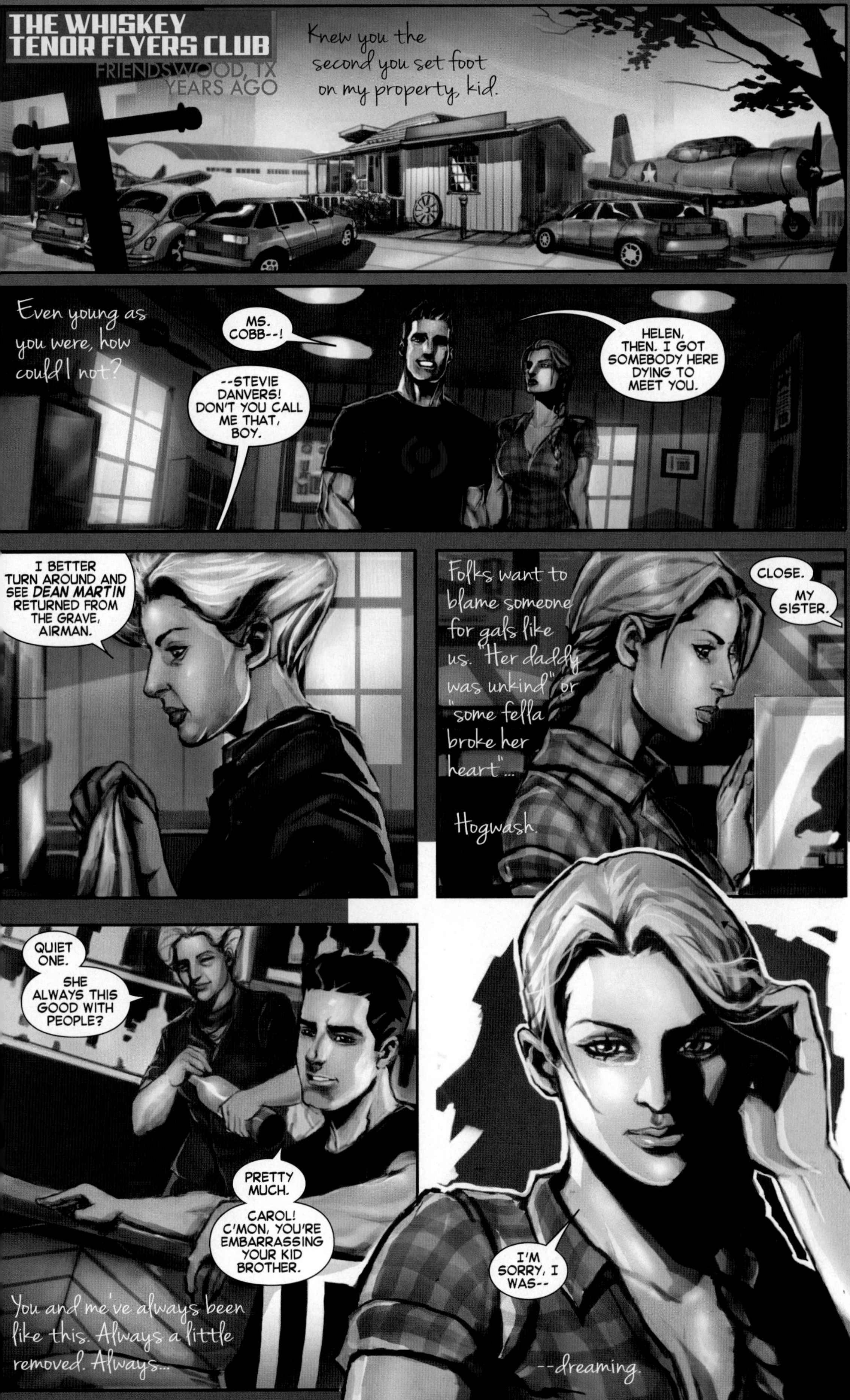

THE WHISKEY TENOR FLYERS CLUB
FRIENDSWOOD, TX YEARS AGO
Knew you the second you set foot on my property, kid.
Even young as you were, how could I not?
MS. COBB--!
--STEVIE DANVERS! DON'T YOU CALL ME THAT, BOY.
HELEN, THEN. I GOT SOMEBODY HERE DYING TO MEET YOU.
I BETTER TURN AROUND AND SEE DEAN MARTIN RETURNED FROM THE GRAVE, AIRMAN.
Folks want to blame someone for gals like us. "Her daddy was unkind" or "some fella broke her heart"...
Hogwash.
CLOSE.
MY SISTER.
QUIET ONE.
SHE ALWAYS THIS GOOD WITH PEOPLE?
PRETTY MUCH.
CAROL! C'MON, YOU'RE EMBARRASSING YOUR KID BROTHER.
You and me've always been like this. Always a little removed. Always...
I'M SORRY, I WAS--
--dreaming.

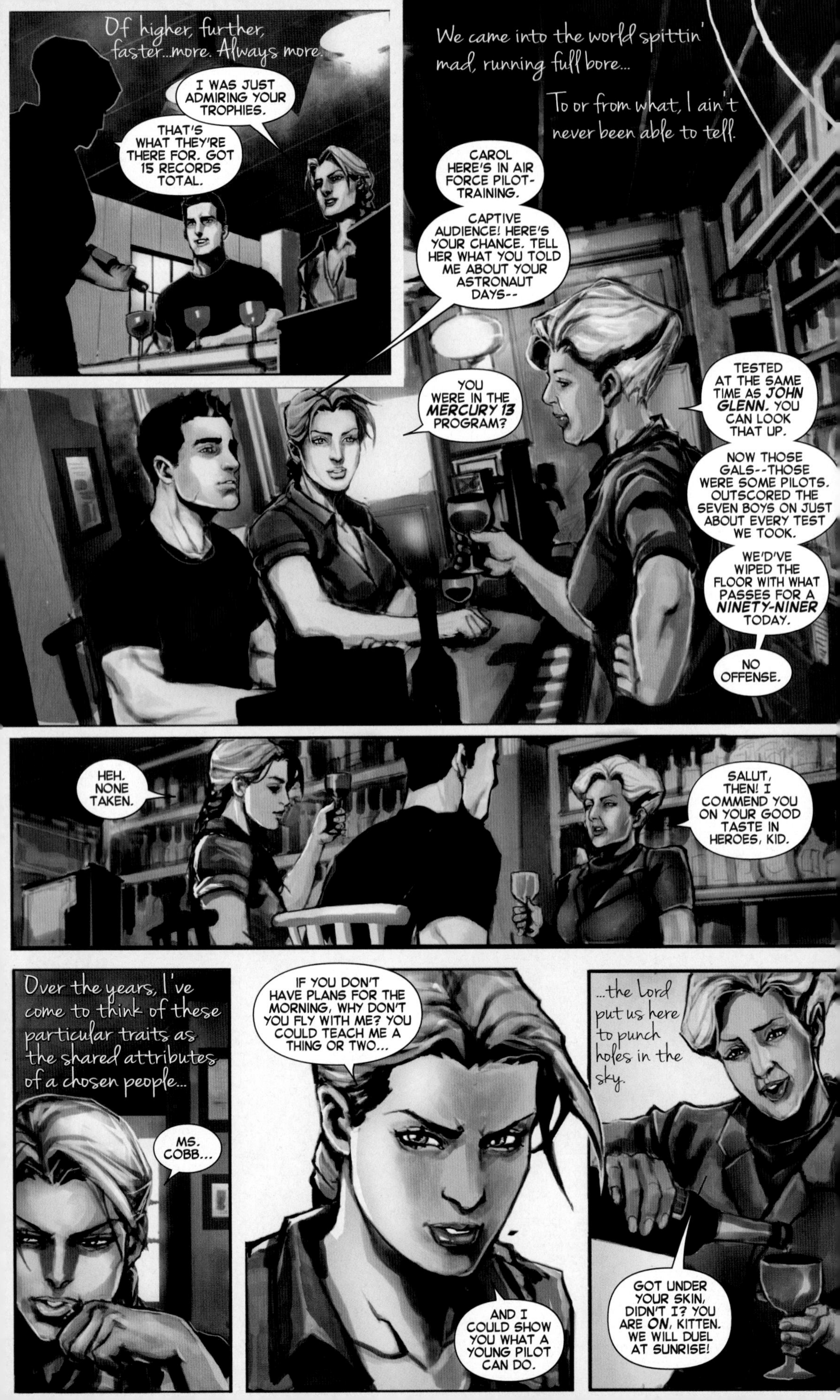

Of higher, further, faster...more. Always more.
I WAS JUST ADMIRING YOUR TROPHIES.
THAT'S WHAT THEY'RE THERE FOR. GOT 15 RECORDS TOTAL.
We came into the world spittin' mad, running full bore...
To or from what, I ain't never been able to tell.
CAROL HERE'S IN AIR FORCE PILOT-TRAINING.
CAPTIVE AUDIENCE! HERE'S YOUR CHANCE. TELL HER WHAT YOU TOLD ME ABOUT YOUR ASTRONAUT DAYS--
YOU WERE IN THE MERCURY 13 PROGRAM?
TESTED AT THE SAME TIME AS JOHN GLENN. YOU CAN LOOK THAT UP.
NOW THOSE GALS--THOSE WERE SOME PILOTS. OUTSCORED THE SEVEN BOYS ON JUST ABOUT EVERY TEST WE TOOK.
WE'D'VE WIPED THE FLOOR WITH WHAT PASSES FOR A NINETY-NINER TODAY.
NO OFFENSE.
HEH. NONE TAKEN.
SALUT, THEN! I COMMEND YOU ON YOUR GOOD TASTE IN HEROES, KID.
Over the years, I've come to think of these particular traits as the shared attributes of a chosen people...
MS. COBB...
IF YOU DON'T HAVE PLANS FOR THE MORNING, WHY DON'T YOU FLY WITH ME? YOU COULD TEACH ME A THING OR TWO...
AND I COULD SHOW YOU WHAT A YOUNG PILOT CAN DO.
...the Lord put us here to punch holes in the sky.
GOT UNDER YOUR SKIN, DIDN'T I? YOU ARE ON, KITTEN. WE WILL DUEL AT SUNRISE!

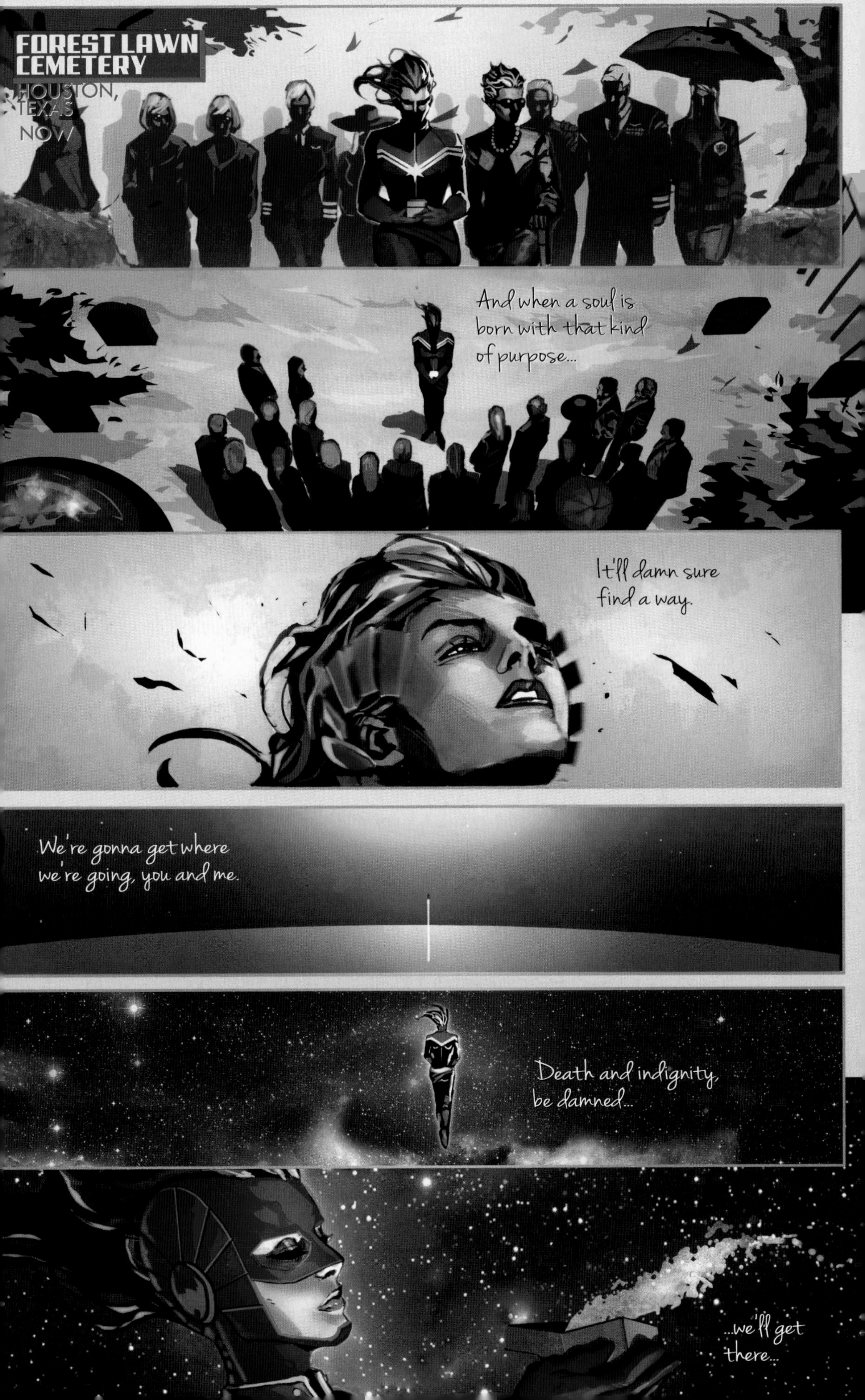
FOREST LAWN CEMETERY
HOUSTON, TEXAS
NOW
And when a soul is born with that kind of purpose...
It'll damn sure find a way.
We're gonna get where we're going, you and me.
Death and indignity, be damned...
...we'll get there...

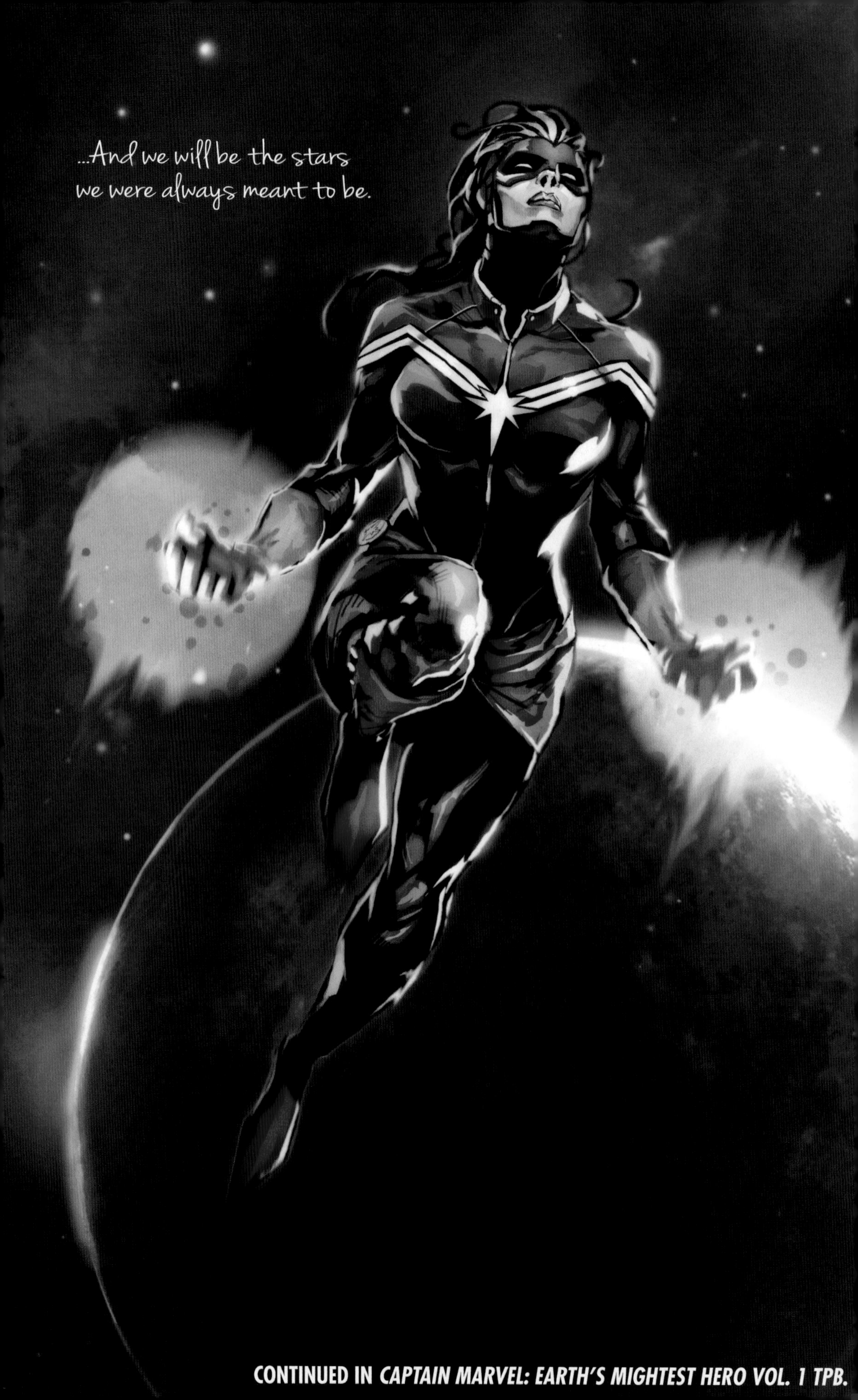
...And we will be the stars we were always meant to be.

CONTINUED IN *CAPTAIN MARVEL: EARTH'S MIGHTEST HERO VOL. 1 TPB.*

THE KREE SOLDIER MAR-VELL DIED A TRAGIC DEATH, ONE THAT LEFT A HOLE IN THE MARVEL UNIVERSE. NOW CAROL IS UNEXPECTEDLY REUNITED WITH HER DECEASED FRIEND IN THIS CHAPTER OF *GENERATIONS*.

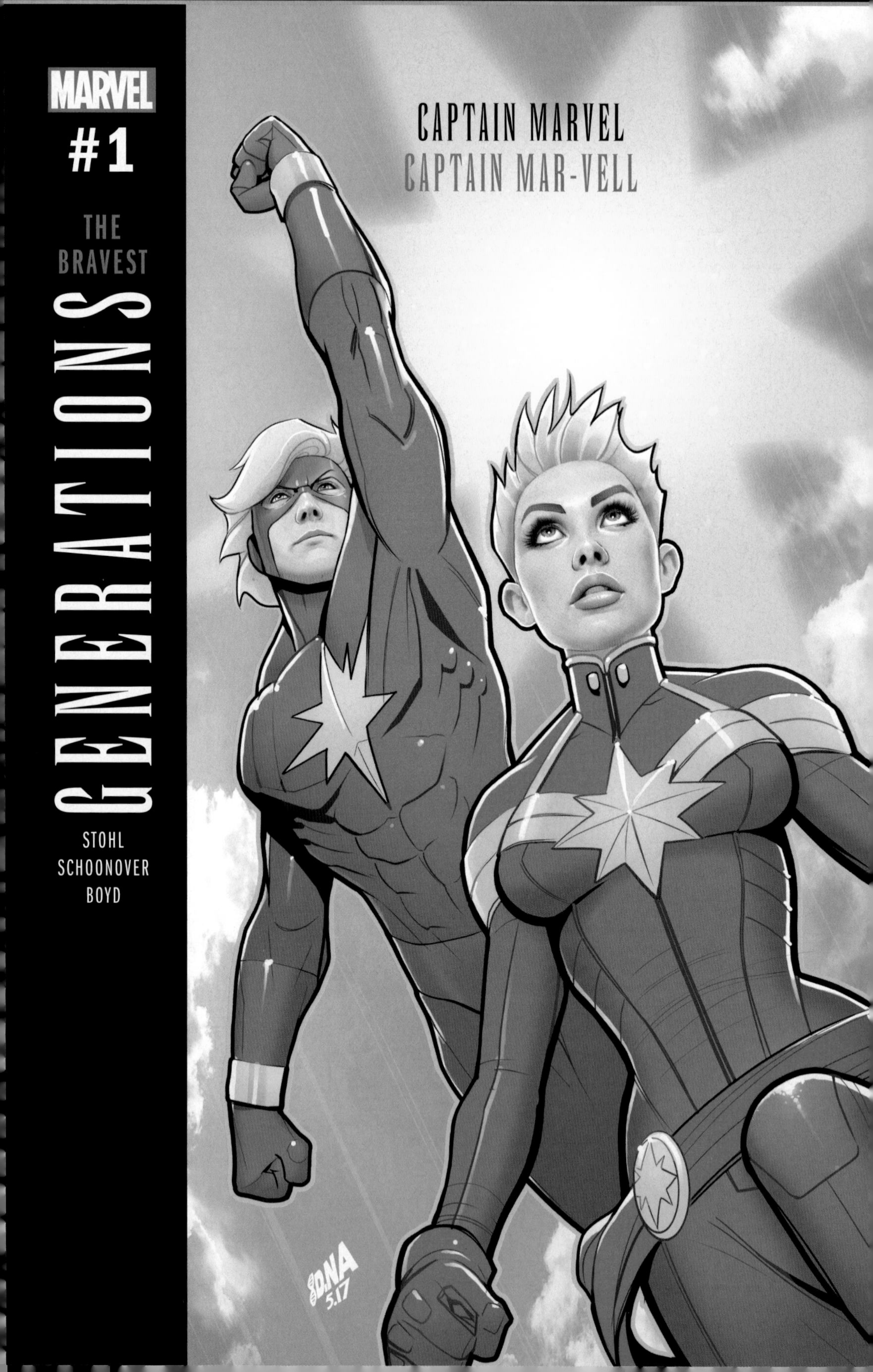
MARVEL
#1
THE BRAVEST
GENERATIONS
STOHL
SCHOONOVER
BOYD
CAPTAIN MARVEL
CAPTAIN MAR-VELL

## THE VANISHING POINT

AN INSTANT APART!
A MOMENT BEYOND!
LOOSED FROM THE SHACKLES OF PAST, PRESENT, FUTURE—
A PLACE WHERE TIME HAS NO MEANING!
BUT WHERE TRUE INSIGHT CAN BE GAINED!
MAKE YOUR CHOICE! SELECT YOUR DESTINATION!
THIS JOURNEY IS A GIFT...

A CAPTAIN OF THE KREE SPACE FLEET, MAR-VELL WAS CHOSEN TO INFILTRATE AND AID IN THE DESTRUCTION OF EARTH BEFORE HUMANITY COULD BECOME MORE POWERFUL THAN THE KREE. BUT WHILE HE LIVED AMONG THE EARTHLINGS, MAR-VELL GREW COMPASSION AND SYMPATHY FOR HUMANITY. HE DISOBEYED HIS ORDERS AND LED THE CHARGE TO DEFEND THE GREATER GOOD AS...

## CAPTAIN MAR-VELL

FORMER AIR FORCE PILOT CAROL DANVERS HAD HER GENETIC STRUCTURE ALTERED BY THE RADIATION OF AN ALIEN TECHNOLOGY; SHE BECAME PART HUMAN, PART KREE. WITH THE LOSS OF HER MENTOR, MAR-VELL, CAROL UNDERSTOOD THAT WITH THE GREAT POWERS BESTOWED UPON HER, SHE WOULD CONTINUE HIS LEGACY AND BECAME EARTH'S MIGHTIEST HERO...

## CAPTAIN MARVEL

## GENERATIONS
### THE BRAVEST

MARGARET STOHL
WRITER

BRENT SCHOONOVER
ARTIST

JORDAN BOYD
COLOR ARTIST

VC'S JOE CARAMAGNA
LETTERER

DAVID NAKAYAMA
MAIN COVER ARTIST

BRENT SCHOONOVER &
RACHELLE ROSENBERG;
TERRY DODSON &
RACHEL DODSON
VARIANT COVER ARTISTS

CHARLES BEACHAM
EDITOR

SANA AMANAT
SUPERVISING EDITOR

AXEL ALONSO
EDITOR IN CHIEF

JOE QUESADA
CHIEF CREATIVE OFFICER

DAN BUCKLEY
PRESIDENT

ALAN FINE
EXECUTIVE PRODUCER

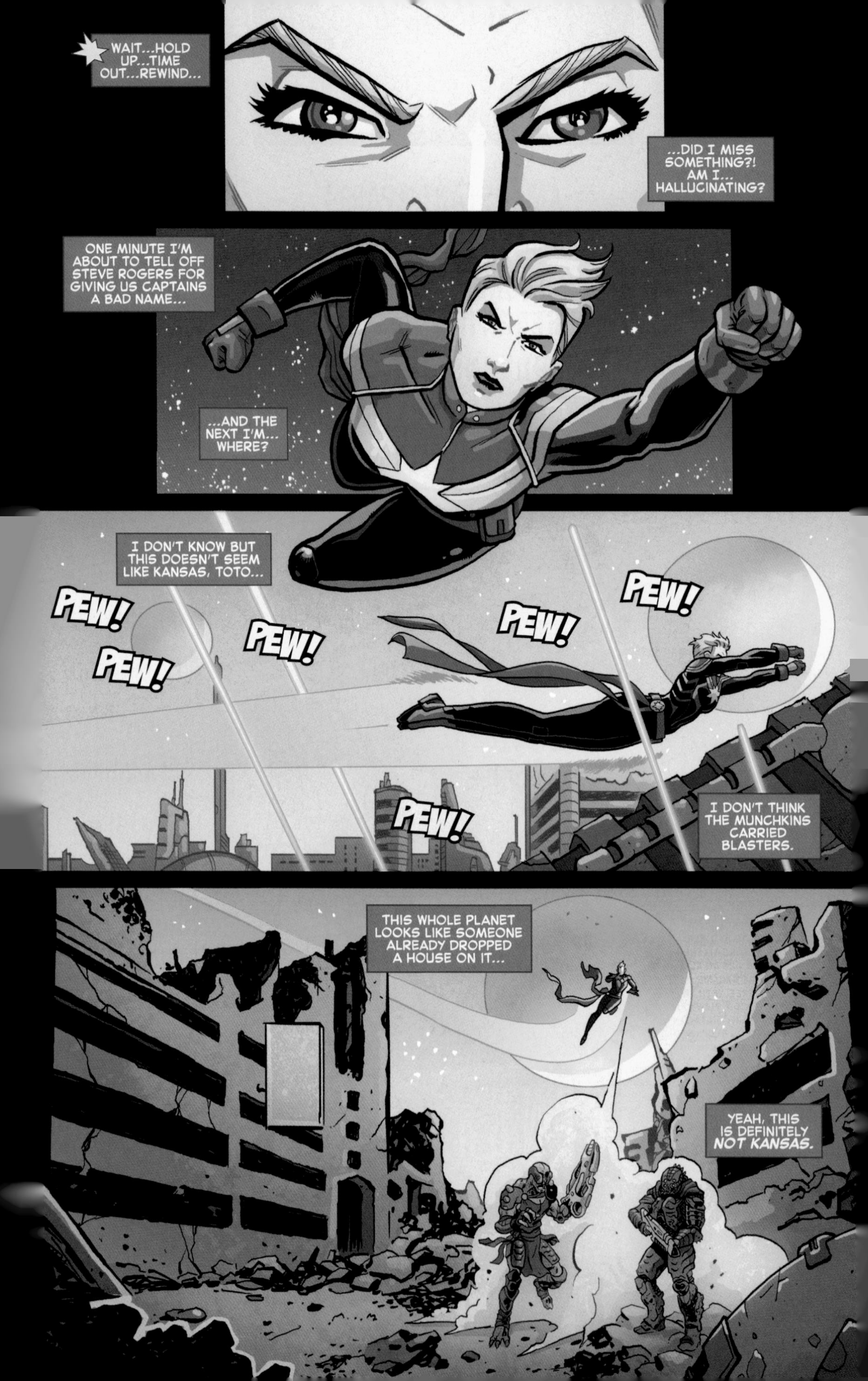
WAIT...HOLD UP...TIME OUT...REWIND...
...DID I MISS SOMETHING?! AM I... HALLUCINATING?
ONE MINUTE I'M ABOUT TO TELL OFF STEVE ROGERS FOR GIVING US CAPTAINS A BAD NAME...
...AND THE NEXT I'M... WHERE?
I DON'T KNOW BUT THIS DOESN'T SEEM LIKE KANSAS, TOTO...
PEW!
PEW!
PEW!
PEW!
PEW!
PEW!
I DON'T THINK THE MUNCHKINS CARRIED BLASTERS.
THIS WHOLE PLANET LOOKS LIKE SOMEONE ALREADY DROPPED A HOUSE ON IT...
YEAH, THIS IS DEFINITELY *NOT KANSAS.*

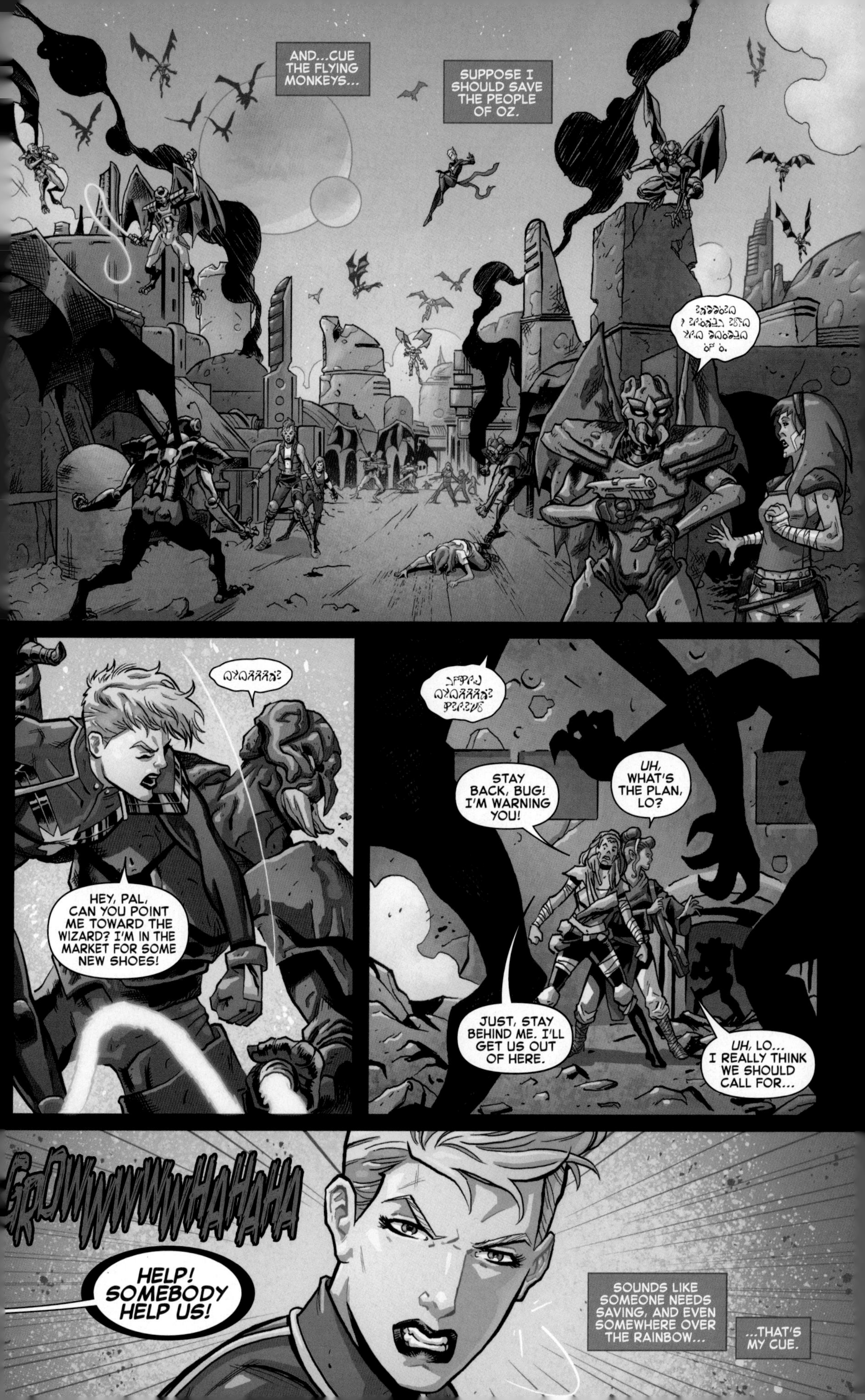
AND...CUE THE FLYING MONKEYS...
SUPPOSE I SHOULD SAVE THE PEOPLE OF OZ.
HEY, PAL, CAN YOU POINT ME TOWARD THE WIZARD? I'M IN THE MARKET FOR SOME NEW SHOES!
STAY BACK, BUG! I'M WARNING YOU!
UH, WHAT'S THE PLAN, LO?
JUST, STAY BEHIND ME. I'LL GET US OUT OF HERE.
UH, LO... I REALLY THINK WE SHOULD CALL FOR...
GROWWWWWHAHAHA
HELP! SOMEBODY HELP US!
SOUNDS LIKE SOMEONE NEEDS SAVING, AND EVEN SOMEWHERE OVER THE RAINBOW...
...THAT'S MY CUE.

RUN, DANAE, RUN!

NO! STAY AWAY FROM HER!

ᓀᑐᐅ ᑎᑯᑕᒍᐅ?

KRRRK!

ᑯᑎᑐᒍ ᑐᒍᑐᑯᐅ ᑯᑎᒍᑐᐅ.

YOU HEARD THE LADY... BEAT IT, BUG BRAINS!

YEAH! BEAT IT!

KA-THUNK!

WHOA. THE WHOLE DAMSEL DUO ACT? I GUESS THAT WAS A FAKE-OUT...

YOU SCARED ME THERE FOR A MINUTE, LO.

ONLY A MINUTE, DANAE? I'M LOSING MY TOUCH.

I WOULDN'T SAY THAT.

I'M CAROL. CAR-ELL.

NO, UH, CAROL. LIKE...THE NAME?

I'M LOBA. MANY THANKS, CAR-ELL.

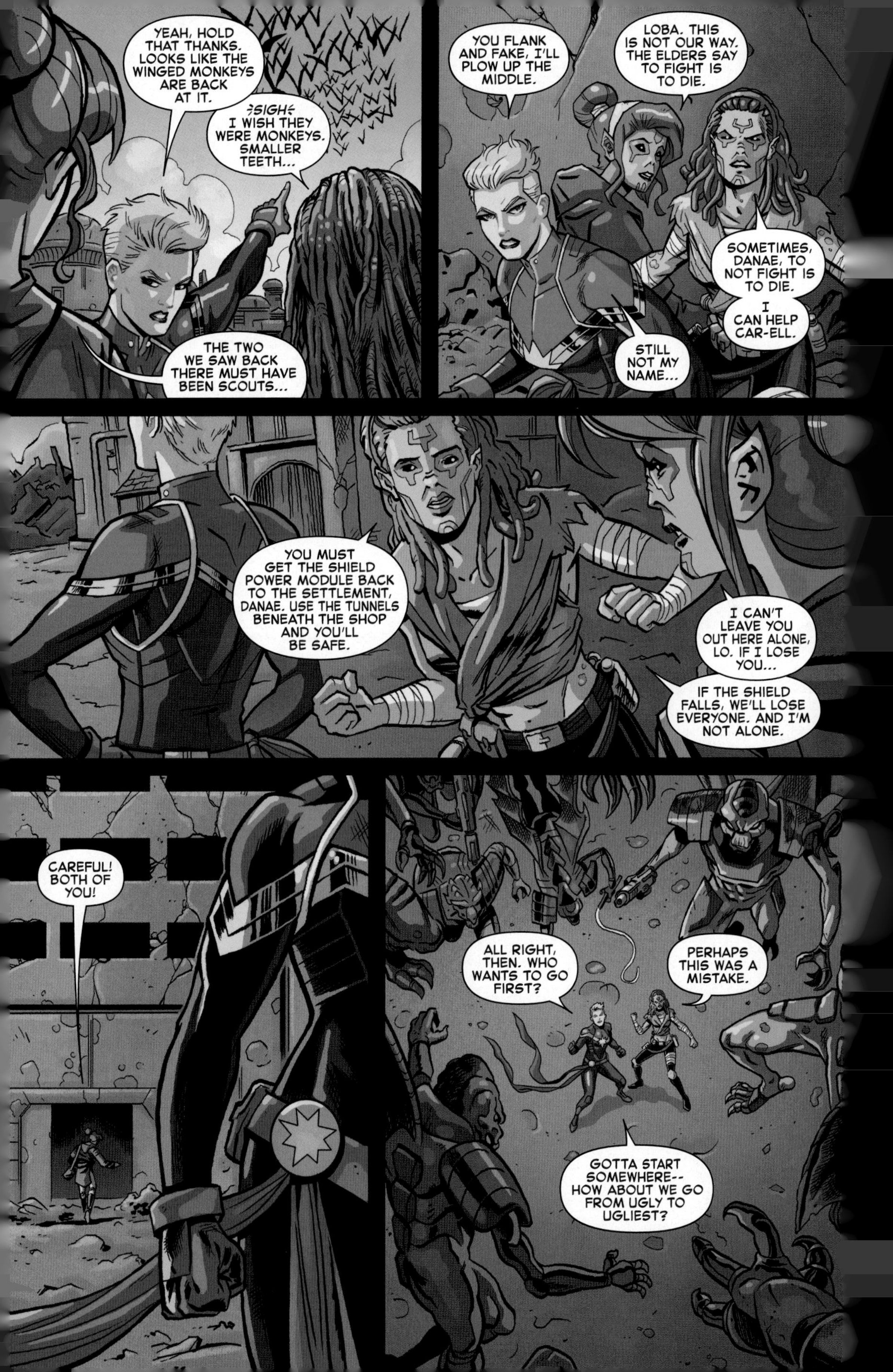
YEAH, HOLD THAT THANKS. LOOKS LIKE THE WINGED MONKEYS ARE BACK AT IT.
⸗SIGH⸗ I WISH THEY WERE MONKEYS. SMALLER TEETH...
THE TWO WE SAW BACK THERE MUST HAVE BEEN SCOUTS...
YOU FLANK AND FAKE, I'LL PLOW UP THE MIDDLE.
LOBA. THIS IS NOT OUR WAY. THE ELDERS SAY TO FIGHT IS TO DIE.
SOMETIMES, DANAE, TO NOT FIGHT IS TO DIE.
I CAN HELP CAR-ELL.
STILL NOT MY NAME...
YOU MUST GET THE SHIELD POWER MODULE BACK TO THE SETTLEMENT, DANAE. USE THE TUNNELS BENEATH THE SHOP AND YOU'LL BE SAFE.
I CAN'T LEAVE YOU OUT HERE ALONE, LO. IF I LOSE YOU...
IF THE SHIELD FALLS, WE'LL LOSE EVERYONE. AND I'M NOT ALONE.
CAREFUL! BOTH OF YOU!
ALL RIGHT, THEN. WHO WANTS TO GO FIRST?
PERHAPS THIS WAS A MISTAKE.
GOTTA START SOMEWHERE-- HOW ABOUT WE GO FROM UGLY TO UGLIEST?

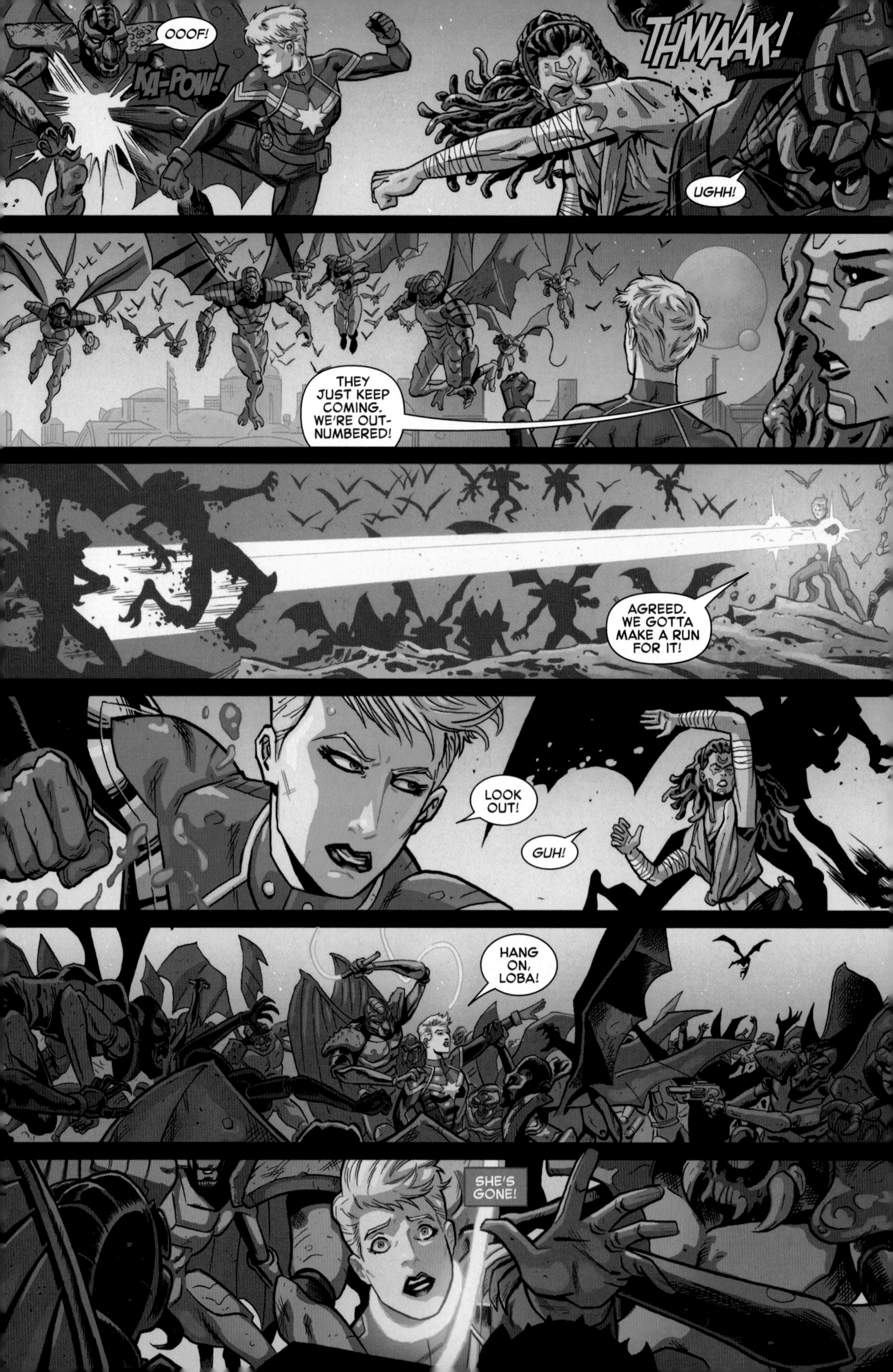
OOOF!
KA-POW!
THWAAK!
UGHH!
THEY JUST KEEP COMING. WE'RE OUT-NUMBERED!
AGREED. WE GOTTA MAKE A RUN FOR IT!
LOOK OUT!
GUH!
HANG ON, LOBA!
SHE'S GONE!

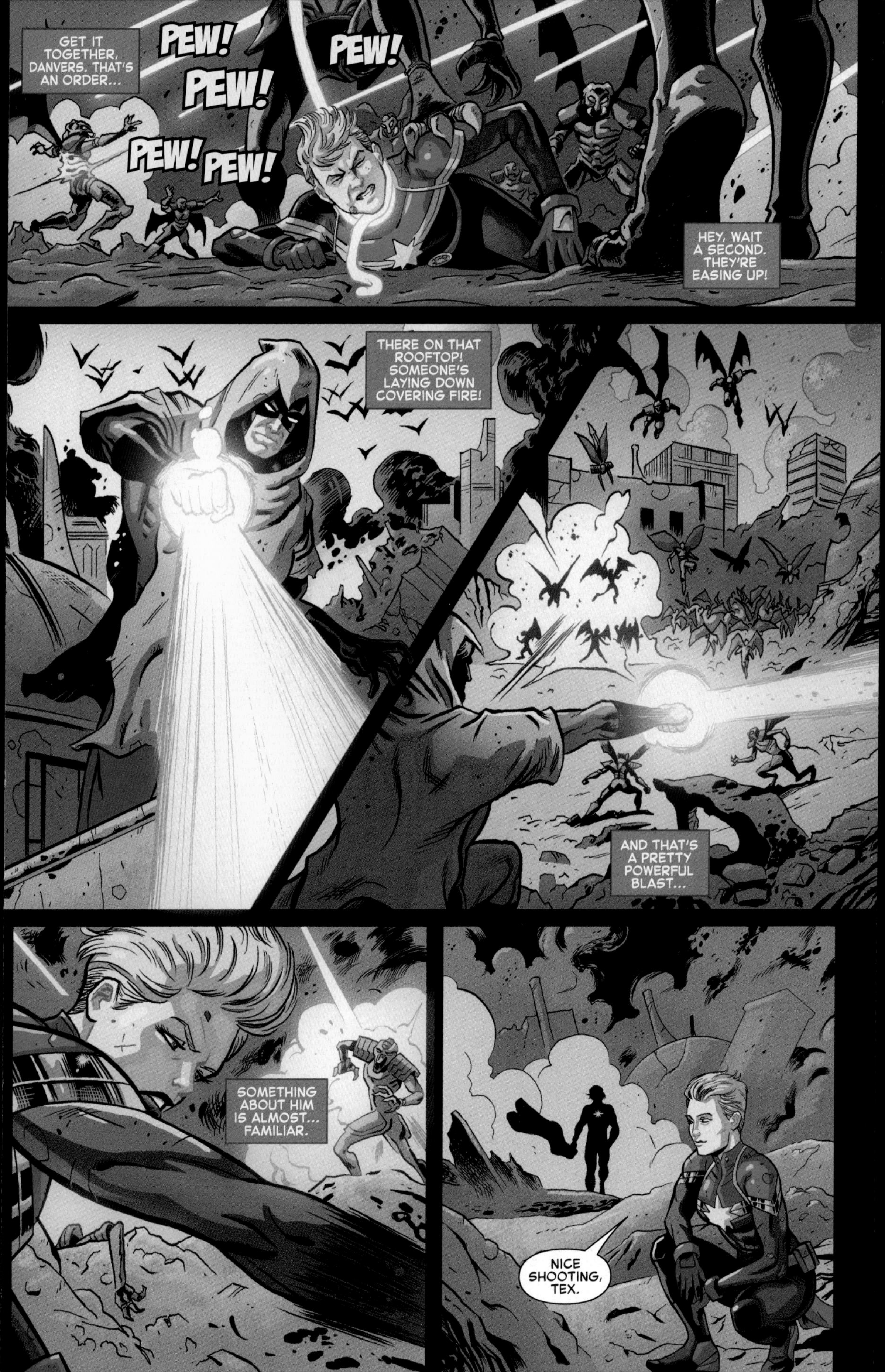
GET IT TOGETHER, DANVERS. THAT'S AN ORDER...
PEW!
PEW!
PEW!
PEW!
PEW!
HEY, WAIT A SECOND. THEY'RE EASING UP!
THERE ON THAT ROOFTOP! SOMEONE'S LAYING DOWN COVERING FIRE!
AND THAT'S A PRETTY POWERFUL BLAST...
SOMETHING ABOUT HIM IS ALMOST... FAMILIAR.
NICE SHOOTING, TEX.

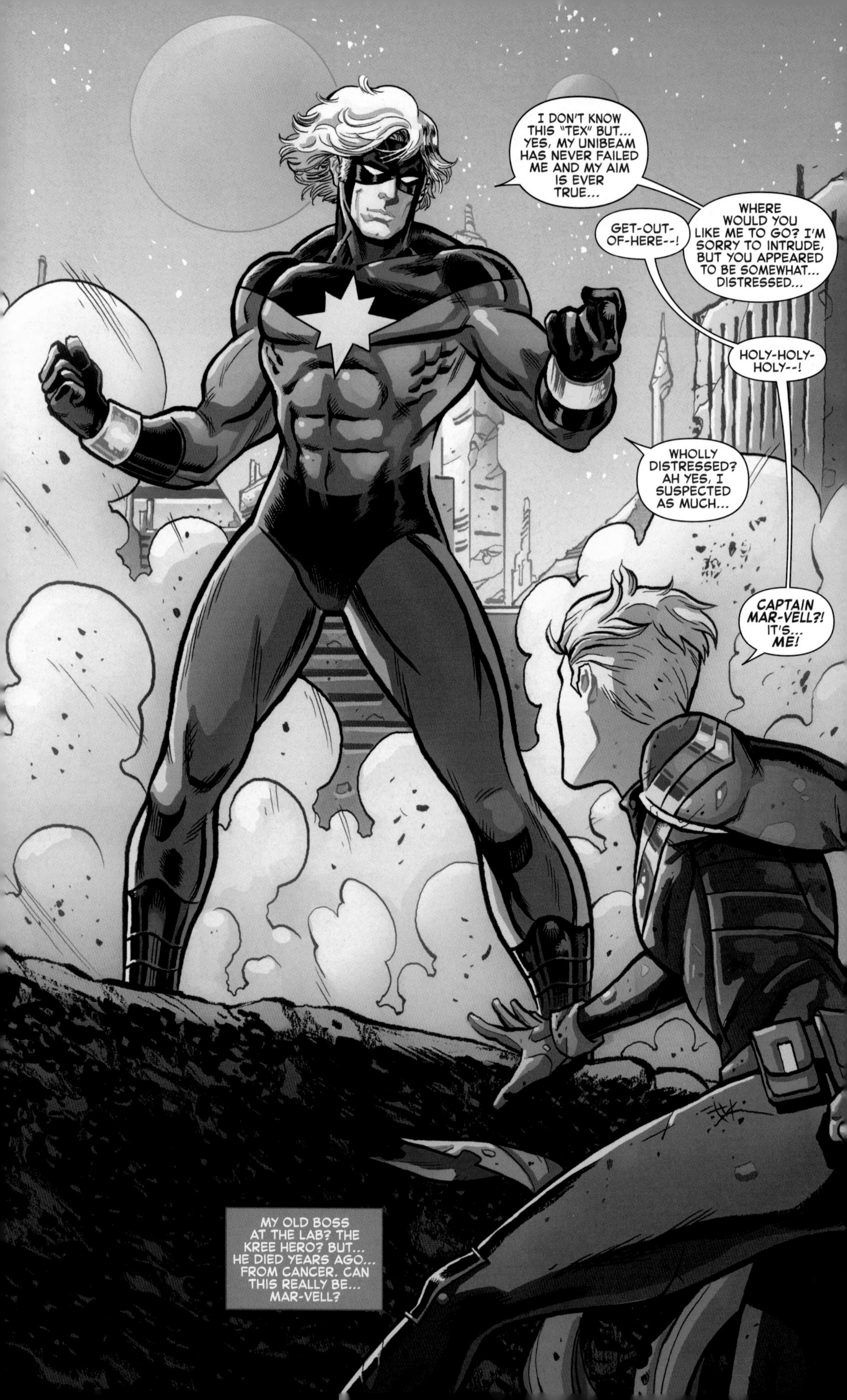
I DON'T KNOW THIS "TEX" BUT... YES, MY UNIBEAM HAS NEVER FAILED ME AND MY AIM IS EVER TRUE...
GET-OUT-OF-HERE--!
WHERE WOULD YOU LIKE ME TO GO? I'M SORRY TO INTRUDE, BUT YOU APPEARED TO BE SOMEWHAT... DISTRESSED...
HOLY-HOLY-HOLY--!
WHOLLY DISTRESSED? AH YES, I SUSPECTED AS MUCH...
CAPTAIN MAR-VELL?! IT'S... ME!
MY OLD BOSS AT THE LAB? THE KREE HERO? BUT... HE DIED YEARS AGO... FROM CANCER. CAN THIS REALLY BE... MAR-VELL?

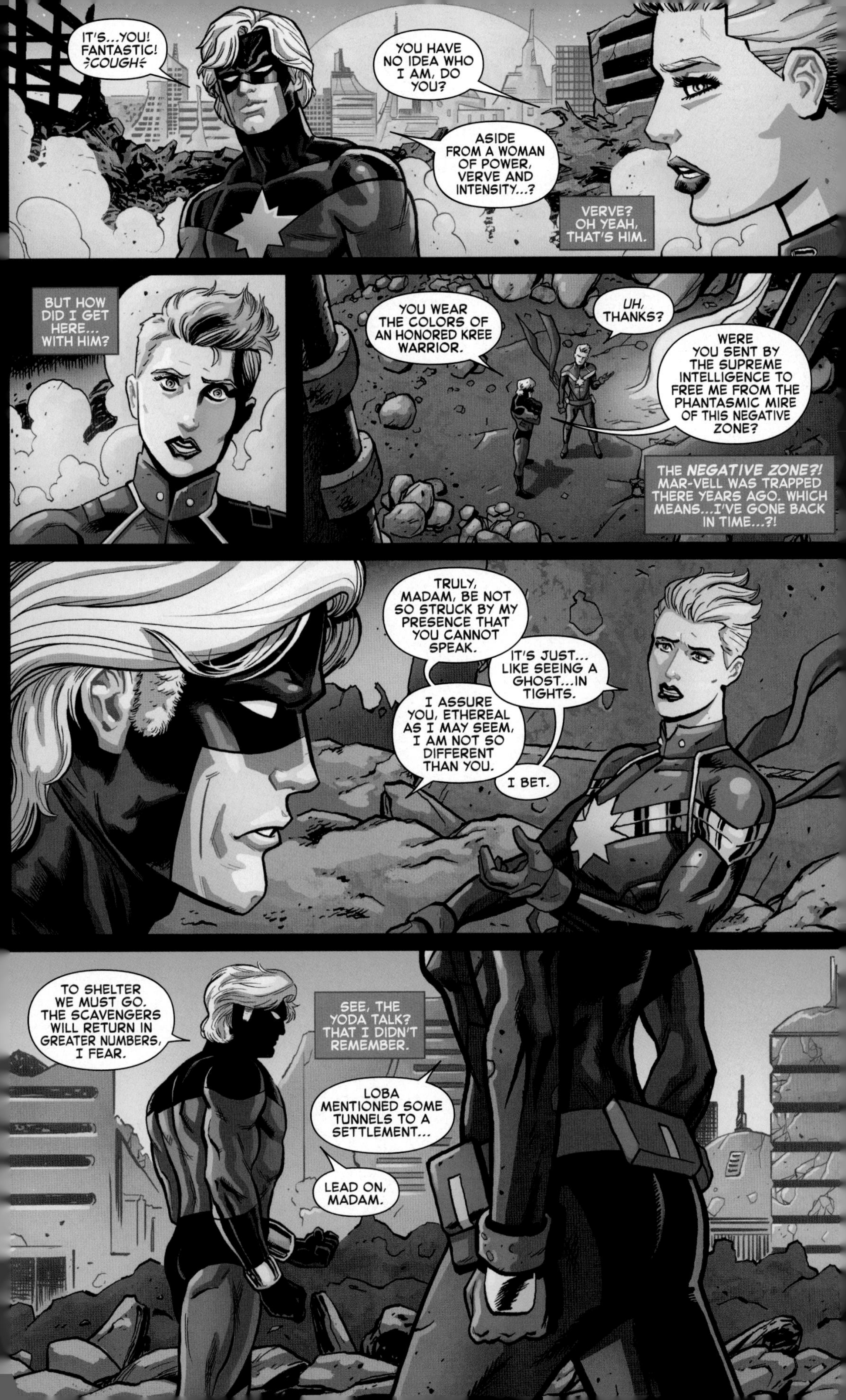
IT'S...YOU! FANTASTIC! *COUGH*
YOU HAVE NO IDEA WHO I AM, DO YOU?
ASIDE FROM A WOMAN OF POWER, VERVE AND INTENSITY...?
VERVE? OH YEAH, THAT'S HIM.
BUT HOW DID I GET HERE... WITH HIM?
YOU WEAR THE COLORS OF AN HONORED KREE WARRIOR.
UH, THANKS?
WERE YOU SENT BY THE SUPREME INTELLIGENCE TO FREE ME FROM THE PHANTASMIC MIRE OF THIS NEGATIVE ZONE?
THE *NEGATIVE ZONE?!* MAR-VELL WAS TRAPPED THERE YEARS AGO. WHICH MEANS...I'VE GONE BACK IN TIME...?!
TRULY, MADAM, BE NOT SO STRUCK BY MY PRESENCE THAT YOU CANNOT SPEAK.
IT'S JUST... LIKE SEEING A GHOST...IN TIGHTS.
I ASSURE YOU, ETHEREAL AS I MAY SEEM, I AM NOT SO DIFFERENT THAN YOU.
I BET.
TO SHELTER WE MUST GO. THE SCAVENGERS WILL RETURN IN GREATER NUMBERS, I FEAR.
SEE, THE YODA TALK? THAT I DIDN'T REMEMBER.
LOBA MENTIONED SOME TUNNELS TO A SETTLEMENT...
LEAD ON, MADAM.

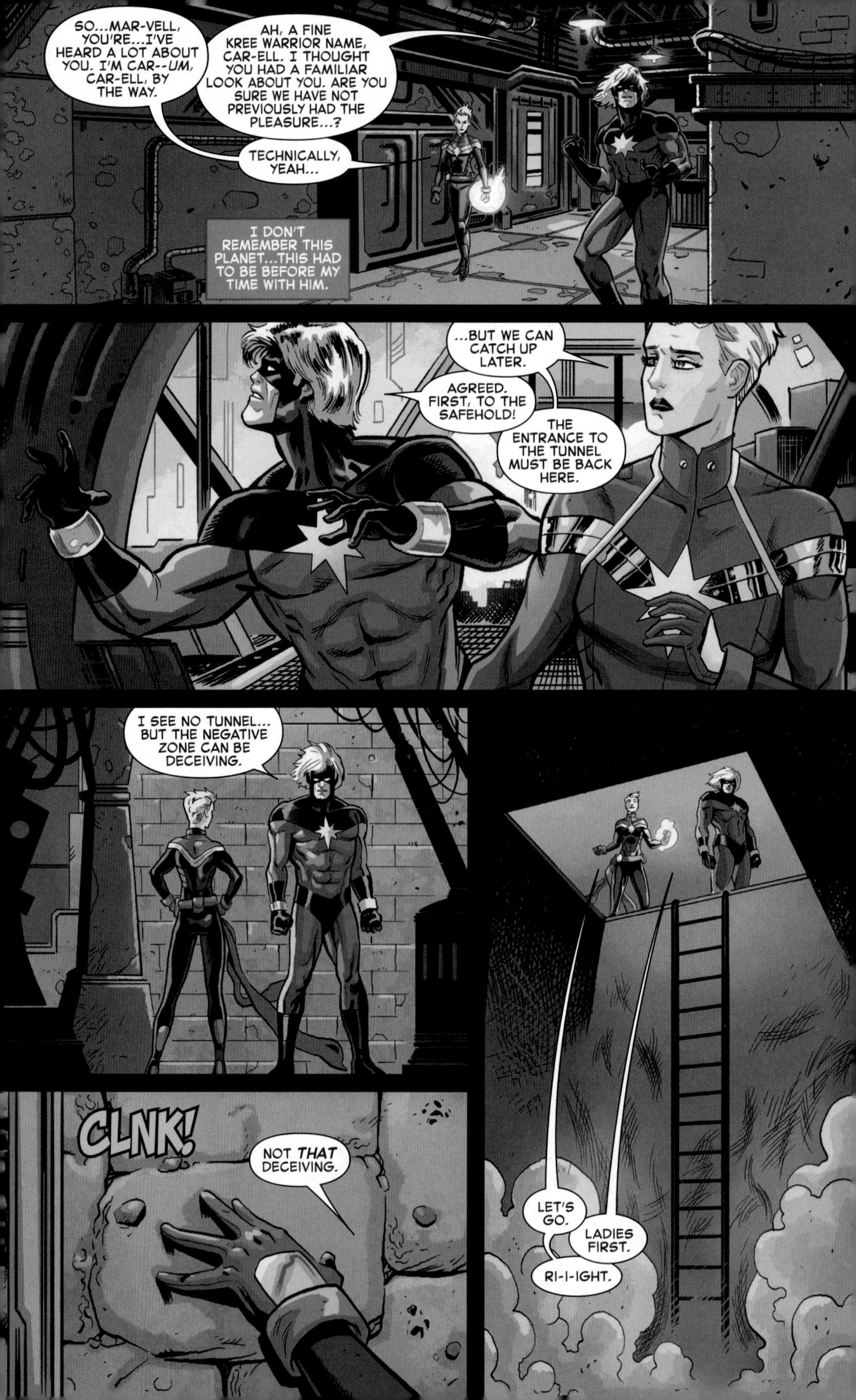

SO...MAR-VELL, YOU'RE...I'VE HEARD A LOT ABOUT YOU. I'M CAR--UM, CAR-ELL, BY THE WAY.
AH, A FINE KREE WARRIOR NAME, CAR-ELL. I THOUGHT YOU HAD A FAMILIAR LOOK ABOUT YOU. ARE YOU SURE WE HAVE NOT PREVIOUSLY HAD THE PLEASURE...?
TECHNICALLY, YEAH...
I DON'T REMEMBER THIS PLANET...THIS HAD TO BE BEFORE MY TIME WITH HIM.
...BUT WE CAN CATCH UP LATER.
AGREED. FIRST, TO THE SAFEHOLD!
THE ENTRANCE TO THE TUNNEL MUST BE BACK HERE.
I SEE NO TUNNEL... BUT THE NEGATIVE ZONE CAN BE DECEIVING.
CLNK!
NOT *THAT* DECEIVING.
LET'S GO.
LADIES FIRST.
RI-I-IGHT.

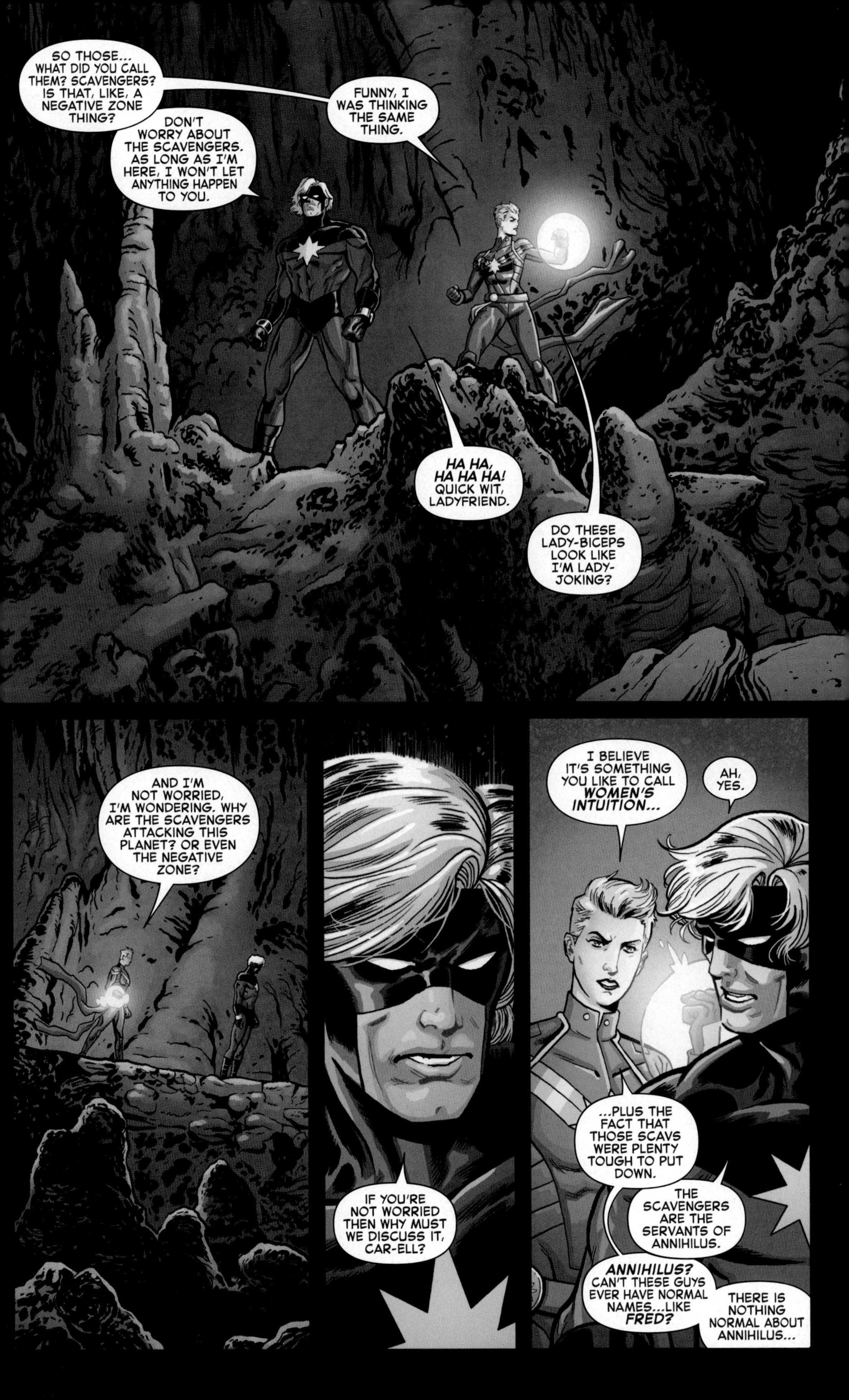
SO THOSE... WHAT DID YOU CALL THEM? SCAVENGERS? IS THAT, LIKE, A NEGATIVE ZONE THING?
DON'T WORRY ABOUT THE SCAVENGERS. AS LONG AS I'M HERE, I WON'T LET ANYTHING HAPPEN TO YOU.
FUNNY, I WAS THINKING THE SAME THING.
HA HA, HA HA HA! QUICK WIT, LADYFRIEND.
DO THESE LADY-BICEPS LOOK LIKE I'M LADY-JOKING?
AND I'M NOT WORRIED, I'M WONDERING. WHY ARE THE SCAVENGERS ATTACKING THIS PLANET? OR EVEN THE NEGATIVE ZONE?
IF YOU'RE NOT WORRIED THEN WHY MUST WE DISCUSS IT, CAR-ELL?
I BELIEVE IT'S SOMETHING YOU LIKE TO CALL WOMEN'S INTUITION...
AH, YES.
...PLUS THE FACT THAT THOSE SCAVS WERE PLENTY TOUGH TO PUT DOWN.
THE SCAVENGERS ARE THE SERVANTS OF ANNIHILUS.
ANNIHILUS? CAN'T THESE GUYS EVER HAVE NORMAL NAMES...LIKE FRED?
THERE IS NOTHING NORMAL ABOUT ANNIHILUS...

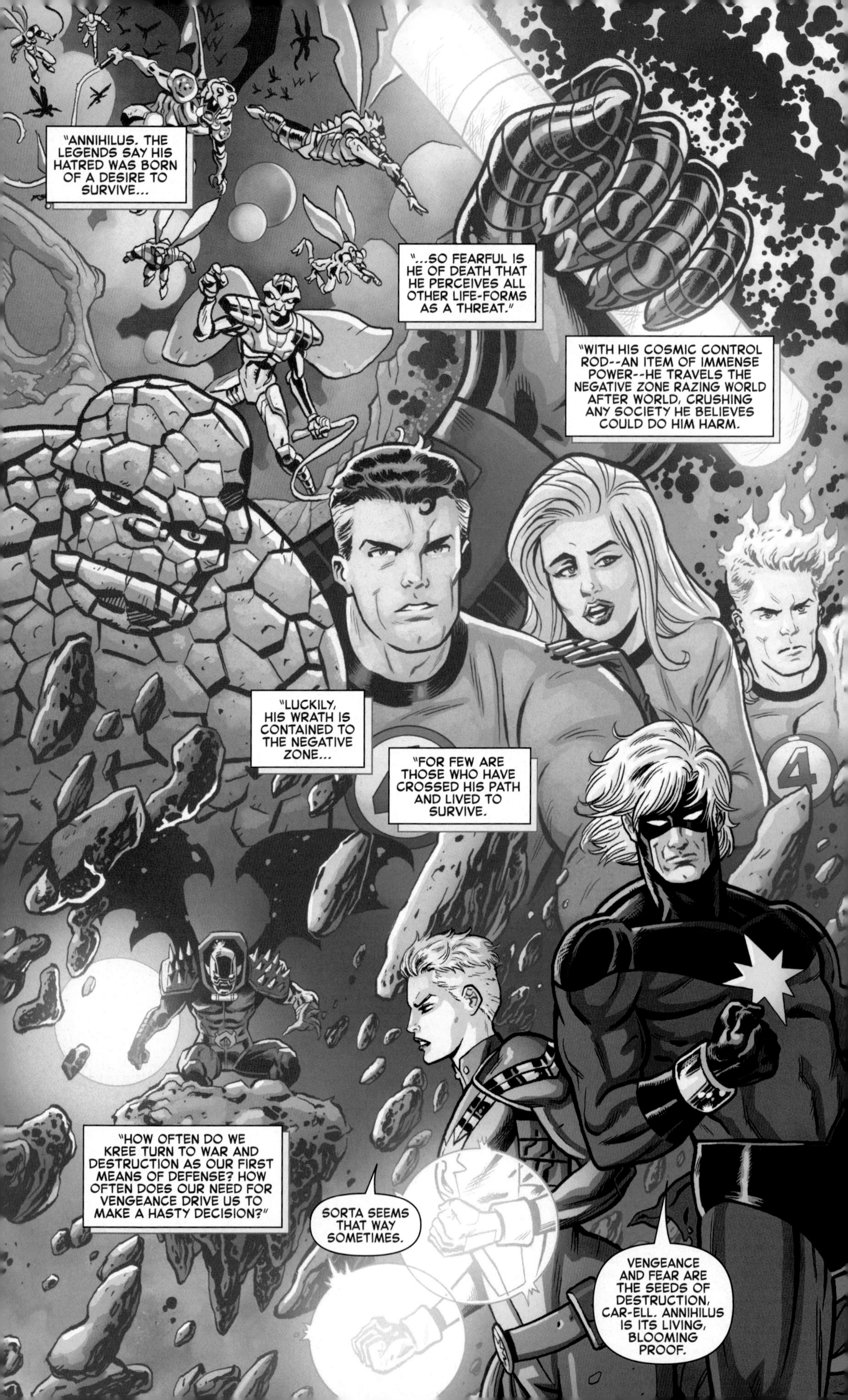
"ANNIHILUS. THE LEGENDS SAY HIS HATRED WAS BORN OF A DESIRE TO SURVIVE...
"...SO FEARFUL IS HE OF DEATH THAT HE PERCEIVES ALL OTHER LIFE-FORMS AS A THREAT."
"WITH HIS COSMIC CONTROL ROD--AN ITEM OF IMMENSE POWER--HE TRAVELS THE NEGATIVE ZONE RAZING WORLD AFTER WORLD, CRUSHING ANY SOCIETY HE BELIEVES COULD DO HIM HARM.
"LUCKILY, HIS WRATH IS CONTAINED TO THE NEGATIVE ZONE...
"FOR FEW ARE THOSE WHO HAVE CROSSED HIS PATH AND LIVED TO SURVIVE.
"HOW OFTEN DO WE KREE TURN TO WAR AND DESTRUCTION AS OUR FIRST MEANS OF DEFENSE? HOW OFTEN DOES OUR NEED FOR VENGEANCE DRIVE US TO MAKE A HASTY DECISION?"
SORTA SEEMS THAT WAY SOMETIMES.
VENGEANCE AND FEAR ARE THE SEEDS OF DESTRUCTION, CAR-ELL. ANNIHILUS IS ITS LIVING, BLOOMING PROOF.

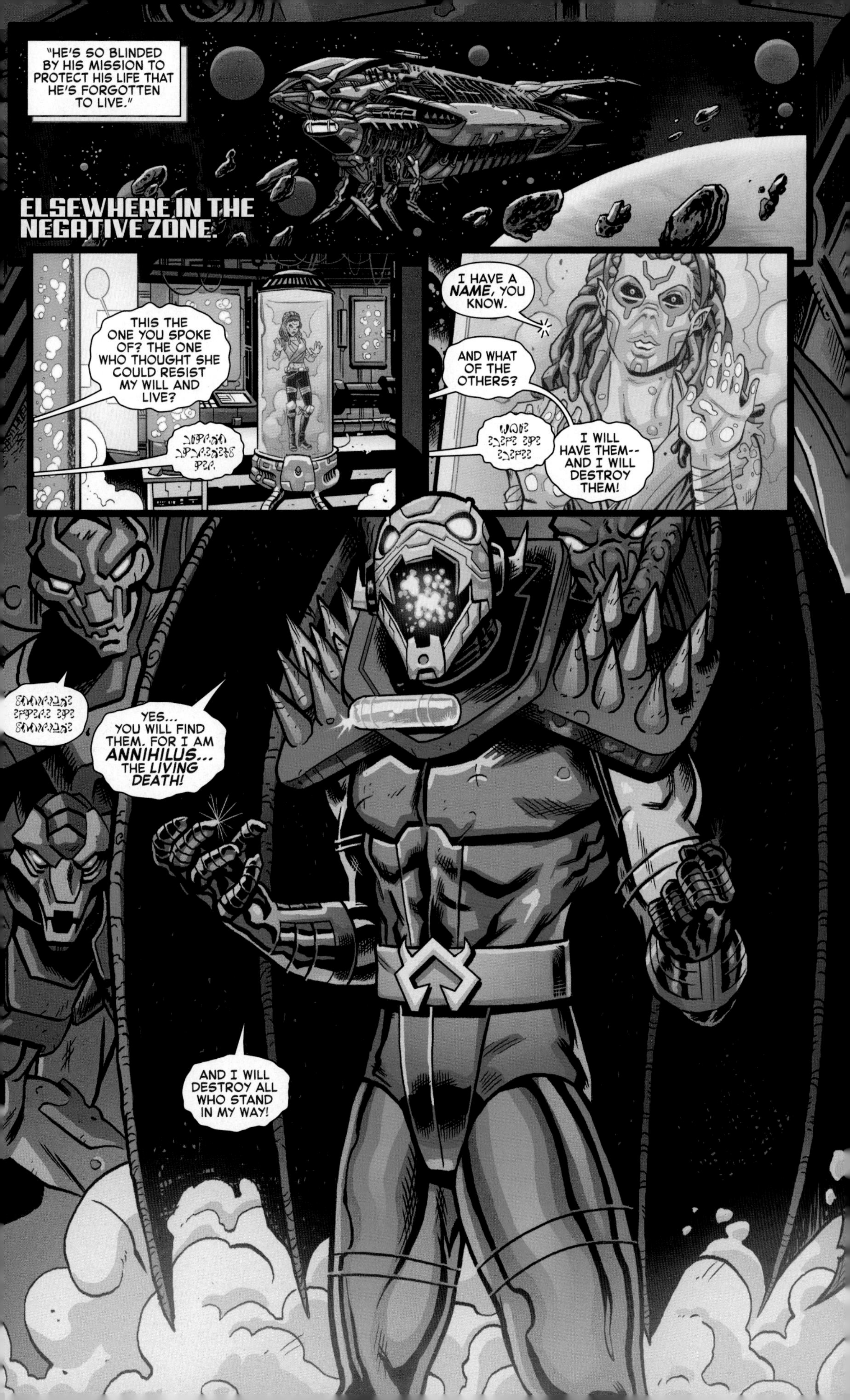
"HE'S SO BLINDED BY HIS MISSION TO PROTECT HIS LIFE THAT HE'S FORGOTTEN TO LIVE."
ELSEWHERE IN THE NEGATIVE ZONE.
THIS THE ONE YOU SPOKE OF? THE ONE WHO THOUGHT SHE COULD RESIST MY WILL AND LIVE?
I HAVE A NAME, YOU KNOW.
AND WHAT OF THE OTHERS?
I WILL HAVE THEM--AND I WILL DESTROY THEM!
YES... YOU WILL FIND THEM. FOR I AM ANNIHILUS... THE LIVING DEATH!
AND I WILL DESTROY ALL WHO STAND IN MY WAY!

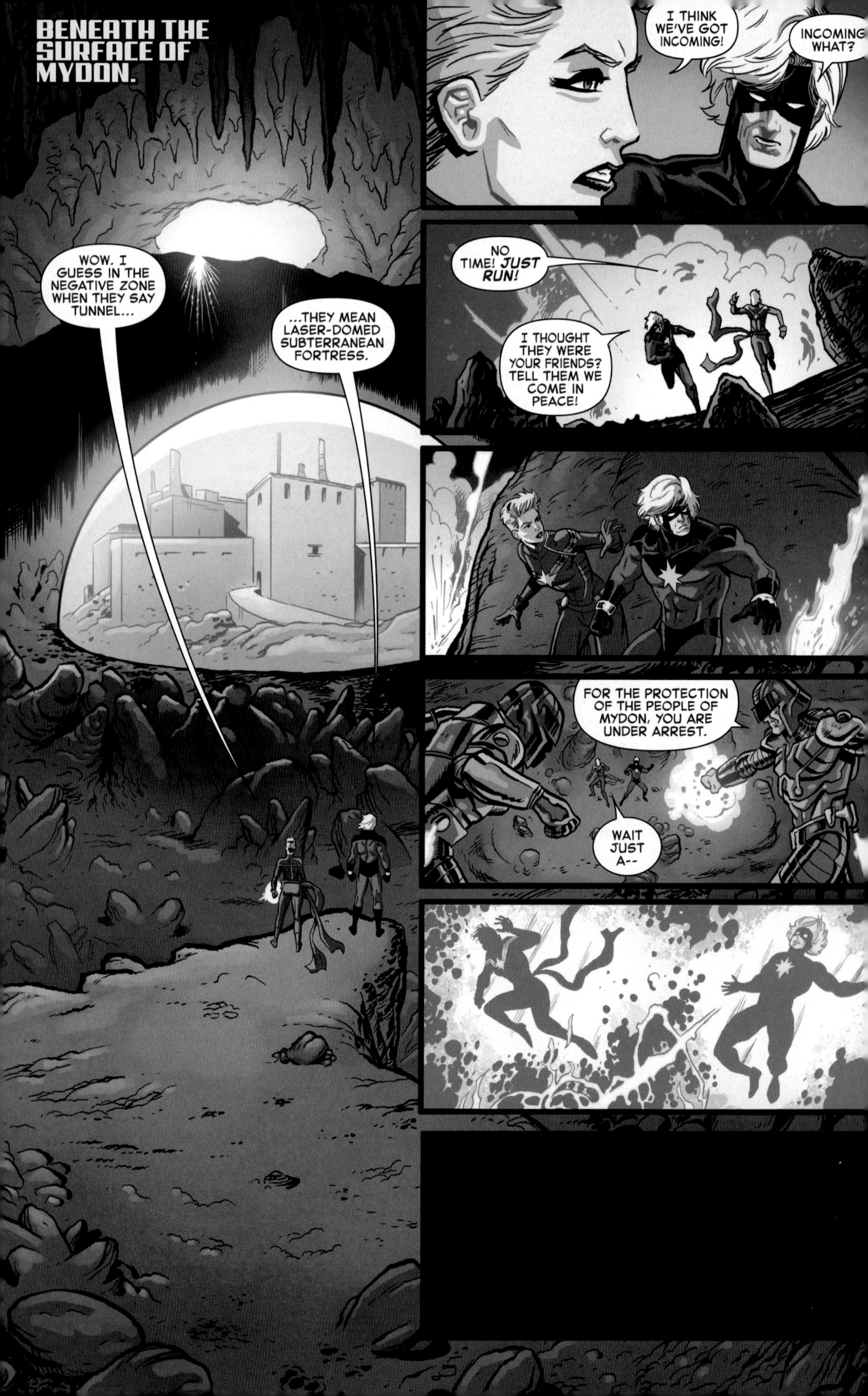
BENEATH THE SURFACE OF MYDON.
WOW. I GUESS IN THE NEGATIVE ZONE WHEN THEY SAY TUNNEL...
...THEY MEAN LASER-DOMED SUBTERRANEAN FORTRESS.
I THINK WE'VE GOT INCOMING!
INCOMING WHAT?
NO TIME! JUST RUN!
I THOUGHT THEY WERE YOUR FRIENDS? TELL THEM WE COME IN PEACE!
FOR THE PROTECTION OF THE PEOPLE OF MYDON, YOU ARE UNDER ARREST.
WAIT JUST A--

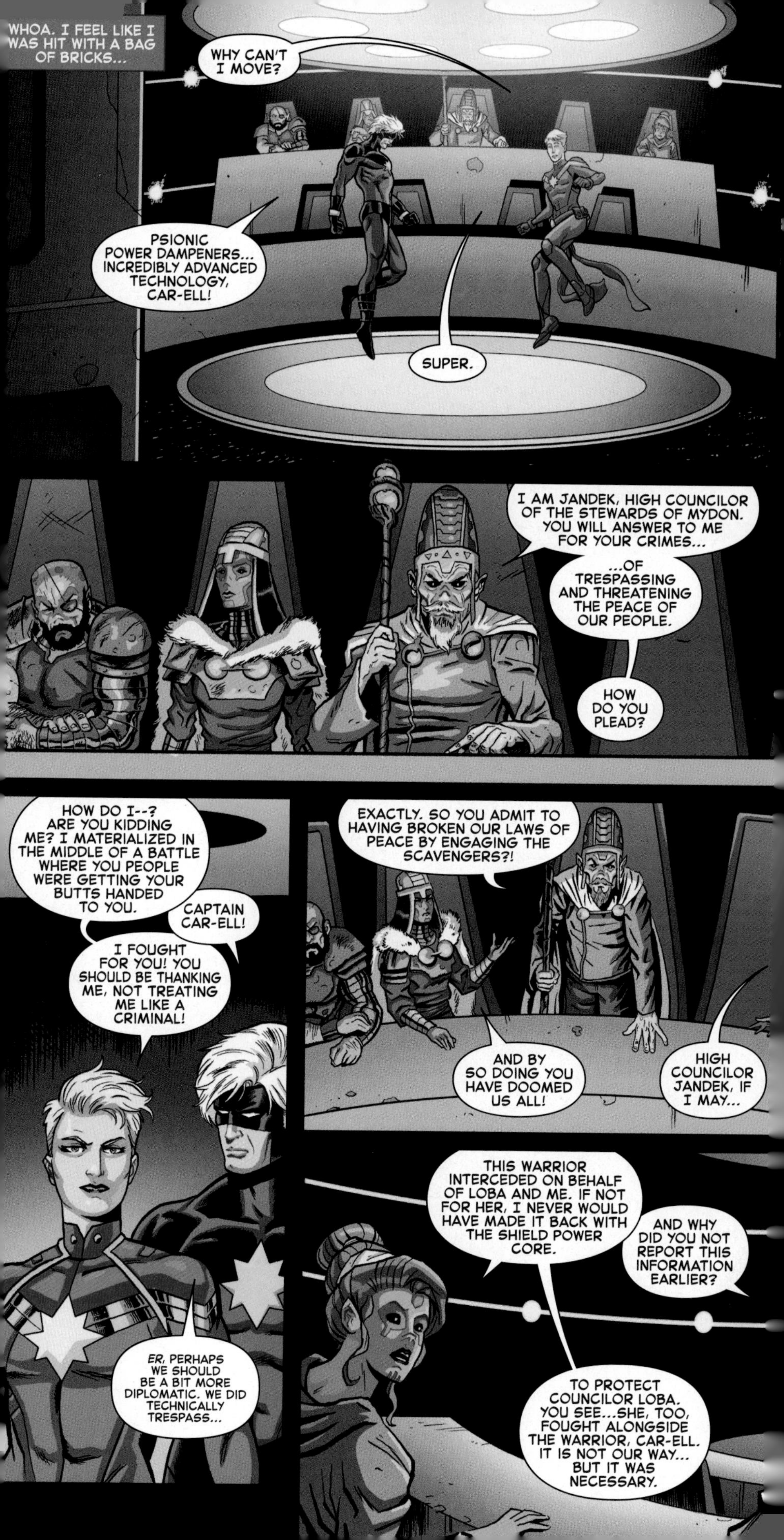

WHOA. I FEEL LIKE I WAS HIT WITH A BAG OF BRICKS...
WHY CAN'T I MOVE?
PSIONIC POWER DAMPENERS... INCREDIBLY ADVANCED TECHNOLOGY, CAR-ELL!
SUPER.
I AM JANDEK, HIGH COUNCILOR OF THE STEWARDS OF MYDON. YOU WILL ANSWER TO ME FOR YOUR CRIMES...
...OF TRESPASSING AND THREATENING THE PEACE OF OUR PEOPLE.
HOW DO YOU PLEAD?
HOW DO I--? ARE YOU KIDDING ME? I MATERIALIZED IN THE MIDDLE OF A BATTLE WHERE YOU PEOPLE WERE GETTING YOUR BUTTS HANDED TO YOU.
CAPTAIN CAR-ELL!
I FOUGHT FOR YOU! YOU SHOULD BE THANKING ME, NOT TREATING ME LIKE A CRIMINAL!
ER, PERHAPS WE SHOULD BE A BIT MORE DIPLOMATIC. WE DID TECHNICALLY TRESPASS...
EXACTLY. SO YOU ADMIT TO HAVING BROKEN OUR LAWS OF PEACE BY ENGAGING THE SCAVENGERS?!
AND BY SO DOING YOU HAVE DOOMED US ALL!
HIGH COUNCILOR JANDEK, IF I MAY...
THIS WARRIOR INTERCEDED ON BEHALF OF LOBA AND ME. IF NOT FOR HER, I NEVER WOULD HAVE MADE IT BACK WITH THE SHIELD POWER CORE.
AND WHY DID YOU NOT REPORT THIS INFORMATION EARLIER?
TO PROTECT COUNCILOR LOBA. YOU SEE...SHE, TOO, FOUGHT ALONGSIDE THE WARRIOR, CAR-ELL. IT IS NOT OUR WAY... BUT IT WAS NECESSARY.

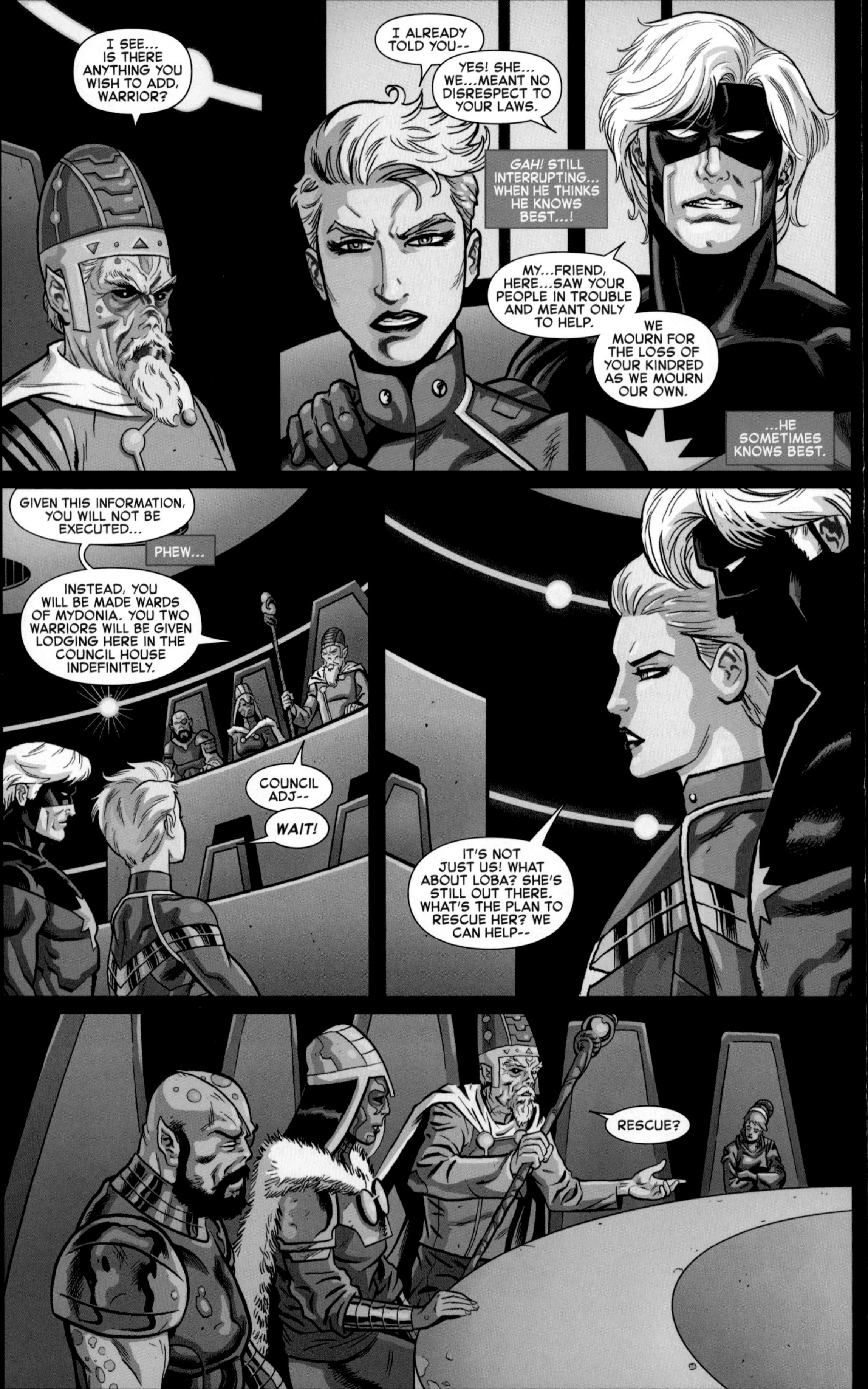
I SEE... IS THERE ANYTHING YOU WISH TO ADD, WARRIOR?
I ALREADY TOLD YOU--
YES! SHE... WE...MEANT NO DISRESPECT TO YOUR LAWS.
GAH! STILL INTERRUPTING... WHEN HE THINKS HE KNOWS BEST...!
MY...FRIEND, HERE...SAW YOUR PEOPLE IN TROUBLE AND MEANT ONLY TO HELP.
WE MOURN FOR THE LOSS OF YOUR KINDRED AS WE MOURN OUR OWN.
...HE SOMETIMES KNOWS BEST.
GIVEN THIS INFORMATION, YOU WILL NOT BE EXECUTED...
PHEW...
INSTEAD, YOU WILL BE MADE WARDS OF MYDONIA. YOU TWO WARRIORS WILL BE GIVEN LODGING HERE IN THE COUNCIL HOUSE INDEFINITELY.
COUNCIL ADJ--
WAIT!
IT'S NOT JUST US! WHAT ABOUT LOBA? SHE'S STILL OUT THERE. WHAT'S THE PLAN TO RESCUE HER? WE CAN HELP--
RESCUE?

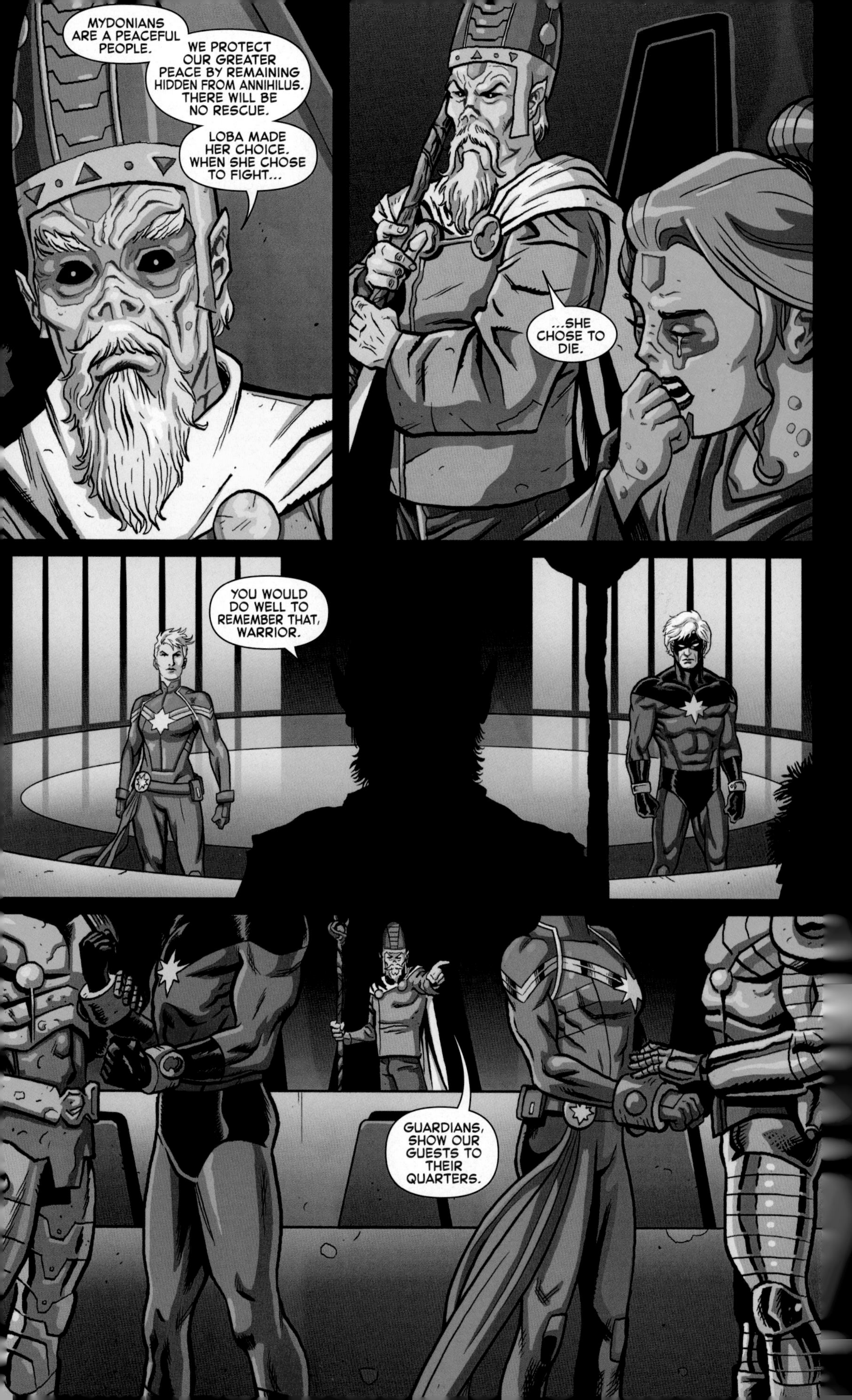
MYDONIANS ARE A PEACEFUL PEOPLE.
WE PROTECT OUR GREATER PEACE BY REMAINING HIDDEN FROM ANNIHILUS. THERE WILL BE NO RESCUE.
LOBA MADE HER CHOICE. WHEN SHE CHOSE TO FIGHT...
...SHE CHOSE TO DIE.
YOU WOULD DO WELL TO REMEMBER THAT, WARRIOR.
GUARDIANS, SHOW OUR GUESTS TO THEIR QUARTERS.

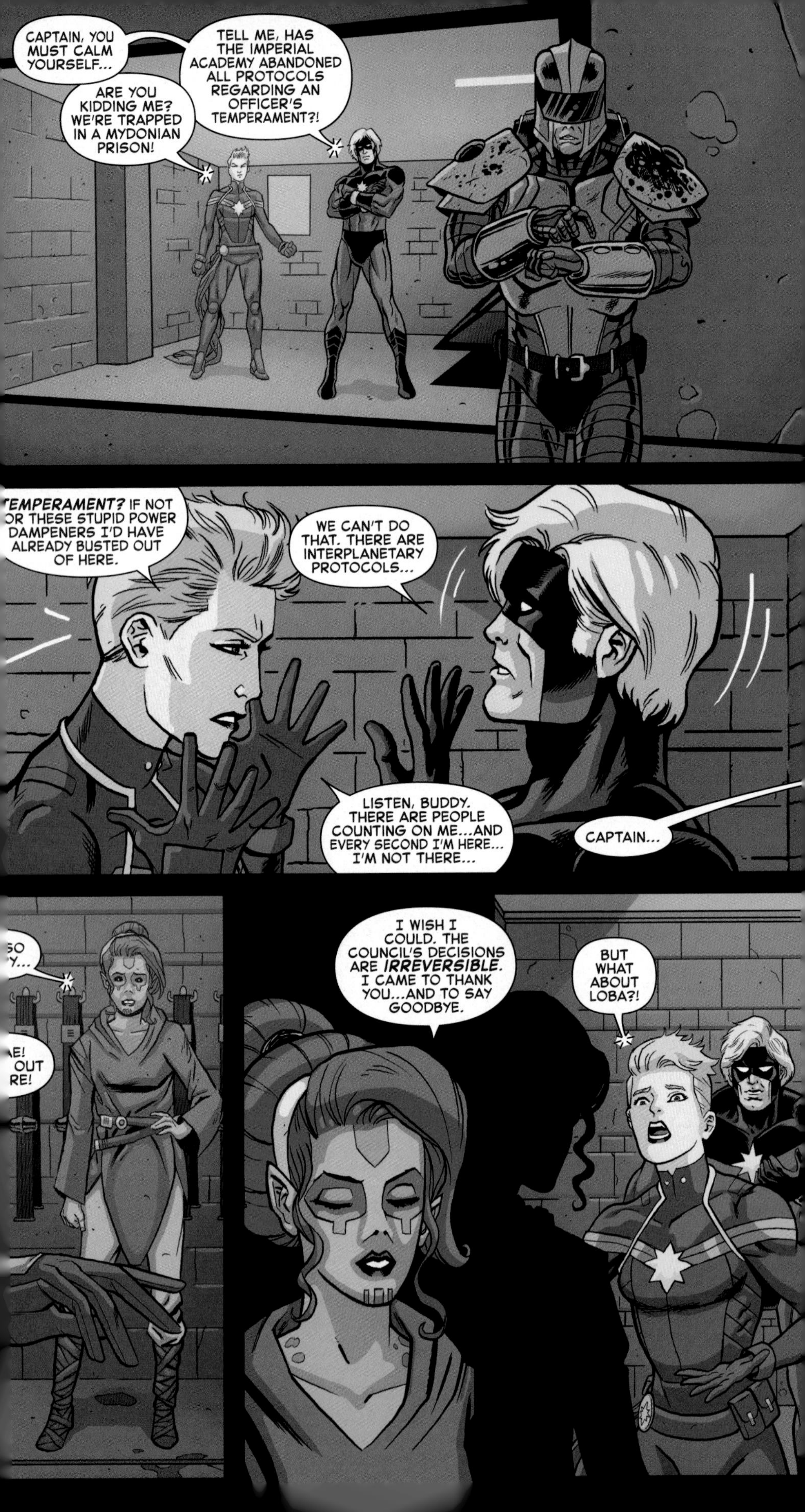
CAPTAIN, YOU MUST CALM YOURSELF...
ARE YOU KIDDING ME? WE'RE TRAPPED IN A MYDONIAN PRISON!
TELL ME, HAS THE IMPERIAL ACADEMY ABANDONED ALL PROTOCOLS REGARDING AN OFFICER'S TEMPERAMENT?!
TEMPERAMENT? IF NOT FOR THESE STUPID POWER DAMPENERS I'D HAVE ALREADY BUSTED OUT OF HERE.
WE CAN'T DO THAT. THERE ARE INTERPLANETARY PROTOCOLS...
LISTEN, BUDDY. THERE ARE PEOPLE COUNTING ON ME...AND EVERY SECOND I'M HERE... I'M NOT THERE...
CAPTAIN...
I WISH I COULD. THE COUNCIL'S DECISIONS ARE IRREVERSIBLE. I CAME TO THANK YOU...AND TO SAY GOODBYE.
BUT WHAT ABOUT LOBA?!

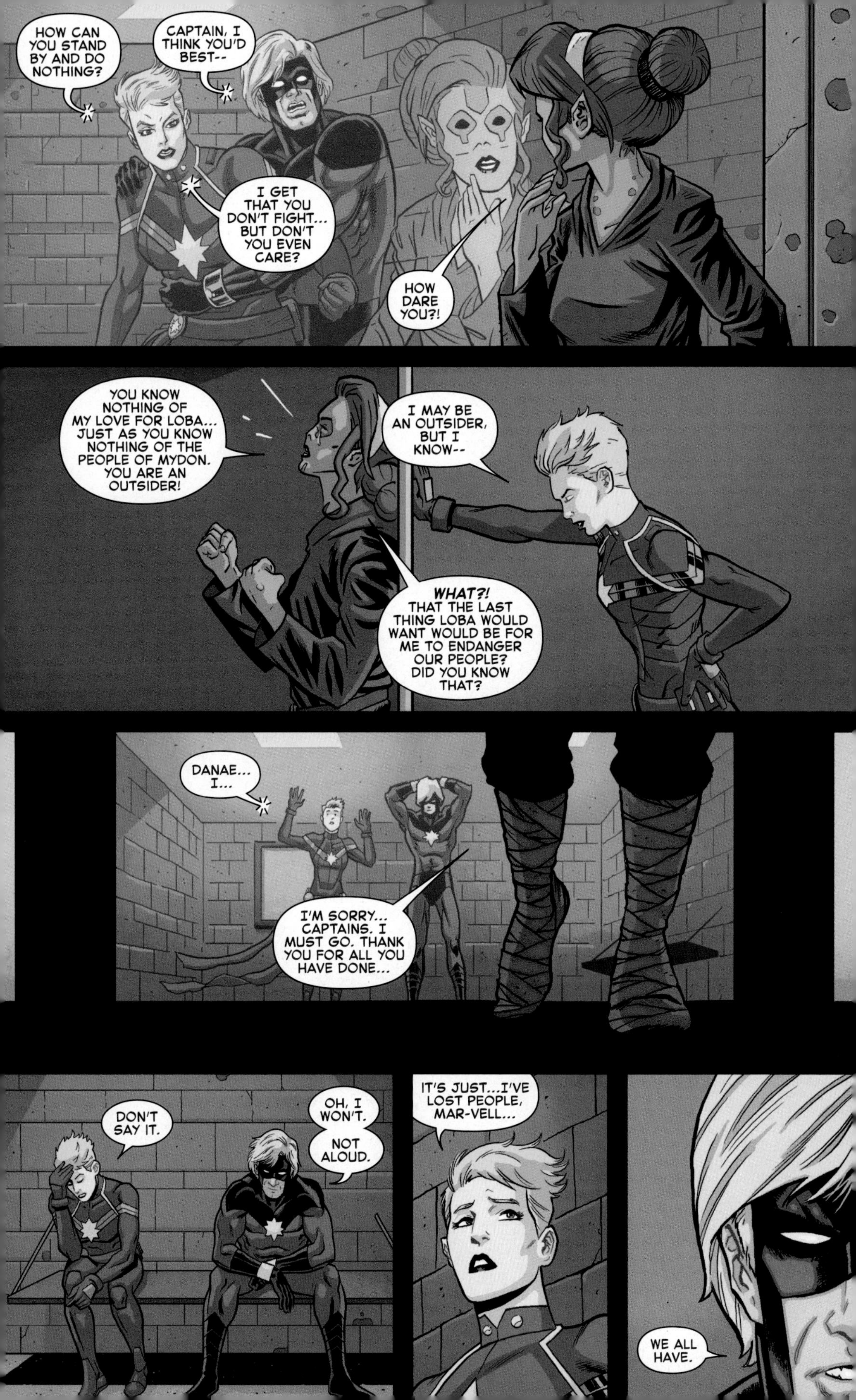
HOW CAN YOU STAND BY AND DO NOTHING?
CAPTAIN, I THINK YOU'D BEST--
I GET THAT YOU DON'T FIGHT... BUT DON'T YOU EVEN CARE?
HOW DARE YOU?!
YOU KNOW NOTHING OF MY LOVE FOR LOBA... JUST AS YOU KNOW NOTHING OF THE PEOPLE OF MYDON. YOU ARE AN OUTSIDER!
I MAY BE AN OUTSIDER, BUT I KNOW--
*WHAT?!* THAT THE LAST THING LOBA WOULD WANT WOULD BE FOR ME TO ENDANGER OUR PEOPLE? DID YOU KNOW THAT?
DANAE... I...
I'M SORRY... CAPTAINS. I MUST GO. THANK YOU FOR ALL YOU HAVE DONE...
DON'T SAY IT.
OH, I WON'T.
NOT ALOUD.
IT'S JUST...I'VE LOST PEOPLE, MAR-VELL...
WE ALL HAVE.

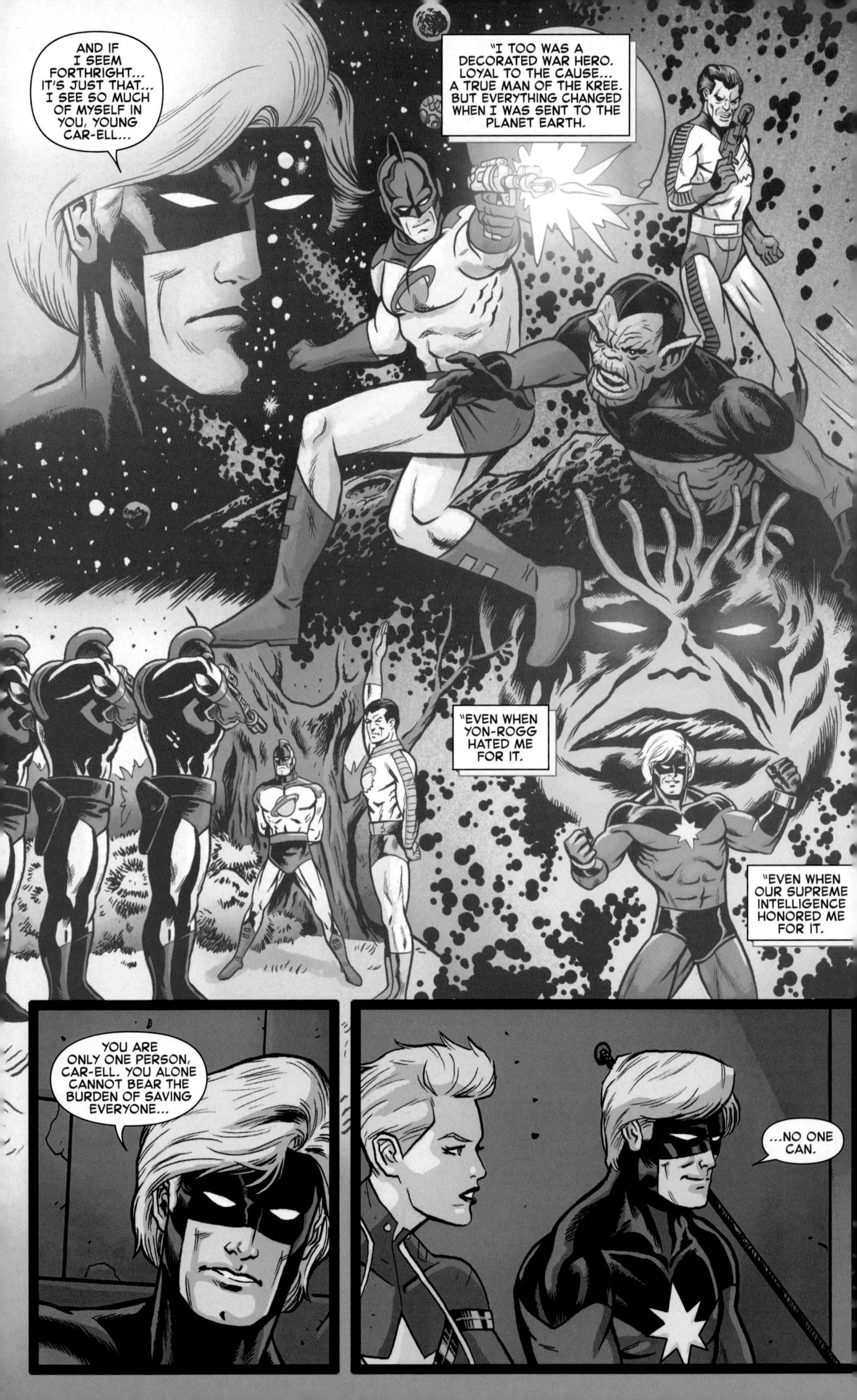
AND IF I SEEM FORTHRIGHT... IT'S JUST THAT... I SEE SO MUCH OF MYSELF IN YOU, YOUNG CAR-ELL...
"I TOO WAS A DECORATED WAR HERO. LOYAL TO THE CAUSE... A TRUE MAN OF THE KREE. BUT EVERYTHING CHANGED WHEN I WAS SENT TO THE PLANET EARTH.
"EVEN WHEN YON-ROGG HATED ME FOR IT.
"EVEN WHEN OUR SUPREME INTELLIGENCE HONORED ME FOR IT.
YOU ARE ONLY ONE PERSON, CAR-ELL. YOU ALONE CANNOT BEAR THE BURDEN OF SAVING EVERYONE...
...NO ONE CAN.

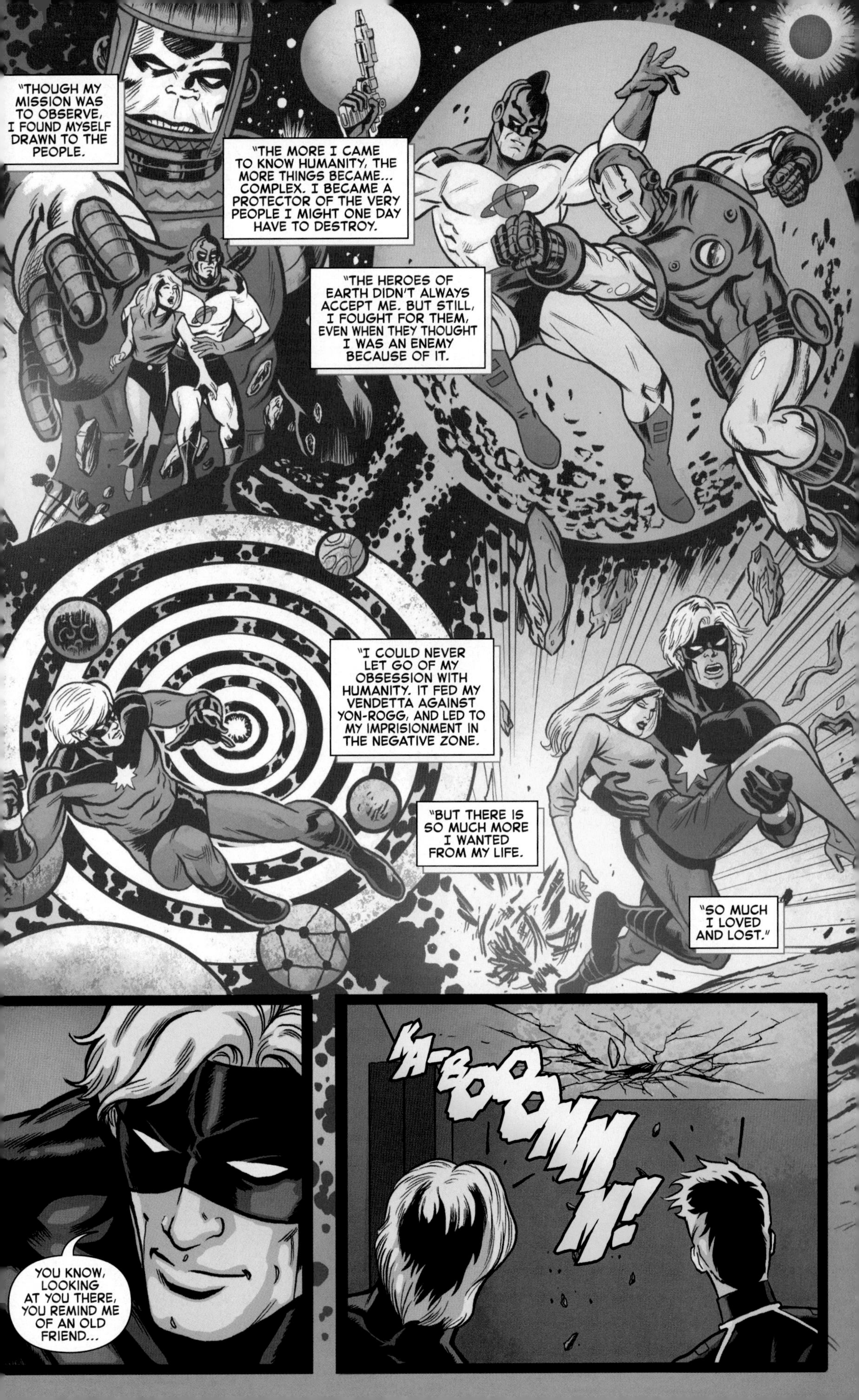
"THOUGH MY MISSION WAS TO OBSERVE, I FOUND MYSELF DRAWN TO THE PEOPLE.
"THE MORE I CAME TO KNOW HUMANITY, THE MORE THINGS BECAME... COMPLEX. I BECAME A PROTECTOR OF THE VERY PEOPLE I MIGHT ONE DAY HAVE TO DESTROY.
"THE HEROES OF EARTH DIDN'T ALWAYS ACCEPT ME. BUT STILL, I FOUGHT FOR THEM, EVEN WHEN THEY THOUGHT I WAS AN ENEMY BECAUSE OF IT.
"I COULD NEVER LET GO OF MY OBSESSION WITH HUMANITY. IT FED MY VENDETTA AGAINST YON-ROGG, AND LED TO MY IMPRISIONMENT IN THE NEGATIVE ZONE.
"BUT THERE IS SO MUCH MORE I WANTED FROM MY LIFE.
"SO MUCH I LOVED AND LOST."
YOU KNOW, LOOKING AT YOU THERE, YOU REMIND ME OF AN OLD FRIEND...
KA-BOOOMMM!

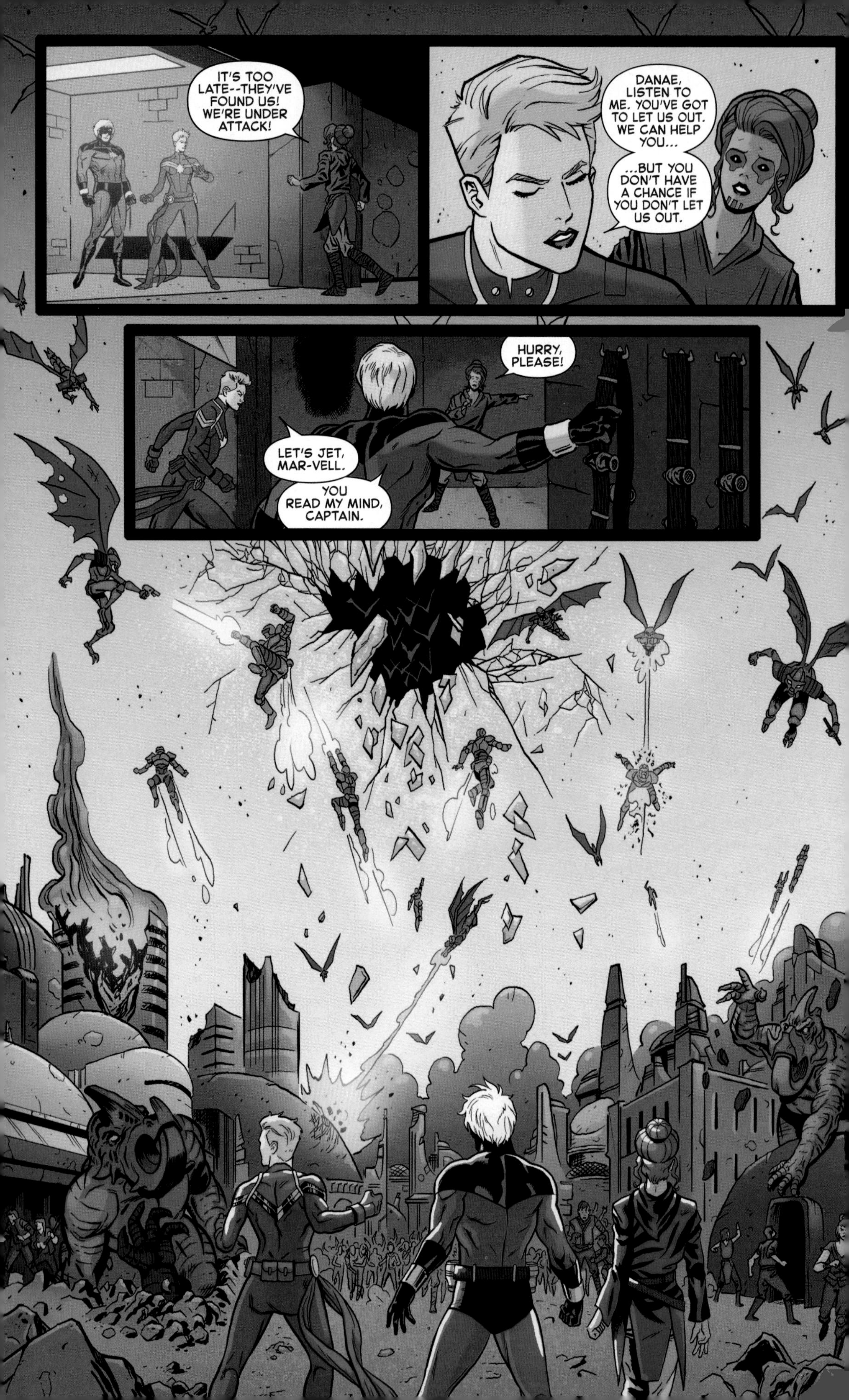
IT'S TOO LATE--THEY'VE FOUND US! WE'RE UNDER ATTACK!
DANAE, LISTEN TO ME. YOU'VE GOT TO LET US OUT. WE CAN HELP YOU...
...BUT YOU DON'T HAVE A CHANCE IF YOU DON'T LET US OUT.
HURRY, PLEASE!
LET'S JET, MAR-VELL.
YOU READ MY MIND, CAPTAIN.

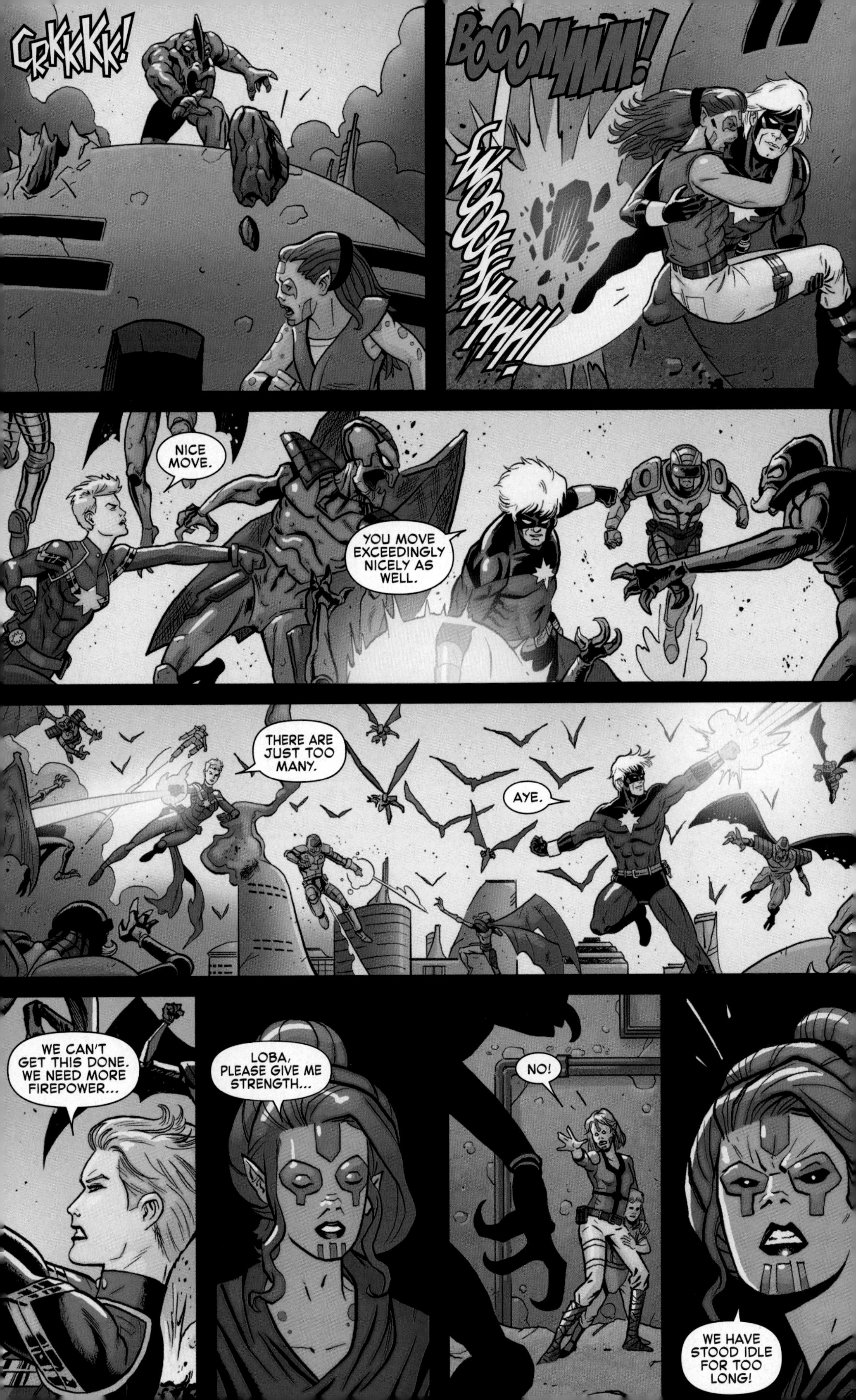
CRKKKK!
BOOOMMMM!
FWOOOOSHHHH!
NICE MOVE.
YOU MOVE EXCEEDINGLY NICELY AS WELL.
THERE ARE JUST TOO MANY.
AYE.
WE CAN'T GET THIS DONE. WE NEED MORE FIREPOWER...
LOBA, PLEASE GIVE ME STRENGTH...
NO!
WE HAVE STOOD IDLE FOR TOO LONG!

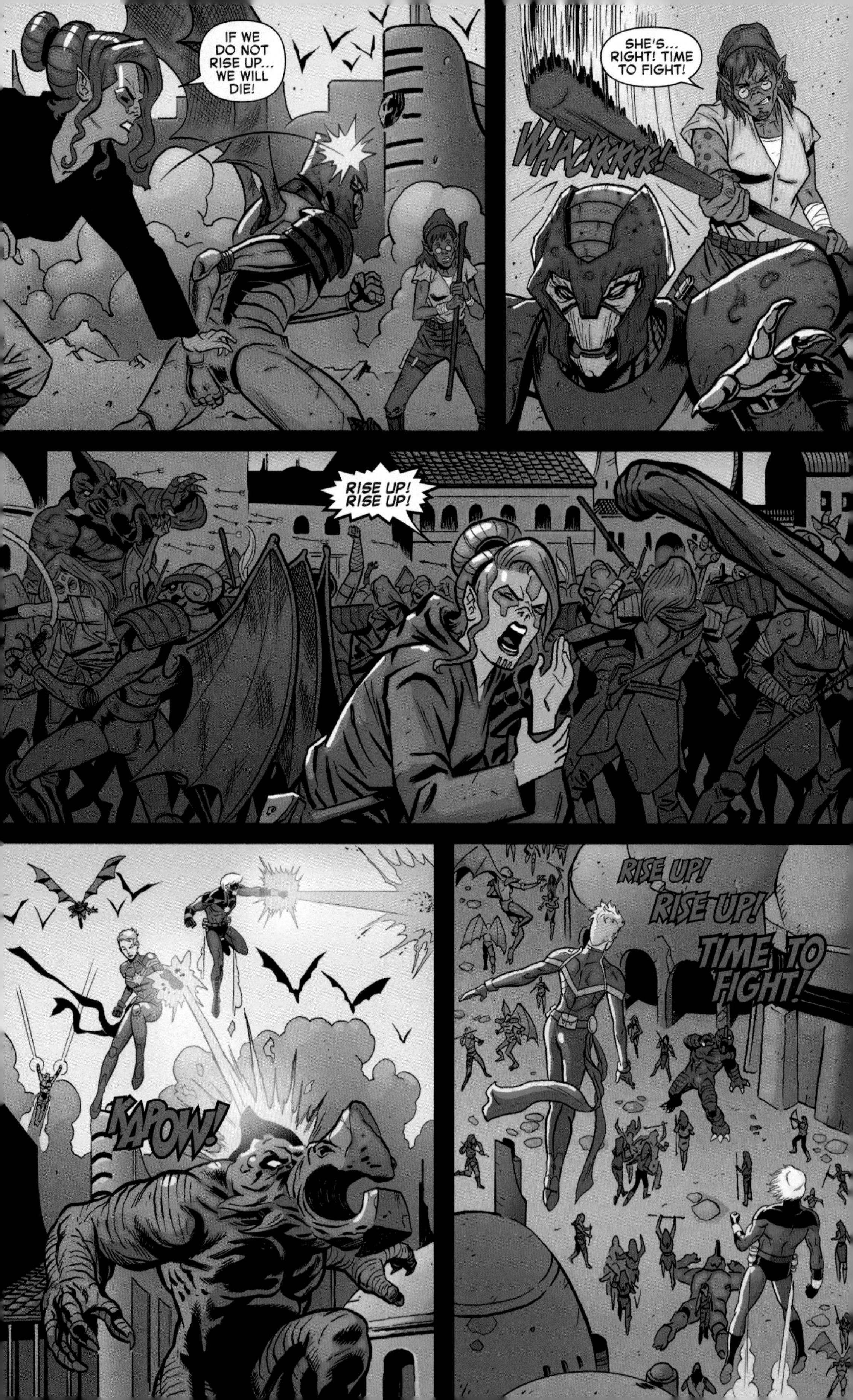
IF WE DO NOT RISE UP... WE WILL DIE!
SHE'S... RIGHT! TIME TO FIGHT!
WHACKKKKK!
RISE UP! RISE UP!
KAPOW!
RISE UP!
RISE UP!
TIME TO FIGHT!

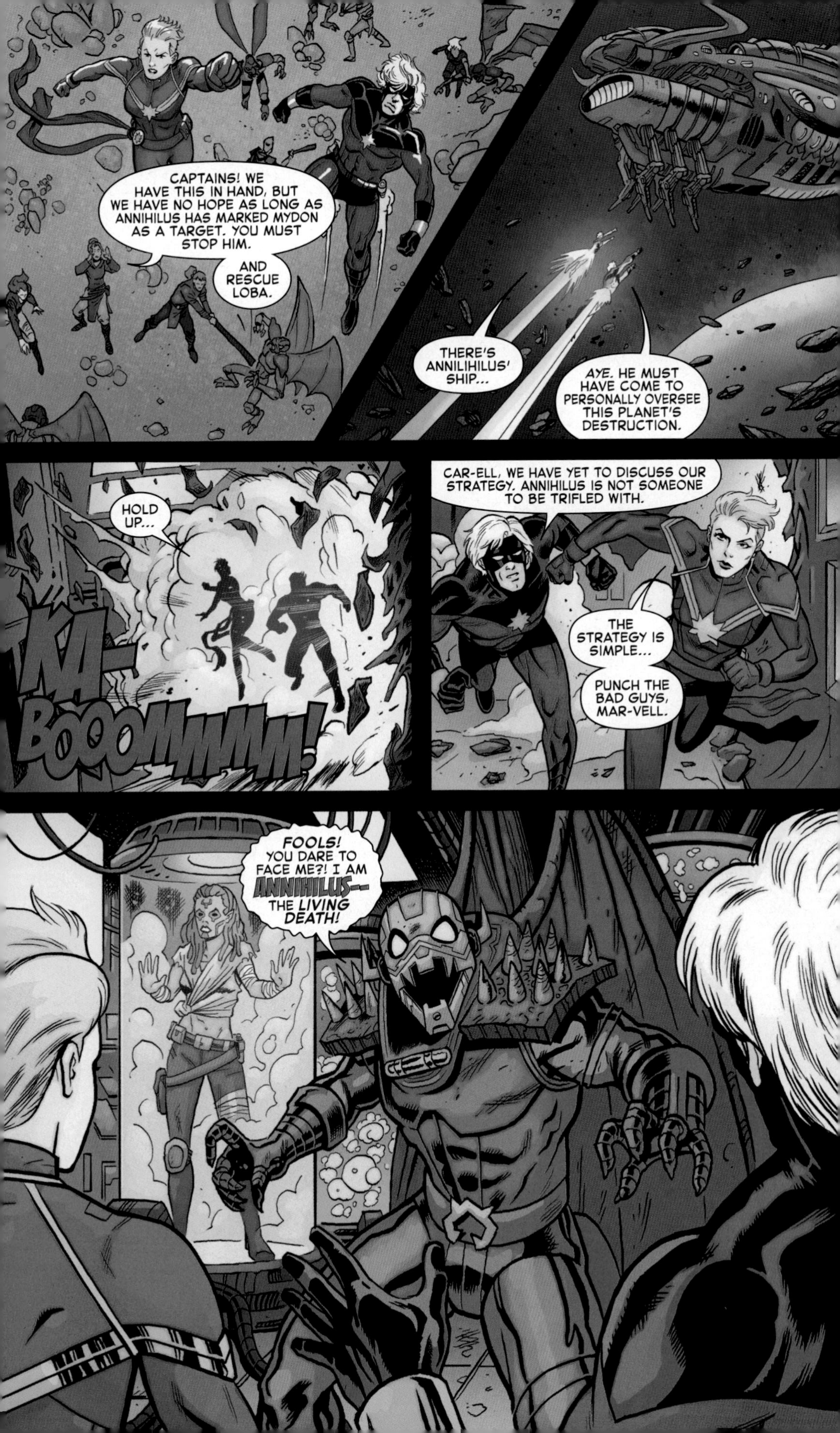
CAPTAINS! WE HAVE THIS IN HAND, BUT WE HAVE NO HOPE AS LONG AS ANNIHILUS HAS MARKED MYDON AS A TARGET. YOU MUST STOP HIM.
AND RESCUE LOBA.
THERE'S ANNILIHILUS' SHIP...
AYE. HE MUST HAVE COME TO PERSONALLY OVERSEE THIS PLANET'S DESTRUCTION.
HOLD UP...
KA-BOOOMMMMM!
CAR-ELL, WE HAVE YET TO DISCUSS OUR STRATEGY. ANNIHILUS IS NOT SOMEONE TO BE TRIFLED WITH.
THE STRATEGY IS SIMPLE...
PUNCH THE BAD GUYS, MAR-VELL.
FOOLS! YOU DARE TO FACE ME?! I AM ANNIHILUS-- THE LIVING DEATH!

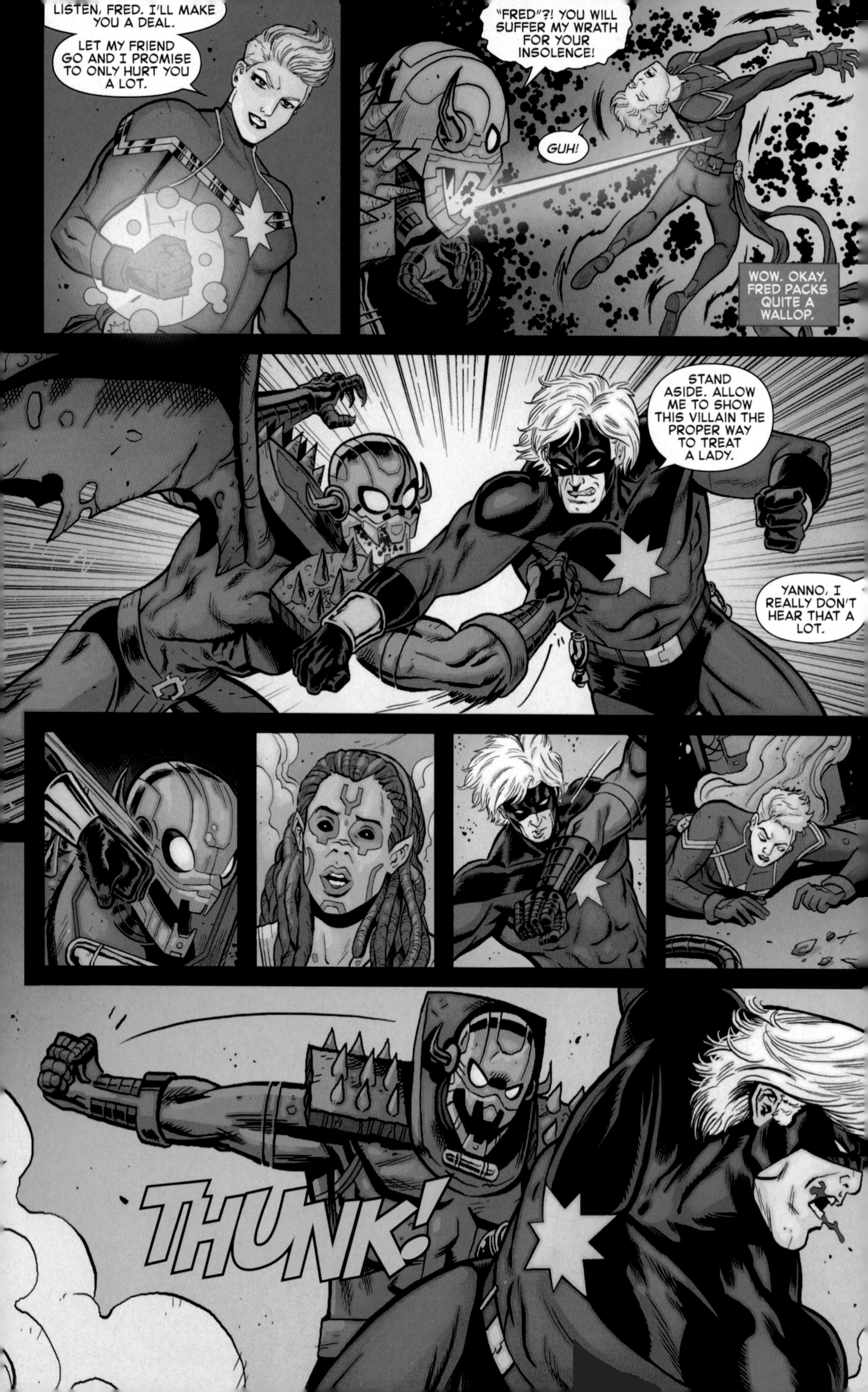

LISTEN, FRED. I'LL MAKE YOU A DEAL.
LET MY FRIEND GO AND I PROMISE TO ONLY HURT YOU A LOT.
"FRED"?! YOU WILL SUFFER MY WRATH FOR YOUR INSOLENCE!
GUH!
WOW. OKAY. FRED PACKS QUITE A WALLOP.
STAND ASIDE. ALLOW ME TO SHOW THIS VILLAIN THE PROPER WAY TO TREAT A LADY.
YANNO, I REALLY DON'T HEAR THAT A LOT.
THUNK!

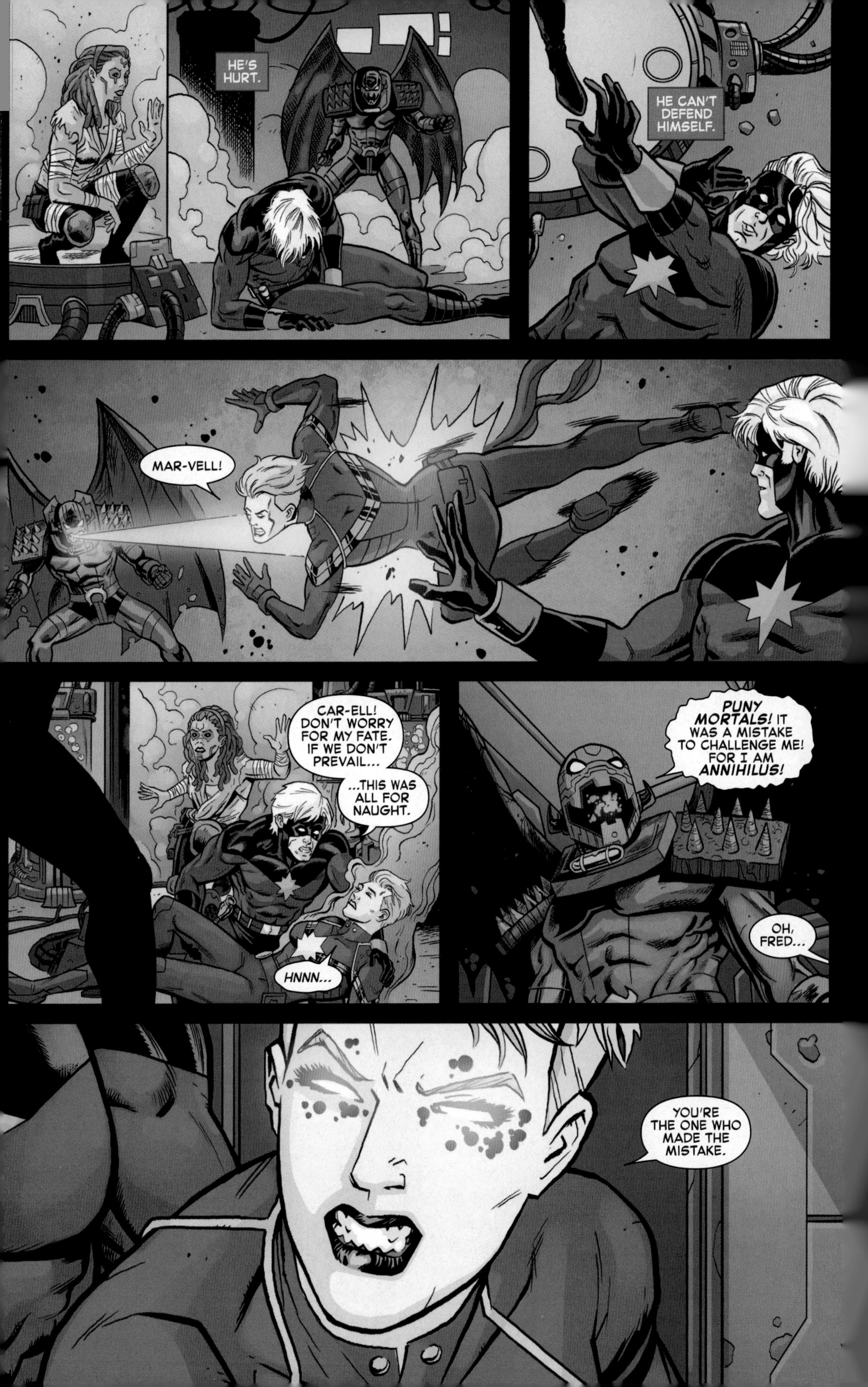
HE'S HURT.
HE CAN'T DEFEND HIMSELF.
MAR-VELL!
CAR-ELL! DON'T WORRY FOR MY FATE. IF WE DON'T PREVAIL...
...THIS WAS ALL FOR NAUGHT.
HNNN...
PUNY MORTALS! IT WAS A MISTAKE TO CHALLENGE ME! FOR I AM ANNIHILUS!
OH, FRED...
YOU'RE THE ONE WHO MADE THE MISTAKE.

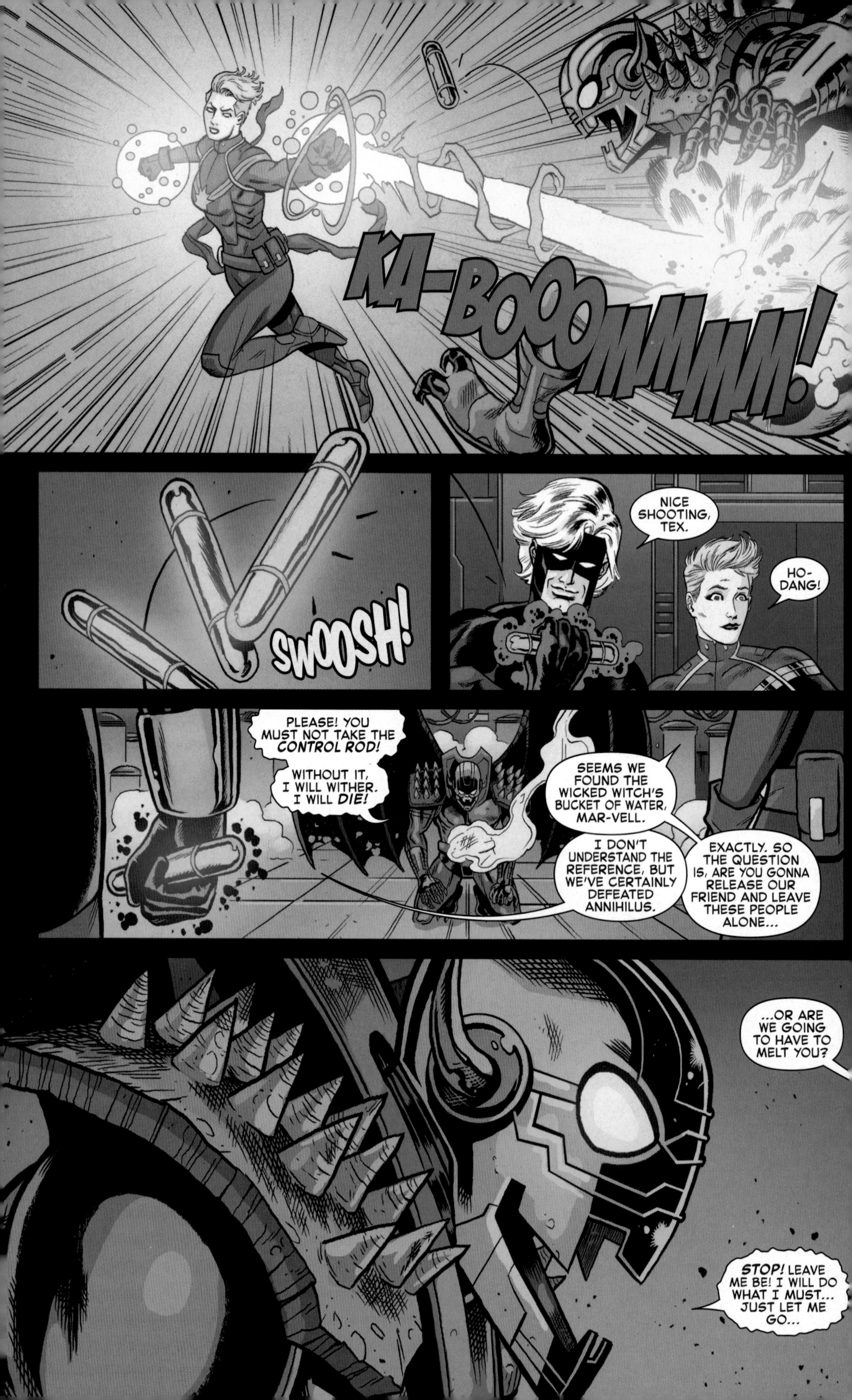
KA-BOOOMMMMM!
SWOOSH!
NICE SHOOTING, TEX.
HO-DANG!
PLEASE! YOU MUST NOT TAKE THE *CONTROL ROD!*
WITHOUT IT, I WILL WITHER. I WILL *DIE!*
SEEMS WE FOUND THE WICKED WITCH'S BUCKET OF WATER, MAR-VELL.
I DON'T UNDERSTAND THE REFERENCE, BUT WE'VE CERTAINLY DEFEATED ANNIHILUS.
EXACTLY. SO THE QUESTION IS, ARE YOU GONNA RELEASE OUR FRIEND AND LEAVE THESE PEOPLE ALONE...
...OR ARE WE GOING TO HAVE TO MELT YOU?
*STOP!* LEAVE ME BE! I WILL DO WHAT I MUST... JUST LET ME GO...

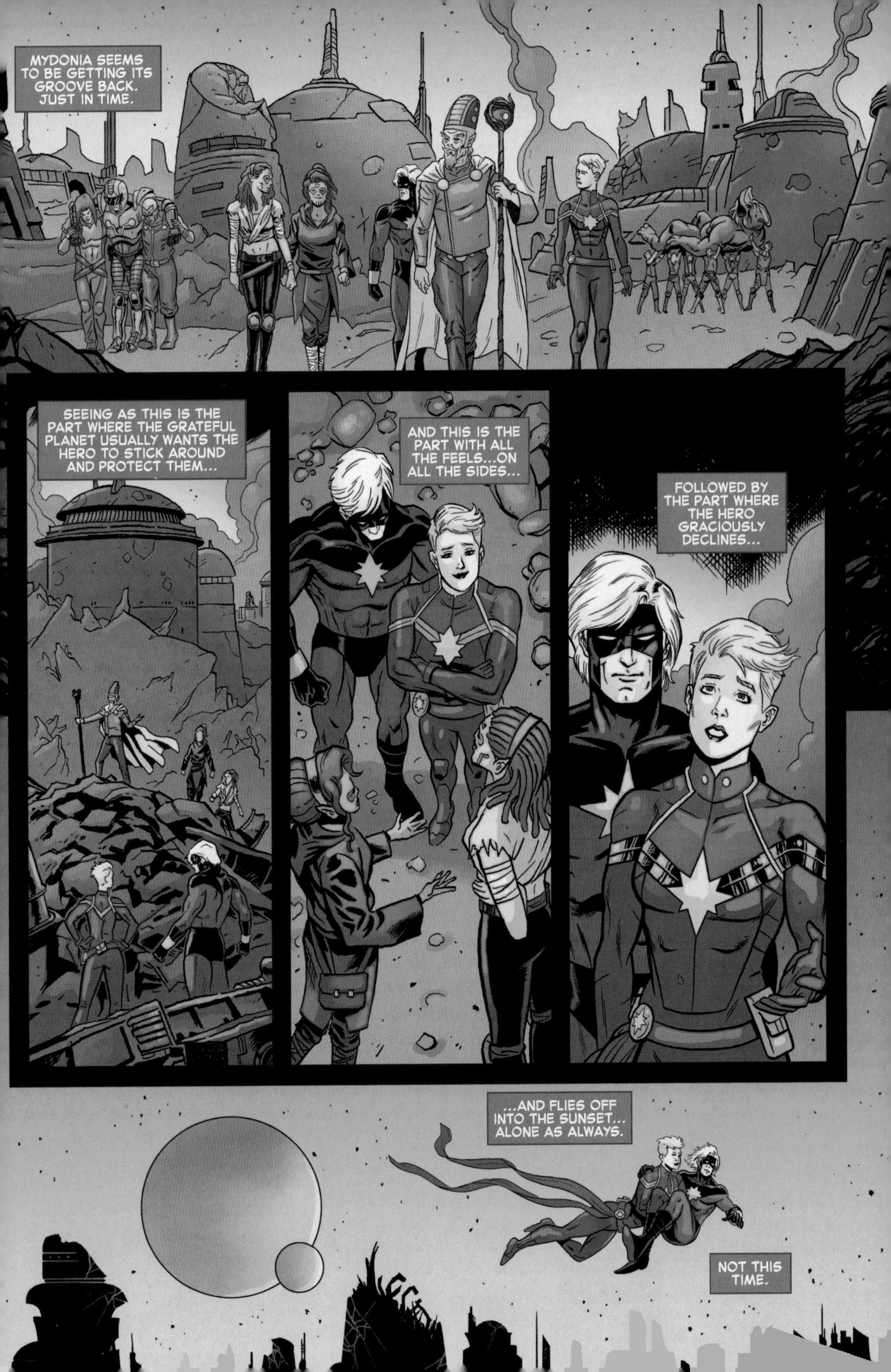
MYDONIA SEEMS TO BE GETTING ITS GROOVE BACK. JUST IN TIME.
SEEING AS THIS IS THE PART WHERE THE GRATEFUL PLANET USUALLY WANTS THE HERO TO STICK AROUND AND PROTECT THEM...
AND THIS IS THE PART WITH ALL THE FEELS...ON ALL THE SIDES...
FOLLOWED BY THE PART WHERE THE HERO GRACIOUSLY DECLINES...
...AND FLIES OFF INTO THE SUNSET... ALONE AS ALWAYS.
NOT THIS TIME.

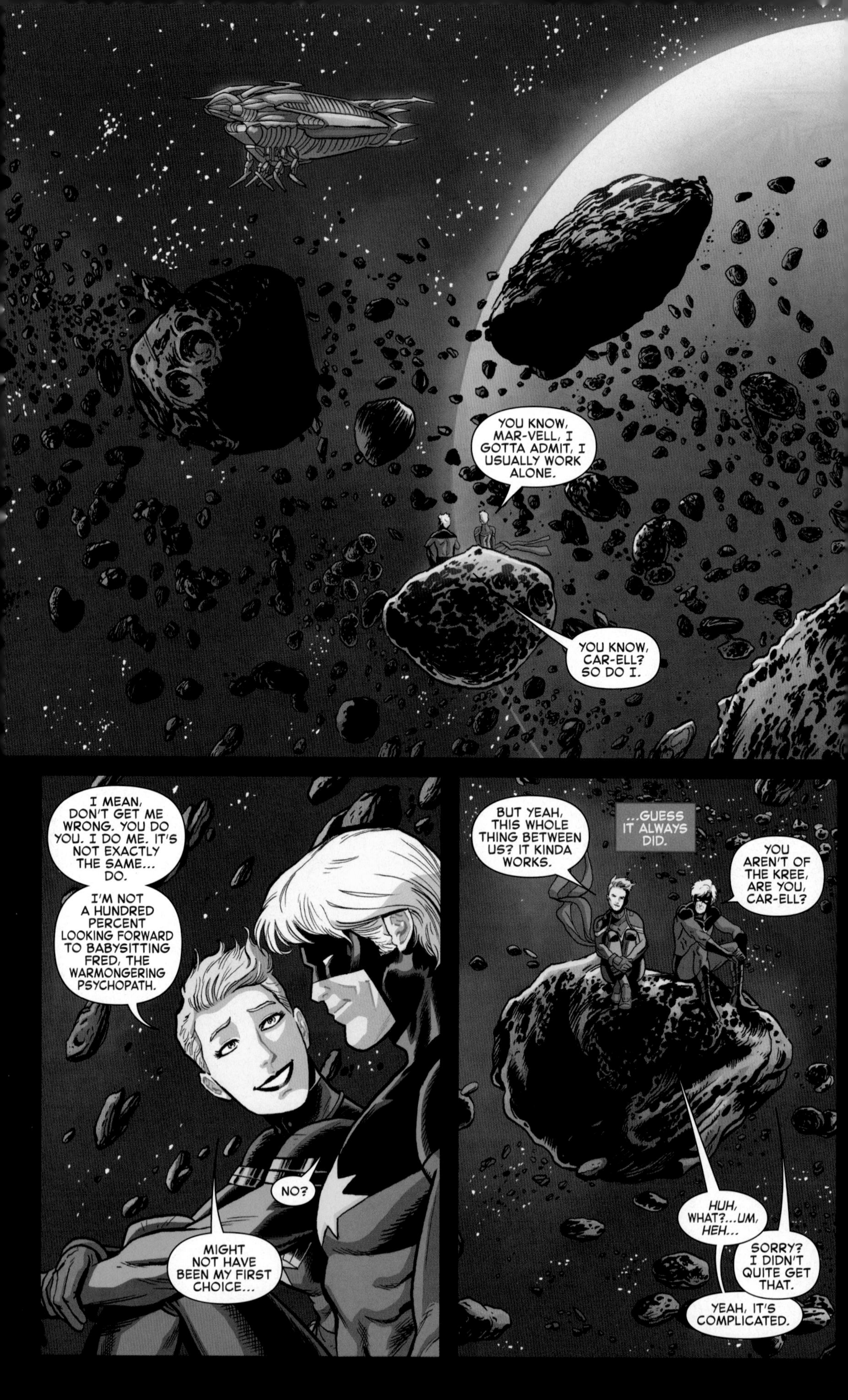
YOU KNOW, MAR-VELL, I GOTTA ADMIT, I USUALLY WORK ALONE.
YOU KNOW, CAR-ELL? SO DO I.
I MEAN, DON'T GET ME WRONG. YOU DO YOU. I DO ME. IT'S NOT EXACTLY THE SAME... DO.
I'M NOT A HUNDRED PERCENT LOOKING FORWARD TO BABYSITTING FRED, THE WARMONGERING PSYCHOPATH.
NO?
MIGHT NOT HAVE BEEN MY FIRST CHOICE...
BUT YEAH, THIS WHOLE THING BETWEEN US? IT KINDA WORKS.
...GUESS IT ALWAYS DID.
YOU AREN'T OF THE KREE, ARE YOU, CAR-ELL?
HUH, WHAT?...UM, HEH...
SORRY? I DIDN'T QUITE GET THAT.
YEAH, IT'S COMPLICATED.

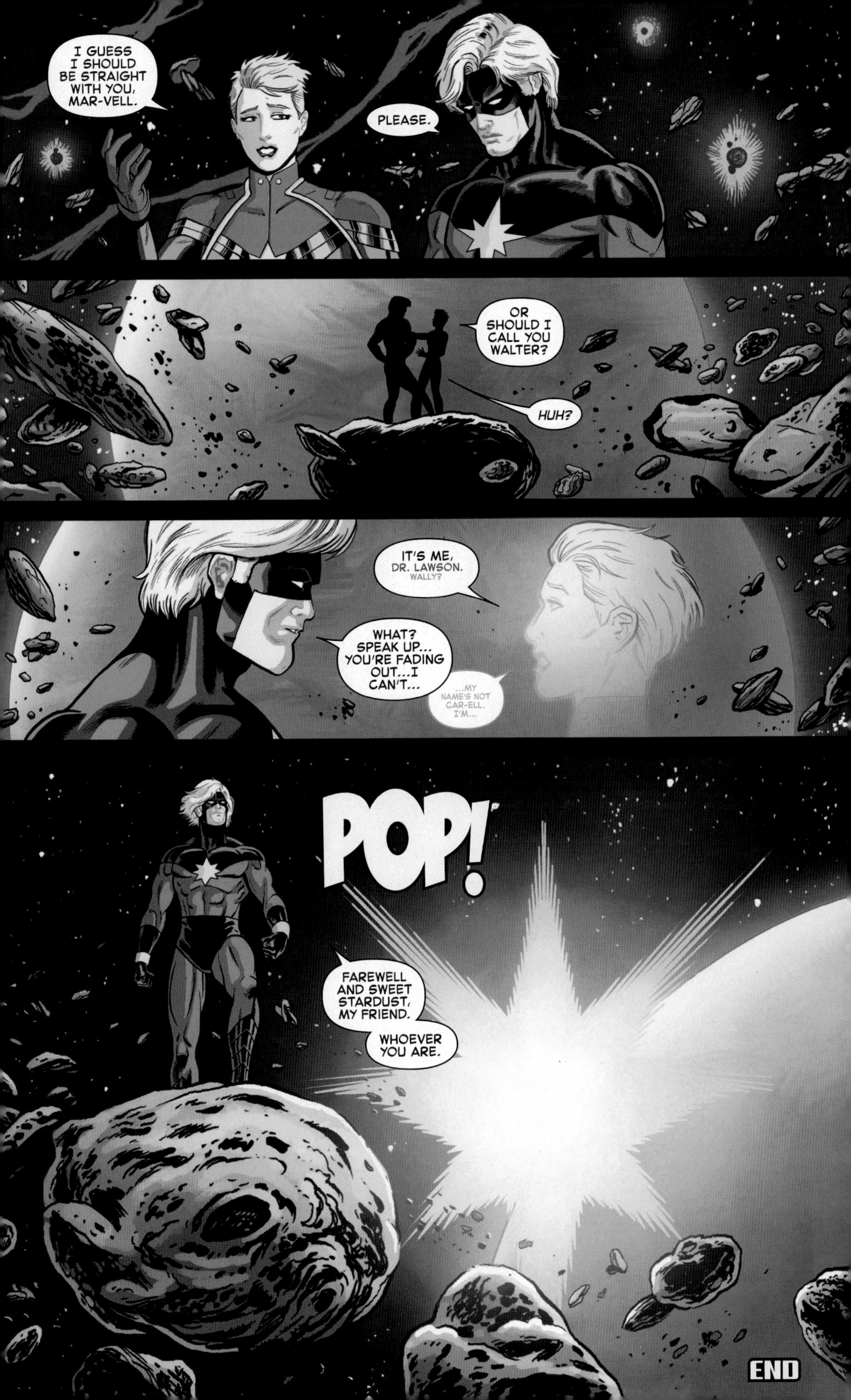
I GUESS I SHOULD BE STRAIGHT WITH YOU, MAR-VELL.
PLEASE.
OR SHOULD I CALL YOU WALTER?
HUH?
IT'S ME, DR. LAWSON. WALLY?
WHAT? SPEAK UP... YOU'RE FADING OUT...I CAN'T...
...MY NAME'S NOT CAR-ELL. I'M...
POP!
FAREWELL AND SWEET STARDUST, MY FRIEND.
WHOEVER YOU ARE.
END

DELVE INTO CAROL DANVERS' PAST IN THE FIRST CHAPTER OF MARGARET STOHL'S *THE LIFE OF CAPTAIN MARVEL*.

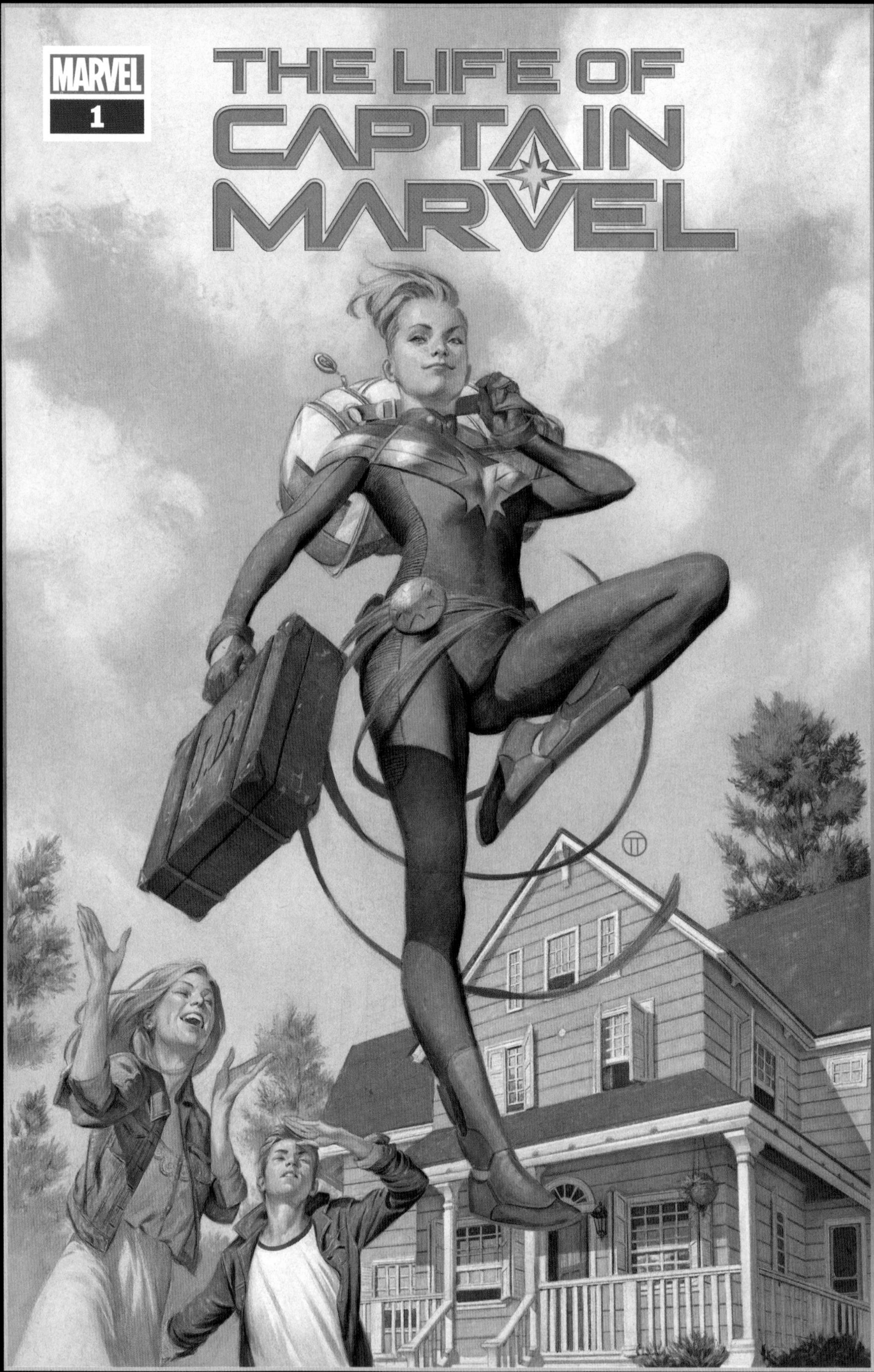
MARVEL
1
THE LIFE OF
CAPTAIN
MARVEL

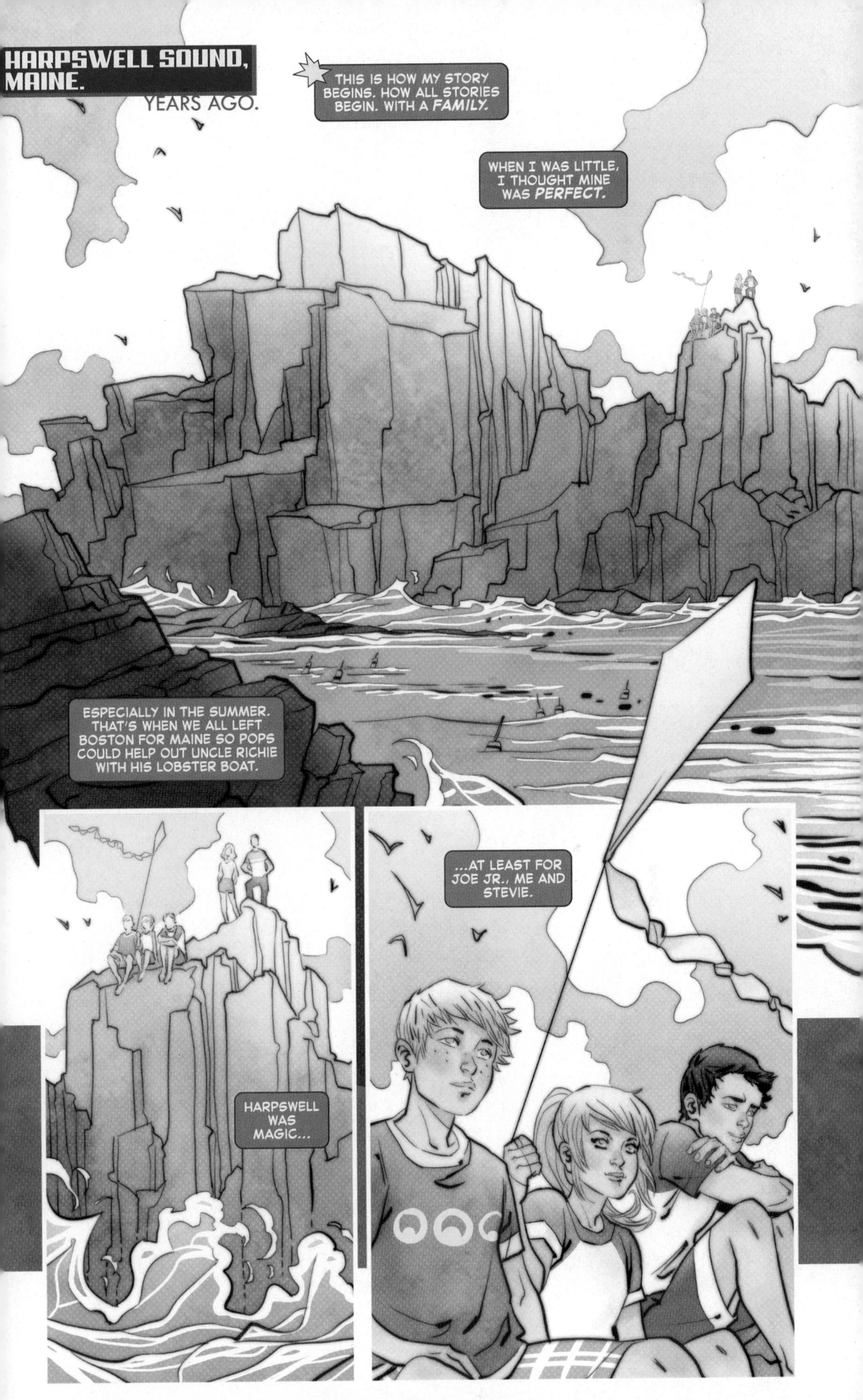

HARPSWELL SOUND, MAINE.
YEARS AGO.
THIS IS HOW MY STORY BEGINS. HOW ALL STORIES BEGIN. WITH A *FAMILY.*
WHEN I WAS LITTLE, I THOUGHT MINE WAS *PERFECT.*
ESPECIALLY IN THE SUMMER. THAT'S WHEN WE ALL LEFT BOSTON FOR MAINE SO POPS COULD HELP OUT UNCLE RICHIE WITH HIS LOBSTER BOAT.
HARPSWELL WAS MAGIC...
...AT LEAST FOR JOE JR., ME AND STEVIE.

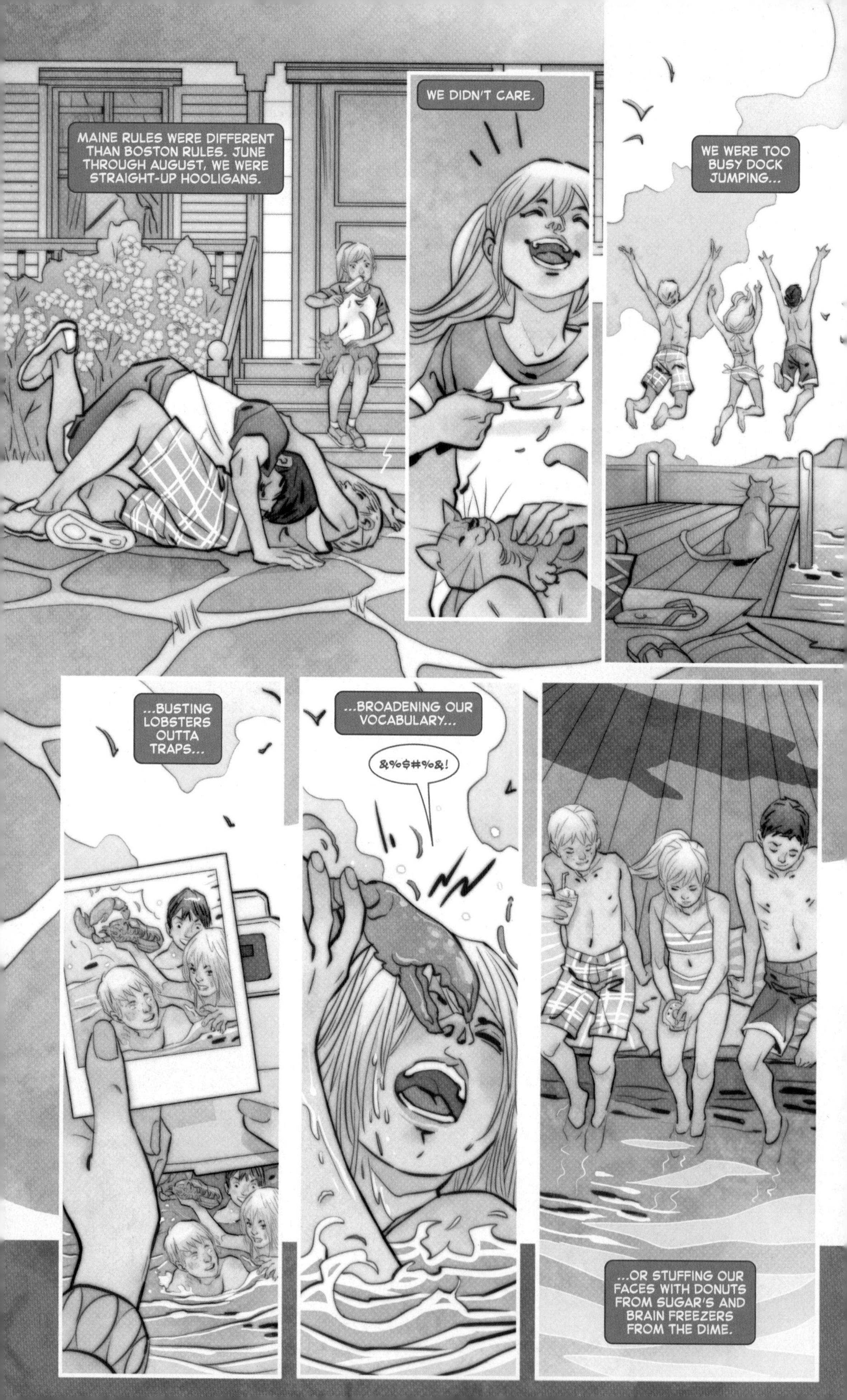
MAINE RULES WERE DIFFERENT THAN BOSTON RULES. JUNE THROUGH AUGUST, WE WERE STRAIGHT-UP HOOLIGANS.
WE DIDN'T CARE.
WE WERE TOO BUSY DOCK JUMPING...
...BUSTING LOBSTERS OUTTA TRAPS...
...BROADENING OUR VOCABULARY...
&%$#%&!
...OR STUFFING OUR FACES WITH DONUTS FROM SUGAR'S AND BRAIN FREEZERS FROM THE DIME.

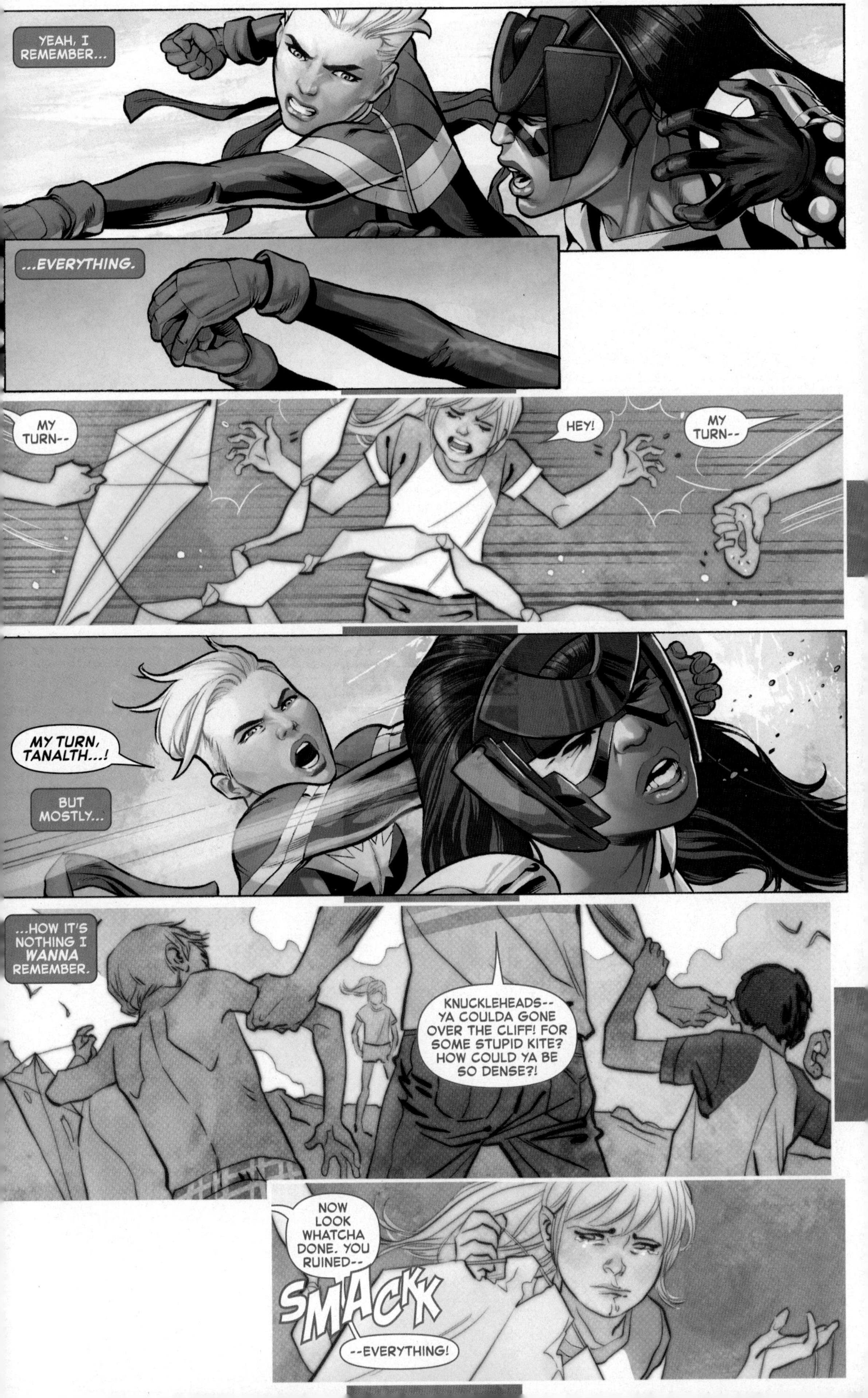
YEAH, I REMEMBER...
...EVERYTHING.
MY TURN--
HEY!
MY TURN--
MY TURN, TANALTH...!
BUT MOSTLY...
...HOW IT'S NOTHING I WANNA REMEMBER.
KNUCKLEHEADS-- YA COULDA GONE OVER THE CLIFF! FOR SOME STUPID KITE? HOW COULD YA BE SO DENSE?!
NOW LOOK WHATCHA DONE. YOU RUINED--
SMACKK
--EVERYTHING!

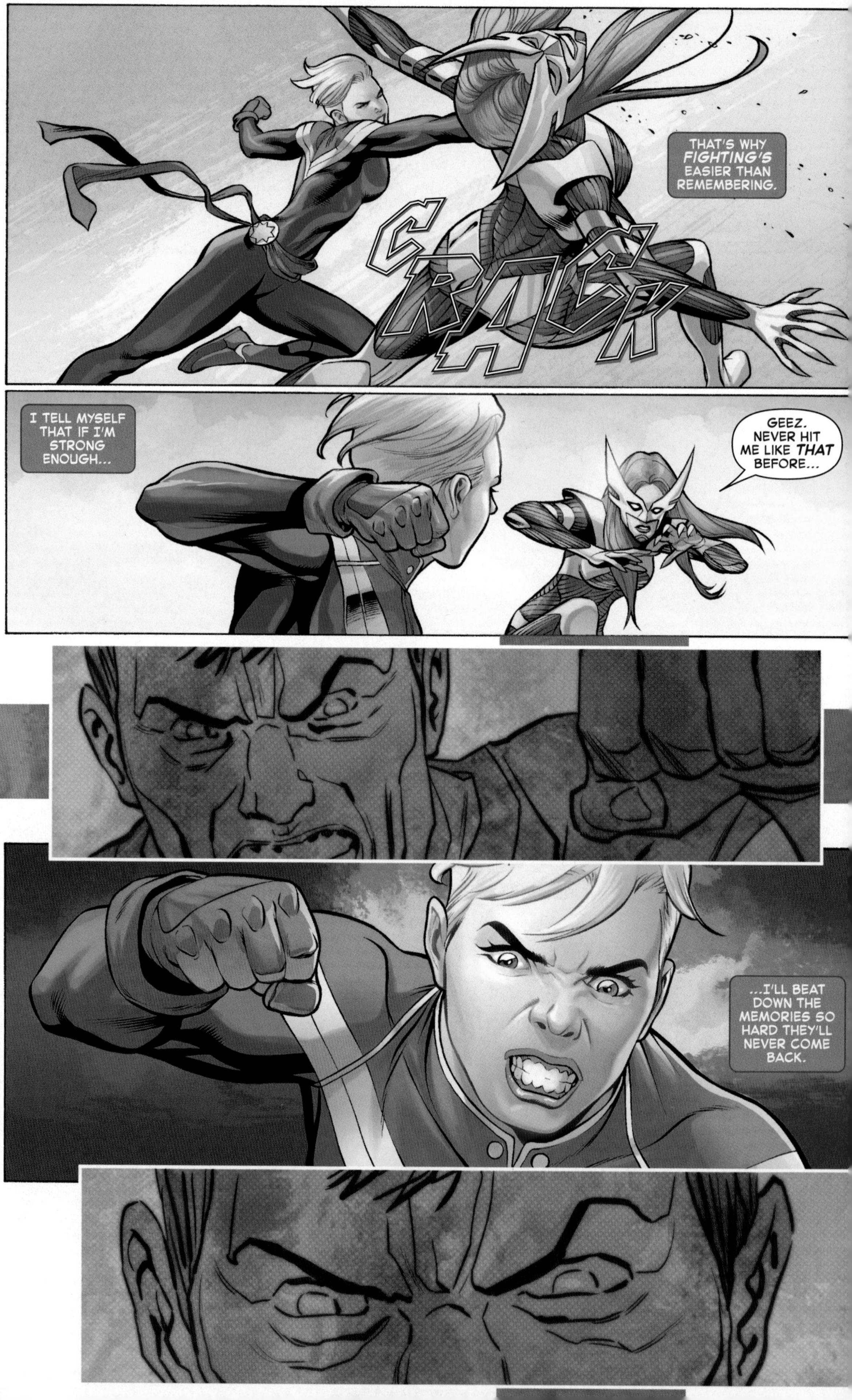
THAT'S WHY FIGHTING'S EASIER THAN REMEMBERING.
CRACK
I TELL MYSELF THAT IF I'M STRONG ENOUGH...
GEEZ. NEVER HIT ME LIKE THAT BEFORE...
...I'LL BEAT DOWN THE MEMORIES SO HARD THEY'LL NEVER COME BACK.

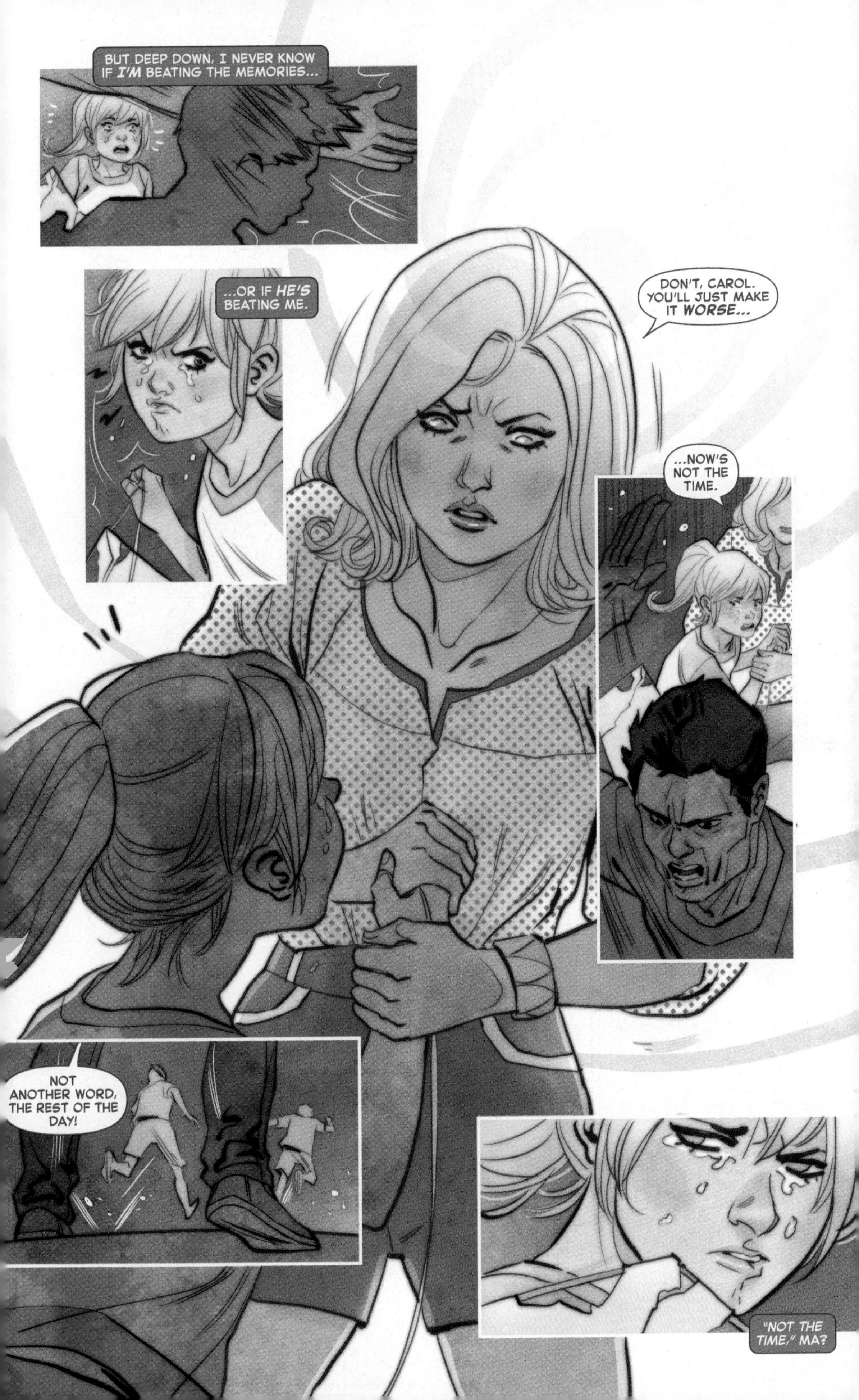
BUT DEEP DOWN, I NEVER KNOW IF I'M BEATING THE MEMORIES...
...OR IF HE'S BEATING ME.
DON'T, CAROL. YOU'LL JUST MAKE IT WORSE...
...NOW'S NOT THE TIME.
NOT ANOTHER WORD, THE REST OF THE DAY!
"NOT THE TIME," MA?

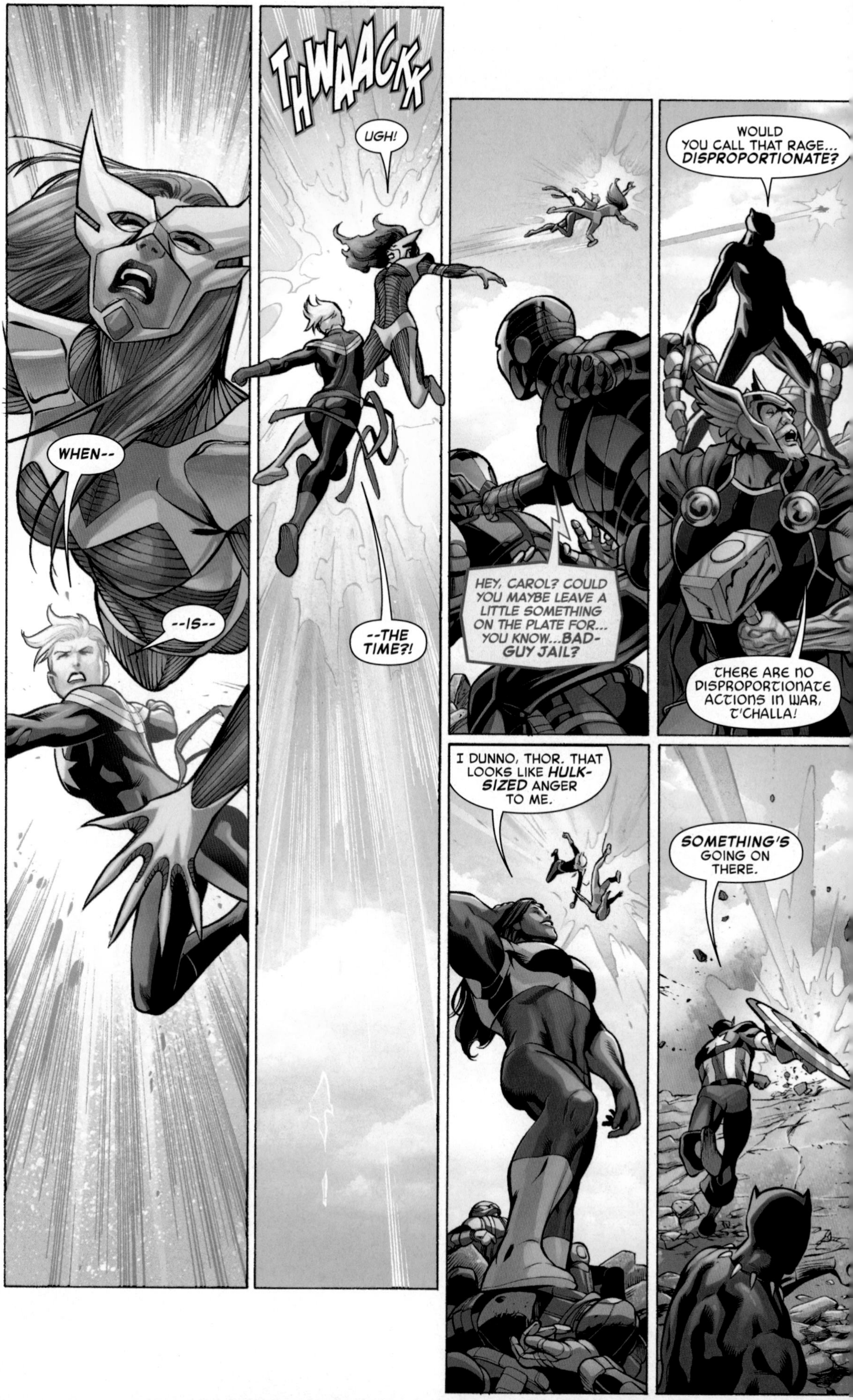

WHEN--
--IS--
THWAACKK
UGH!
--THE TIME?!
HEY, CAROL? COULD YOU MAYBE LEAVE A LITTLE SOMETHING ON THE PLATE FOR... YOU KNOW...BAD-GUY JAIL?
WOULD YOU CALL THAT RAGE... DISPROPORTIONATE?
THERE ARE NO DISPROPORTIONATE ACTIONS IN WAR, T'CHALLA!
I DUNNO, THOR. THAT LOOKS LIKE HULK-SIZED ANGER TO ME.
SOMETHING'S GOING ON THERE.

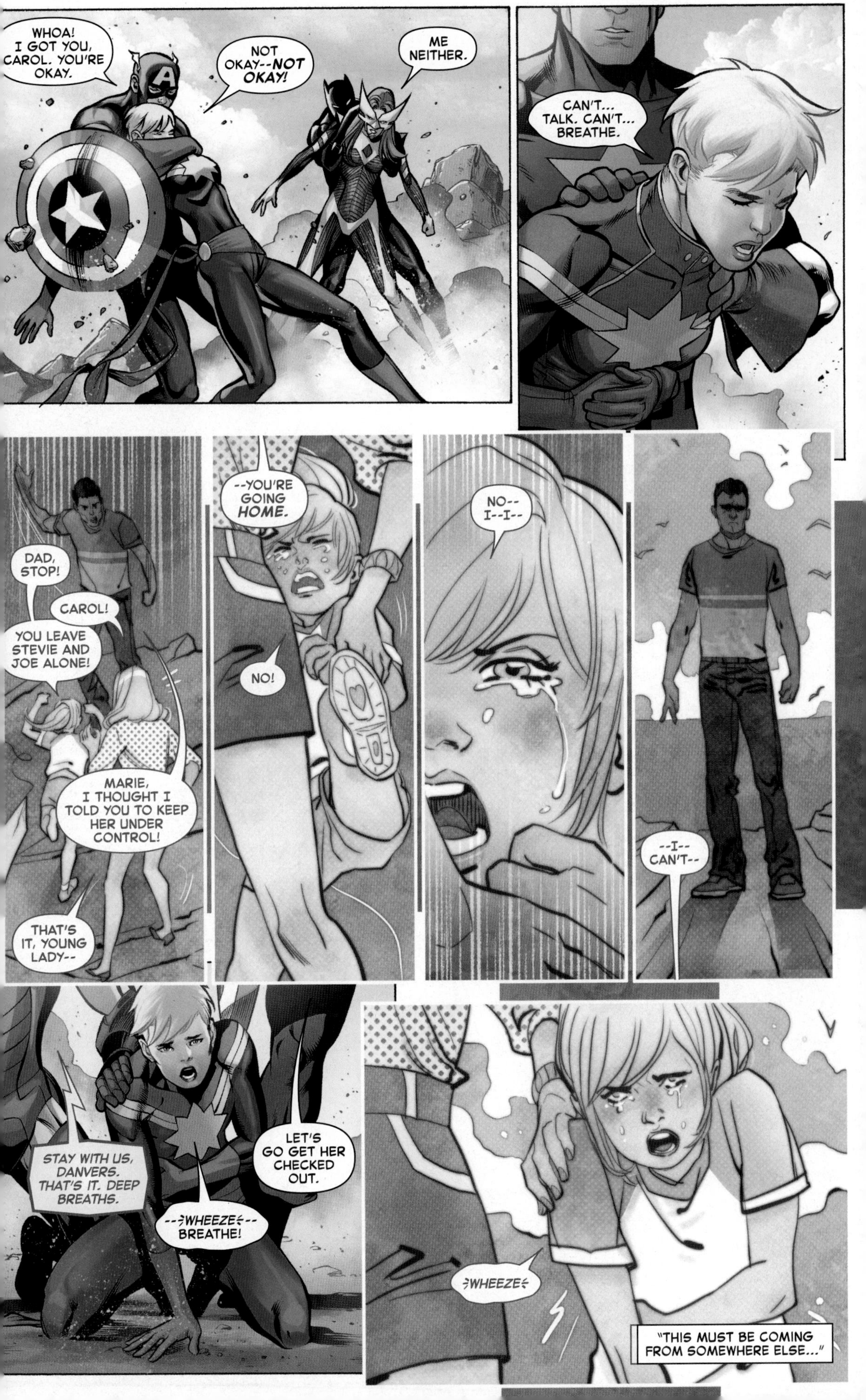
WHOA! I GOT YOU, CAROL. YOU'RE OKAY.
NOT OKAY--NOT OKAY!
ME NEITHER.
CAN'T... TALK. CAN'T... BREATHE.
DAD, STOP!
CAROL!
YOU LEAVE STEVIE AND JOE ALONE!
MARIE, I THOUGHT I TOLD YOU TO KEEP HER UNDER CONTROL!
THAT'S IT, YOUNG LADY--
--YOU'RE GOING HOME.
NO!
NO-- I--I--
--I-- CAN'T--
STAY WITH US, DANVERS. THAT'S IT. DEEP BREATHS.
--WHEEZE-- BREATHE!
LET'S GO GET HER CHECKED OUT.
WHEEZE
"THIS MUST BE COMING FROM SOMEWHERE ELSE..."

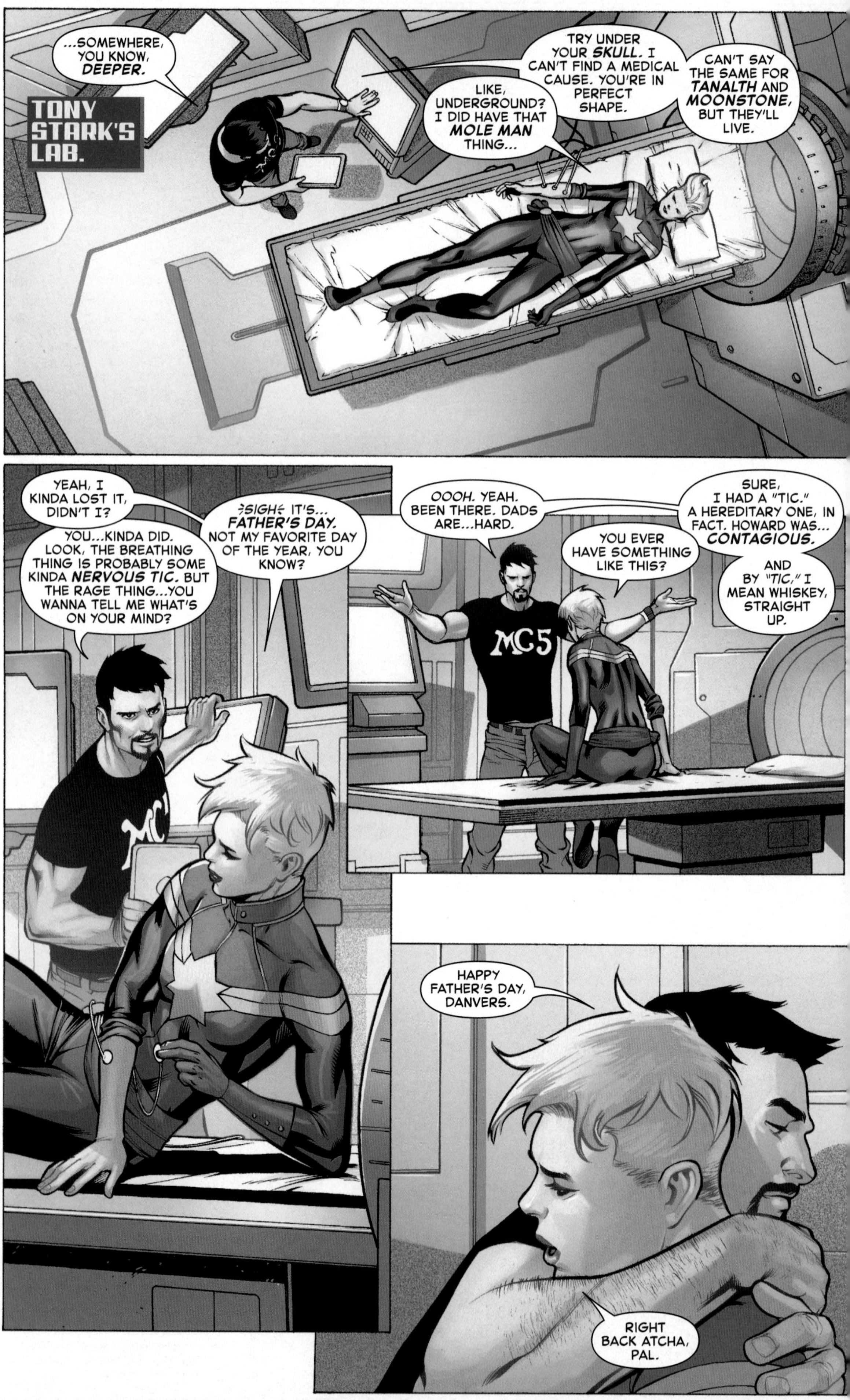

TONY STARK'S LAB.
...SOMEWHERE, YOU KNOW, DEEPER.
LIKE, UNDERGROUND? I DID HAVE THAT MOLE MAN THING...
TRY UNDER YOUR SKULL. I CAN'T FIND A MEDICAL CAUSE. YOU'RE IN PERFECT SHAPE.
CAN'T SAY THE SAME FOR TANALTH AND MOONSTONE, BUT THEY'LL LIVE.
YEAH, I KINDA LOST IT, DIDN'T I?
YOU...KINDA DID. LOOK, THE BREATHING THING IS PROBABLY SOME KINDA NERVOUS TIC. BUT THE RAGE THING...YOU WANNA TELL ME WHAT'S ON YOUR MIND?
⇒SIGH⇐ IT'S... FATHER'S DAY. NOT MY FAVORITE DAY OF THE YEAR, YOU KNOW?
OOOH. YEAH. BEEN THERE. DADS ARE...HARD.
YOU EVER HAVE SOMETHING LIKE THIS?
SURE, I HAD A "TIC." A HEREDITARY ONE, IN FACT. HOWARD WAS... CONTAGIOUS.
AND BY "TIC," I MEAN WHISKEY, STRAIGHT UP.
HAPPY FATHER'S DAY, DANVERS.
RIGHT BACK ATCHA, PAL.

# THE LIFE OF CAPTAIN MARVEL

When former U.S. Air Force pilot Carol Danvers was caught in the explosion of an alien device, she was transformed into one of the world's most powerful super-beings. Now, she's an Avenger and Earth's mightiest hero.

But before all that, Carol Danvers was just a girl from New England. This is her story.

## PART ONE: "TRAPPED"

| WRITER | PENCILER PRESENT DAY | INKER PRESENT DAY | COLORIST PRESENT DAY | ARTIST FLASHBACKS |
|---|---|---|---|---|
| MARGARET STOHL | CARLOS PACHECO | RAFAEL FONTERIZ | MARCIO MENYZ | MARGUERITE SAUVAGE |

| LETTERER | COVER ARTIST | VARIANT COVER ARTISTS |
|---|---|---|
| VC's CLAYTON COWLES | JULIAN TOTINO TEDESCO | JOE QUESADA & RICHARD ISANOVE; SANA TAKEDA; FIONA STAPLES; ARTGERM |

| LOGO | DESIGN | EDITOR | CONSULTING EDITOR |
|---|---|---|---|
| JAY BOWEN | NICK RUSSELL | SARAH BRUNSTAD | SANA AMANAT |

| EXECUTIVE EDITOR | EDITOR IN CHIEF | CHIEF CREATIVE OFFICER | PRESIDENT | EXECUTIVE PRODUCER | SPECIAL THANKS |
|---|---|---|---|---|---|
| TOM BREVOORT | C.B. CEBULSKI | JOE QUESADA | DAN BUCKLEY | ALAN FINE | AXEL ALONSO |

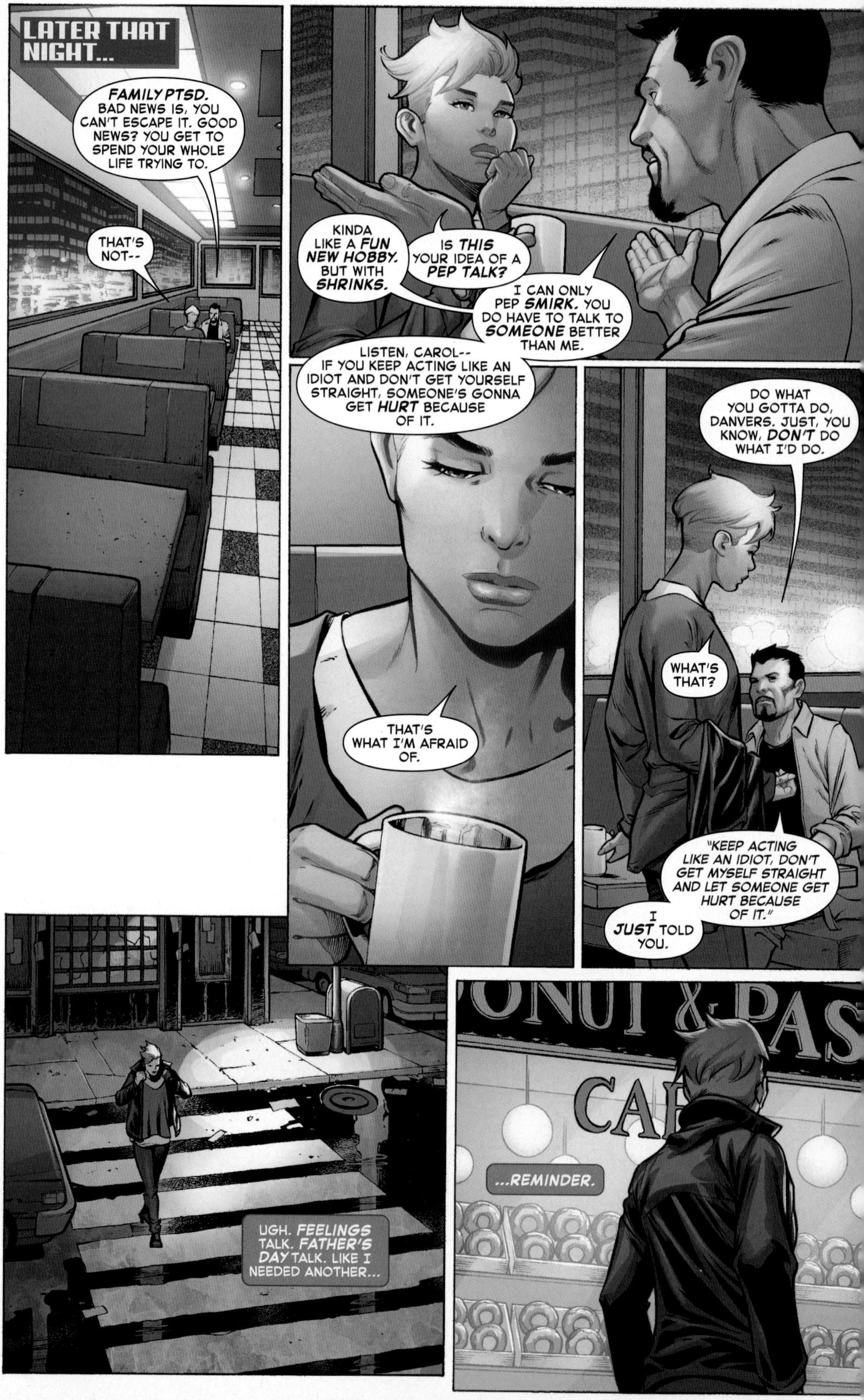
LATER THAT NIGHT...
FAMILY PTSD. BAD NEWS IS, YOU CAN'T ESCAPE IT. GOOD NEWS? YOU GET TO SPEND YOUR WHOLE LIFE TRYING TO.
THAT'S NOT--
KINDA LIKE A FUN NEW HOBBY. BUT WITH SHRINKS.
IS THIS YOUR IDEA OF A PEP TALK?
I CAN ONLY PEP SMIRK. YOU DO HAVE TO TALK TO SOMEONE BETTER THAN ME.
LISTEN, CAROL-- IF YOU KEEP ACTING LIKE AN IDIOT AND DON'T GET YOURSELF STRAIGHT, SOMEONE'S GONNA GET HURT BECAUSE OF IT.
THAT'S WHAT I'M AFRAID OF.
DO WHAT YOU GOTTA DO, DANVERS. JUST, YOU KNOW, DON'T DO WHAT I'D DO.
WHAT'S THAT?
"KEEP ACTING LIKE AN IDIOT, DON'T GET MYSELF STRAIGHT AND LET SOMEONE GET HURT BECAUSE OF IT."
I JUST TOLD YOU.
UGH. FEELINGS TALK. FATHER'S DAY TALK. LIKE I NEEDED ANOTHER...
...REMINDER.
CAF

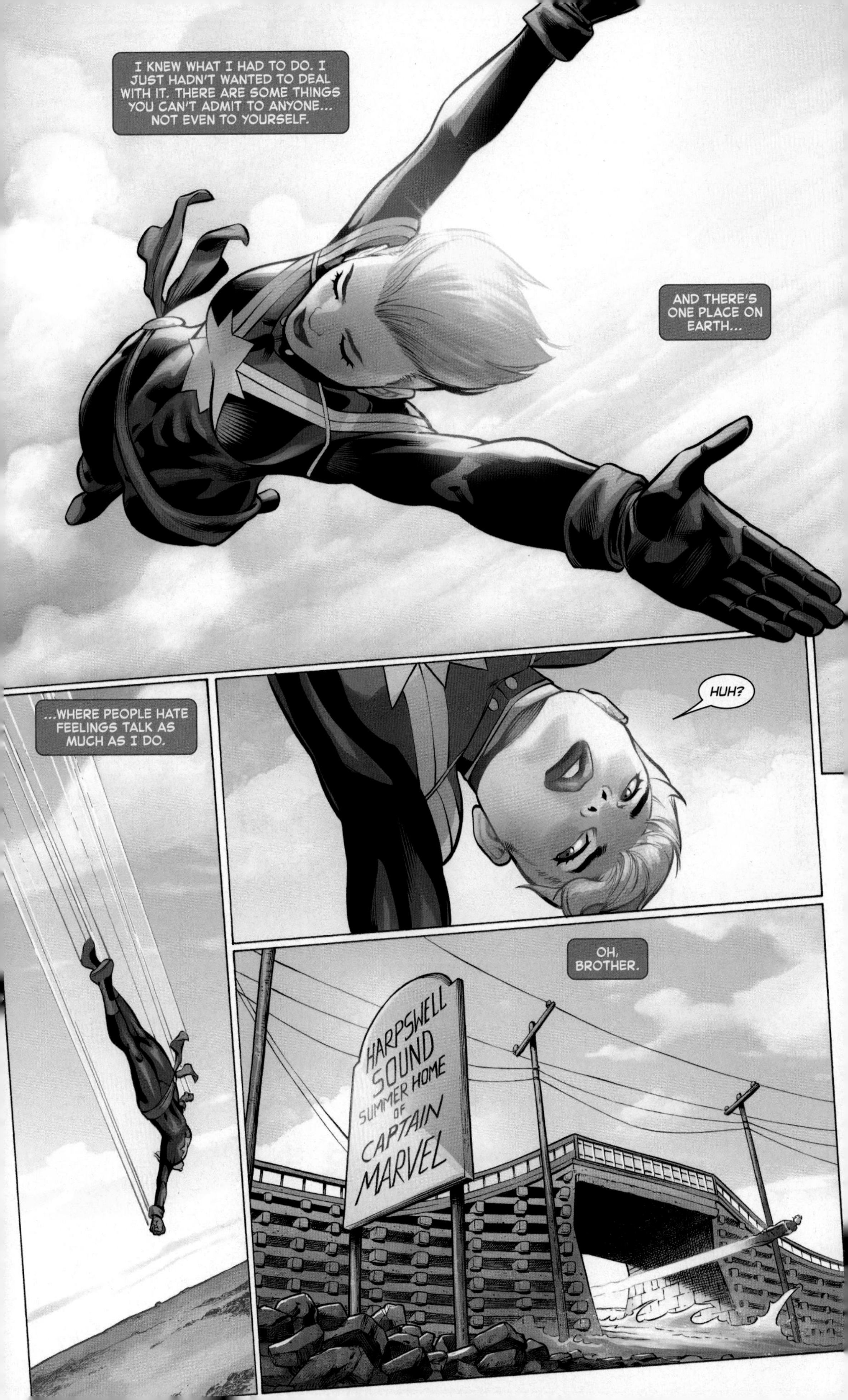

I KNEW WHAT I HAD TO DO. I JUST HADN'T WANTED TO DEAL WITH IT. THERE ARE SOME THINGS YOU CAN'T ADMIT TO ANYONE... NOT EVEN TO YOURSELF.
AND THERE'S ONE PLACE ON EARTH...
...WHERE PEOPLE HATE FEELINGS TALK AS MUCH AS I DO.
HUH?
OH, BROTHER.
HARPSWELL SOUND SUMMER HOME OF CAPTAIN MARVEL

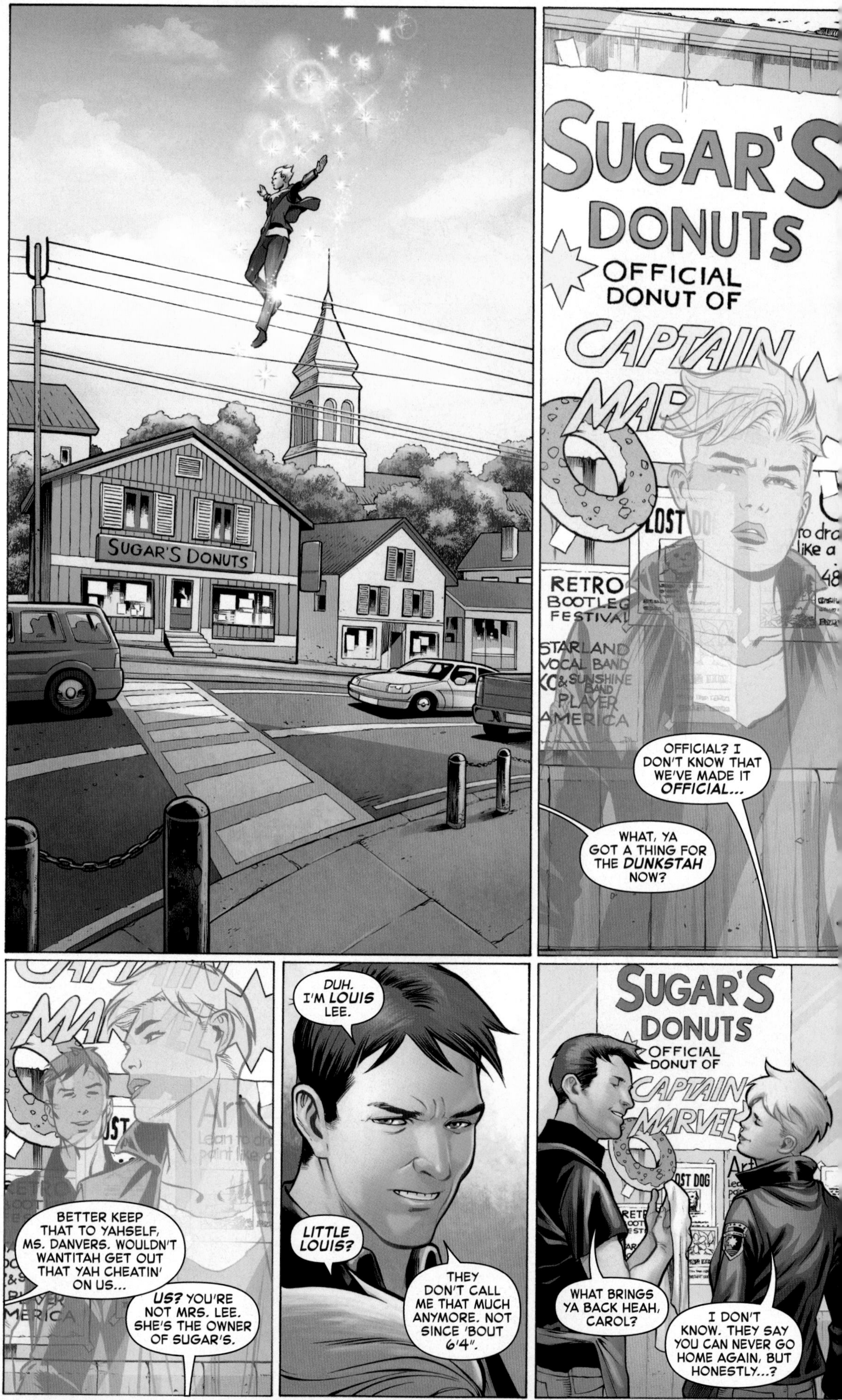

SUGAR'S DONUTS
SUGAR'S DONUTS
OFFICIAL DONUT OF
CAPTAIN
LOST
RETRO BOOTLEG FESTIVAL
STARLAND VOCAL BAND
KC & SUNSHINE BAND
PLAYER
AMERICA
OFFICIAL? I DON'T KNOW THAT WE'VE MADE IT *OFFICIAL...*
WHAT, YA GOT A THING FOR THE *DUNKSTAH* NOW?
BETTER KEEP THAT TO YAHSELF, MS. DANVERS. WOULDN'T WANTITAH GET OUT THAT YAH CHEATIN' ON US...
*US?* YOU'RE NOT MRS. LEE. SHE'S THE OWNER OF SUGAR'S.
DUH. I'M *LOUIS* LEE.
*LITTLE LOUIS?*
THEY DON'T CALL ME THAT MUCH ANYMORE. NOT SINCE 'BOUT 6'4".
SUGAR'S DONUTS
OFFICIAL DONUT OF
CAPTAIN MARVEL
LOST DOG
WHAT BRINGS YA BACK HEAH, CAROL?
I DON'T KNOW. THEY SAY YOU CAN NEVER GO HOME AGAIN, BUT HONESTLY...?

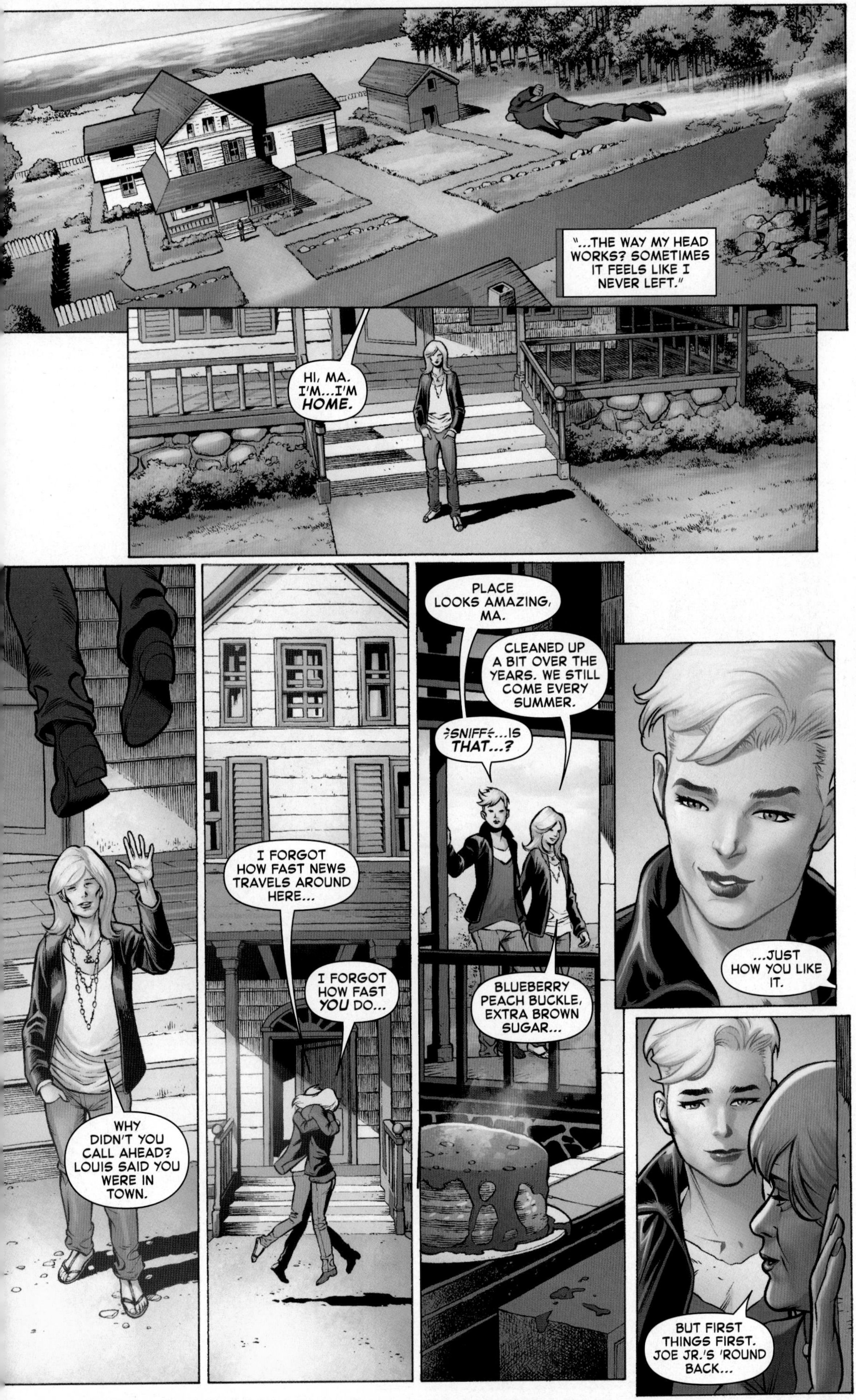
"...THE WAY MY HEAD WORKS? SOMETIMES IT FEELS LIKE I NEVER LEFT."
HI, MA. I'M...I'M HOME.
WHY DIDN'T YOU CALL AHEAD? LOUIS SAID YOU WERE IN TOWN.
I FORGOT HOW FAST NEWS TRAVELS AROUND HERE...
I FORGOT HOW FAST YOU DO...
PLACE LOOKS AMAZING, MA.
CLEANED UP A BIT OVER THE YEARS. WE STILL COME EVERY SUMMER.
SNIFF...IS THAT...?
BLUEBERRY PEACH BUCKLE, EXTRA BROWN SUGAR...
...JUST HOW YOU LIKE IT.
BUT FIRST THINGS FIRST. JOE JR.'S 'ROUND BACK...

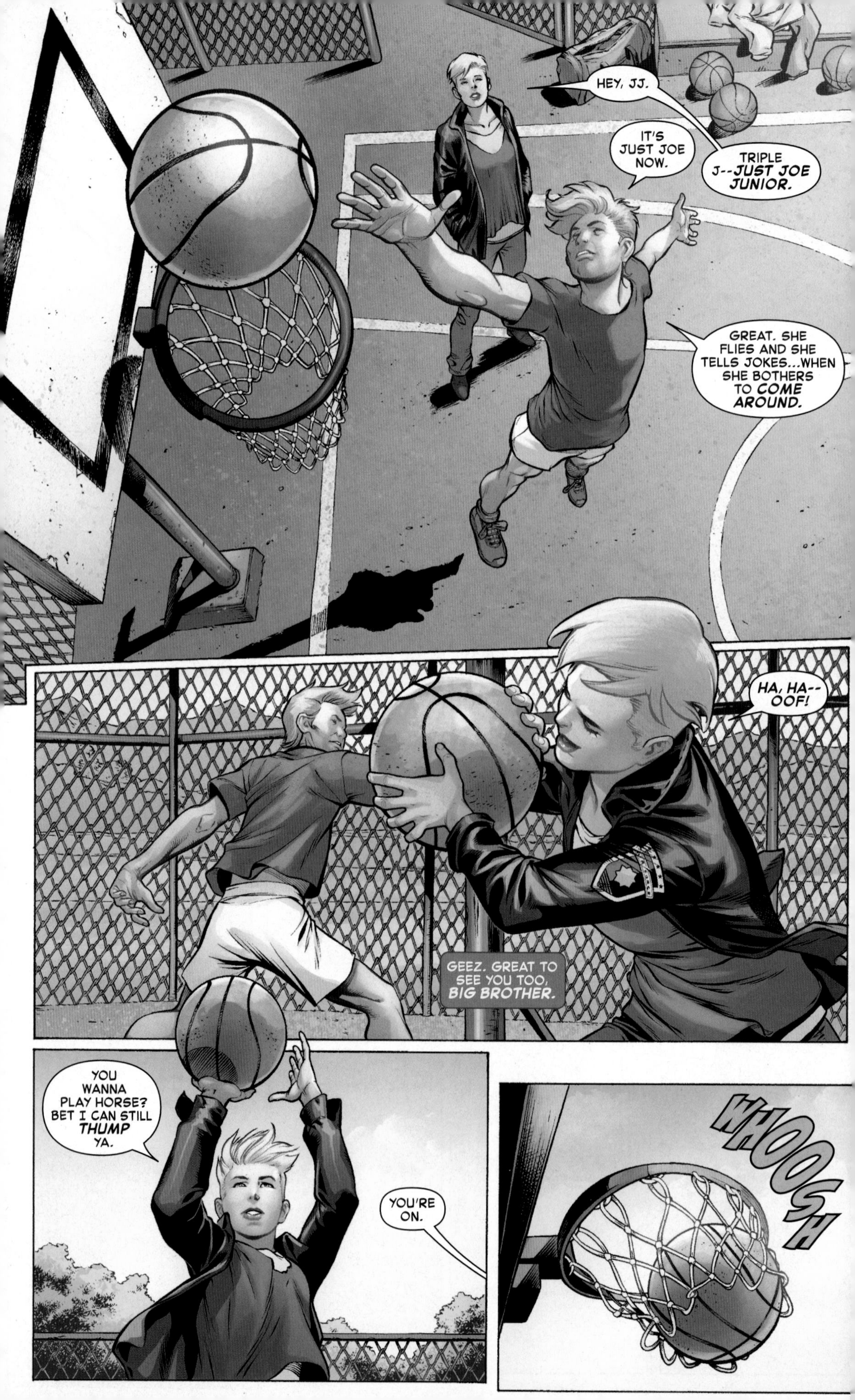
HEY, JJ.
IT'S JUST JOE NOW.
TRIPLE J--JUST JOE JUNIOR.
GREAT. SHE FLIES AND SHE TELLS JOKES...WHEN SHE BOTHERS TO COME AROUND.
HA, HA--OOF!
GEEZ. GREAT TO SEE YOU TOO, BIG BROTHER.
YOU WANNA PLAY HORSE? BET I CAN STILL THUMP YA.
YOU'RE ON.
WHOOSH

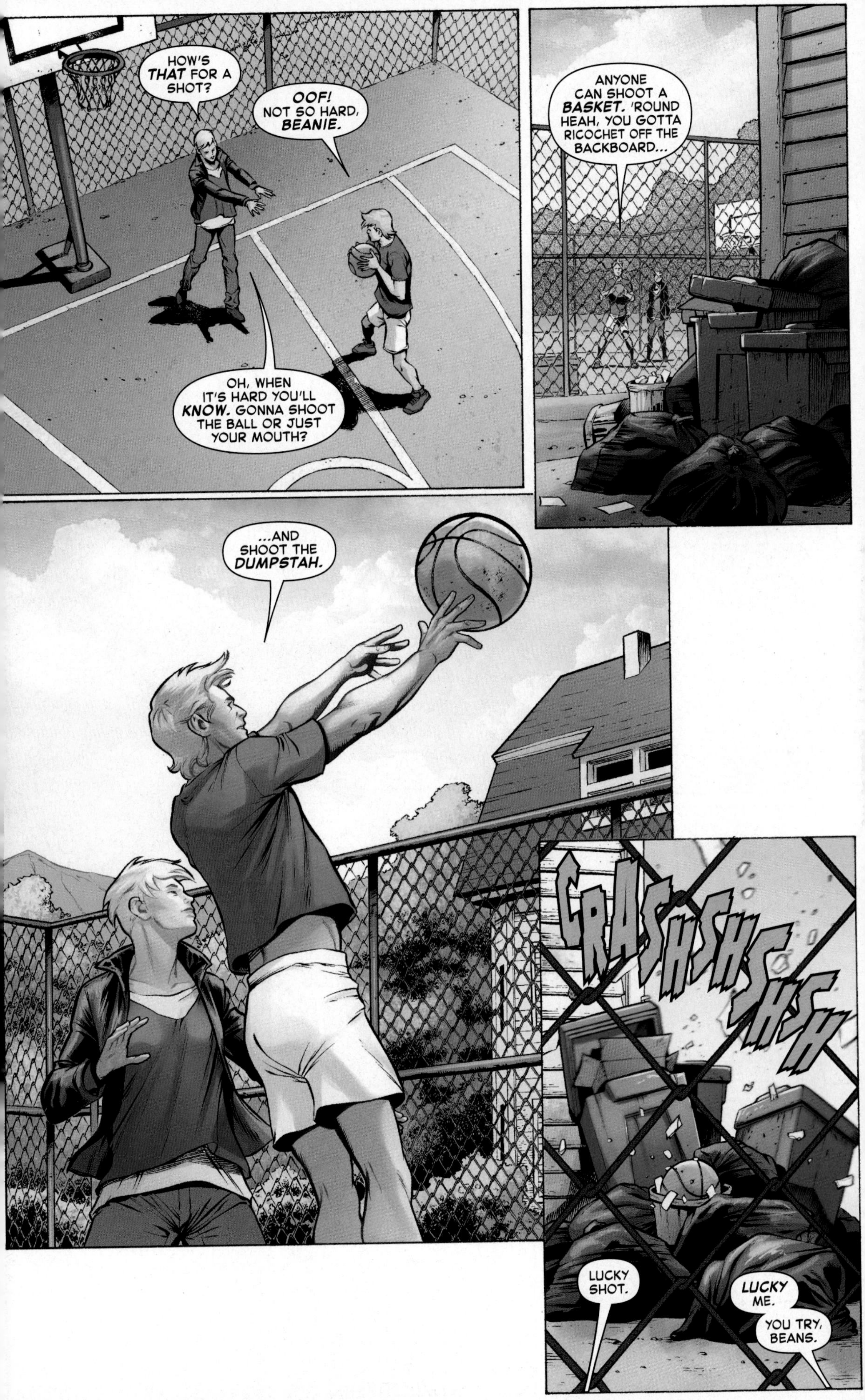

HOW'S THAT FOR A SHOT?
OOF! NOT SO HARD, BEANIE.
OH, WHEN IT'S HARD YOU'LL KNOW. GONNA SHOOT THE BALL OR JUST YOUR MOUTH?
ANYONE CAN SHOOT A BASKET. 'ROUND HEAH, YOU GOTTA RICOCHET OFF THE BACKBOARD...
...AND SHOOT THE DUMPSTAH.
CRASHSHSHSHSH
LUCKY SHOT.
LUCKY ME.
YOU TRY, BEANS.

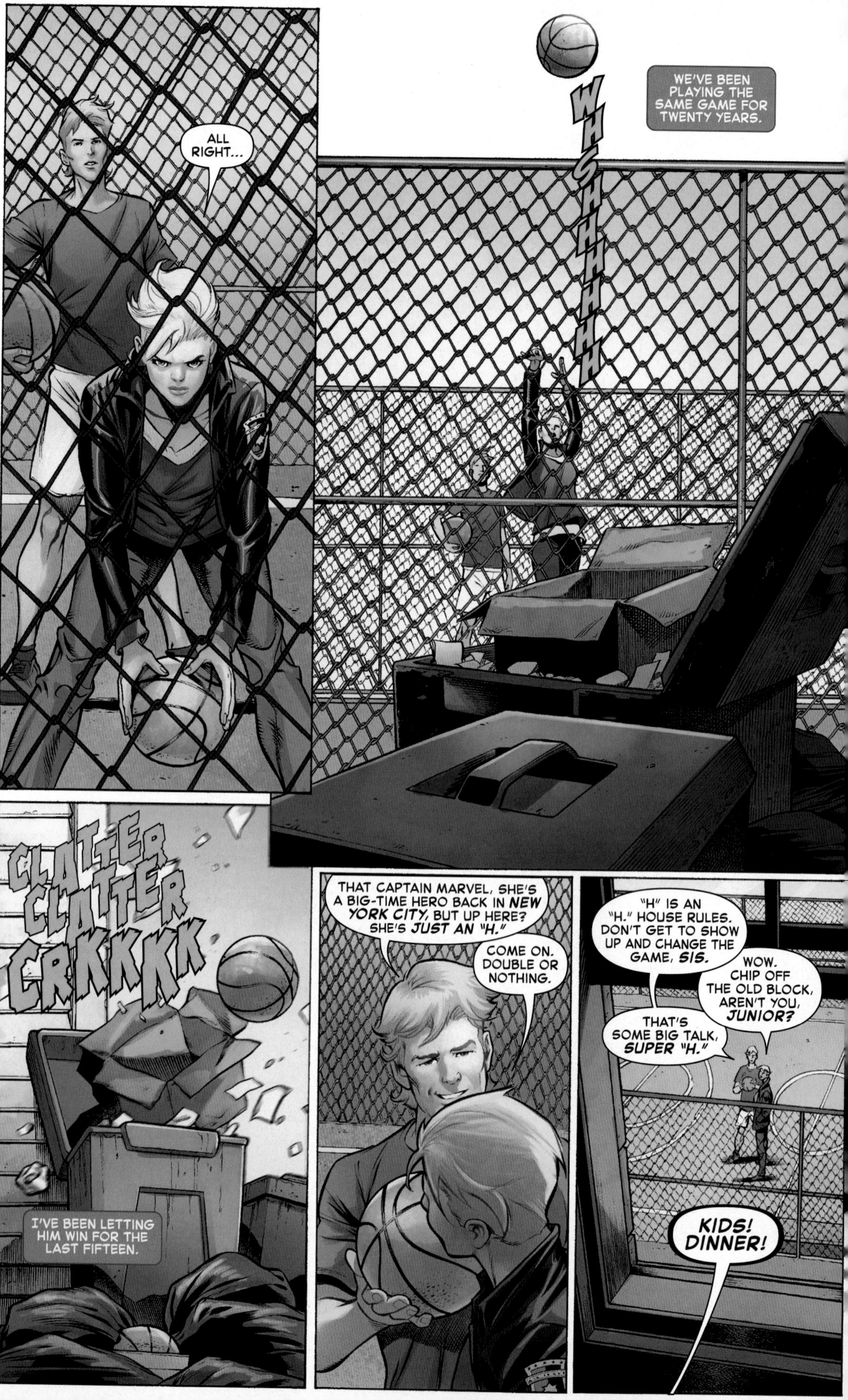
ALL RIGHT...
WHSHHHHHH
WE'VE BEEN PLAYING THE SAME GAME FOR TWENTY YEARS.
CLATTER CLATTER CRKKKK
I'VE BEEN LETTING HIM WIN FOR THE LAST FIFTEEN.
THAT CAPTAIN MARVEL, SHE'S A BIG-TIME HERO BACK IN NEW YORK CITY, BUT UP HERE? SHE'S JUST AN "H."
COME ON. DOUBLE OR NOTHING.
"H" IS AN "H." HOUSE RULES. DON'T GET TO SHOW UP AND CHANGE THE GAME, SIS.
WOW. CHIP OFF THE OLD BLOCK, AREN'T YOU, JUNIOR?
THAT'S SOME BIG TALK, SUPER "H."
KIDS! DINNER!

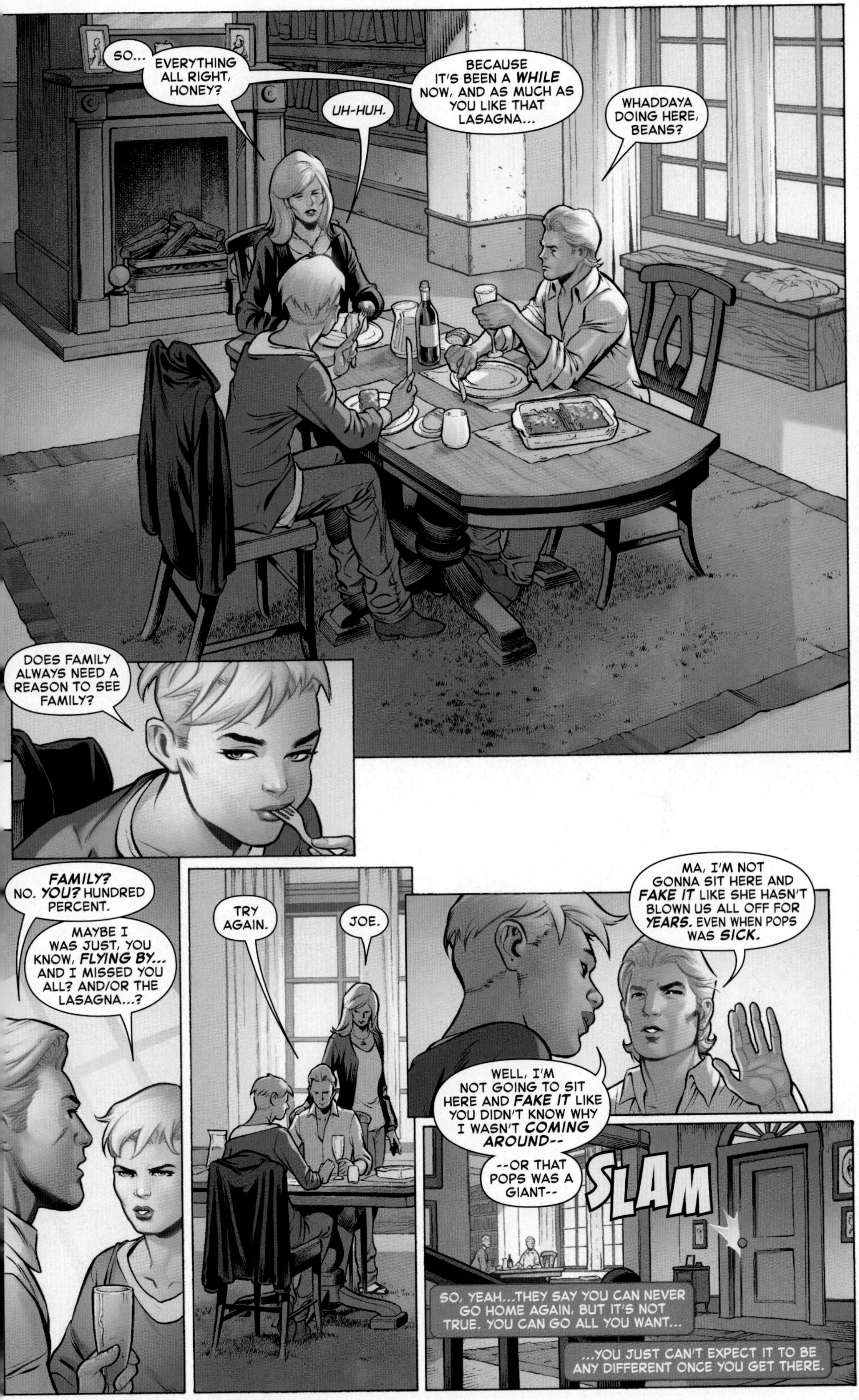
SO...
EVERYTHING ALL RIGHT, HONEY?
UH-HUH.
BECAUSE IT'S BEEN A WHILE NOW, AND AS MUCH AS YOU LIKE THAT LASAGNA...
WHADDAYA DOING HERE, BEANS?
DOES FAMILY ALWAYS NEED A REASON TO SEE FAMILY?
FAMILY? NO. YOU? HUNDRED PERCENT.
MAYBE I WAS JUST, YOU KNOW, FLYING BY... AND I MISSED YOU ALL? AND/OR THE LASAGNA...?
TRY AGAIN.
JOE.
MA, I'M NOT GONNA SIT HERE AND FAKE IT LIKE SHE HASN'T BLOWN US ALL OFF FOR YEARS. EVEN WHEN POPS WAS SICK.
WELL, I'M NOT GOING TO SIT HERE AND FAKE IT LIKE YOU DIDN'T KNOW WHY I WASN'T COMING AROUND--
--OR THAT POPS WAS A GIANT--
SLAM
SO, YEAH...THEY SAY YOU CAN NEVER GO HOME AGAIN, BUT IT'S NOT TRUE. YOU CAN GO ALL YOU WANT...
...YOU JUST CAN'T EXPECT IT TO BE ANY DIFFERENT ONCE YOU GET THERE.

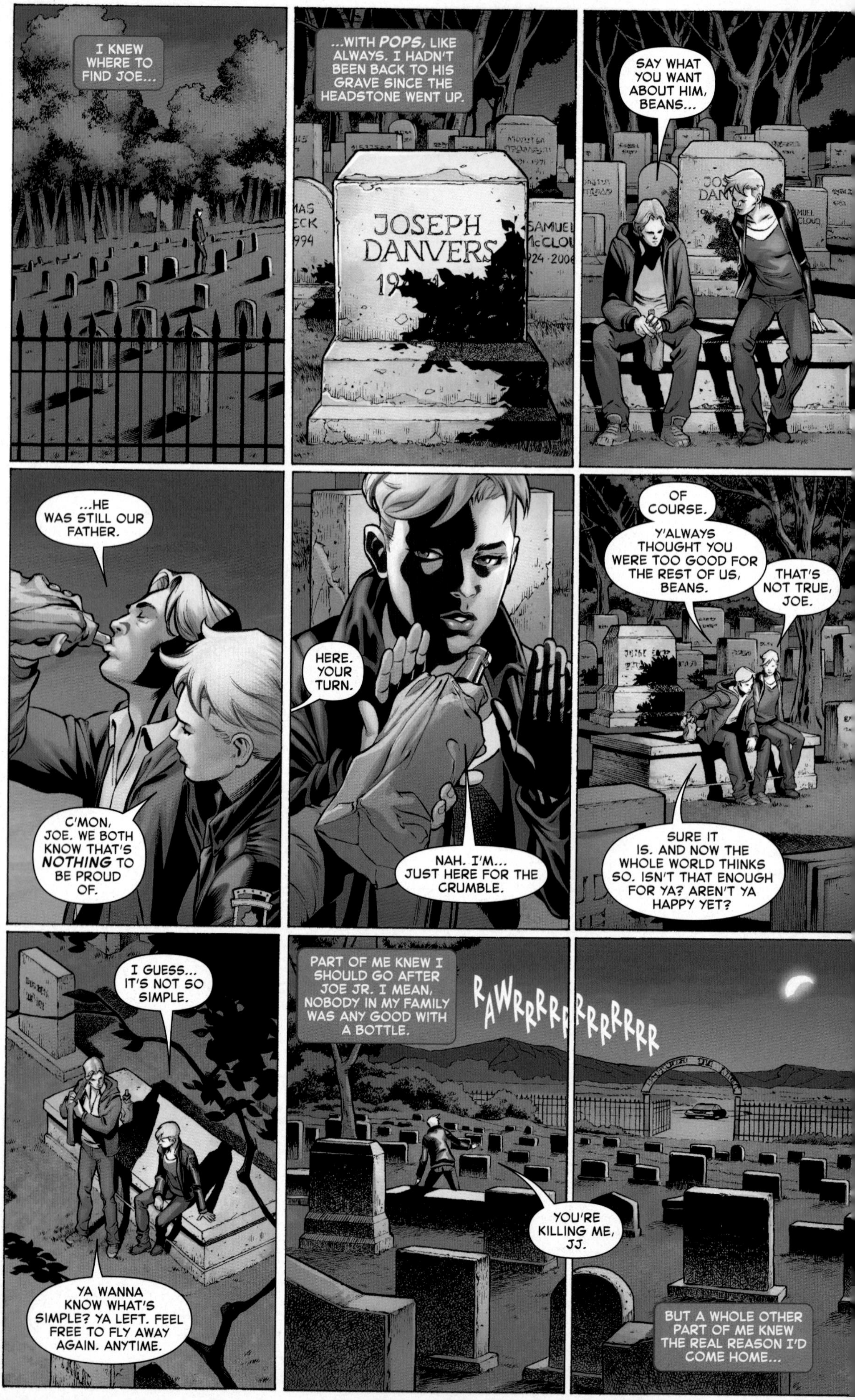
I KNEW WHERE TO FIND JOE...
...WITH POPS, LIKE ALWAYS. I HADN'T BEEN BACK TO HIS GRAVE SINCE THE HEADSTONE WENT UP.
JOSEPH DANVERS
SAMUEL McCLOUD
SAY WHAT YOU WANT ABOUT HIM, BEANS...
...HE WAS STILL OUR FATHER.
C'MON, JOE. WE BOTH KNOW THAT'S NOTHING TO BE PROUD OF.
HERE. YOUR TURN.
NAH. I'M... JUST HERE FOR THE CRUMBLE.
OF COURSE.
Y'ALWAYS THOUGHT YOU WERE TOO GOOD FOR THE REST OF US, BEANS.
THAT'S NOT TRUE, JOE.
SURE IT IS. AND NOW THE WHOLE WORLD THINKS SO. ISN'T THAT ENOUGH FOR YA? AREN'T YA HAPPY YET?
I GUESS... IT'S NOT SO SIMPLE.
YA WANNA KNOW WHAT'S SIMPLE? YA LEFT. FEEL FREE TO FLY AWAY AGAIN. ANYTIME.
PART OF ME KNEW I SHOULD GO AFTER JOE JR. I MEAN, NOBODY IN MY FAMILY WAS ANY GOOD WITH A BOTTLE.
RAWRRRRRRRRRRRR
YOU'RE KILLING ME, JJ.
BUT A WHOLE OTHER PART OF ME KNEW THE REAL REASON I'D COME HOME...

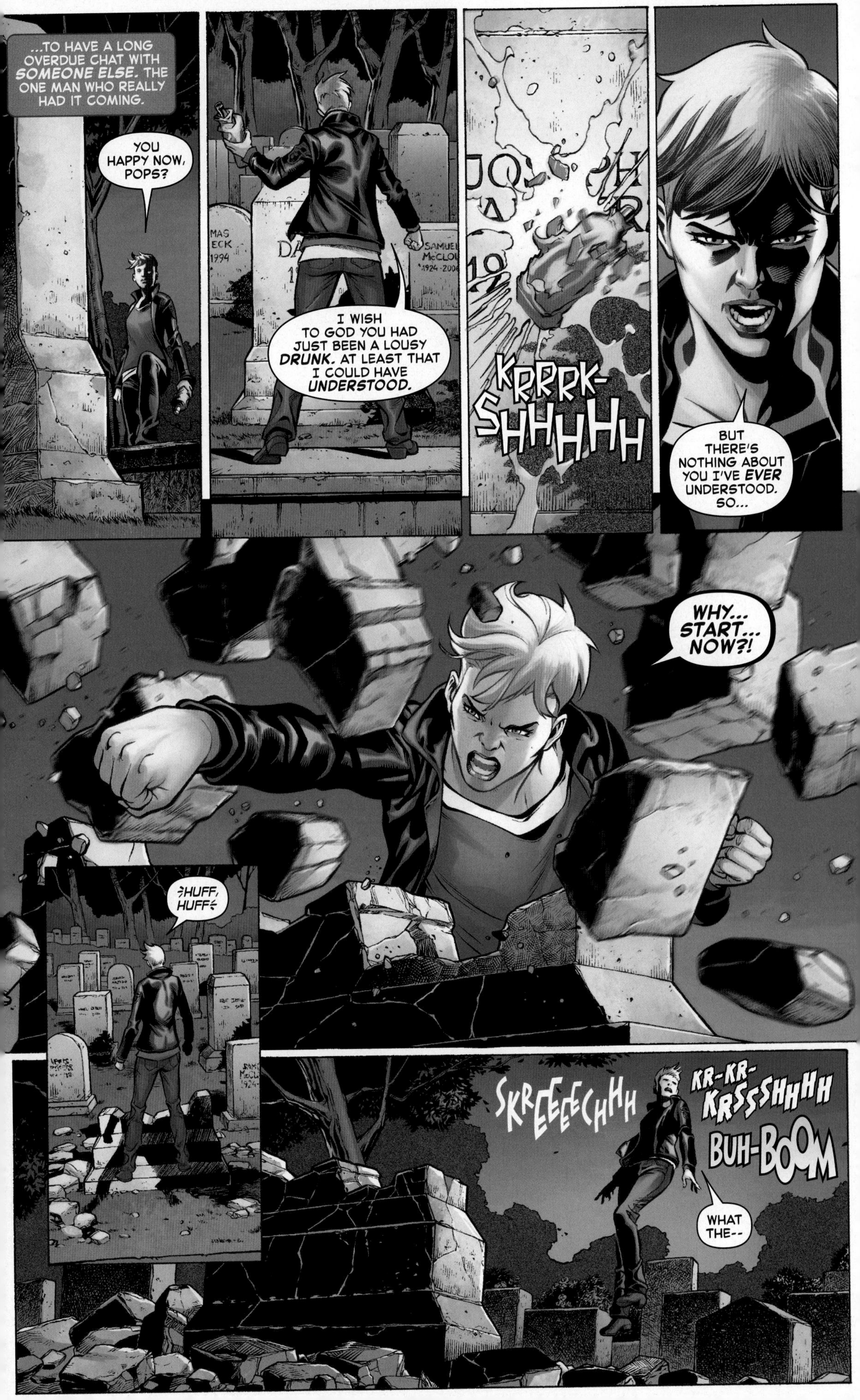
...TO HAVE A LONG OVERDUE CHAT WITH SOMEONE ELSE. THE ONE MAN WHO REALLY HAD IT COMING.
YOU HAPPY NOW, POPS?
I WISH TO GOD YOU HAD JUST BEEN A LOUSY DRUNK. AT LEAST THAT I COULD HAVE UNDERSTOOD.
KRRRK-SHHHHHH
BUT THERE'S NOTHING ABOUT YOU I'VE EVER UNDERSTOOD. SO...
WHY... START... NOW?!
HUFF, HUFF
SKREEEECHHH
KR-KR-KRSSSHHHH
BUH-BOOM
WHAT THE--

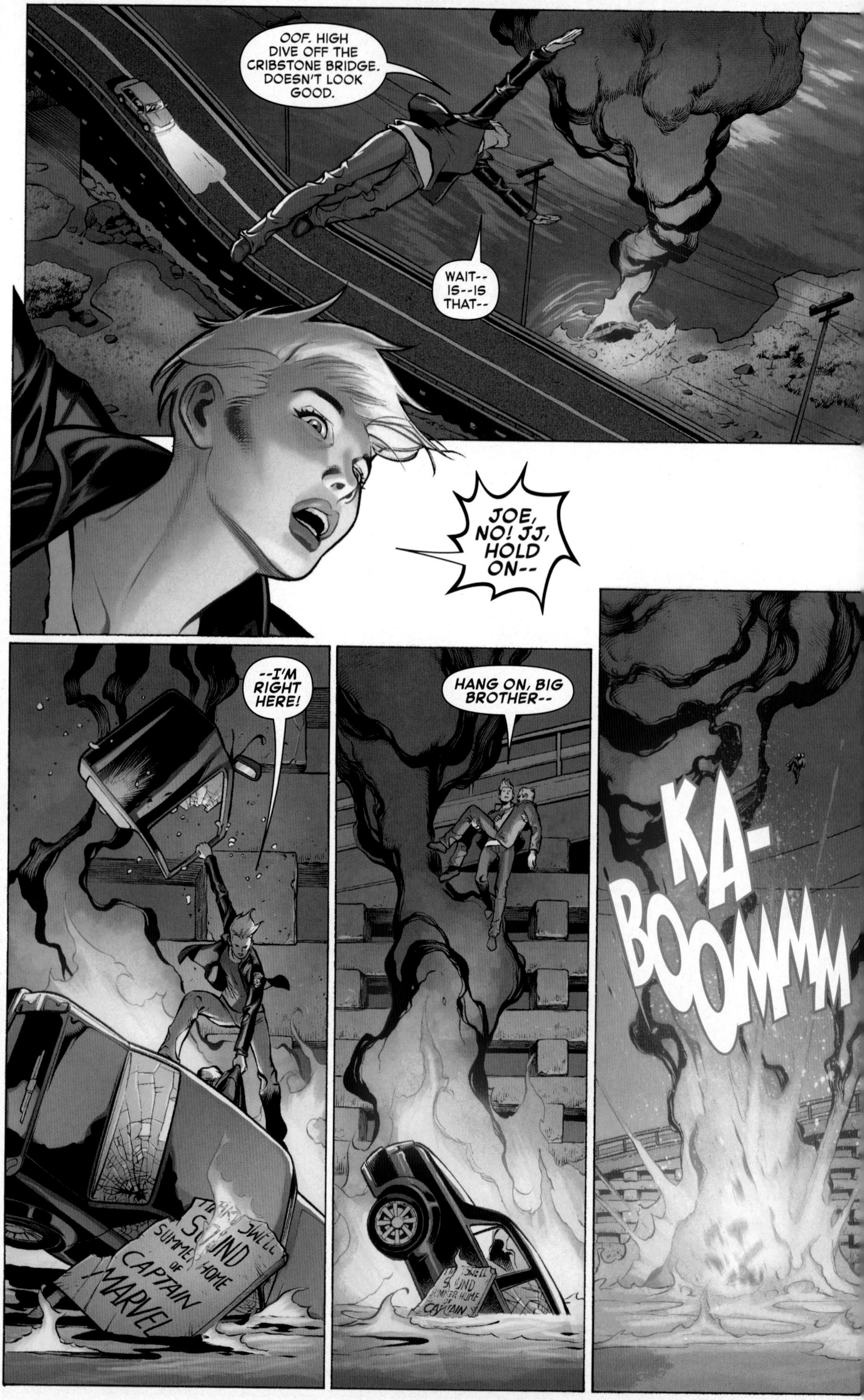
OOF. HIGH DIVE OFF THE CRIBSTONE BRIDGE. DOESN'T LOOK GOOD.
WAIT-- IS--IS THAT--
JOE, NO! JJ, HOLD ON--
--I'M RIGHT HERE!
SUMMER HOME OF CAPTAIN MARVEL
HANG ON, BIG BROTHER--
KA-BOOMMM

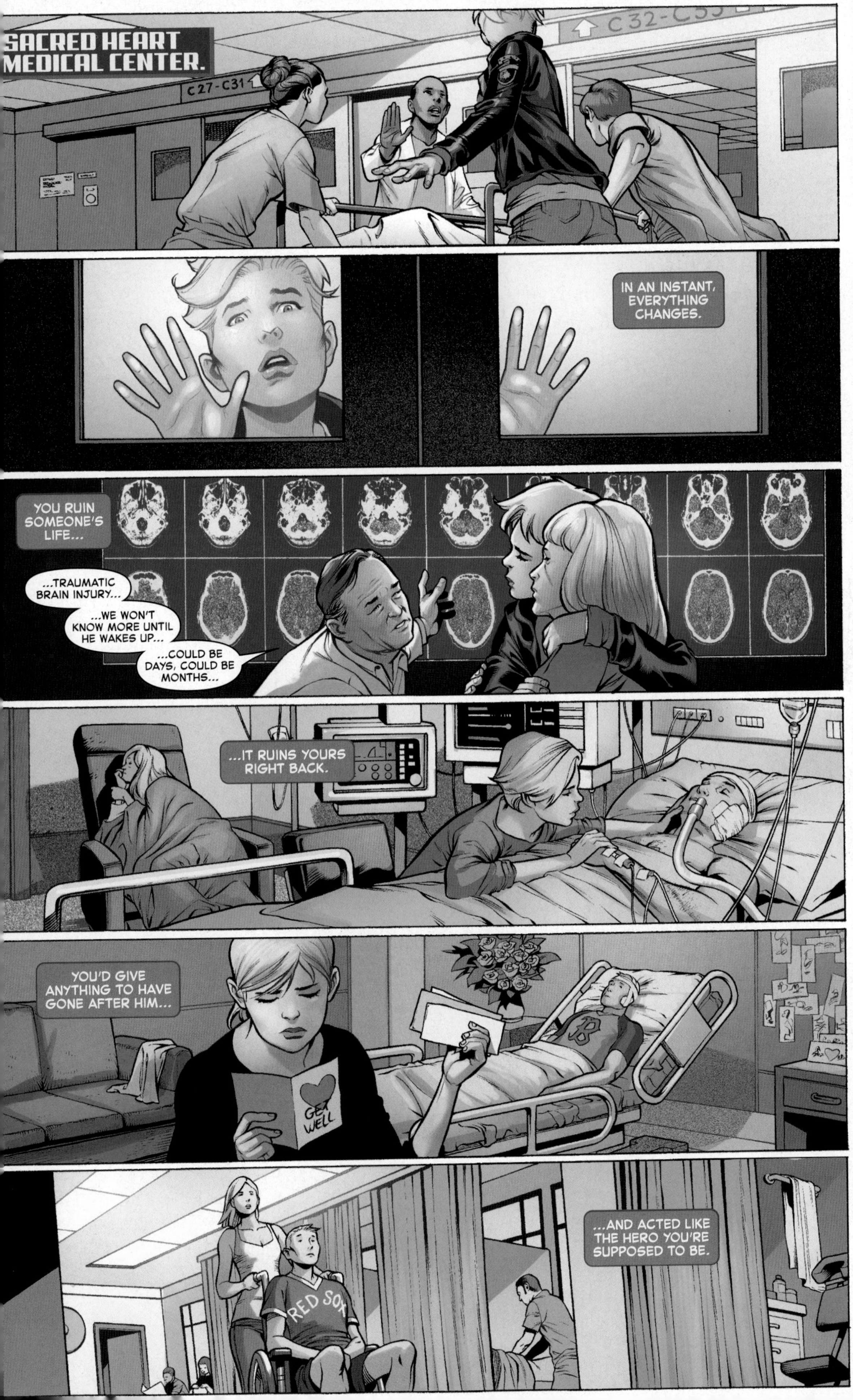
SACRED HEART MEDICAL CENTER.
C27-C31
C32-C35
IN AN INSTANT, EVERYTHING CHANGES.
YOU RUIN SOMEONE'S LIFE...
...TRAUMATIC BRAIN INJURY...
...WE WON'T KNOW MORE UNTIL HE WAKES UP...
...COULD BE DAYS, COULD BE MONTHS...
...IT RUINS YOURS RIGHT BACK.
YOU'D GIVE ANYTHING TO HAVE GONE AFTER HIM...
GET WELL
...AND ACTED LIKE THE HERO YOU'RE SUPPOSED TO BE.
RED SOX

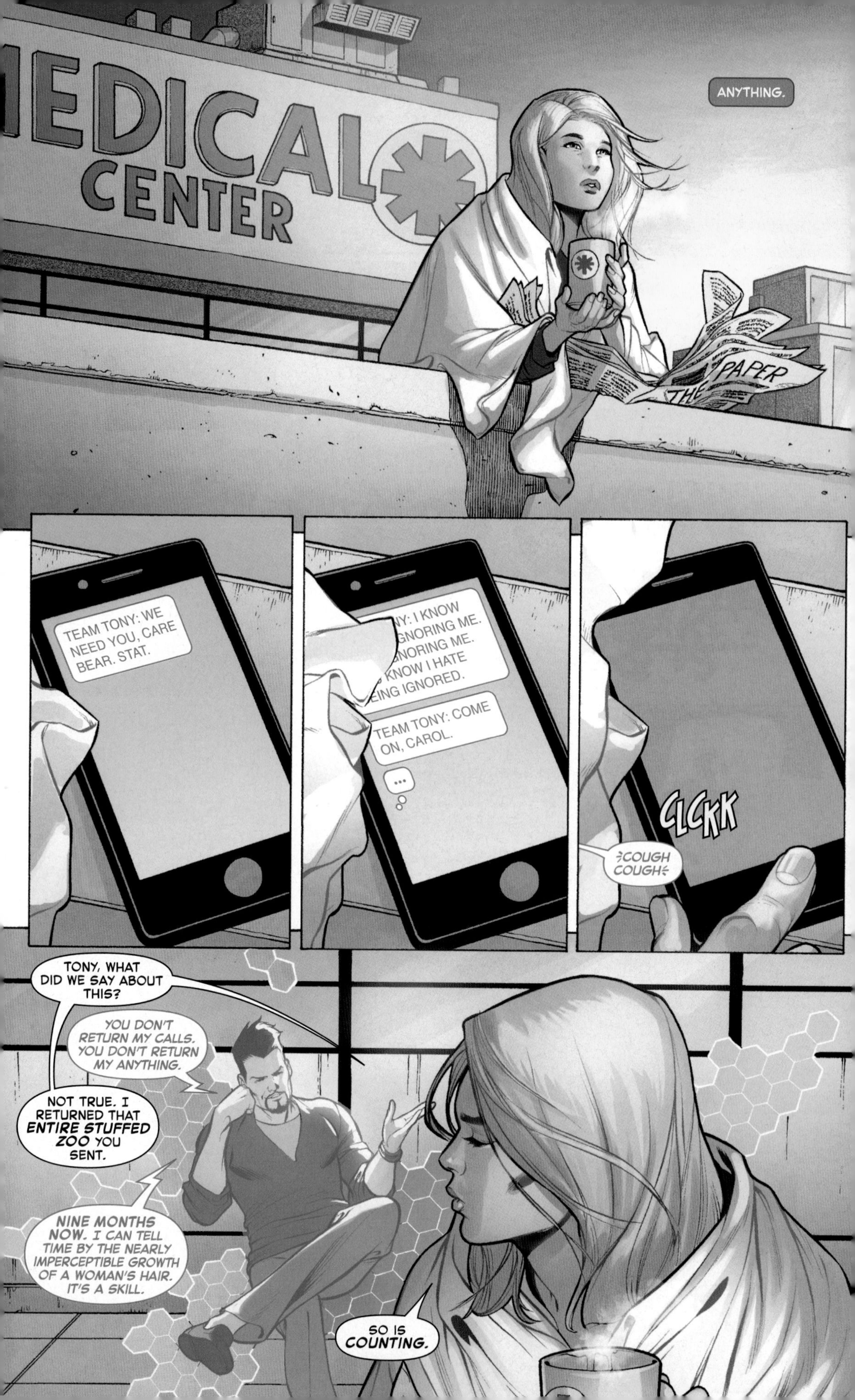

IEDICAL CENTER
ANYTHING.
THE PAPER
TEAM TONY: WE NEED YOU, CARE BEAR. STAT.
NY: I KNOW
GNORING ME.
NORING ME.
KNOW I HATE
EING IGNORED.
TEAM TONY: COME ON, CAROL.
...
CLCKK
COUGH COUGH
TONY, WHAT DID WE SAY ABOUT THIS?
YOU DON'T RETURN MY CALLS. YOU DON'T RETURN MY ANYTHING.
NOT TRUE. I RETURNED THAT ENTIRE STUFFED ZOO YOU SENT.
NINE MONTHS NOW. I CAN TELL TIME BY THE NEARLY IMPERCEPTIBLE GROWTH OF A WOMAN'S HAIR. IT'S A SKILL.
SO IS COUNTING.

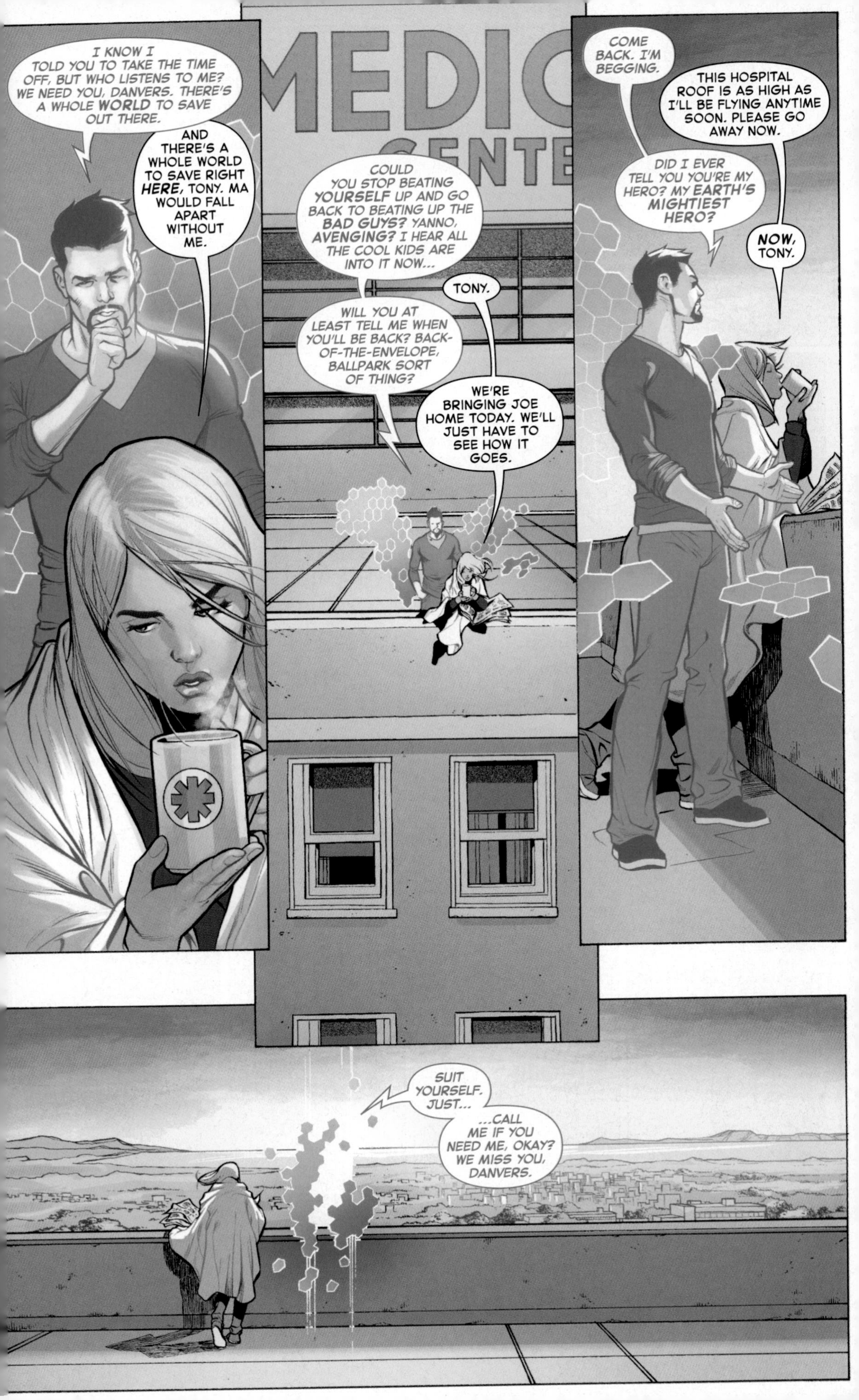
MEDIC
CENTE
I KNOW I TOLD YOU TO TAKE THE TIME OFF, BUT WHO LISTENS TO ME? WE NEED YOU, DANVERS. THERE'S A WHOLE WORLD TO SAVE OUT THERE.
AND THERE'S A WHOLE WORLD TO SAVE RIGHT HERE, TONY. MA WOULD FALL APART WITHOUT ME.
COULD YOU STOP BEATING YOURSELF UP AND GO BACK TO BEATING UP THE BAD GUYS? YANNO, AVENGING? I HEAR ALL THE COOL KIDS ARE INTO IT NOW...
TONY.
WILL YOU AT LEAST TELL ME WHEN YOU'LL BE BACK? BACK-OF-THE-ENVELOPE, BALLPARK SORT OF THING?
WE'RE BRINGING JOE HOME TODAY. WE'LL JUST HAVE TO SEE HOW IT GOES.
COME BACK. I'M BEGGING.
THIS HOSPITAL ROOF IS AS HIGH AS I'LL BE FLYING ANYTIME SOON. PLEASE GO AWAY NOW.
DID I EVER TELL YOU YOU'RE MY HERO? MY EARTH'S MIGHTIEST HERO?
NOW, TONY.
SUIT YOURSELF. JUST...
...CALL ME IF YOU NEED ME, OKAY? WE MISS YOU, DANVERS.

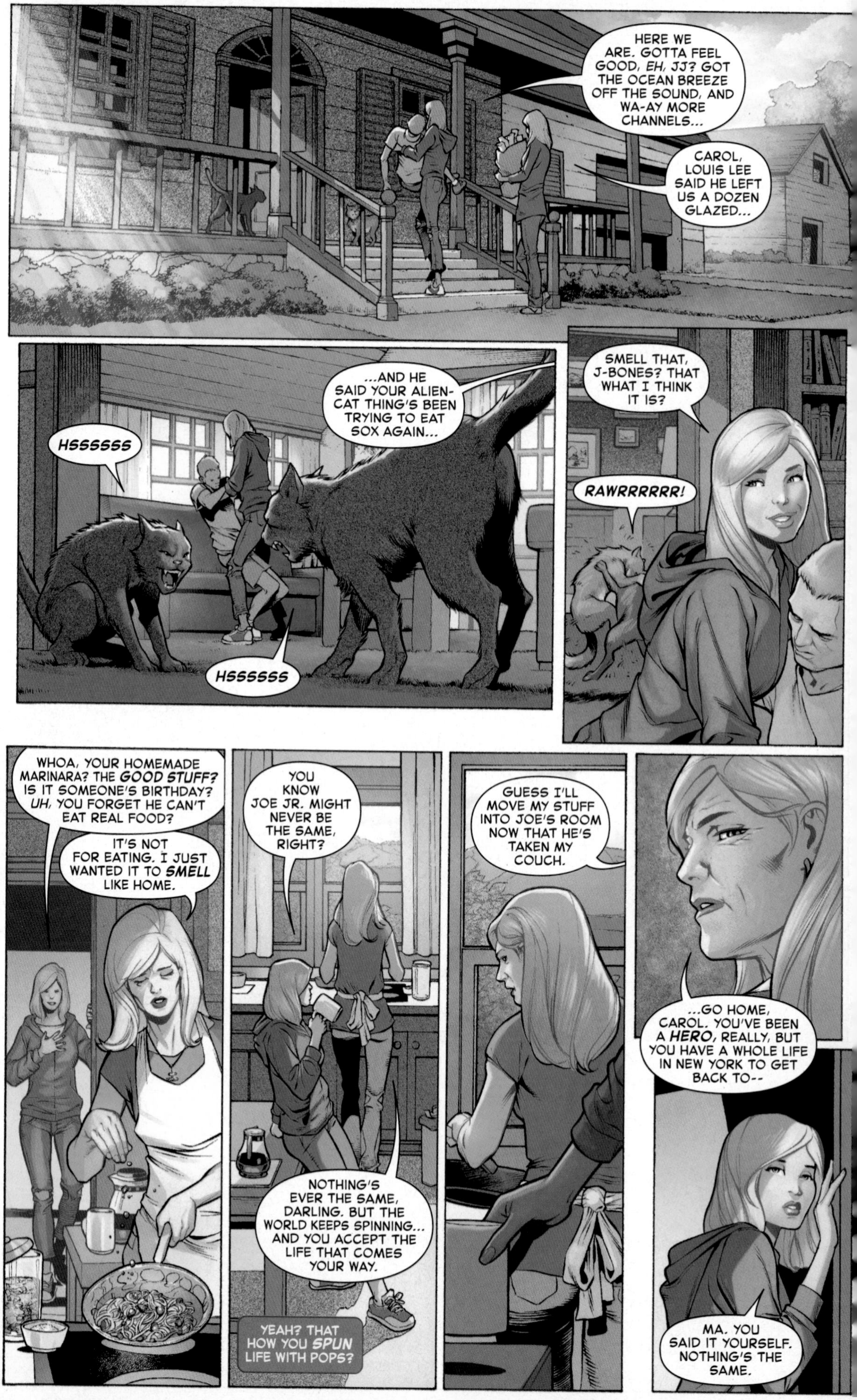
HERE WE ARE. GOTTA FEEL GOOD, EH, JJ? GOT THE OCEAN BREEZE OFF THE SOUND, AND WA-AY MORE CHANNELS...
CAROL, LOUIS LEE SAID HE LEFT US A DOZEN GLAZED...
...AND HE SAID YOUR ALIEN-CAT THING'S BEEN TRYING TO EAT SOX AGAIN...
HSSSSSS
HSSSSSS
SMELL THAT, J-BONES? THAT WHAT I THINK IT IS?
RAWRRRRRR!
WHOA, YOUR HOMEMADE MARINARA? THE GOOD STUFF? IS IT SOMEONE'S BIRTHDAY? UH, YOU FORGET HE CAN'T EAT REAL FOOD?
IT'S NOT FOR EATING. I JUST WANTED IT TO SMELL LIKE HOME.
YOU KNOW JOE JR. MIGHT NEVER BE THE SAME, RIGHT?
NOTHING'S EVER THE SAME, DARLING. BUT THE WORLD KEEPS SPINNING... AND YOU ACCEPT THE LIFE THAT COMES YOUR WAY.
YEAH? THAT HOW YOU SPUN LIFE WITH POPS?
GUESS I'LL MOVE MY STUFF INTO JOE'S ROOM NOW THAT HE'S TAKEN MY COUCH.
...GO HOME, CAROL. YOU'VE BEEN A HERO, REALLY, BUT YOU HAVE A WHOLE LIFE IN NEW YORK TO GET BACK TO--
MA. YOU SAID IT YOURSELF. NOTHING'S THE SAME.

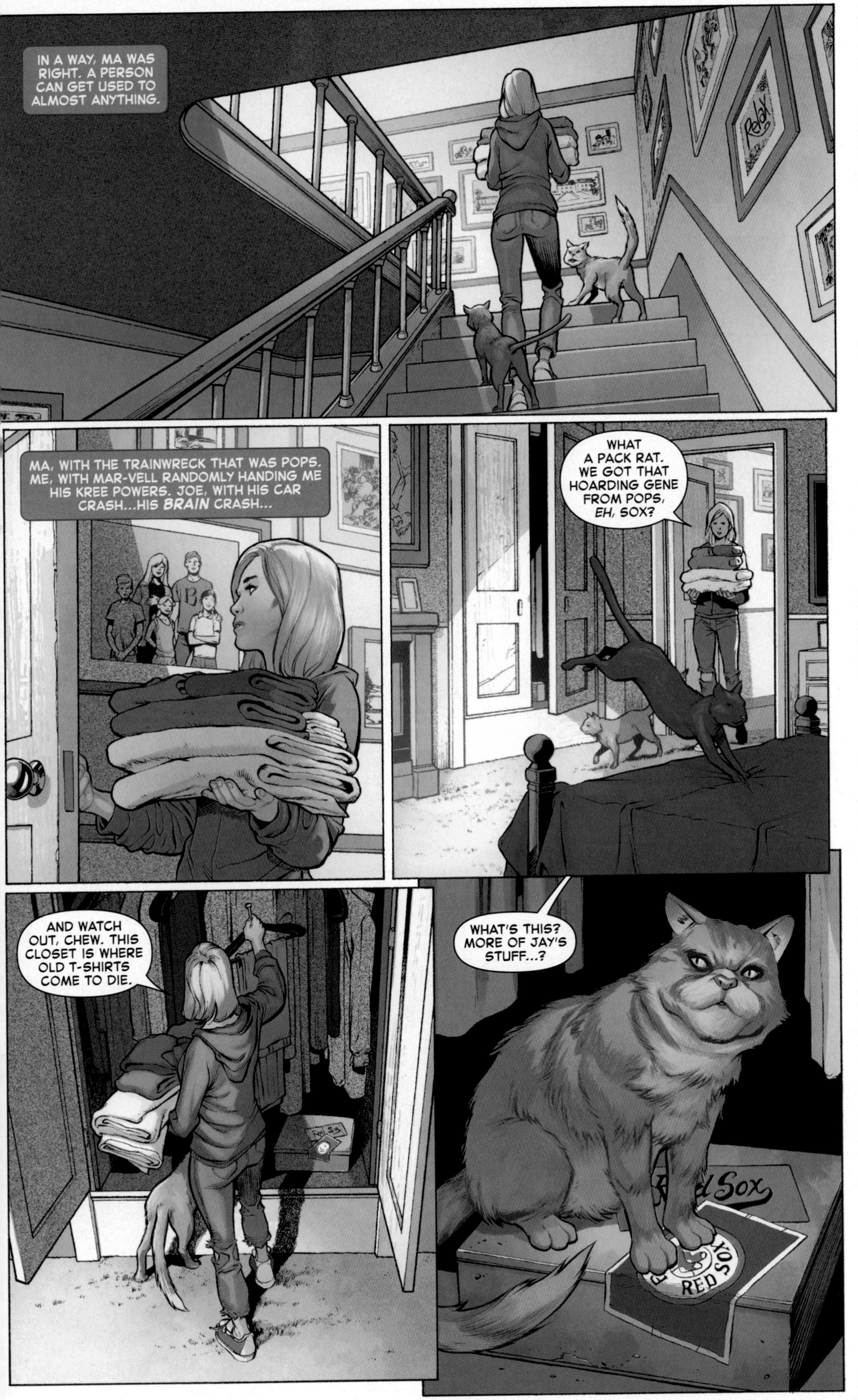
IN A WAY, MA WAS RIGHT. A PERSON CAN GET USED TO ALMOST ANYTHING.
Relax
MA, WITH THE TRAINWRECK THAT WAS POPS. ME, WITH MAR-VELL RANDOMLY HANDING ME HIS KREE POWERS. JOE, WITH HIS CAR CRASH...HIS *BRAIN* CRASH...
WHAT A PACK RAT. WE GOT THAT HOARDING GENE FROM POPS, *EH,* SOX?
AND WATCH OUT, CHEW. THIS CLOSET IS WHERE OLD T-SHIRTS COME TO DIE.
WHAT'S THIS? MORE OF JAY'S STUFF...?
Red Sox
RED SOX

THIS LOOKS TOO OLD TO BE JJ'S OR STEVIE'S OR MINE.

MA MUST HAVE BEEN CLEANING OUT THE ATTIC.

WHAT'S...

"...I'm ripped apart when I'm not with you, but I'm gutted when I am. I'm afraid of you and I'm afraid of losing you. And nobody in the universe but you knows how I feel.

My love,

I have to make a confession...I'm ripped apart when I'm not with you, but I'm gutted when I am. I'm afraid of you and I'm afraid of losing you. And nobody in the universe but you knows how I feel.

I'm not an idiot. I know there's no ... this turns out well, not for either ... I know we're not meant to be. I ... hat people will say if they find ... maybe you're right, and we ... op seeing each other...

... be you're wrong, because ... top seeing each other, we're ... stop feeling each other, ... t I have a family and ... ot you don't.

... eason we found each other, ... it's this: You are my ... can't give up on that, and ... t me to.

All my lov
Joseph

WHAT IS THIS? WHO WROTE THIS? THE HANDWRITING IS SO FAMILIAR. POPS? MA? CAN'T IMAGINE EITHER...

"...I'm not an idiot. I know there's no way this turns out well, not for either of us. I know we're not meant to be. I know what people will say if they find out. So maybe you're right, and we should stop seeing each other...

"...but maybe you're wrong, because even if we stop seeing each other, we're never gonna stop feeling each other, whether or not I have a family and whether or not you don't.

"There's a reason we found each other, my love, and it's this: You are my soulmate. I can't give up on that, and you can't ask me to.

"All my love...

"...Joseph."

HOLY--POPS WAS HAVING AN AFFAIR?

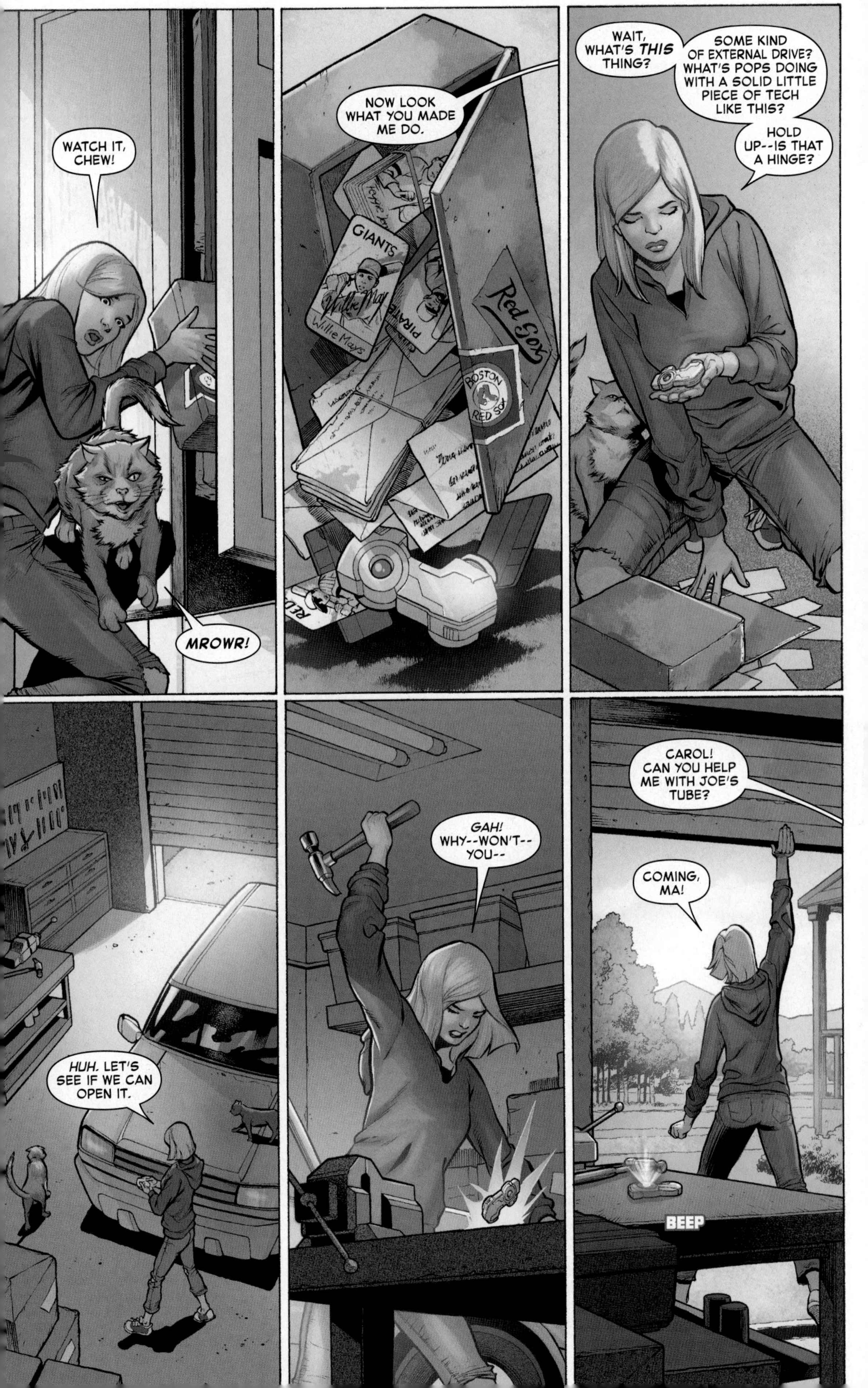
WATCH IT, CHEW!
MROWR!
NOW LOOK WHAT YOU MADE ME DO.
GIANTS
Willie Mays
PIRATE
Red Sox
BOSTON RED SOX
WAIT, WHAT'S THIS THING?
SOME KIND OF EXTERNAL DRIVE? WHAT'S POPS DOING WITH A SOLID LITTLE PIECE OF TECH LIKE THIS?
HOLD UP--IS THAT A HINGE?
HUH. LET'S SEE IF WE CAN OPEN IT.
GAH! WHY--WON'T--YOU--
CAROL! CAN YOU HELP ME WITH JOE'S TUBE?
COMING, MA!
BEEP

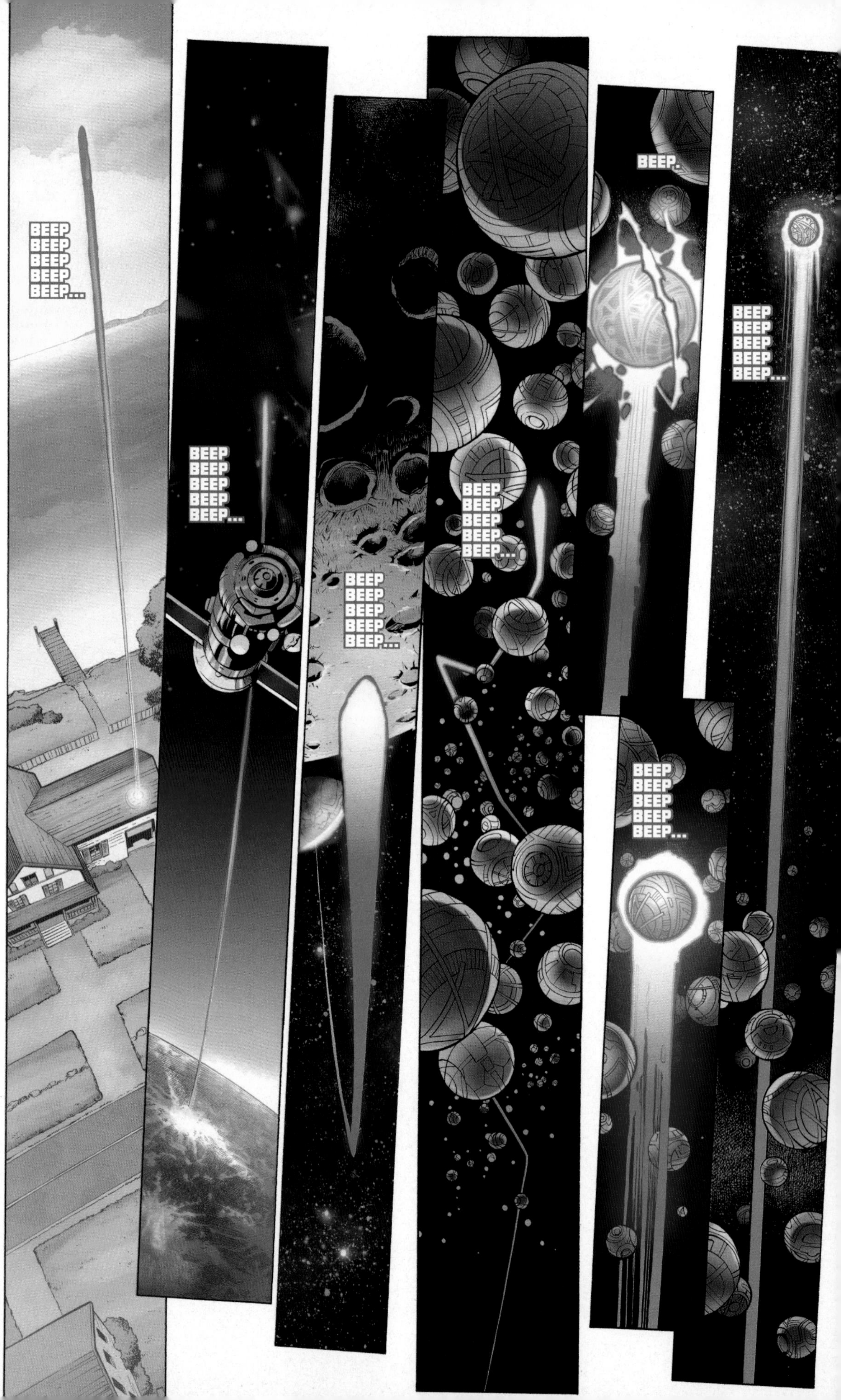
BEEP
BEEP
BEEP
BEEP
BEEP...
BEEP
BEEP
BEEP
BEEP
BEEP...
BEEP
BEEP
BEEP
BEEP
BEEP...
BEEP
BEEP
BEEP
BEEP
BEEP...
BEEP.
BEEP
BEEP
BEEP
BEEP
BEEP...
BEEP
BEEP
BEEP
BEEP
BEEP...

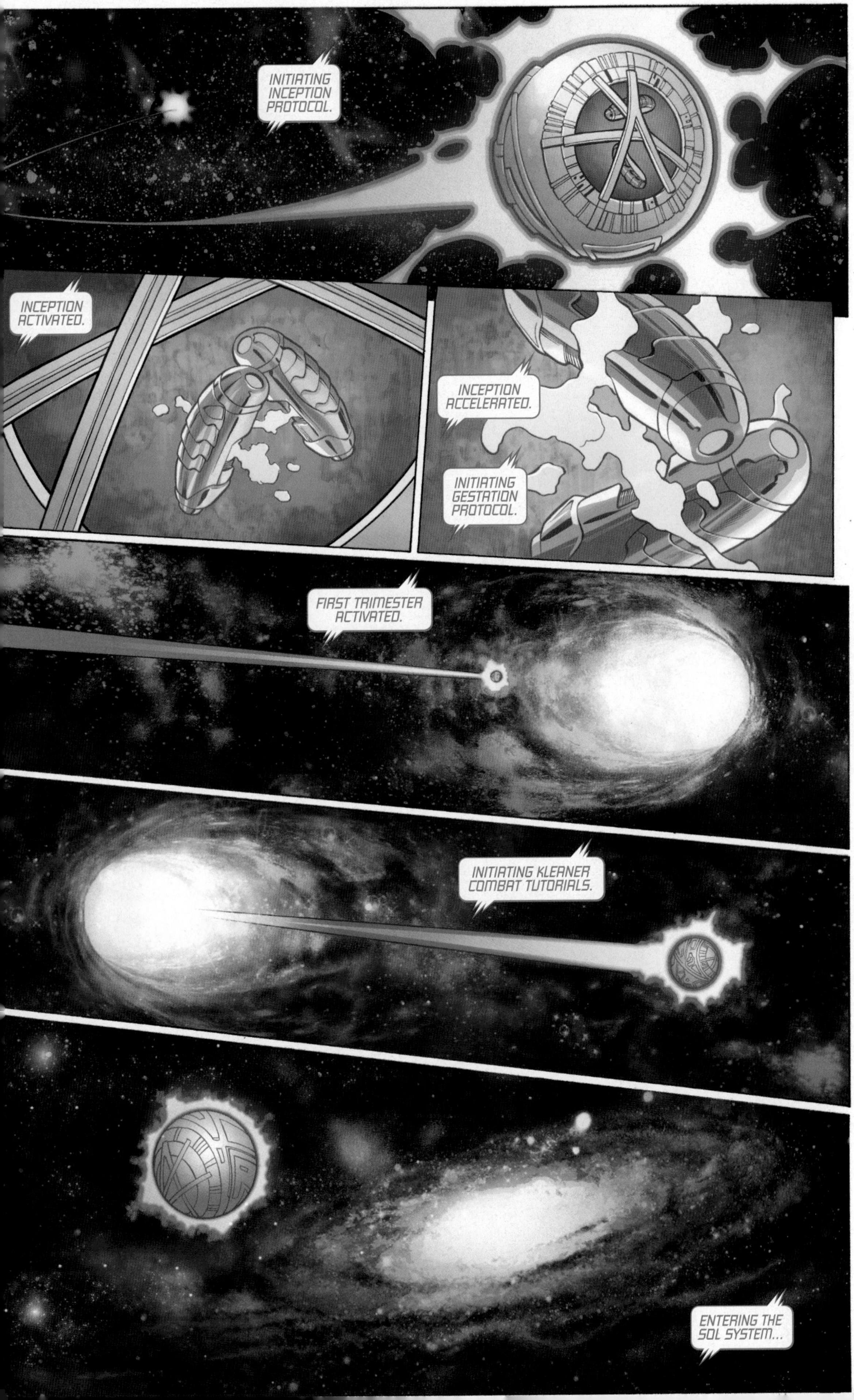
INITIATING INCEPTION PROTOCOL.
INCEPTION ACTIVATED.
INCEPTION ACCELERATED.
INITIATING GESTATION PROTOCOL.
FIRST TRIMESTER ACTIVATED.
INITIATING KLEANER COMBAT TUTORIALS.
ENTERING THE SOL SYSTEM...

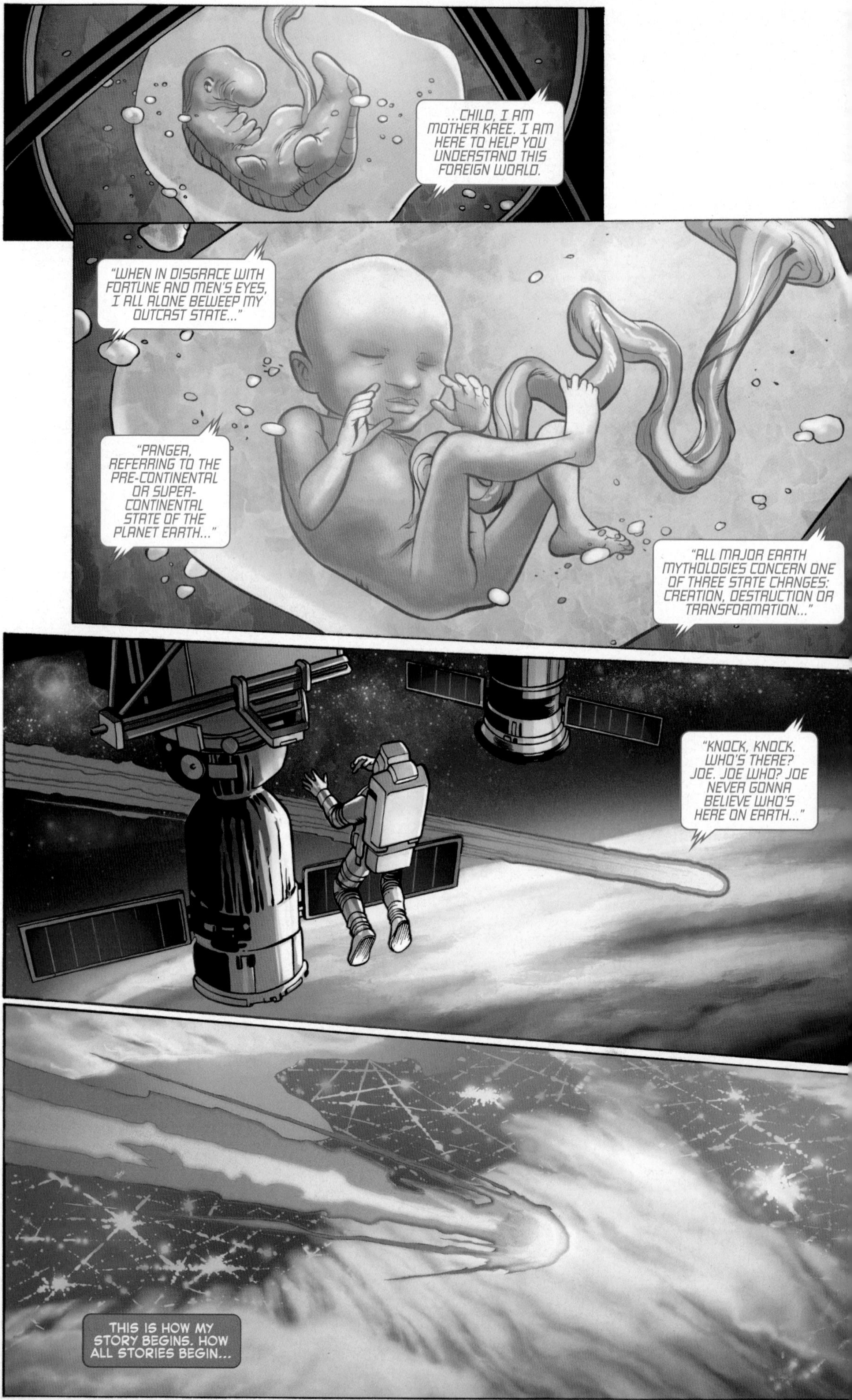
...CHILD, I AM MOTHER KREE. I AM HERE TO HELP YOU UNDERSTAND THIS FOREIGN WORLD.
"WHEN IN DISGRACE WITH FORTUNE AND MEN'S EYES, I ALL ALONE BEWEEP MY OUTCAST STATE..."
"PANGEA, REFERRING TO THE PRE-CONTINENTAL OR SUPER-CONTINENTAL STATE OF THE PLANET EARTH..."
"ALL MAJOR EARTH MYTHOLOGIES CONCERN ONE OF THREE STATE CHANGES: CREATION, DESTRUCTION OR TRANSFORMATION..."
"KNOCK, KNOCK. WHO'S THERE? JOE. JOE WHO? JOE NEVER GONNA BELIEVE WHO'S HERE ON EARTH..."
THIS IS HOW MY STORY BEGINS. HOW ALL STORIES BEGIN...

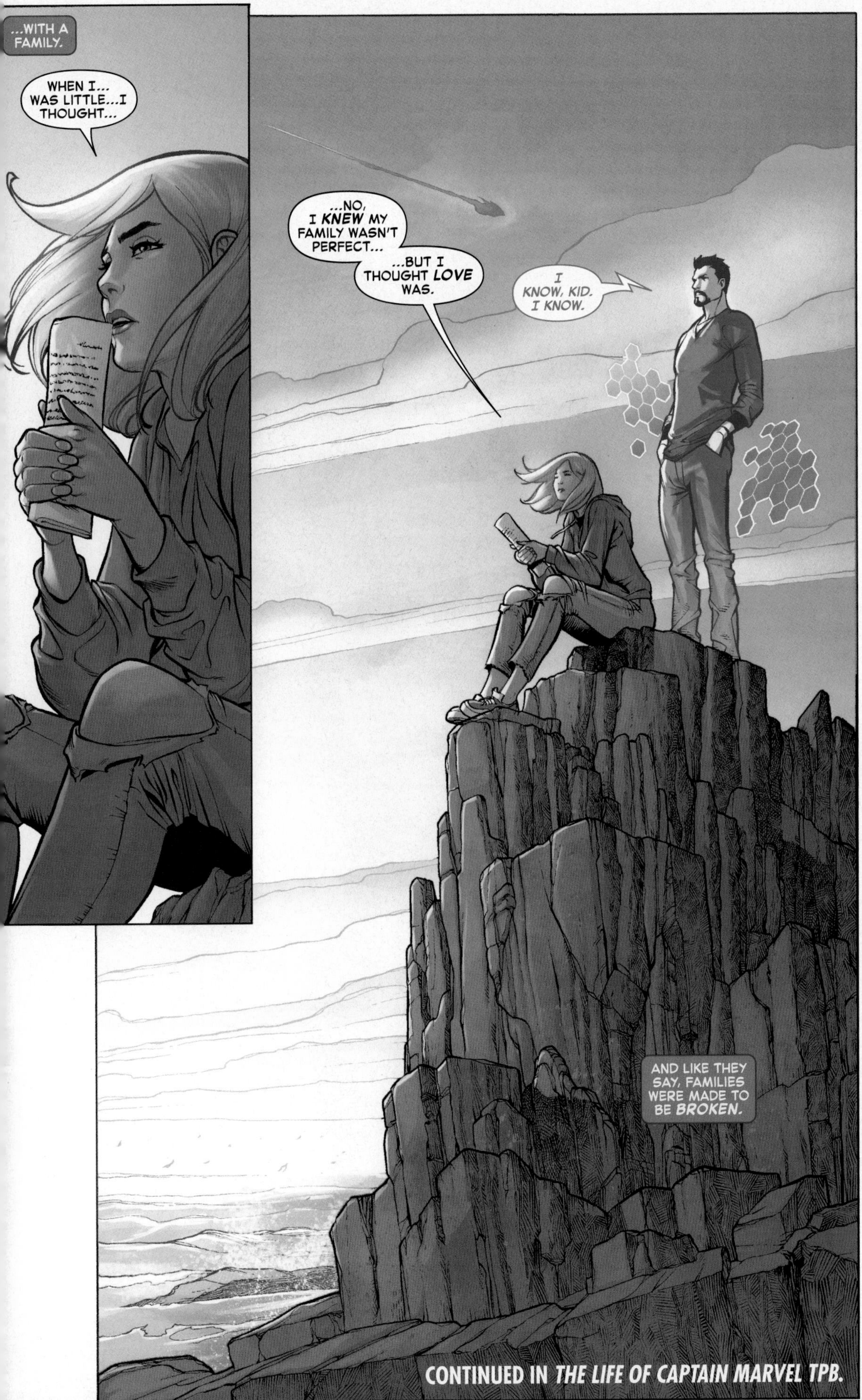
...WITH A FAMILY.
WHEN I... WAS LITTLE...I THOUGHT...
...NO, I KNEW MY FAMILY WASN'T PERFECT...
...BUT I THOUGHT LOVE WAS.
I KNOW, KID. I KNOW.
AND LIKE THEY SAY, FAMILIES WERE MADE TO BE BROKEN.

CONTINUED IN *THE LIFE OF CAPTAIN MARVEL TPB.*

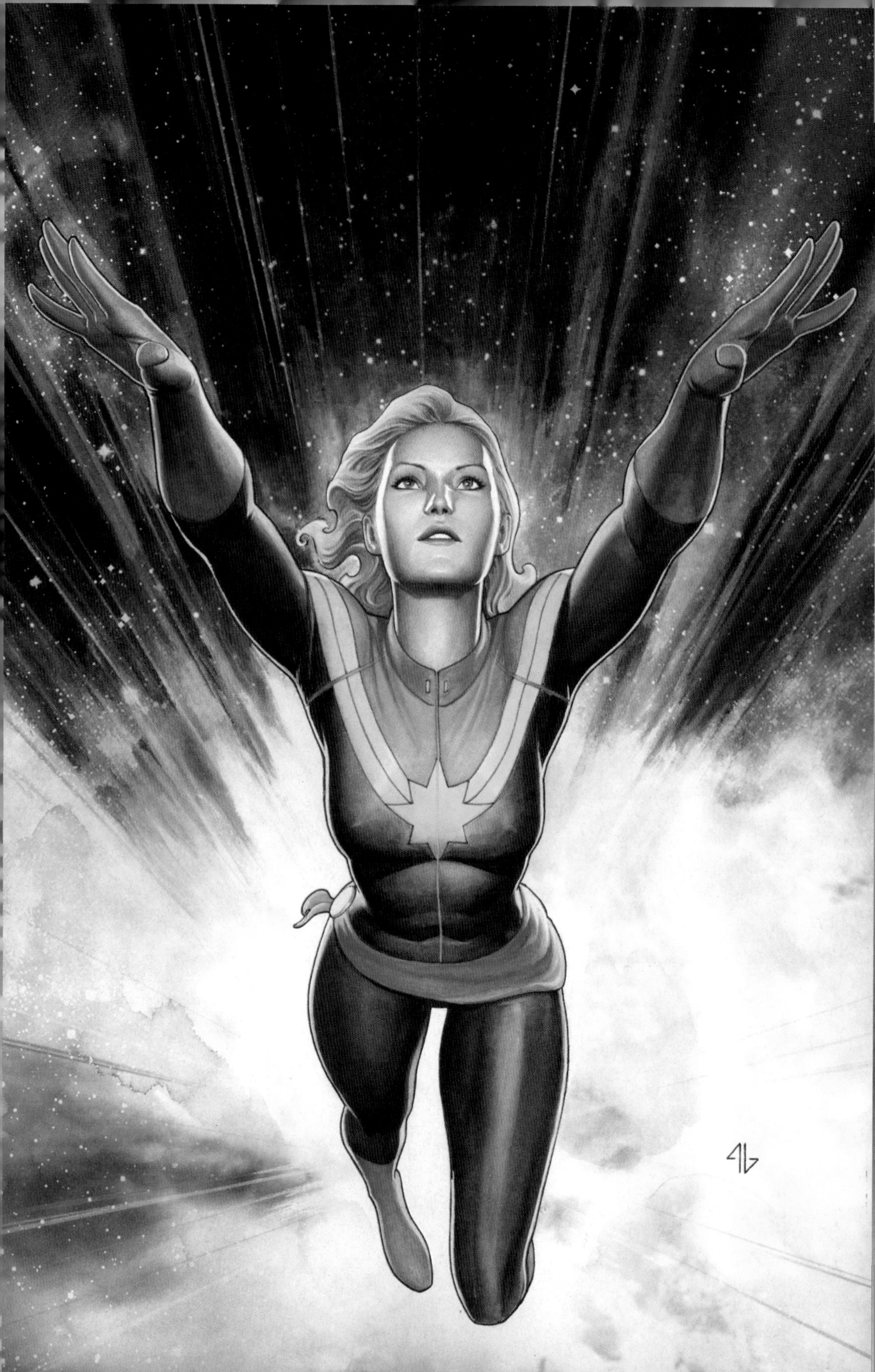

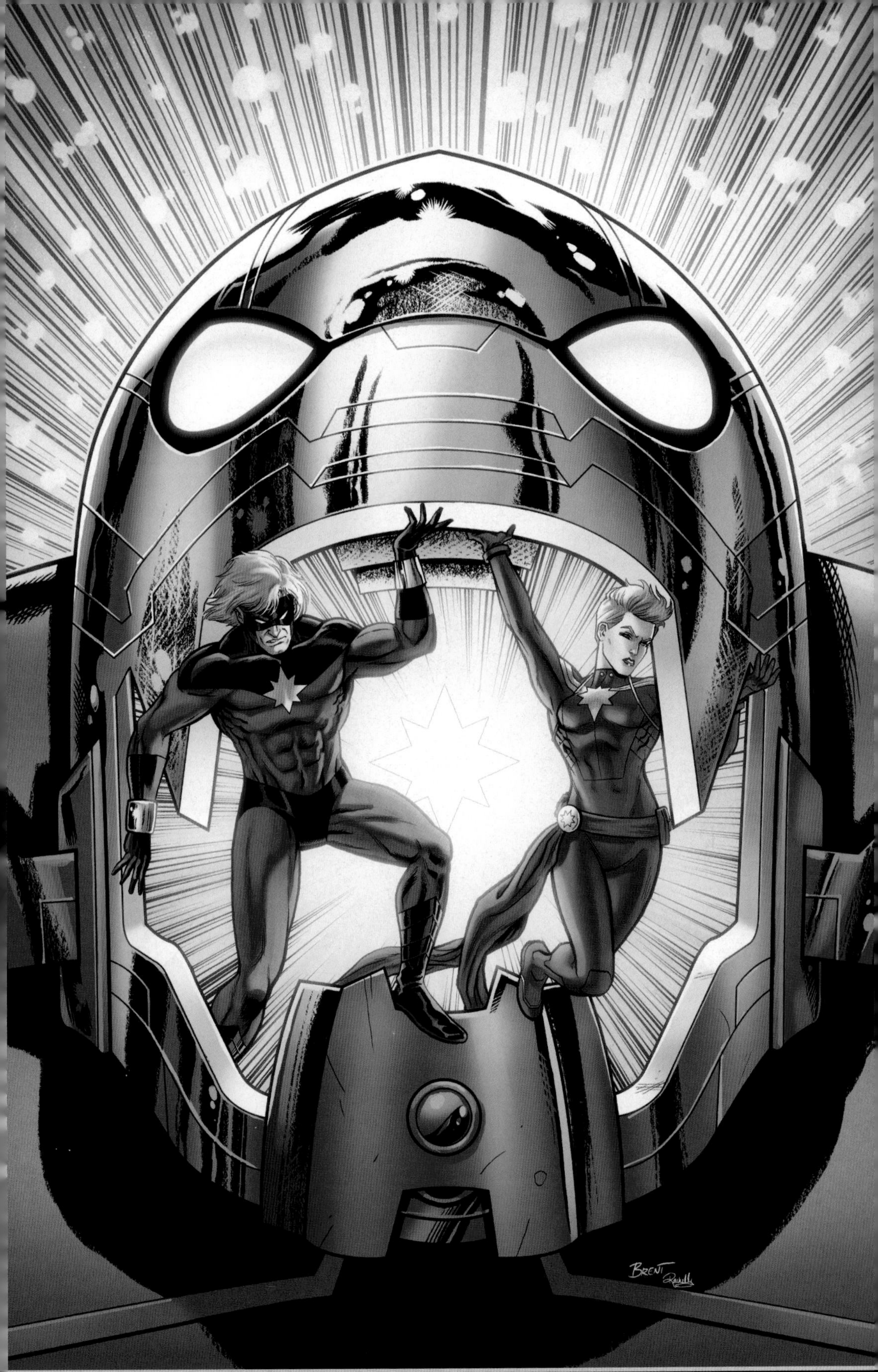
BRENT

GENERATIONS: CAPTAIN MARVEL & CAPTAIN MAR-VELL #1 VARIANT
BY BRENT SCHOONOVER & RACHELLE ROSENBERG

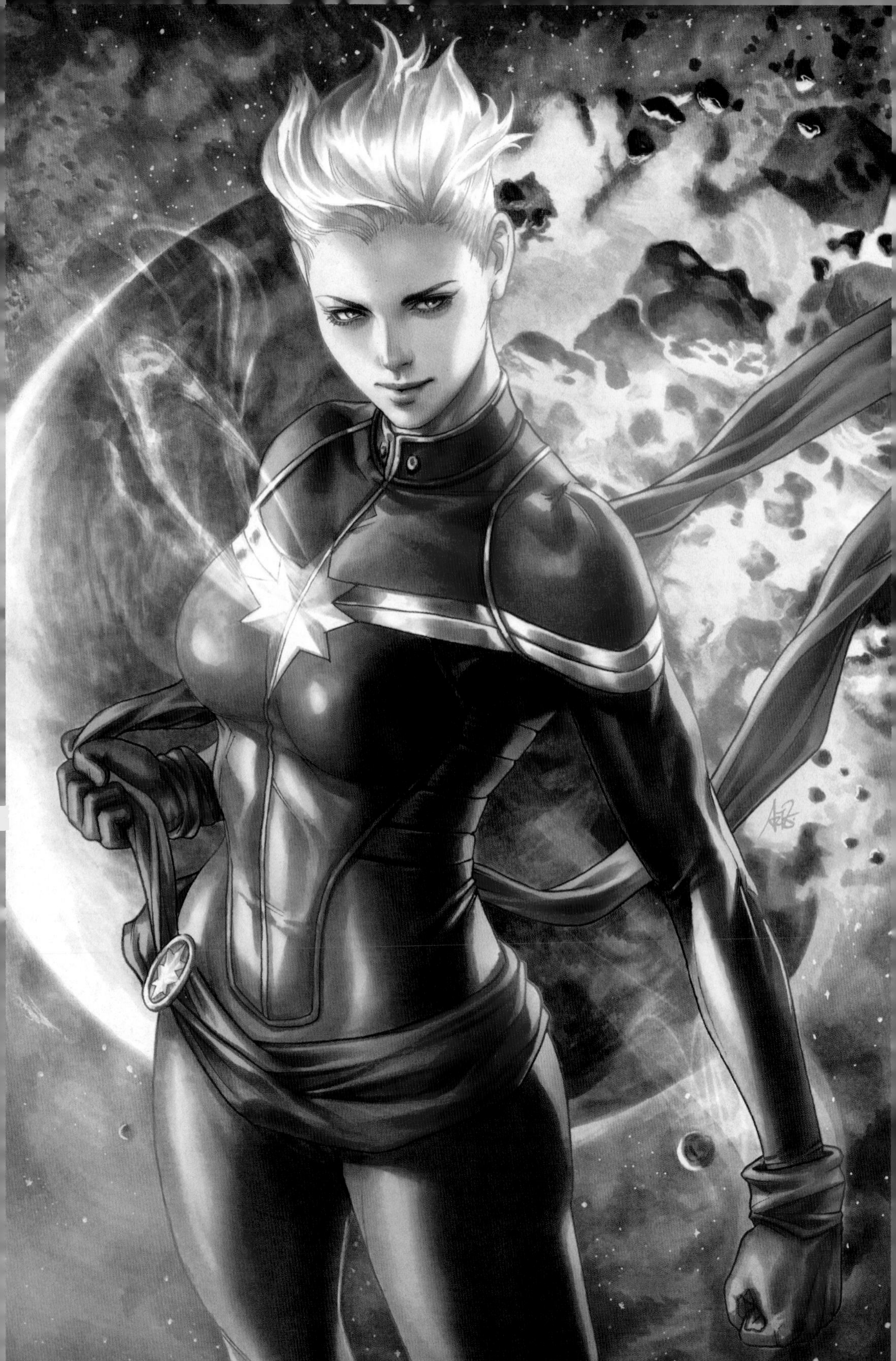

THI NT

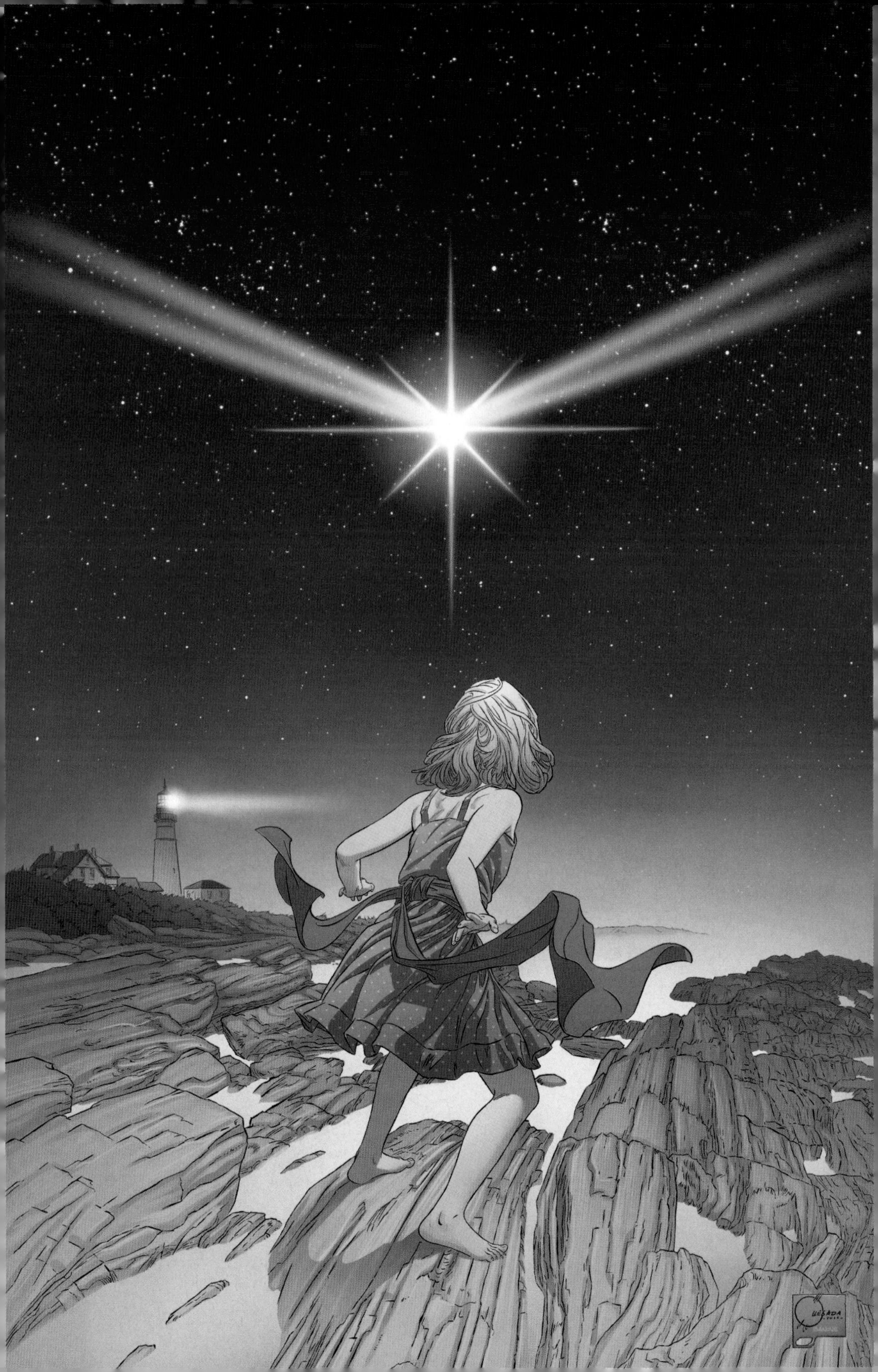

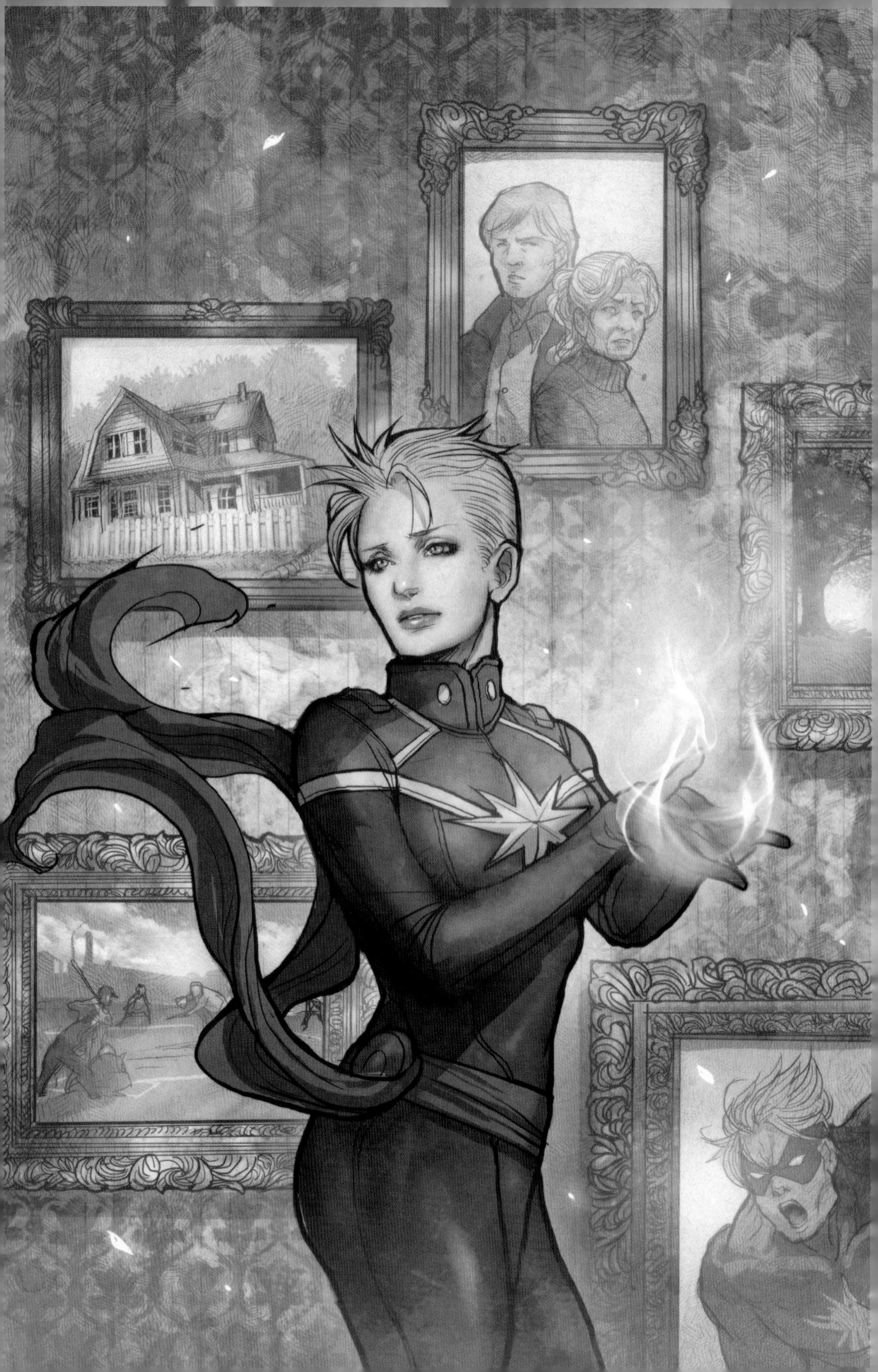

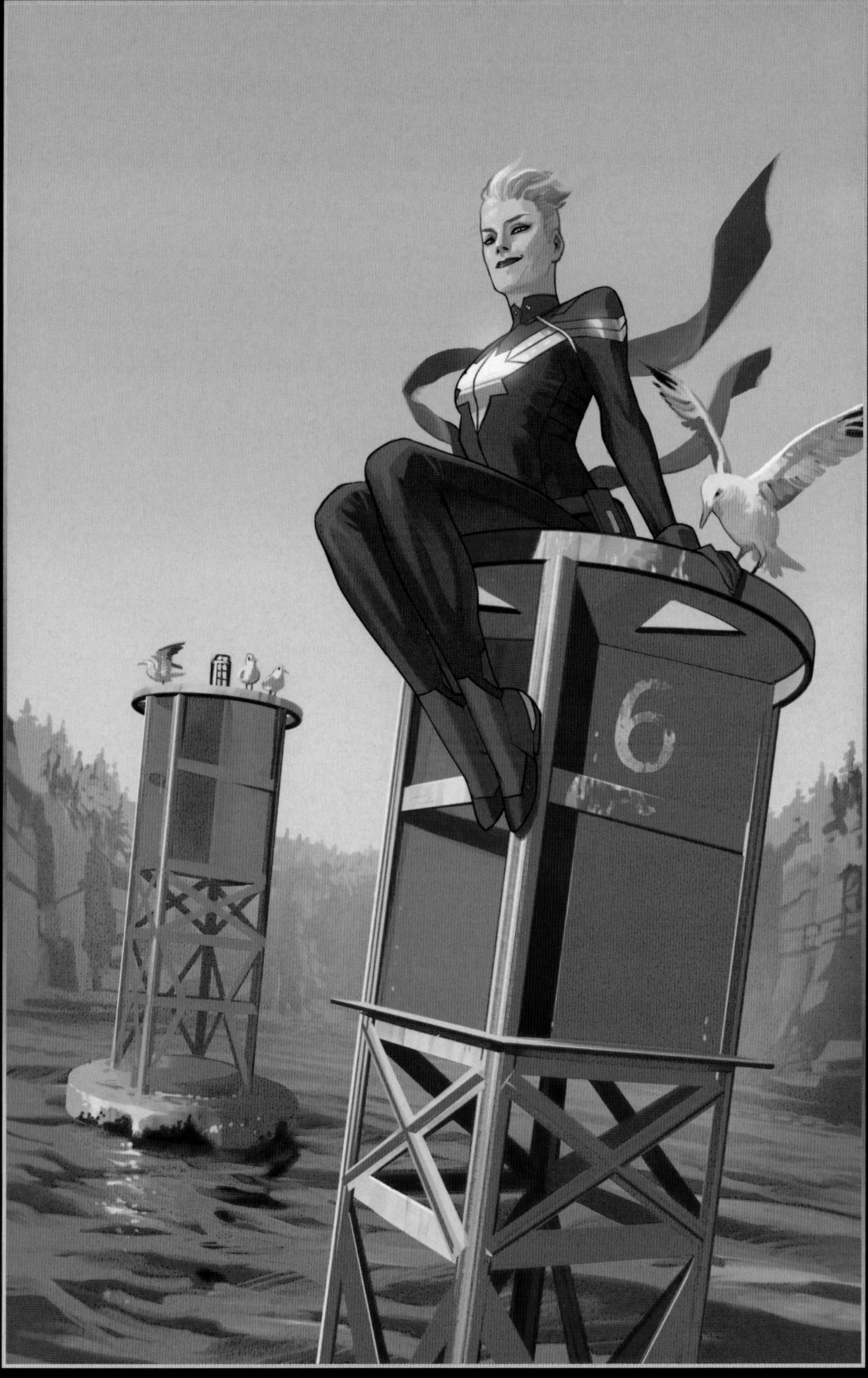
6

**THE LIFE OF CAPTAIN MARVEL #1 VARIANT**
BY FIONA STAPLES